ADO.NET Programming in Visual Basic .NET

Steve Holzner

Bob Howell

Prentice Hall PTR
Upper Saddle River, New Jersey 07458
www.phptr.com

Library of Congress Cataloging-in-Publication Data

A CIP catalog record of this book can be obtained from the Library of Congress

Production Supervisor: Wil Mara
Acquisitions Editors: Mark Taub/Jill Harry
Developmental Editor: Jim Markham
Cover Design: Nina Scuderi
Cover Design Director: Jerry Votta
Editorial Assistant: Noreen Regina
Marketing Manager: Dan DePasquale
Buyer: Maura Zaldivar

Publishing as Prentice Hall Professional Technical Rerefence
Upper Saddle River, New Jersey 07458

Prentice Hall books are widely used by corporations and government agencies for training, marketing, and resale.

For information regarding corporate and government bulk discounts, please contact Corporate and Government Sales, at 1-(800)-382-3419, or corpsales@pearsontechgroup.com.

Printed in the United States of America
10 9 8 7 6 5 4 3 2 1

ISBN 0-13-101881-7

Pearson Education LTD.
Pearson Education Australia PTY, Limited
Pearson Education Singapore, Pte. Ltd.
Pearson Education North Asia Ltd.
Pearson Education Canada, Ltd.
Pearson Educación de Mexico, S.A. de C.V.
Pearson Education—Japan
Pearson Education Malaysia, Pte. Ltd.

Contents

7 The ADO .NET DataSet 181

8 Data Binding in Windows Forms 229

DEDICATION

For my late wife, Gida, who typed the last period,
and without whose support this book would not have been possible.

I miss you honey.

—B. H.

Introduction

Welcome to *ADO .NET Programming in Visual Basic .NET.* As a fellow VB programmer and developer, I wrote this book for two reasons:

- To introduce the VB Classic (VB Version 6.0 and prior versions) programmer to VB .NET and ADO .NET and take some of the version shock out of the transition.
- To introduce non-VB programmers who have experience in other platforms (specifically Java or C++) to the advantages of database programming with the new .NET platform.

My intent is not necessarily to win you over and get you to switch platforms. That is the job of Microsoft's marketing people. My intent is to show that .NET is a radical departure from previous versions of VB and that it is a first-class tool for serious development.

A Disruptive Release

When I first started working with the beta versions of Visual Studio .NET, I could see from the very beginning that this was going to be a disruptive release, a term I adapted from sociology. In sociology, disruptive innovation refers to the invention of something so revolutionary that it changes the basic rules by which the society functions. The automobile, airplane, and personal computer are all examples of disruptive innovation.

Once the automobile was invented there was no reason to further develop horse-drawn buggies. So by calling VB .NET a disruptive release I mean that Visual Studio .NET is such a radical departure from what most VB Classic programmers are used to that it would require almost complete retraining to bring them to the point of being as productive as they were in their prior VB version. Having programmed in VB since Version 1.0, I remembered what the conversion from VB 3 to VB 4 entailed. That was the last time Microsoft radically changed the language to support 32-bit programming and operating systems such as Windows 95 and NT.

Microsoft also switched from the VB-specific VBX format component model to the new (at the time) OCX OLE-based component model. This caused a lot of consternation and discussion (read whining and complaining) among the programming community. If that seemed difficult, this time is not even remotely as easy. That was a breeze compared to this.

VB .NET

As I worked with Visual Studio .NET, however, I could see that this was much better than what we had in the past. VB Classic had grown from basically a scripting tool to a sophisticated development platform capable of creating line-of-business class systems. It also became bloatware, meaning the package became so large and cumbersome that with each new revision, we had to learn a whole new set of tools and wizards.

In the wider world of programming, VB Classic is an anomaly. It has its own proprietary IDE, its own runtime, a peculiar syntax, and its own proprietary forms package. None of these items works very well with other languages. VB Classic grew out of the early BASICs that came with old microcomputers. I remember Level II BASIC, the language that ran on my old (circa 1979) Radio Shack TRS-80 Model I, also known as the "Trash-80." While it still used line numbers, GoSubs, and Returns, it had the same basic syntax as VB Classic. That language evolved into GW-Basic that came with the original MS-DOS.

We then had Quick Basic, a cheap compiled version of GW-Basic. Then there was the Basic Professional Development System, a fully compiled and linked BASIC language for MS-DOS development. Finally came VB 1.0, which kept much of the syntax, statements, and functions of the older languages to try to win those programmers over to Windows development. If you don't believe that VB Classic evolved from those early languages, you should know that VB 6 still supports line numbers, GoSub, - Return, and GoTo. It also supports On … GoSub, an early form of a Select - Case statement. Microsoft doesn't advertise this, but it does work. Try it sometime. VB Classic has maintained that evolutionary path up until VB .NET.

With VB .NET, we now have a fully object-oriented programming language that rivals other languages, such as Java. The forms package is generic and no longer limited to use with just VB. You can actually pass entire forms across a network connection. While much of the syntax is the same (it is, after all, still BASIC), it has been standardized and brought into conformance with other languages. You no longer pass values into functions by reference as the default. The default is now by value, which is how virtually *all* other languages do it. Unfortunately, this will make transitioning difficult for many VB Classic programmers. This book is designed to ease that transition, and avoid the mistakes and wrong turns I made while hacking through it myself.

ADO .NET PROGRAMMING

ADO .NET programming has a special connection with Visual Studio .NET, and we'll see both packages at their best and most powerful in this book.

These two packages—ADO .NET and Visual Studio .NET—are specifically designed to work together. Visual Studio bends over backward to make using ADO .NET easy, and I'll cover the Visual Studio .NET database tools like the Project Explorer, the various data adapter and dataset configuration tools, the query builder, and more in depth. In fact, the natural environment for ADO .NET programming is Visual Studio .NET—and I think you'll agree as you read this book.

If this book is titled *ADO .NET Programming in Visual Basic .NET*, why do I keep referring to Visual Studio? Well, in the past, VB (and its variants, VBScript and VB For Applications) was the most natural environment for ADO database programming. The other Visual Studio tools (Visual C++, Visual Interdev, Visual FoxPro) could all use ADO, but since ADO was designed around the COM (Component Object Model) architecture, VB was the easiest way to use the package. With the advent of Visual Studio .NET, this has all changed.

Visual Studio .NET no longer uses COM as its underlying architecture. Instead it uses the Extensible Markup Language (XML) and Simple Object Access Protocol (SOAP). (You can still use your old COM objects in .NET, even ADO, but that is outside the scope of this book.) The common language runtime (CLR) interpreter allows all of the managed languages (VB, Managed C++, and C#) to utilize a common set of data types and interfaces so they can all use the same objects interchangeably. In fact, you can write components in C# and use them in VB and vice-versa. So while we will use VB .NET syntax in all of the examples and demonstrations in the book, the principles we are sharing will apply equally to C#.

WHAT'S IN THIS BOOK?

This book covers ADO .NET programming using VB .NET, which means there's a great deal of material to work with: the basics of the ADO .NET object model, Web Services, typed and untyped DataSets, DataAdapters, ASP .NET, and DataBinding. ADO .NET is intended to be the future of data access as far as Microsoft is concerned, and we'll see it all here.

TYPOGRAPHIC CONVENTIONS

For sanity's sake, I promise to adhere to the following conventions:

- Headings will divide major sections within a chapter.
- Certain terms, such as keywords, clauses, statements, methods, and parameters, will be in a fixed typeface (the `where` clause).
- Code examples will be printed in the same fixed typeface to make them easier to read:

```
Public Sub Example()
  Some Code
End Sub
```

- When you see indented text in a different typeface like this:

VB 6—That means that this section is specifically for VB 6 programmers who are making the jump to .NET. If you never programmed in VB 6 you can skip these sections.

That's it. I like to keep things simple.

WHAT YOU WILL NEED

The short answer is that you will need Microsoft Visual Studio .NET Professional Version or higher. Any machine that will run that will be capable of executing the examples in the book. If you are not sure if your machine will run Visual Studio .NET, the requirements are:

- A Pentium II 300mhz or higher. I have successfully run Visual Studio on a Pentium II 300mhz Notebook. I recommend a faster machine if possible. NO Pentiums or 486s.
- At least 256 megabyte (MB) of random access memory (RAM); ' 512 MB is preferred. Unless you have access to a server, you will also need to run the Microsoft Database Engine (MSDE) or SQL Server 2000 and

Internet Information Server (IIS) services so this memory is not all yours.

- I can't see using a display with anything less than 1024×768 resolution, unless you have really great eyesight. A 17-inch monitor is also preferred.
- A 10-gigabyte (GB) hard drive. Visual Studio .NET fully installed takes a whopping 1.7 GB! You will need to install the Microsoft Developer Network (MSDN) library that comes with it.
- Microsoft Windows NT 4 Workstation with Service Pack 6, 2000 Professional or XP Professional. The IDE will not run on Windows 95, 98, or Millennium Edition Me. (Programs developed for the .NET framework will run on Windows 98 and Me, but you must have NT 4 or higher for development. It may run on XP Home; check with Microsoft on this.
- Access to MSDE or SQL Server 7.0 or 2000. The MSDE comes with Visual Studio .NET Professional Edition. We will not be using the Jet Engine (Microsoft Access). This is because Microsoft Access does not support stored procedures or triggers. You will also need the Northwind database. This comes with the full versions of SQL Server, but when I installed the MSDE, it was not there.

If the entry price of Visual Studio .NET Professional makes you unhappy (the nonupgrade version is about $800), you can get a free 60-day evaluation copy from Microsoft. Or you can get your boss to buy it for you. Just convince him or her that the next big project cannot be done without it! Microsoft will love you and so will I. There is a "Standard" version of VB .NET on the market. It has a really great price, but, unfortunately, it lacks too many features to make it usable for this book.

You will also need some programming experience. It's good if you've programmed in previous versions of VB, but experience with any Basic language will do. If you've programmed in another object-oriented language, even better. Some experience with databases is also desirable. A decent understanding of basic SQL (Select, Update, Insert, and Delete) will help a great deal; we are not going to attempt to teach SQL. We will give you the basics, but there are other great books on SQL. The purpose of this book is to teach you how to use ADO .NET from within VB .NET and that is what we shall do. When you finish this book, you will be well-equipped to begin developing serious business applications in VB .NET.

USING THE FTP SITE

This is an explanation of the structure of the book's FTP site and how to download and access the projects. The projects are all in their completed state. There are no intermediate "under construction" steps for the code.

The projects are all in directories named for the chapter they belong to, e.g, ADOBook01 contains the projects for Chapter 1, and so forth.

Within the chapter directories are folders for each project named with the chapter and a project number. For example ADOBook01-01 is for the first project in Chapter 1.

Downloading and Using Projects

In order to access the FTP site you will need an FTP Client. There is a command-line version that comes with Windows, but the easiest way is to just use your Web broser. Open Internet Explorer, for example, and type http://www.phptr.com/howell into the address bar. From there you can simply drag and drop directories to your machine using Windows Explorer.

For Windows Forms projects, all you have to do is download the entire folder to the location of your choice, create a new blank solution in the IDE, and simply add the project to it.

Web projects are a little more complicated. Follow these instructions and you should have minimal problems—

1. Download the project into your wwwroot folder for IIS, wherever that is on your system. By default it is in c:\inetpub.
2. You can then try to open the web project directly using "File|Open|Project From Web". In most cases this should work.
3. If that does not work, then create a new Web Project and add each file from the location you downloaded to it one at a time. All paths in the projects are relative to the project root so it should not be a problem.

If you get any messages stating that "Source Code Control cannot be found" or something of the sort, you can just continue and remove the projects from source control. I went through and removed them all, but sometimes the messages pop up anyway. If you want to avoid these altogether, before opening the project, delete any files ending in .scc or .vsscc from the project root folder. You should remove all of the "read-only" file attributes as well if any are set. If you have Visual SourceSafe on you system it will then prompt you to add then project to it. If you do not have Visual SourceSafe you will not be prompted about source control.

CHAPTER 1

Visual Basic .NET Database Programming

This book is about accessing databases in Visual Basic (VB) .NET, Microsoft's latest incarnation of the popular development tool and programming language that revolutionized Windows application development. With this release, Microsoft has departed from the traditional VB paradigm by introducing object-oriented programming to VB for the first time. Microsoft has also changed lanes in its approach to database access. Until now, all of the past technologies (DAO, RDO, ADO) have relied on a connected model, where a connection to the database was maintained throughout the user's session. With ADO .NET, this has been reversed. Now we are going to a disconnected model, where connections are established just long enough to read or update the data, then closed.

Because of these changes, we will be discussing ADO .NET and VB in detail. We will be looking at how object-oriented programming is implemented in VB, as this is necessary to understand how ADO .NET works.

To alleviate version shock, we will jump right in to creating a simple database form in VB. This is not intended to be a complete discussion of ADO .NET or VB. That will come later. This chapter is intended to show you that *you can do this!* Remember there was a time when Windows programming was new to us and we thought we would never get it. We all managed to learn it and we will also manage to learn this new paradigm. As a matter of fact, that is the purpose of this book: to make you a productive VB .NET database programmer. We will not look at every property and method of every class out there. We will show you the most productive practices and give you a thorough understanding of how to use ADO .NET with VB. We will then leave it to you to dig deeper and go build something.

DATABASE ACCESS IN VB .NET

.NET is a set of application interfaces implemented as a .NET class library. This class library is used by VB .NET (and the other managed code languages, C# and managed C++) to provide programmatic access to databases. There are three basic kinds of classes.

- Connection
- Command and DataAdapter
- DataSet

`Connection` classes provide the properties and methods needed to open a channel to a database. This may be a network connection, in the case of SQL Server or other server-based database systems, or a file handle, in the case of desktop databases such as Microsoft Access (JET) databases or Excel files.

`Command` and `DataAdapter` classes provide the means to execute queries and return data from the database objects referenced by the open database connection.

`DataSet` classes (containing `DataTable` and `DataView` objects) provide a local data cache to store the results of queries that return data. The DataSet classes have no relationship to the `Command` or `DataAdapter` class that was used to retrieve the data. `DataSet` can be used as a standalone data storage object without any relationship to an external database. This is a very powerful set of classes that forms the heart of ADO .NET.

The basic process for accessing data is to open a connection to a database using a Connection object, and then use a `DataAdapter` object to execute an SQL query against the database and stream the data into a `DataTable` inside a `DataSet` object. Then you would close the database connection. ADO .NET automates much of this processing.

The basic process for updating a database from data residing in a `DataTable` inside a `DataSet` is to open a connection, then execute the `Update` method of the `DataAdapter` object and reference the `DataSet` object containing the data you wish to update. You can also execute standalone SQL statements that update data (`Insert`, `Update`, `Delete`) by using a `Command` object directly.

Both the processes for reading and updating can use stored procedures instead of SQL statements.

VB 6—VB 6 coders had a plethora of database access tools. There was Data Access Object (DAO), Remote Data Object (RDO), DAO Direct, and ActiveX Data Object (ADO). You also had a choice of whether to use object libraries, data controls, or a combination. Each of these tools came with a data control, a visual component that you could drop on a form. These provided simple database access and a visual navigation control. With VB .NET your choices are much simpler. Basically, you have ADO .NET. There is no visual navigation control in ADO .NET. (We will develop our own in Chapter 11.) You can choose which set of client classes to use: the SQL client classes, which provide high-performance access to SQL Server Version 7.0 and 2000 databases, or the OLEDB client classes, which provide access to older SQL Server databases, Oracle, Access, Excel, Flat files, and the other OLE DB providers, as well as any ODBC-compliant database system. There is a way to access these older technologies using VB .NET, through Component Object Model (COM) Interop. We will not be covering these in this book. If you need to port an application to VB .NET quickly, these may be of interest to you. Be warned that although you will have programmatic access to the object libraries, you will not be able to use the VB .NET control binding mechanism to bind controls to them. If your application really must still use ADO, RDO, or DAO, it is better left in VB 6. Any new applications should be developed using ADO .NET from the beginning.

The ADO .NET Class Library

ADO .NET is implemented in the .NET environment as a set of classes which belong to the `System.Data` namespace. A namespace is a logical grouping of classes. A namespace usually compiles into a single dynamic link library (DLL) but it doesn't have to. When we want to access the classes in a namespace, we have to create a reference to it. This is similar to creating a reference to a COM object library in VB 6. The good news here is that when we create a project in VB .NET, the `System.Data` namespace is included automatically.

The `System.Data` library is divided into three major branches as illustrated in Figure 1.1. The top level contains the classes that make up the `DataSet` object. The `System.Data.SqlClient` level contains the SQL Server-optimized `SqlConnection` and `SqlDataAdapter` classes. The `System.Data.OleDb` level contains the general-purpose OLEDB `OleDbConnection` and `OleDbDataAdapter` classes.

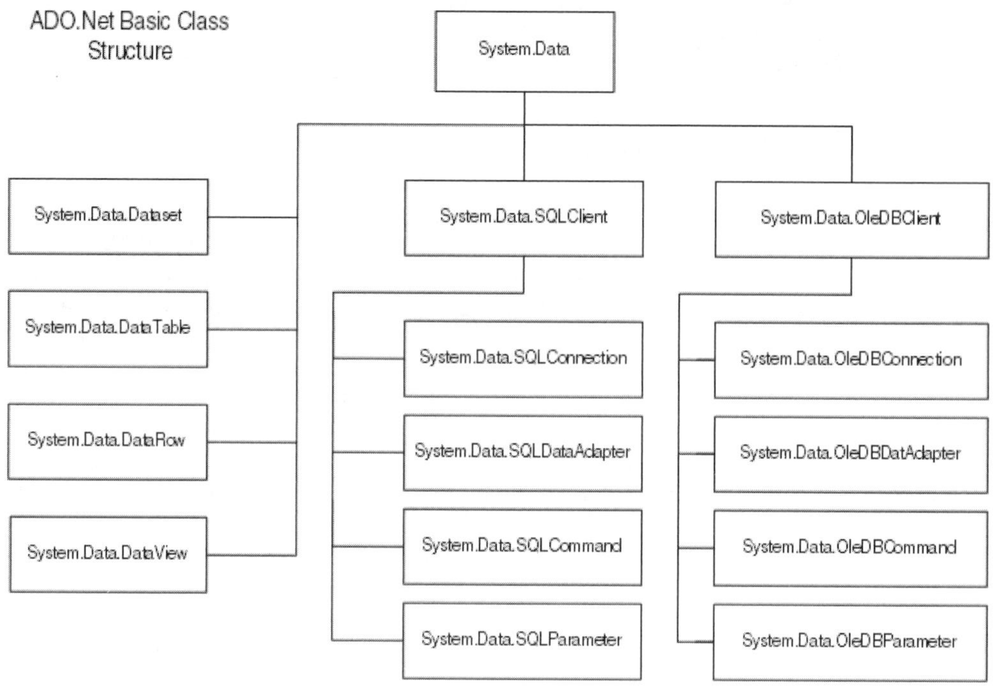

FIGURE 1.1 The ADO .NET class structure (simplified).

The `OleDb` classes are for accessing non-SQL Server databases such as Oracle and Access. These two namespaces are on parallel levels. Since we will be using SQL Server in all of our examples, we will concentrate on the `SqlClient` classes. The `OleDBClient` classes are very similar; however, there are a few differences, mainly with how `OleDBDataAdapter` handles parameters. When I demonstrate these differences I will use an Access database (.mdb) file, since most of us would not have access to an Oracle database (myself included).

Let's take a quick tour:

- SqlConnection—Handles all communications with the server, including connecting to databases, authenticating users and resource management. For ADO users, it is similar to the ADO `Connection` object. Connections are identified through a `ConnectionString` property. This contains information such as server name, database name, user name, and password. For you veterans, the Connection string is similar in format to an ODBC Data Source Name (DSN) string. The good news is that you don't have to remember the arcane syntax of the Connection string. The SqlConnection object will build one for you.

- SqlCommand—Basically wraps an SQL statement. This statement can be a select query, a query that updates the database, or a stored procedure call. `SqlCommand` must reference an `SqlConnection` object for it to work. Because ADO .NET uses a disconnected architecture, the command object establishes a connection only when needed. You can force it to connect using the `Open` method of the Connection object. Use the `SqlCommand` object to execute SQL statements directly on the database. The most obvious use is for updating the database using dynamic SQL. This is where you build your SQL statement programmatically, then send it to the server for execution. I prefer this method because it provides the most control. The `Command` class also contains the parameters collection, which contains any parameter objects needed to execute the query, such as stored procedure parameters (input and output) and ODBC-style placeholder parameters within an SQL statement.
- SqlParameter—Represents a parameter to be passed to a stored procedure or a placeholder in an SQL statement. You can create your parameters manually or have ADO .NET create them for you by parsing your SQL statement or by fetching them from the stored procedure.
- SqlDataAdapter—Contains up to four `SqlCommand` objects, one each to `Select`, `Insert`, `Update`, and `Delete`. The `DataAdapter` class functions as a mediator between the `DataSet` and the database. Remember we said that ADO .NET is an inherently disconnected architecture? This class is used to fetch data from the database and fill the tables in the `DataSet`. It is also used to update the database with changes made to the `DataSet`. The `DataAdapter` is also responsible for marshaling, or converting, data types from native .NET types to those supported by the underlying database.
- DataSet—The main class you will work with programmatically. The `DataSet` can be bound to Windows Forms controls and ASP .NET controls. It is roughly analogous to the `Recordset` object of ADO but it is much more powerful. The `DataSet` is more like an in-memory database all by itself. It contains tables, keys, constraints, and relations. As a matter of fact, you can use a `DataSet` as a stand-alone in-memory database. It has no direct relationship to any external database. The other important thing about `DataSets` is that they persist themselves as Extensible Markup Language (XML). You can save a `DataSet` to disk as an XML document. Likewise, when a `DataSet` needs to move from computer to computer across a network, it does so using an XML stream. Let's look at the subcomponents of the `DataSet` class.

- DataTable—The DataTable is an in-memory representation of a database table. It contains rows and columns. It is a fully database system-independent representation of the data. In other words, no matter which in which database system your data resides (SQL Server, Oracle, etc.) the data will look the same. The DataTable contains the following collections:
  - Columns collection—A collection of DataColumn objects that define the metadata of the table.
  - Rows collection—The rows of data returned from the database or some other source.
  - Constraints—A collection of constraints placed on the columns. A constraint is a primary key, unique index, and so forth. These are inherited from the source database table.
  - Tables collection—A collection of all the DataTables in the DataSet. It is indexed numerically and by the table name.
  - Relations—Defines the relationship between DataTables. It is analogous to a foreign key or declarative referential integrity (DRI). The Relations collection contains all of the Relations objects in a DataSet.
- DataReaders—There are two versions of this class: SqlDataReader and OleDbDataReader. Both provide a way to read forward-only cursorless data streams from a database. This is the most efficient way to read data from a database. The drawback is that the data cannot be updated using one of these classes. However if you need to read lots of data with blinding speed, and plan to use some other way of updating it or updating isn't necessary (with a report, for example), then this is the class to use. The class is also very useful in batch (command-line) programs.
- DataView—Used to implement data binding. It also contains methods for navigating, editing, sorting, searching, and filtering the data in a Datatable. For you VB 6 veterans, many of the old Recordset methods can be found here. Each Datatable has a default view manager, but you can create several and apply them one at a time to the Datatable to quickly change sorts, filters, and so forth. This is a powerful class for displaying data.

The General Process for Accessing a Database

Creating an SQL Server or Microsoft Data Engine (MSDE) database connection, accessing and updating the data, and closing the connection take 18 steps:

1. Create an instance of the SqlConnection class.
2. Format a Connection string with the server name, database name, user name, and password. Assign the string to the `ConnectionString` property of the SqlConnection class.
3. Create an instance of an SqlCommand class.
4. Format a `Select` statement and assign it to the `CommandText` property of the SqlCommand class.
5. Create another SqlCommand class.
6. Assign the SqlCommand object's `Connection` property to the SqlConnection you just created.
7. Format an SQL Update statement and assign it to the `CommandText` property.
8. Create an instance of the SqlDataAdapter class.
9. Assign the Select command object to the DataAdapter's `SelectCommand` property.
10. Assign the Update command object to the DataAdapter's `UpdateCommand` object.
11. Create an instance of a DataSet class.
12. Open the connection using the SqlConnection object's `Open` method.
13. Use the `Fill` method of the DataAdapter to fill the DataSet with a DataTable containing the data returned from the SQL Select command.
14. Close the connection using the SqlConnection object's `Close` method.
15. Using the DataSet's DataTables collection, programmatically manipulate the data in the `Rows` property of the DataTable.
16. Open the connection again using the SqlConnection object's `Open` method.
17. Use the `Update` method of the DataAdapter to flush the changes back to the database.
18. Close the connection using the SqlConnection object's `Close` method.

YOUR FIRST ADO .NET PROGRAM

We will now create a simple command-line program using ADO .NET. We will access a table, list the rows to the console, and close the connection.

1. Begin by opening the Visual Studio integrated development environment (IDE).

2. Next select the File|New|NewProject menu item. The New Project dialog opens. On the left you will notice a tree view with several different types of project groups listed: VB, Visual C# and Visual C++, and others.
3. Select the VB tree node. In the list view on the right you will see a number of project templates.
4. Scroll down and select Console Application.
5. Change the name of the project to ADOBook1. If you wish, you can create a subfolder under the default location so you can group the projects.
6. Click OK.

Visual Studio creates a VB console application with one module named Module1. It is also creates a Sub Main procedure to act as the program entry point.

```
Module Module1
  Sub Main()
  End Sub
End Module
```

VB 6—In VB 6 you could not create a console application easily. It was possible, but involved application program interface (API) calls and lots of arcane syntax. Even so-called batch programs with only a Sub Main() function still ran as a Windows code image. This was always one of the big complaints of the C/C++ crowd and Unix programmers moving to the Windows platform. As a participant in both realms, I could understand their frustration. Some jobs simply do not require the overhead of the windowing environment. This is especially true of server-side applications that do no more than massage data, such as batch billing and posting programs. Well, Microsoft finally addresses this issue in VB .NET. It only took *seven* versions!

Look at the Project Explorer. Expand the References node. Notice that there are three namespaces: System, System.Data, and System.XML. These are the basic namespaces required to write a console database application.

Now let's add code. First we want to declare our objects and variables. Enter the following declarations right after the Sub Main() declaration:

```
Dim cn As New SqlClient.SqlConnection()
Dim ad As New SqlClient.SqlDataAdapter()
Dim cmd As New SqlClient.SqlCommand()
Dim ds As New DataSet()
Dim strCn As String
Dim strSQL As String
Dim row As DataRow
```

Notice how the IDE automatically indents for you. My advice is to get used to this. If you used a different formatting standard (or none at all) in the past, you can adjust the IDE to your standard but I advise against it. The defaults conform to the VB coding standards set forth by Microsoft. I am a strong proponent of coding standards as they give the code a uniform look and feel within an organization. This is important when several generations of coders must work with a program.

VB 6—In VB 6 it was not considered good practice to declare object variables using the `New` keyword. This would cause bizarre behavior because merely referencing the variable would cause an instance to be created. This is no longer true in VB .NET. Instances of classes are created when they are declared if they are declared as New. Because the .NET common language runtime (CLR) uses garbage collection, you do not have to be as concerned about releasing references to objects (by assigning them to Nothing). In addition, you can assign an object variable to Nothing in VB .NET even if it was declared `As New`. You can also have some stay over when the object is destroyed by calling the `Dispose` method. This does not actually destroy the object. It marks it for garbage collection, so there is not really full control, but it is better than nothing.

Now go ahead and add the rest of the code:

```
Try
' NOTE: Replace the name MyServer with the name of your server.
' ALSO: Be sure to use a user name and password that is valid for your
server.
  strCn = "Server=MyServer;Initial
Catalog=Northwind;UID=adobook;pwd=xxxx"
  cn.ConnectionString = strCn
  strSQL = "Select * from Customers"
  cmd.CommandText = strSQL
  ad.SelectCommand = cmd
  ad.SelectCommand.Connection = cn
  ad.Fill(ds)
  For Each row In ds.Tables(0).Rows
    Console.WriteLine(CStr(row.Item("CustomerID")) & vbTab &
CStr(row.Item("CompanyName")))
  Next
Catch errobj As Exception
  Console.WriteLine(errobj.Message)
End Try
```

Take note of the Try, Catch, End Try blocks of code. This is the new structured error-handling construct of VB .NET. This replaces the `On Error`... method of older versions of VB. When an error occurs within the Try block, control jumps to the first Catch block that references the Error Object returned by the system. The Error Object's root class is Exception. All other custom error classes derive from this class. Therefore, since we are catching all errors that send an Exception class, this will catch the error and assign the exception object to the errobj variable. Once the Catch exception code executes, control passes to the first statement after the End Try, which in this case is the end of the program.

Compiling the Program

Now we must compile the program. Point to the Build menu and select Build ADOBook01-01. We don't want to just run the project. This would compile the program, and start a console session, but the program would execute too fast to see the results. Instead let's start our own console session by using a special command prompt from the Visual Studio .NET program menu. This is the same command prompt (cmd.exe), but sets up all the correct environment variables for running .NET programs. You may want to drag a copy to the command bar or desktop for easy access. It is found in the Start menu, Programs, Microsoft Visual Studio .NET, Microsoft Visual Studio .NET Tool, Visual Studio .NET Command Prompt.

Once you have the console session running, navigate to the folder where your program executable resides using the cd command. Be sure to put path names with spaces inside double quotes. By default, all .NET compilers put their executables in a "bin" folder immediately under the folder where you have your source code. Run the program by typing ADOBook1 at the command prompt. After a second (depending on your machine's speed and the location of SQL Server or MSDE), a list of customer IDs and names should appear on the screen, after which the command prompt will reappear. Let's take a look at the program line-by-line.

```
strCn = "Server=MyServer;Initial Catalog=Northwind;UID=adobook;pwd=xxxx"
cn.ConnectionString = strCn
```

These two lines set up the ConnectionString. I like to assign my string properties to string variables first and then assign the string variable to the property. This is so I can examine the string while debugging in case I formatted it incorrectly. Substitute the name of your server and use a user name and password that will allow access to your server. The user name and password in the example are not real. Note that we did not specify a provider (SQLOLEDB.1) as we would have had to in VB 6. This is because we are using the SqlClient classes and it is assumed we are connecting to SQL Server. If we were using the OleDbClient classes we would have had to include the OLEDB provider in the Connection string.

These next four lines set up the DataAdapter:

```
strSQL = "Select * from Customers"
cmd.CommandText = strSQL
cmd.Connection = cn
ad.SelectCommand = cmd
```

Notice that DataAdapter contains the SqlCommand object cmd. The command object in turn contains the SQL statement and a reference to the Connection object. As we said, the DataAdapter acts as the mediator between the DataSet and the database or data source.

So far, all we have done is set up the objects. We have not actually opened a Connection or read any data. The next line does all of this for us.

```
ad.Fill(ds)
```

The `Fill` method of the DataAdapter opens the connection, executes the SQL statement, and caches the results in a DataTable object in the DataSet (ds). It then closes the connection. Remember, we are working under the assumption of inherently disconnected and sessionless data access. This is a good thing, because your SQL Server will not have to maintain 3,000 open connections for all concurrent users. Additionally, we did not have to release any of the objects. When an object goes out of scope, the garbage collector automatically releases the reference and deallocates the memory. There is a way to force an object to dereference itself, but we will look at that later. In most cases it is not necessary.

AN ADO .NET WINDOWS FORM PROGRAM

Now it's time to create a simple database form. There are two ways to accomplish this: use the data form wizard or build it ourselves. Using the wizard is quick but we wouldn't learn anything. As you will learn, when you begin the build, a Windows form is considerably more complex than the console application.

VB 6—In VB 6 the easiest way to create a data form without using wizards was by using the ADO Data Control. You could drop this on a form and by setting a few properties you could gain access to your database. Then you could drop some data-bound controls on the form, set the `DataSource` and `DataField` properties and you were done. You didn't have to write any code. The Data Control handled all the details for you. Not so with VB .NET. Since ADO .NET is a disconnected protocol, there is a lot more to creating a data form. There is no Data Control. The database will not be updated automatically, so we will have to write code for this. We will have to write code to navigate through the data as well.

The purpose of this exercise is to demonstrate the basics of creating a data-bound Windows form. We will not explain every aspect of the code here. We want only to get started. We will go into much more detail in later chapters so hang in there.

Begin by closing any open solutions. Next create a project. When the New Project dialog opens, select Windows Application under the VB .NET templates. Name the Project ADOBook2. The IDE will create a project and it will also create a Windows form called Form1.vb. The form designer should be displayed. For you VB 6 coders this should look similar to a new VB 6 application. Switch to Code view by clicking the Code button in the Project Explorer. You should see something like the image in Figure 1.2.

You can see that the form inherits from the Windows.Forms.Form base class. There is also a collapsed region. Regions are new in VB .NET. Basically they enable the programmer to hide code. This is only cosmetic—any user can open the region and view or edit what's inside. The main purpose is for code organization and the ability to tidy up the display. Expand the region by clicking the plus box next to it. You will see a bunch of code that was

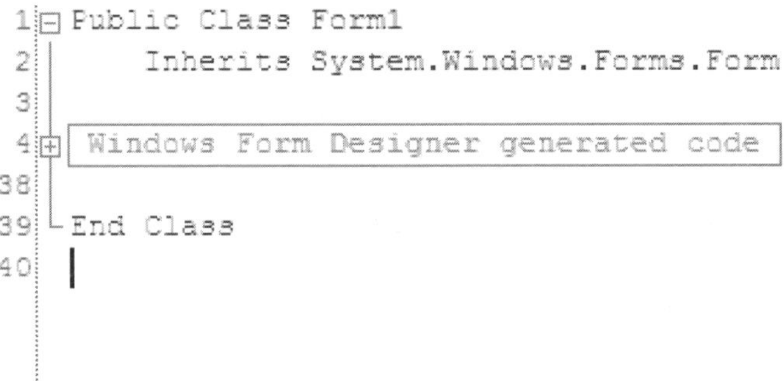

FIGURE 1.2 Empty Windows form code.

added by the forms designer. Do not modify this code. The form designer will maintain this area of code for you. We will explain this code in detail in a later chapter. Go ahead and collapse the region again. Go back to the form designer.

Now we have to begin adding the data components to the form. There is a real easy way to do this. Open Server Explorer. This should be rolled up on the left side of the designer window and should appear as a vertical tab. If you hover the mouse pointer over the tab, it should unroll. (If you have turned off animation or have messed with the IDE since you installed it, the Server Explorer may not be readily seen. I will leave it up to you to find it. Check the View menu.)

Open the subtree for one of the listed servers with the SQL Server on it that you are using. Expand the SQL Servers node. Under this node find the Northwind database. Expand it. Expand the Tables folder. Find the Customers table. (See Figure 1.3.) Now drag the Customers table onto the form and drop it anywhere. Two components appear in the component area under the form. There is an SqlConnection1 object and an SqlDataAdapter1 object.

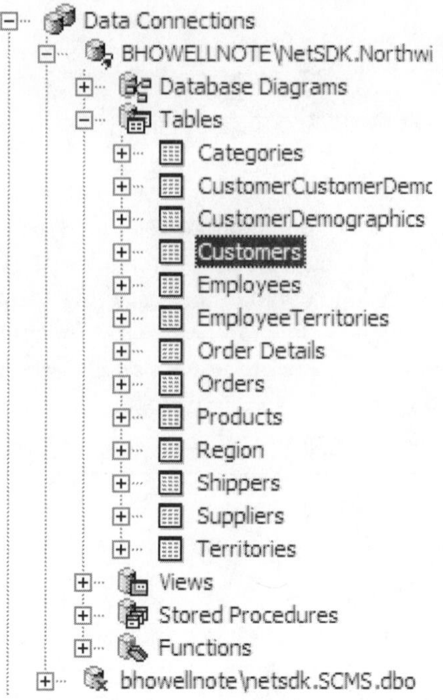

FIGURE 1.3 The Server Explorer.

VB 6—In VB 6 nonvisual controls appeared on the form at design time. They were actually visual controls that had no visual interface, so they were invisible at runtime. With VB .NET there is a new type of class called a component class. These are part of the `Component` model and are not visual. They can be dropped on any form or component that supports the `IComponentModel` interface. This enables us to visually create components that contain other components. My advice is to create all of your components using the `Component` model. This makes creating and using them much easier and saves a lot of coding effort.

Right-click on SqlDataAdapter1. Select Generate DataSet from the context menu. When the dialog opens, check Add to designer when finished. Accept the defaults and click Finished. A new DataSet will appear in the designer. This is a typed DataSet. What actually happened is that the IDE generated a whole new class, inherited from the DataSet class that was customized using the SQL statement in the DataAdapter. The DataSet you created is a type of the class just generated. In this way, it is easy to create more instances of the same DataSet object by typing the DataSet. It took me a while to figure all this out so if you are lost, stay with it. We will clear it all up in later chapters. For now just accept it at face value.

Creating the Visual Interface

Let's switch tracks and start creating the visual design of the form. Start by rolling out the toolbox by hovering your mouse pointer over it. Select the TextBox control. Drop it on your form. Next move and resize it so it is positioned in a convenient place. If you've never done any visual design before, this is a simple matter of grabbing the control's handles (the tiny black boxes that appear when you select the control) and dragging them to a new size. Move the control by clicking on the grab border and dragging the control to where you want it. Next do the same thing with a Label control. Position the label next to the text box. Change the text property of the label control to Customer ID. Change the name of the text box to txtCustomerID. To set the data binding for the text box, click on the text box to select it. Select the property labeled (`DataBindings`). Click the plus box to expand the property. Your Properties window should look like that shown in Figure 1.4.

Select the property labeled `Text`. This is not the same as the regular text property. This is telling VB to bind the `Text` property to the selected field in the DataSet. Drop down the list of selections for the `Text` property. You will see the DataSet we just created listed. Expand the DataSet and you will see the Customers DataTable. Expand that and find—and select—the column

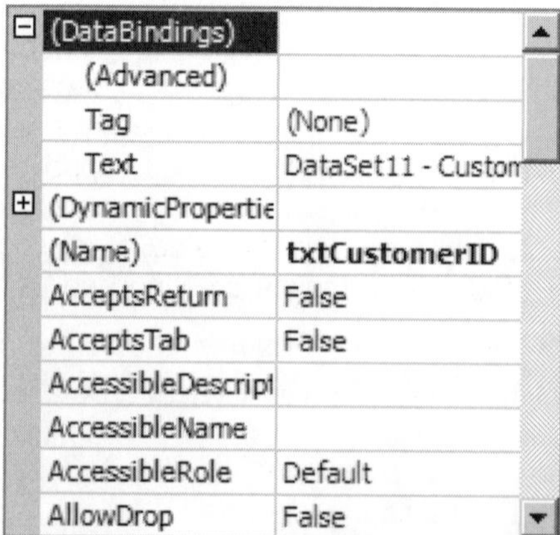

(DataBindings)
(Advanced)
Tag (None)
Text DataSet11 - Custom
(DynamicPropertie
(Name) txtCustomerID
AcceptsReturn False
AcceptsTab False
AccessibleDescript
AccessibleName
AccessibleRole Default
AllowDrop False

FIGURE 1.4 The Properties window.

CustomerID. You have just bound the control to the CustomerID field in DataSet1. Now scroll down the Properties window until you see the regular text property. Notice there is a database symbol next to the property name. This indicates that this property has been bound. Repeat this process for the following database fields: CompanyName, ContactName, Address, City, Region, PostalCode, and Country. When you are done your form should look like Figure 1.5.

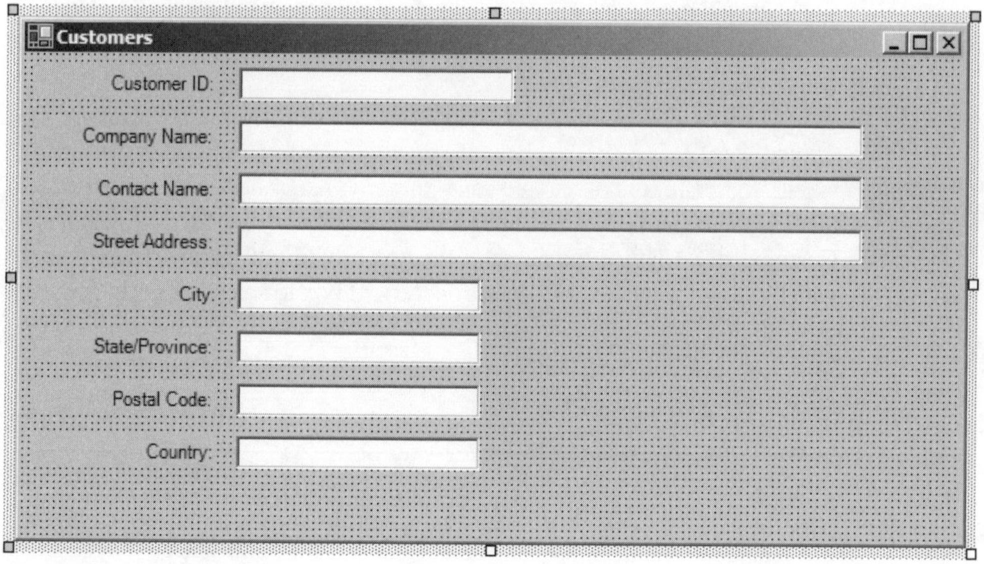

FIGURE 1.5 The basic user interface design.

VB 6—In VB 6 you could only bind what the control author designated as bindable. In addition, you had to set the `DataSource` property to either an ADO Data Control or a Recordset object in code. You could also set the property to a data environment object. You then set the `DataField` property to the column you wanted to bind to. The `DataField` property could only bind to one property, usually text or caption depending on the control. In VB .NET, the property that displays text to the `Text` property has been standardized. There are no more `Caption` properties. This is in line with the Windows API, making changing a Label to a TextBox real easy. All you have to do is change its declaration and initializer. No more global search and replace Text for Caption. VB .NET also allows you to bind to any property, as long as the data types are compatible. If you open Advanced... in the (`DataBindings`) property, you will see what I mean in Figure 1.6.

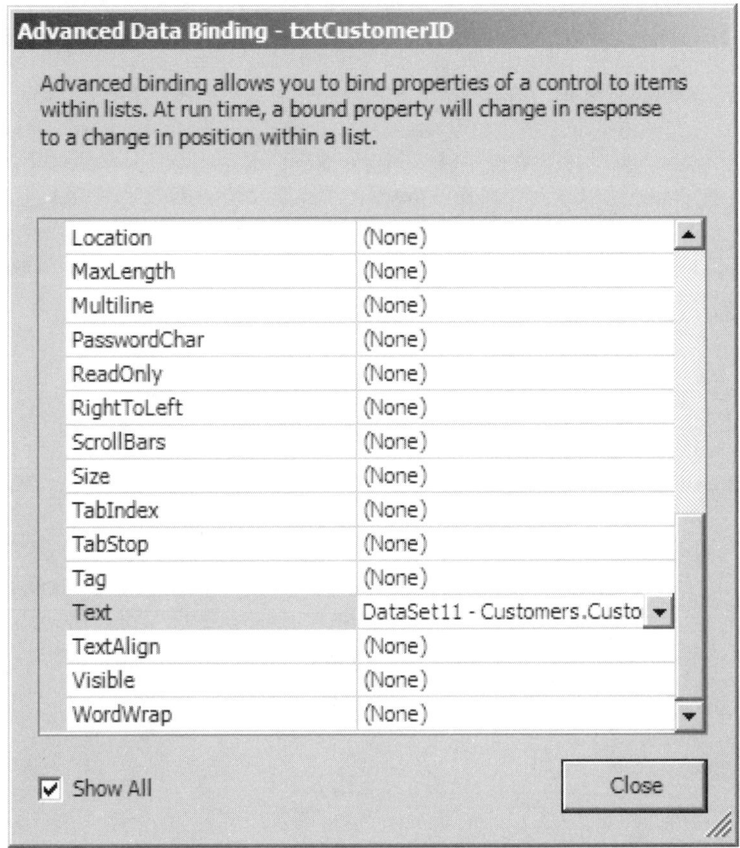

FIGURE 1.6 The advanced data binding dialog.

Getting Data from the Database

Now compile and run the project. You should get a form with blank controls. What happened to the data binding? Why doesn't it show any data? Remember we said that ADO .NET is disconnected. This means that there is no way for the DataSet to know where you want to pull the data from unless you tell it programmatically. I personally think that this is a flaw in ADO .NET. I agree with the concept of disconnected data, but I think there should be a property you can set either on the DataSet, to tell it which DataAdapter to link to, or on the DataAdapter to tell it which DataSet to manage. You could set this at design time, or leave it blank and do it programmatically. At any rate, right now the only way to do it is programmatically. We could have it populate the DataSet when the form starts, but I'd rather use a command button for now. This will also enable us to refresh the data later on. Drop a command button on the form. Name it btnLoad. Change the `Text` property of the button to Get Data. Double-click on the button and the code window opens with the button's Click event precreated. Enter the following code:

```
Private Sub LoadData()
  Dim dsTemp As New DataSet1()

  Try
    SqlDataAdapter1.Fill(dsTemp)
    DataSet11.Clear()
    DataSet11.Merge(dsTemp)
  Catch errobj As Exception
    MsgBox(errobj.Message)
  End Try
End Sub

Private Sub btnLoad_Click(ByVal sender As System.Object, _
      ByVal e As System.EventArgs) Handles btnLoad.Click
  LoadData()
End Sub
```

I prefer to make my procedures that actually do the work into separate procedures instead of putting the code directly into the event procedure. This enables me to reuse the code if I need to perform the same function from somewhere other than the event. Why do I go through the trouble of creating a temporary DataSet to fill? It has to do with a peculiar effect of data binding. If I filled the DataSet directly we would have to re-bind all of the controls programmatically. By merging the DataSets it doesn't require the re-binding.

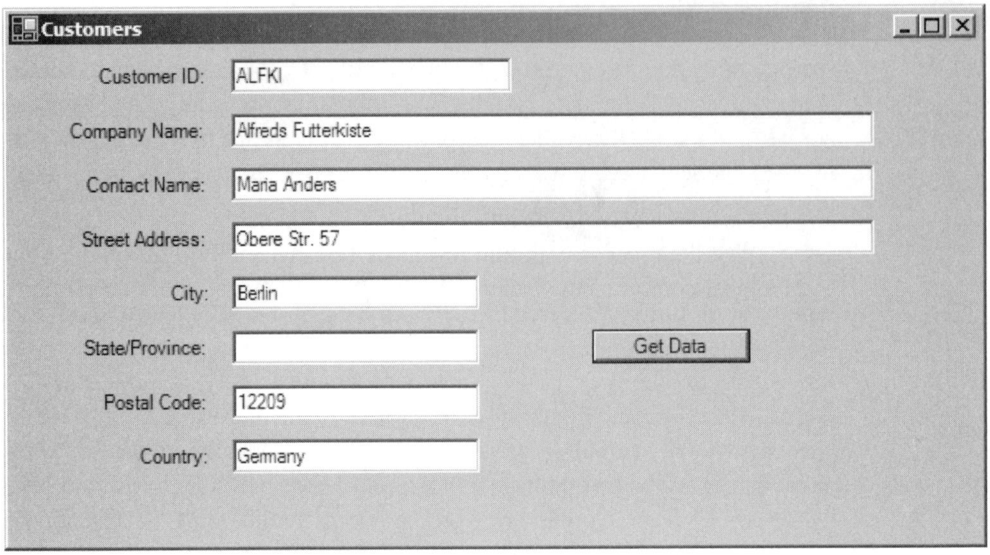

FIGURE 1.7 The form with the button on it.

This is what the documentation says. I tried it the other way and it seems to work fine. I would still go with the recommended practice.

Compile and run the project. When the form opens, click the Get Data button. The controls should fill with data. Your form should look like Figure 1.7.

Navigating the Records

This is great but how do we navigate the records? We'll have to create navigation buttons. We'll use the typical First, Previous, Next, and Last buttons. When we are done what we will have is a group of controls that resembles the old Data Control from previous versions of VB. It will not be a true data control; we will create one of these in Chapter 11.

Begin by dropping a panel control on the form and sizing it so it is long horizontally and short vertically. The panel control is new to VB .NET. We will use the panel as a container for the other controls we will use.

VB 6—In previous versions of VB, if you wanted to group controls you had to use a Frame control and turn off the border, or use a Picture Box, which comes with a lot of overhead. Microsoft addressed this issue with the panel control. It is a simple control to be used for grouping other controls. It has low overhead and includes properties for positioning and arranging the controls it contains.

Next, add four command buttons to the control, one each for the four functions. Name them, in order, btnFirst, btnPrev, btnNext, and btnLast. Be sure to name them as listed. To make the buttons align properly we will use the `Dock` property. Select btnFirst. Scroll down the Properties window until you find the `Dock` property. Click the down arrow. What appears is a graphical representation of the docking enumeration. Select left by clicking the button that is all the way on the left. Figure 1.8 should help.

Repeat the process with btnPrev. Dock btnNext and btnLast on the right. Add a label control to the panel. Use the fill setting for its docking property. This is the center button in the drop down. This causes the label control to fill up the remaining area of the panel not used by the four buttons.

For the `Text` property of the buttons, we will use greater-than (>) and less-than (<) signs to represent the four functions. Change the `Text` property of btnFirst to <<, btnPrev to <, btnNext to >, and btnLast to >>. Your panel should look like Figure 1.9.

Open the code window and enter the following procedures:

```
Private Sub btnNext_Click(ByVal sender As System.Object, _
  ByVal e As System.EventArgs) Handles btnNext.Click
  Me.BindingContext(DataSet11, "Customers").Position += 1
  UpdatePos()
End Sub

Private Sub btnLast_Click(ByVal sender As System.Object, _
  ByVal e As System.EventArgs) Handles btnLast.Click
  Me.BindingContext(DataSet11, "Customers").Position =
Me.BindingContext(DataSet11, "Customers").Count - 1
  UpdatePos()
End Sub
```

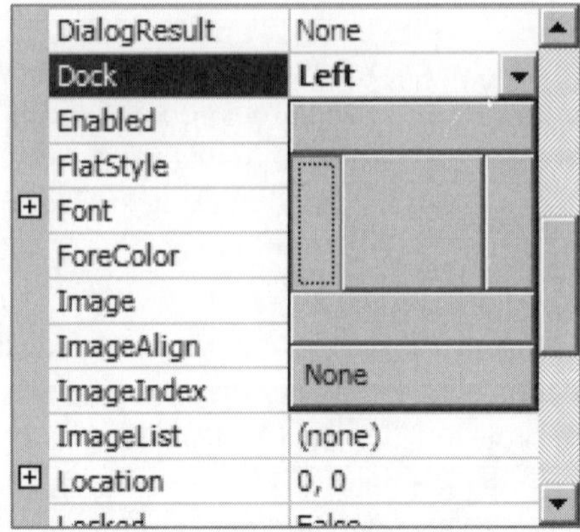

FIGURE 1.8 The dock graphical representation.

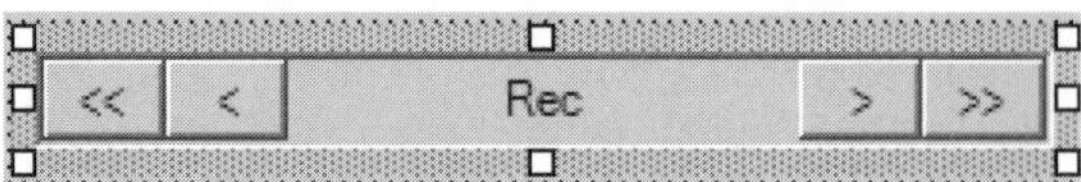

FIGURE 1.9 The data navigator.

```
Private Sub btnFirst_Click(ByVal sender As System.Object, _
  ByVal e As System.EventArgs) Handles btnFirst.Click
  Me.BindingContext(DataSet11, "Customers").Position = 0
  UpdatePos()
End Sub

Private Sub btnPrev_Click(ByVal sender As System.Object, _
  ByVal e As System.EventArgs) Handles btnPrev.Click
  Me.BindingContext(DataSet11, "Customers").Position -= 1
  UpdatePos()
End Sub

Private Sub UpdatePos()
  lblRecs.Text = "Record " & Me.BindingContext(DataSet11, _
   "Customers").Position + 1 & " of " & _
   Me.BindingContext(DataSet11, "Customers").Count
End Sub
```

There are two items worth noting in these procedures:

- The `BindingContext` property
- The use of arithmetic assignment operators

The `BindingContext` property connects the DataSet's DataTable object to the controls on the form. We will investigate the BindingContext object in detail in a later chapter. The basic function of the BindingContext is to keep track of the current row position and to manage the editing of records through the form. Familiarity with the BindingContext object is essential to working with data-bound controls on a form. UpdatePos updates the caption on the Navigation control. It will have additional functionality later on.

VB .NET now supports the +=, -=, *=, and /= operators, a la C/C++. Hallelujah! (The increment and decrement unary operators would be nice too!)

Compile and run the project. Click the Get Data button. The form should fill with data. Click the navigation buttons. The controls should change with the rows. The form should look like the one shown in Figure 1.10.

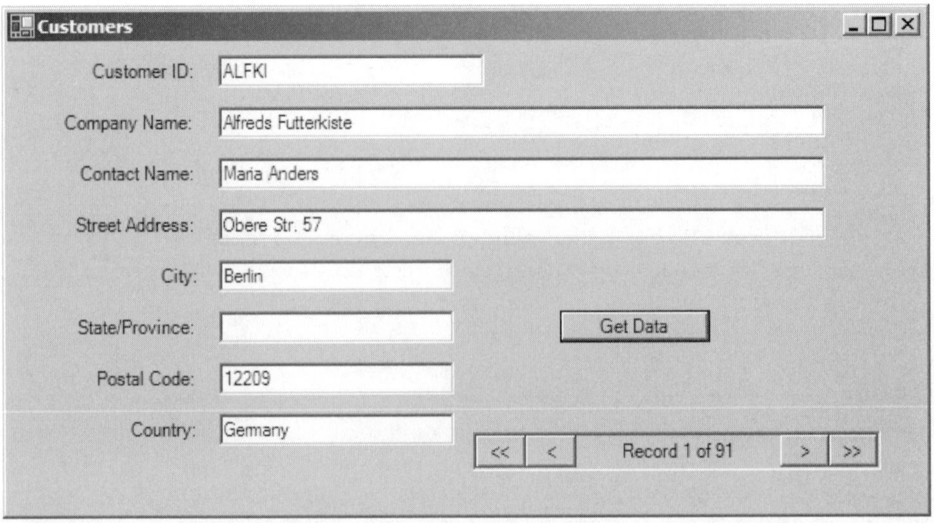

FIGURE 1.10 The form with the navigator on it.

Adding and Deleting Rows

Next we have to add functionality to add and delete records. We also must create a way to update the data source with the changes. First, let's tidy up. Dock the panel controls with the navigation buttons to the bottom of the form. Next, drop four more buttons onto the form. Name them btnAdd, btnDelete, btnSave, and btnReject. Change the text captions to look like the form in Figure 1.10. Drop a picture box on the form. Change the image property to the save.bmp bitmap in the Graphics folder in the Visual Studio folders under Program Files. Size the picture box to the size of the bitmap. Name this control picDirty. We will use this as an indicator that changes have been made to the data. The finished form designer should look like Figure 1.11.

Before we can save our changes to the database, we have to be able to make changes. To edit a record, you can just type the new data over the existing. How do we add and delete records? Let's put that functionality in first. Add the following event procedures for the Add New and Delete buttons:

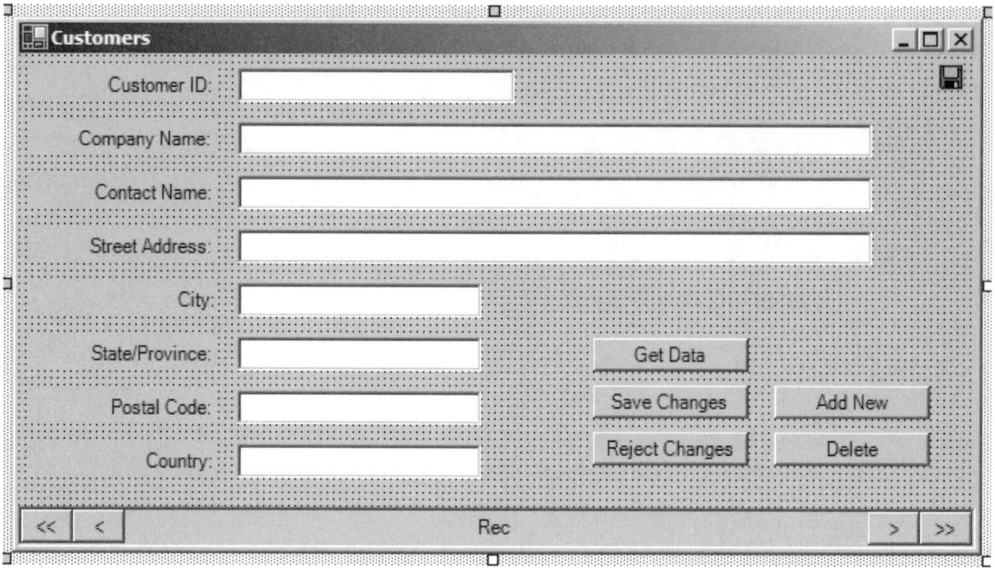

FIGURE 1.11 The final design of the form.

```
Private Sub btnAdd_Click(ByVal sender As System.Object, _
  ByVal e As System.EventArgs) Handles btnAdd.Click
  Me.BindingContext(DataSet11, "Customers").EndCurrentEdit()
  Me.BindingContext(DataSet11, "Customers").AddNew()
End Sub

Private Sub btnDelete_Click(ByVal sender As System.Object, _
  ByVal e As System.EventArgs) Handles btnDelete.Click

DataSet11.Tables("Customers").DefaultView.Delete((Me.BindingContext(Dat
aSet11, "Customers").Position))
  UpdatePos()
End Sub
```

TIP—Double-click the button control to create an empty event procedure template. The event used depends on the default event for the control, but the default event for the button is the click event.

These two procedures open a new row for adding, and deleting, the current row, respectively. They do nothing to update the database. They only enable editing the DataSet. Try the code. Compile and run the project. Click the Add New button. The controls should all blank out. Fill in some data. Click the Next button. The record counter should now say 92 records. Go back to the record you just entered. Click Delete. The record counter should now go back to 91 records.

Updating the Database

Next, we want to add the ability to update the database. Add the following event procedures to the form:

```
Private Sub btnSave_Click(ByVal sender As System.Object, _
  ByVal e As System.EventArgs) Handles btnSave.Click
  Dim dsTemp As DataSet1

  Me.BindingContext(DataSet11,
"Customers").EndCurrentEdit()
  If DataSet11.HasChanges Then
    dsTemp = CType(DataSet11.GetChanges, DataSet1)
    SqlDataAdapter1.Update(dsTemp)
    DataSet11.AcceptChanges()
  End If
  UpdatePos()
End Sub
```

This procedure performs four basic functions for saving changed data in a DataSet. First we call the `EndCurrentEdit` method of the binding context. This has the same effect as if we moved off the row using the visual interface. It ends the editing session and saves the changed values in the controls to the DataTable in the DataSet. There is a complementary method called `CancelCurrentEdit` which discards changes made on the screen and restores the original values.

Next, we call the `HasChanges` method. This method returns true (1) if the DataSet has any changed, added, or deleted rows. If there were changes, we store them in a temporary DataSet. We do this so we can minimize network traffic. Since we are using a local SQL Server, the effect of this is minimal, but if the DataSet were large and we had a wide area network (WAN) connection to the server, minimizing traffic has major benefits. To get the changed rows into a temporary DataSet, we call the `GetChanges` method of the DataSet. This gets the changes from all of the DataTable objects in the DataSet. Since we only have one, this is not a consideration right now, but it may be in the future. Note the call to the CType function. This is because the `GetChanges` method returns an untyped DataSet. In order for the assignment to work, we have to typecast the DataSet to the DataSet1 type that was created when we created the typed DataSet. That is what the CType function does.

We then call the update method of the DataAdapter and pass it the temporary DataSet we just created. This does an atomic update of the database, meaning it employs an implicit transaction automatically. If there were multiple tables to be updated, they would all succeed or all fail. You can override this functionality. We will see how in a later chapter.

The last statement in the if block causes the DataSet to reset all the change flags on the rows. The way the DataSet knows which rows have changed is that each row has a Changed, Added, or Deleted flag. This is how it knows which rows to extract when the `GetChanges` method is called. The `AcceptChanges` method simply resets the flags so we know any changes were flushed to the database. Finally, we call the UpdatPos procedure to update the navigation label.

Compile and run the project. Make some changes to a row. Click the Save Changes button. The data will be written to the database. Try adding some rows, saving the data and deleting some rows. (Don't delete any of the rows that were originally in the Northwind database.) You should look at the table from outside the application to see the data being changed. You can use the Server Explorer for this purpose. If you navigate to the Customers table and double-click it, a grid will open showing the data in the table. You will have to refresh the grid after each change is made through our program.

Finishing Touches

A final couple of finishing touches and our first Windows data form will be finished. What if our user decides to discard the changes that he made? We can easily add this feature. We already placed a Reject Changes button on our form. We will use this button for this purpose. Add the following event procedure to the form:

```
Private Sub btnReject_Click(ByVal sender As System.Object, _
  ByVal e As System.EventArgs) Handles btnReject.Click
  Me.BindingContext(DataSet11,
"Customers").CancelCurrentEdit()
  DataSet11.RejectChanges()
  UpdatePos()
End Sub
```

This code cancels any edits on the current row. It then calls the `RejectChanges` method of the DataSet object. This method effectively rolls back any changes made since the DataSet was filled or since the last call to the `AcceptChanges` method. Any deleted rows will reappear, any added rows will vanish, and any changes to existing rows will be restored to their original values. We will examine how the DataSet does this in a later chapter.

It would also be nice for the user of our form to know if any changes were made to the DataSet so it can be saved. We will employ two visual cues for this purpose. We will enabled/disable the Save and Reject Changes buttons, and we will use a bitmap of a floppy disk to indicate that the data has changed.

First we will enable/disable the Save Changes and Reject Changes buttons. The buttons should only be enabled if there are changes to save. I prefer this method to displaying a message box to inform the user of an error after the fact. If there are no changes to save, just disable the buttons. That way the user cannot make a mistake.

To do this, we must make sure the buttons are disabled by default. Open the form designer and select the Save Changes button. Go to the Properties window and find the enabled property. Set it to false. Next do the same thing with the Reject Changes button. Remember the picture box we added with the bitmap of the floppy disk? We will also use this as a cue. When there are changes to be saved, the floppy icon will appear. If you haven't already done so, name the picture box picDirty. Now add the following code to the UpdatePos procedure.

```
Private Sub UpdatePos()
  lblRecs.Text = "Record " & Me.BindingContext(DataSet11, _
   "Customers").Position + 1 & " of " & _
   Me.BindingContext(DataSet11, "Customers").Count
  picDirty.Visible = DataSet11.HasChanges
  btnSave.Enabled = DataSet11.HasChanges
      btnReject.Enabled = DataSet11.HasChanges
End Sub
```

This is the only change you should need. Since this procedure is called each time the DataSet is updated, the visual cues will always be correct. Compile and run the program. Try deleting a row. Click the Reject Changes button. The row reappears. Add a row. Click Reject Changes. The new row disappears. Try making some changes. Save them to the database. Notice the cues change appropriately. Congratulations! Your new data form is finished!

SUMMARY

This was quite a beginning. We've already come a long way. We looked at what databases are, their history, and how they are structured. We took a quick tour of ADO .NET and discovered its basic components. We then built a console database application to demonstrate the basic approach to accessing data with ADO .NET. Then we took a look at a full-featured Windows database application with full updating capability. We learned that ADO .NET is a powerful but very complex tool. We've only scratched the surface in this chapter. In the chapters that follow we will dig deep. Let's continue the journey, shall we?

CHAPTER 2

Object-Oriented Programming in Visual Basic .NET

Object-oriented programming (OOP) is perhaps one of the most misused and abused buzz phrases in the industry today, and this is largely the fault of VB. What! Am I about to commit authorial suicide? Not really. I am not about to launch into a tirade about how VB is a toy language not worthy of notice by *real* computer science professionals who program exclusively in C++ under some Unix variant. Those discussions have long been rendered moot just by the sheer success of VB and its relatively wide acceptance in the workplace. Just about everywhere you look, there is VB being used, even if just for prototyping.

Yet, the widespread adoption of VB is the cause of the misunderstanding of the concepts of OOP. Many VB programmers think they are using OOP when they are really using COM. Despite extensive efforts to educate about and promote OOP, most VB programmers I have met do not use it, understand it, or know why they should use it. They see it as an arcane and complex way of doing what they are already doing using procedural code. One of the reasons for this is that until this version you could use some OOP techniques, but overall they were clunky and difficult to implement. Since most programmers tend to take the path of least resistance, they usually avoided OOP and used procedural techniques.

VB .NET is fully object oriented. You will no longer be able to pretend ignorance or hide behind VB 6's lack of OOP support. While it is *possible* to program in VB .NET using a non-OOP approach, it bends over backward to encourage the use of OOP techniques and design methodology. A full cost-benefit analysis of why OOP is the way to go is beyond the scope of this book. However, to really understand VB .NET and the way its tools and ADO .NET are implemented requires at least a cursory examination of OOP and how it is implemented in VB. Even if you never create a class and use only the built-in design tools, you are using OOP, so get ready to leave the world of procedural programming behind and jump right in and learn some of the terms and techniques of OOP.

A Thumbnail Sketch of OOP

Until this version, VB was not object oriented in a strictly academic sense. While it is true that VB 6 uses objects and can create classes, they are not true classes in the OOP paradigm. They are really COM objects, and there's an important difference. For a language to be truly object oriented, it must support the following capabilities:

- Encapsulation—Data in a class must be able to be fully hidden from the rest of the program. The language must provide a mechanism for controlling this access. Moreover, the class must be self-sufficient, with no external dependencies other than its immediate parent.
- Inheritance—Classes derived from other classes must have a mechanism for inheriting the functionality and data of the parent class.
- Polymorphism—Literally many forms, it means that methods can have many signatures and the compiler determines which member to call based on the parameters given.

Terms and Definitions

Since VB 6 was not an object-oriented language, you may not be familiar with some of the terms. Let's begin with definitions: .

- Class—A programming entity that contains members and methods for accessing the members. A class becomes a data type so that identifiers can be declared that reference instances of the class. The class is not an object; it is the definition of an object. Classes can inherit from other classes and can be inherited by other classes.

- Object—An instance of a class. Once a class is declared and instantiated it becomes an object. There can be many objects of the same class.
- Structure—A structure is similar to a class in that it can contain members and methods, but it cannot be inherited. It is also considered a value class, meaning it does not have to be initialized as new. Simply declaring a variable as the structure type creates an instance. This is an advanced form of the VB 6 user-defined type. I will use the term *class* to refer to both classes and structures, except where their behavior is different.
- Member—A member is data or methods that are defined within a class definition. They are commonly referred to as member variables, Member Methods, or just members.
- Methods—Methods are procedures that are defined as public and control access to the member data. They can also perform operations on the data, such as printing a report or saving it to disk.
- Properties—Properties are like methods but can appear on the left side of an assignment. They are primarily used as access control mechanisms to provide a way to get and update the member data.
- Class hierarchy—The family tree of a class library. Also called an inheritance tree, it shows the relationship between all of the classes in the library.
- Derived class—A class that was inherited from another.
- Parent class—The class from which the current class was derived.
- Base class—Same as parent class.
- Abstract class—This type of class cannot be instantiated. It is meant to act as a template for other classes and must be derived from to be used. In an abstract class, some methods must be overridden.
- Overloading—Overloading is how we implement polymorphism. You can have many procedures with the same name, as long as the parameter list is different by the data type and/or number of the parameters. This is an important distinction. The names of the parameters don't matter; it's the data types that make the procedures unique.
- Overriding—A method of a derived class can add functionality to that provided by the parent class.
- Nested class—A class declared within another class. Nested classes become subtypes of the type defined by the outer class.
- Interface—Those methods and properties visible to the "outside" from the class. These comprise the way users of your class interact with it.
- Access modifier—This is part of the class access mechanism. The access modifier appears as the first keyword in a procedure or variable declara-

tion. Access modifiers can be applied to members and classes and have slightly different meanings when used with each.

- Events—Events are the programming construct used to pass notifications back from one class (called the event source) to the listening class (called the event sink or target).
- Event handler—A procedure in a listening class that is designated to handle or process the event(s) being sent by the event source.
- Delegate—Part of the event model. A delegate is similar to a function pointer except that it contains information about the function's parameter signature and containing class. Delegates are used mainly to dynamically wire events to procedures at runtime.

Now let's look at some of the less obscure ways OOP is used in VB. This will not be an exhaustive discussion. That is best left for a book on OOP. We will examine the most commonly used techniques as applied to VB. We will also try to help you avoid some common pitfalls.

ENCAPSULATION

Encapsulation means that all of the members of a class and the processes to be performed on those members must be contained within the class they reside in. Another way of saying this is that the class must contain everything it needs to store and operate in the data it defines. That means, for example, if a class contains date data, it must also contain the information and procedures required to format and print the data, if that is a required function of the class. In pure form, it also means that the class should not have to rely on any external data or procedures, but be entirely self-contained. In this sense, the class can be seen as a complete program unto itself.

Besides containing data and the procedures to be performed on the data, the class also must have a way of sharing this information and knowledge with the outside world. In OOP parlance, this is called the interface. The mechanism used to control how much of this information is shared is called the access control system. In VB .NET, this is implemented via access control modifiers that can be used for classes and members.

When applied to members they mean:

- Private—This means that the member variable or procedure is accessible only from within this class. It is invisible to other classes.

- Public—The member is accessible from any other class with no restrictions. Note that this does not mean it is a global variable; the class containing the member still has to be instantiated.
- Protected—This is similar to private; except that the member can be accessed from any inherited classes as well as the current class. It cannot be accessed from other classes.
- Friend—Friend members are similar to public members except they can only be accessed from within the same assembly. As long as the class is declared in the current project, you can see friend members, but if the class is declared in another project, the friend members are invisible.

You can combine protected and friend. This causes the member to be accessible in inherited classes outside the current project, but it still retains friend access within the project of the inherited class. It will be accessible from other classes within the project of the inherited class but not from outside the project.

When applied to classes or structures they mean:

- Private—The class (or structure) is accessible from only within the current class. It cannot be declared outside the class. Valid for nested classes only.
- Public—The class is accessible with no restrictions.
- Protected—Applies to nested classes only. The nested class is available to inherited classes, but not outside the branch of the inheritance tree.
- Friend— The class is available inside the current project, but not outside it.

As with member access modifiers, Protected and Friend can be combined with similar behavior as for members, but only on nested classes.

INHERITANCE

VB supports full inheritance as per the OOP specification. It does not support multiple inheritance. Multiple inheritance is where a class can inherit from more than one base class, effectively merging the functionality of the two. There has been much discussion in academic circles as to whether this should even be included in the OOP specification. It can be confusing and even dangerous so Microsoft left it out of VB. It is available in C++ if you really must use it. To create a class that inherits from a base class use the `Inherits` keyword in the declaration of a class.

```
Public Class MyClass
  Inherits System.Windows.Forms.Form

End Class
```

This class declaration creates a class called `MyClass`, which inherits the `Windows.Forms.Form` class. In other words, this creates a new form class. The `inherits` clause must be on the next line of text after the class declaration or you will generate a syntax error. Classes do not have to inherit from any other class.

```
Public Class MyClass

End Class
```

This declaration is perfectly valid. If inherited from it will become the root class of a new inheritance tree.

Classes can be defined that *cannot* be inherited from:

```
Public NotInheritable Class MyClass
  Inherits System.Windows.Forms.Form

End Class
```

This is useful if you are writing some classes you wish to sell commercially and you don't want your customers pirating your code by inheriting from it and then selling a new product. It is also useful in a secure environment where you don't want the users of your class to override functionality.

Classes can also be defined that *must* be inherited from:

```
Public MustInherit Class MyClass
  Inherits System.Object

End Class
```

This creates an abstract class. These are classes you want to use as a template for defining other classes. Abstract classes should only inherit from other abstract classes. If you try to create an abstract class by inheriting a nonabstract class, it will allow it, but you will not be able to use it in the IDE designer. You will get an error saying that it cannot instantiate the abstract class.

Constructors and Finalizers

Constructors and finalizers are special procedures that a class uses to create and destroy itself. Every class must have at least one constructor, called a default constructor. If you do not provide one, VB assumes there is a blank constructor. Without at least one public constructor, the class could never be instantiated. Sometimes this behavior is desirable if you don't want the class to have the ability to be instantiated directly. In VB, the constructor must be a subprocedure named `New`. In other languages, the constructor(s) must have the same name as the class. I do not know why Microsoft did not continue this convention. There is one advantage to it; when you change the name of a class you do not have to remember to rename every constructor as well. For that reason, perhaps it is a better way of naming constructors. Constructors may be overloaded. As a matter of convention, most OOP programmers create at least one constructor with no parameters, but this is not required. Inherited classes must declare their own constructor, even if one is declared in its base class. To use the base class's constructor, you must explicitly call it like this:

```
MyBase.New()
```

If used, it must be the first line of code in the constructor. If you look at the way constructors are implemented, you are really calling the class's constructor when you use the `New` keyword. Suppose we have a class:

```
Public Class ClassA

Private intA as Integer

Public Sub New()
    IntA = 1
End Sub

End Class
```

When we create an instance of the class using the `New` keyword, we are really calling the new procedure:

```
Private mA as New ClassA()

Or

Private mA as ClassA

mA = New ClassA()
```

We could use the constructor to pass in initialization data. This is used very often:

```
Public Class ClassA

Private intA as Integer

Public Sub New()
     IntA = 1
End Sub

Public Sub New(ByVal IntIN as Integer)
  IntA = IntIn
End Sub

End Class

Private mA as New ClassA(12)
```

In this example, we have overloaded the constructor. If the programmer uses the default constructor, `intA` gets assigned a default value of one. If the programmer uses the second constructor, he can pass in any value he wants to initialize `intA`.

Finalizers

Finalizers are typically used to clean up before a class is destroyed. In other OOP languages, these are used to deallocate memory, close files, and so forth. In C++ they are called destructors and are named by using a tilde (~) followed by the class name. In VB .NET they are named `Finalize` and cannot have any parameters. Finalizers cannot be overloaded because they are called implicitly and not under programmer control. In most cases finalizers are not needed in VB .NET because the CLR uses a garbage collection mechanism to automatically deallocate memory and generally clean up after a class is destroyed. Even if you use a finalizer, you still cannot be sure an object has been fully destroyed by the garbage collector.

```
Public Sub Finalize()
  ' Destroy something
End Sub
```

The finalizer will be called automatically when the use count for the object drops to zero. Finalizers cannot be called under programmer control.

POLYMORPHISM

Polymorphism is the ability of a class to take on different functionality based on the context in which it is used. Polymorphism is chiefly implemented in most OOP languages using techniques called method overloading, overriding, and shadowing.

Overloading

Overloading is how we can create methods that have the same name but accept many different argument parameters. We can overload methods we create and we can overload methods we override. Suppose we want to create a function that, if passed numbers, adds the two numbers and returns the result, but if passed strings, concatenates the strings and returns the result.

```
Public Function Add(ByVal intA As Integer, _
ByVal intB As Integer) as Object
  Dim intC As Integer

  intC = intA + intB
  Return intC
End Function

Public Function Add(ByVal strA As String, _
ByVal strB As String) as Object
  Dim strC As String

  strC = strA & strB
  Return strC
End Function
```

There are a couple of things to notice in the example. First, both versions of the `Add` function return data types of `Object`. While the overloaded functions can have different parameters, they must return the same type. Since `Object` is the root class of the entire class library, it can accept any data type. This is currently the only way to return data of different types from an overloaded function. Second, they don't include the keyword `Overloads`. This is because as long as they are declared in the same class, the overload is implicit. The only time we need to explicitly use `Overloads` is when we are overloading a method in the base class. Suppose the first function were in `ClassA`. If in `ClassB` we want to overload it, we would use this syntax:

`ClassA` Function:

```
Public Overridable Function Add(ByVal intA As Integer, _
ByVal intB As Integer) As Object
  Dim intC As Integer

  intC = intA + intB
  Return intC
End Function
```

`ClassB` (inherits `ClassA`) Function:

```
Public Overloads Function Add(ByVal strA As String, _
ByVal strB As String) As Object
  Dim strC As String

  strC = strA & strB
  Return strC
End Function
```

Note that this does not override the function. The original function in `ClassA` is still available. If you include `Overrides` and `Overloads` in the same declaration you will generate an error.

Overriding

When a class inherits from another class, it has all the properties and methods of the first class. Without doing anything, you can access all of them. However, what is the point of inheriting? It isn't just to create another data type with the same functionality as the first. The point of inheriting is to retain the functionality of the first, and add more and change some of the existing. Adding more functionality is easy. We just add more properties and methods to implement the new functionality. However, what if we want to change or enhance existing functionality. Do we have to create it all over again? That would seem to undo the benefits of inheritance. This is where overriding comes in.

We can override a method in the parent class and replace its functionality with new. Suppose a class has this method:

```
Public Overridable Function Sum(ByVal intA As Integer, _
ByVal intB As Integer) As Integer
  Dim intC As Integer

  intC = intA + intB
  Return intC

End Function
```

Note `Overridable` in the declaration. This enabled the function to be overridden in a derived class. In the derived class we can then override the function and make it do something else:

```
Public Overrides Function Sum(ByVal intA As Integer, _
ByVal intB As Integer) As Integer
  Dim intC As Integer

  intC = intA - intB
  Return intC

End Function
```

The function template can be created easily by selecting `(Overrides)` in the class drop down on the code window and then selecting the method you wish to override in the method drop down. This override actually changes the `Sum` method to a subtraction, not advisable in real life, but okay for illustration. Suppose we want to use the existing functionality and then add to it. We can do this:

```
Public Overrides Function Sum(ByVal intA As Integer, _
ByVal intB As Integer) As Integer
  Dim intC As Integer
  Dim intD As Integer

  intC = MyBase.Sum(intA, intB)
intD = intA * intC
  Return intD

End Function
```

This overridden method calls the parent (or base) class's `add` method first, preserving the existing functionality, using the `MyBase` keyword. It then performs additional processing on the result of the call to the `base-class` method before returning it to the caller. In actual practice we would not make a `Sum` method do anything but add the two arguments, but it is an extreme example of how you can change the functionality in derived classes.

Shadowing

Shadowing masks the `Overridable` method in the base class with a method of the same name. The parameter signature does not have to be the same. It effectively creates a method with the same name as a method in the base class, but they are completely independent from each other. ***Do not use***

this. I can't think of one good reason to use the `Shadows` keyword. Moreover, there is a way to shadow a method without even knowing it, called an implicit shadow. Just for completeness I will demonstrate both ways. That way you can avoid implicit shadows.

We will use our `Sum` procedure described earlier. First, the explicit shadow:

```
Public Shadows Function Sum(ByVal strA As String, _
                                        ByVal StrB As String) As
String
  Dim strC As String

  strC = strA & strB
  Return strC
End Function
```

Notice that the parameters are strings this time. We could also have just as legally done this:

```
Private Shadows Sub Sum()
  ' Do nothing
End Sub
```

This would effectively mask the method from the users of your class. This is one of the possible uses of the `Shadows` keyword that I grudgingly will allow.

Here is one that I've seen experienced OOP programmers stumble over:

```
Public Overridable Function Sum(ByVal intA As Integer, _
        ByVal intB As Integer) As Integer
  Dim intC As Integer

  intC = intA * intB
  return intC
End Function
```

Notice that it multiplies the two arguments. Here is the real insidious thing about it. Because we declared this as `Overridable`, it implicitly shadows the method in the base class. The IDE does warn you about this, but it is easy to dismiss the warning without paying much attention to it. What will happen here is that any classes derived from this one will multiply the two arguments, because we have masked the functionality of the base class and replaced it with this method.

The bottom line is do not shadow. It creates a dangerous, confusing class structure and should not be used. If anyone can come up with a valid reason to use shadows, I would appreciate an email at mailto:*bob@emanageservice.com.*

EVENTS AND DELEGATES

Events are part of what we call the `Callback Mechanism`. One way of looking at OOP is by using a communications paradigm. Objects communicate with each other by sending and receiving messages. Messages are received using methods and properties. Messages are sent via *callbacks* or events. Classes can *fire* events anytime they want to *notify* any class that's *listening* for some action. The class that's listening for the event can then take appropriate action, or do nothing. Thus we can say that we have event senders and event listeners. Another more academic way of saying this is that there are event *sources* and event *sinks*. VB provides a very robust event system.

The first and most basic way of creating and using events is as follows:

1. In the source class, declare the event you wish to use, like this:

```
Public Class Seinfeld

Public Event WeirdThingHappens(ByVal strSomeArg As String)

End Class
```

2. In the listening class where the source class has been declared using the `WithEvents` keyword and instantiated, create an event handler, like this:

```
Private WithEvents mJerry As New Seinfeld()

Private Sub SomeWeirdEventHandler(ByVal strSomeArg As
String) _
Handles mJerry.WeirdThingHappens
  MsgBox(StrSomeArg)
End Sub
```

3. In the source class where you want to fire the event, add code like this:

```
Public Class Seinfeld

Public Event WeirdThingHappens(ByVal strSomeArg As String)
```

```
Private Sub SomethingWeirdHappens()
  RaiseEvent WeirdThingHappens("What's up with that? Yada
yada yada.")
End Sub

End Class
```

Delegates

A delegate is an object that contains a reference to a procedure. Delegates enable events to be wired at runtime. When we say we *wire* an event, it means that we connect the event to an event handler. The most basic way to do this at runtime is to use the `AddHandler` keyword. Suppose we have the same event and source class defined earlier. Suppose also that we do not know what we want the program to do at design time. One of two possible event handlers must be invoked depending on some user input. If the user sets a variable to `1`, then one handler is invoked; any other value and a second handler is invoked. At some point in the code, after the user has set the value, you can wire the event on the fly, like this:

```
Private Sub SetHandler()
  If intUser = 1 then
    Addhandler mJerry.WeirdThingHappens, AddressOf HandlerA
  Else
    Addhandler mJerry.WeirdThingHappens, AddressOf HandlerB
  End If
End Sub

Private Sub HandlerA(ByVal strSomeArg As String)
MsgBox(StrSomeArg)
End Sub

Private Sub HandlerB(ByVal strSomeArg As String)
Console.WriteLine(StrSomeArg)
End Sub
```

One of the important items to note in the example is that both event handlers are regular procedures and they both have the same parameter signature as the event itself. These are the requirements of event handlers. You will generate an error if the parameter signatures do not match the signature of the event. Another item to note is the use of the `AddressOf` operator. This operator returns a delegate to the procedure that follows. As we mentioned earlier, a delegate is similar to a function pointer in C. However, it is a more powerful object if it contains the address of a procedure, and information about the class the procedure belongs to and the parameter signature of the procedure. This enables VB to validate that the delegate actually points to a valid procedure.

VB 6—In VB 6 there was an `AddressOf` operator as well. This operator was much different though. The VB 6 `AddressOf` operator returned a pointer to a procedure, and the procedure could only be in a standard module. It was mainly used to provide function pointers to Windows APIs that required callbacks, such as window enumerators and window message functions. In VB .NET it returns a reference type that is an object. The object contains information about the procedure including the class it is in and its parameter signature.

In VB 6 you could only handle events by their predefined procedure name. The event handlers had to be in a class module of some type (class, form, usercontrol, etc). In VB .NET there is no such restriction. Events can be handled anywhere, including modules. (In VB .NET standard modules are classes as well.) In addition, you can wire an event handler to an object that is declared locally within a procedure. This was not possible in VB 6.

There is a lot more to delegates than we have covered here. Delegates can be declared directly and assigned to variables. We will not delve into this now. They are a very powerful feature of VB .NET and have many uses besides handling events. However, these are beyond the scope of this book. Indeed there could be an entire book on delegates and the reflection classes. Perhaps someone will write one someday.

SUMMARY

We have now had a brief introduction into the world of OOP. This should be enough to enable you to understand the terminology and to see how ADO .NET uses OOP technology. We have only really scratched the surface of what is possible using OOP technology in VB. I encourage you to investigate further.

Next we move on to looking at the Visual Studio IDE and the available database tools.

CHAPTER 3

Visual Basic .NET Database Tools

Tools, tools, tools. It's funny, but if I were asked to name the one thing that has changed the most since the 1980s, as far as programming is concerned, I would have to say it is the tools available to the programmer. As far as the programming itself goes, we really aren't doing much more real work than we were 15 years ago. We're basically making screens, updating data, creating reports, and doing background (now called server-side) processing. Yes, it's a lot cheaper and a lot faster and a lot more complicated. In 1985, $40,000 got me a COBOL compiler for the Data General Minicomputer I programmed, and it was just that, a compiler. No editor (one came with the operating system), no IDE, no tools, just a command-line compiler and a bunch of thick books. No database tools either. If you wanted a database you had to shell out another $20,000 to $40,000, depending on the number of users. Moreover, all you got was indexed sequential access method (ISAM) which came with a database manager and some backup and integrity-checking utilities. There was also a very primitive query tool.

The first IDEs came with some of the MS-DOS PC-based software, such as dBase by Ashton-Tate and Boland's Paradox. I remember seeing my first real IDE in 1987 when I picked up a copy of Borland's Turbo-Pascal (which came on a single 5-inch diskette shrink-wrapped with the book). It had a color-coded editor (which I didn't even know about with my monochrome monitor), on-the-fly syntax checking, and built-in compiler. I was impressed. By the way, this is the tool that would evolve into Delphi a few years later.

Even though I was impressed by the IDE, I could never quite swallow Pascal, with its weird block syntax.

It wasn't until VB 1.0 for Windows appeared that I felt that the IDE had finally found its stride. Since then it seems to be more about tools than programming. Originally intended to boost programmer productivity, the tools have become an entity unto themselves, causing programmers to spend more time learning the tools than the actual language. This has created a knowledge gap, where many of today's programmers are just tool users. I have read articles recently advocating dumping the IDE and returning to the simpler days of text editors and command lines.[1] I would not go that far, but I agree that the IDE can mask enough of the intricacies of programming that it can create a tendency toward laziness. However I also believe that the benefits of the IDE far outweigh the liabilities. Imagine trying to manage one of today's multimodule, multiproject solutions without an IDE with integrated source control. What a nightmare!

Some of my projects have literally hundreds of source files. The real-time syntax checking saves a lot of compile-edit-compile iterations. The dynamic online help is a lifesaver. Interactive debuggers have saved me thousands of hours scouring for bugs. This is not to mention the myriad other aids like spy++, the OLE tools, and so forth. Tools should enhance, not mask, a programmer's abilities. This is what the integrated database tools do in Visual Studio .NET. Without ever leaving the IDE, a programmer can create databases, tables, stored procedures, database diagrams, and views. In this chapter, we will look at the IDE and the tools provided to help with database programming.

A Roadmap of the IDE

With this version of Visual Studio, Microsoft finally achieved its goal of unifying the development environments into one IDE. Until this version, VB had its own IDE separate from the standard IDE used for C++ and other languages. One reason for this was because VB was an interpreted language while the others were compiled. Another reason was because VB developed along a separate evolutionary path than the other Microsoft development tools. The VB debugger was proprietary, but had an edit-and-continue feature that made C++ programmers jealous. There were many integrated tools, such as the database manager and data environment designer, that were not available in the other IDE.

1. Bradley S. O'Hearne, "10 Reasons to Dump Your Java IDE," May 1, 2002, DevX web site: URL: *http://www.devx.com/free/hotlinks/2002/ednote050102/ednote050102.asp*

The new IDE has some equivalents to the tools in the old IDE, but many have been combined into the Server Explorer, and some are made obsolete by the radical changes in VB itself. (See Figure 3.1.) Others have been incorporated into the various designers.

Take a look at the IDE startup screen. Notice that nowhere does it say anything about VB. This is because the same IDE is now used for VB, C#, and C++, as well as any number of other third-party languages supported by .NET, including COBOL. By default, the Start page shows in the main workspace at startup. This is just an embedded web browser window. It doubles as the display for the online help, which is all in HTML now, and also as a portal to the various .NET web sites that Microsoft thought you might be interested in. I will leave it up to you to explore the pages. If you really hate this, you can turn it off through the Options dialogs. I initially turned it off, but I found some of the resources rather useful, and it is a quick way of opening your last project with a single mouse click, so I leave it on now. The IDE with a Windows application open is shown in Figure 3.2.

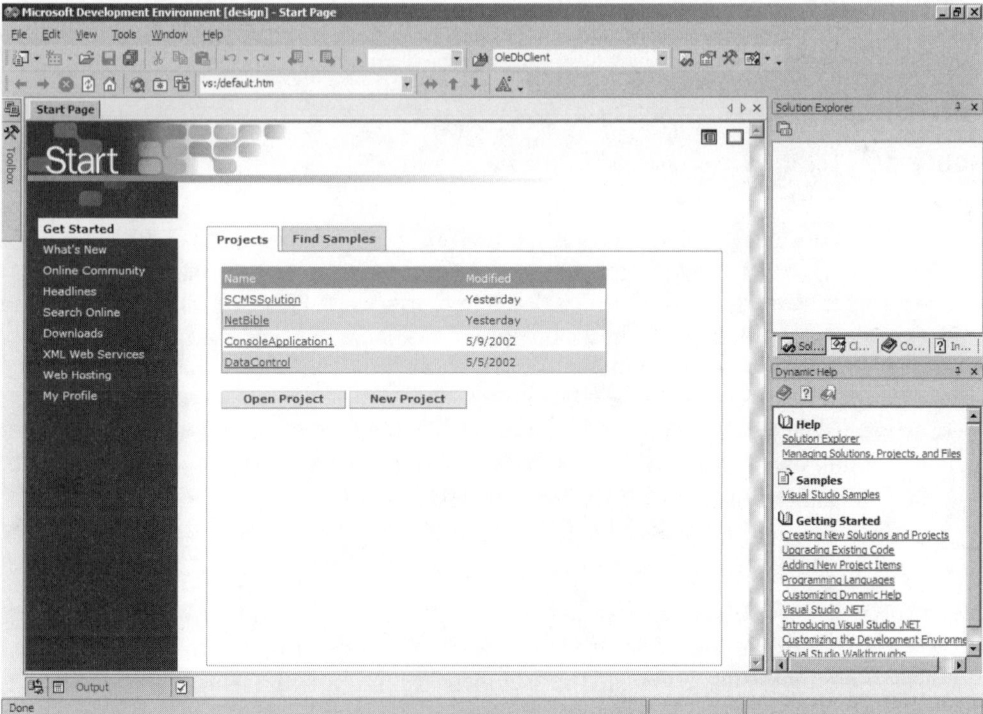

FIGURE 3.1 The opening screen of the Visual Studio IDE.

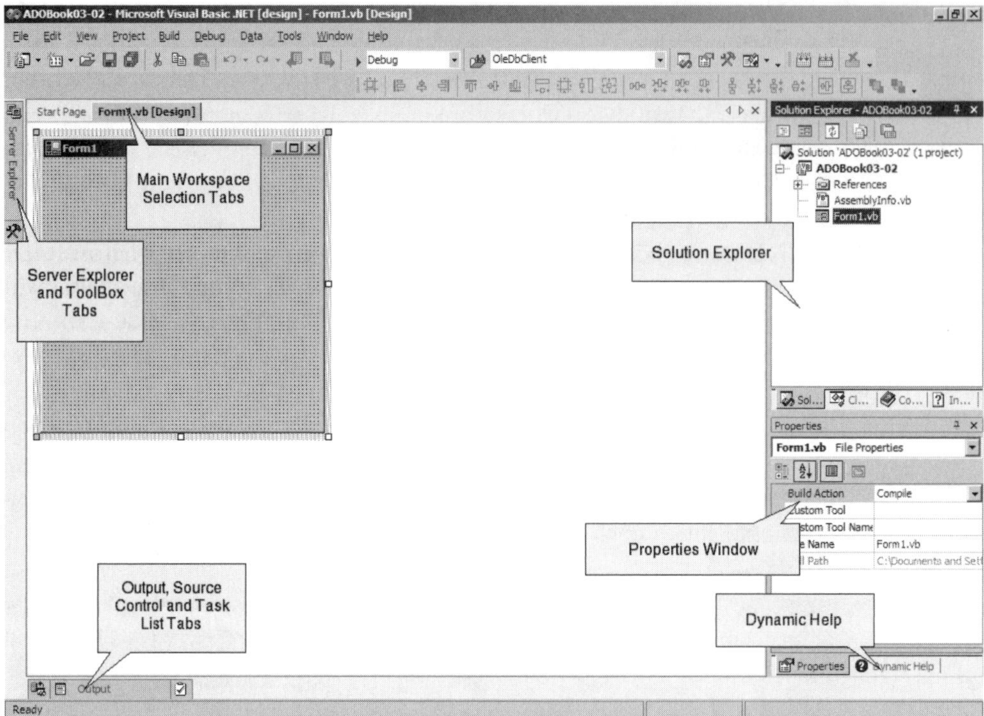

FIGURE 3.2 The IDE with a new Windows application open.

VB 6—I don't know if you are one of these holdouts, like I was. In VB 6 and prior versions, the IDE supported a single-document interface (SDI) display mode. This was a holdover from the 16-bit Windows IDEs. In this mode most of the windows, including the designers, displayed as top-level floating windows, allowing the desktop to show through. Since I started with VB 1, I tended to prefer this mode to the newer multiple-document interface (MDI) style used in VB 5 and VB 6. The SDI mode is no longer supported, so we had best get used to the new tabbed view. If you can afford a larger monitor, use a high screen resolution, such as 1280x1024. Otherwise you will have to get used to scrolling the designers around if your forms cannot fit into the workspace.

The main workspace is the center of attention. This is where the various designers and code windows appear, surrounded by the many controls and tools available to you. The user interface (UI) uses a modified version of MDI layout called a tabbed view. All of the MDI child windows appear as tabs in the main workspace.

Two items of the IDE stand out: the Dynamic Help window, rollaway ancillary windows, and the solution explorer.

Dynamic Help takes F1 Help one-step further by automatically displaying all relevant Help topics each time the cursor is positioned over a keyword or a designer is open. I found this tool especially handy when first learning VB .NET and left it turned on because it did not slow down my typing, even on my slower laptop (300mhz PII).

Rollaway ancillary windows first appeared in the standard Microsoft IDE in a prior version. However, this is the first time the feature is available with VB so it is probably new to most of you. With the rollaway feature, some of the less frequently used windows roll out of the way and collapse into a tab when not needed, much like a window shade. When the user hovers the mouse pointer over the window's tab, the window rolls out. Most of the dockable windows have this option. It is enabled by clicking the pushpin icon.

In previous versions of VB the solution explorer was called the project explorer. It retains that function except that group projects are now called solutions. It also has a direct connection to the underlying file system. If you rename a file in VB, the IDE renames it on disk. If you delete a file from a project, it deletes it from disk. The good news is that it sends the file to the recycle bin so it can be recovered. If you want only to remove the file from the project, use the Remove From Project menu item instead. The solution explorer also allows you to act recursively on projects and solutions for things like source control functions. The solution now has properties that you can use to customize build types and other items.

The output window displays the results of program compiles. The task window displays compile-time errors that need to be fixed. These are linked directly to the source code windows so that when an error is fixed, it disappears from the task list. You can also jump directly to an error by double-clicking on the task. You can also use the task list to make notes to yourself, and so forth. This list persists between sessions.

If you have source code control, such as Visual SourceSafe, there is now a window that shows the status of all checked-out files. SourceSafe comes with the Enterprise Version of Visual Studio and higher. If you have SourceSafe Version 6.0 installed as a separate product, it will work with Visual Studio .NET Professional. A handy addition in this version is the inclusion of dynamic checkout. With this feature, if you attempt to edit a file that is checked-in, the environment will either prompt you for a checkout or silently check the file out, depending on your preferences. If you ever made substantial changes to a file only to discover that it was not checked out and somehow the read-only attribute got toggled off, you will appreciate this feature.

Working our way around, we come to the toolbox. The toolbox contains icons for Windows controls, database tools, and other components. It changes its contents based on the context. For example, if we are designing a web page, it will display the web controls. One annoying feature is that the Control tab doesn't show if you are in a code window. If you want to see what controls are available, you have to open a designer window first. I've seen more than one programmer mystified as to where all the controls went.

There are two main tools for managing databases in Visual Studio. Server Explorer allows you to create databases, manage tables and views, and create stored procedures and triggers. The database project allows you to manage scripts associated with the solution you are creating. With the database project you can create scripts to perform data definition language (DDL) and data manipulation language (DML) functions. DDLs are transact-SQL scripts that manage the database schema. DMLs are transact-SQL scripts that manage the data in the database. DDL and DML can be (and often are) combined in the same script.

OPENING OR CREATING A PROJECT

To create a project, click the New Project button. Alternatively, you can go through the File menu as well. The new project dialog appears.

Figures 3-3 and 3-4 show the project types available for VB.

A similar list appears for C#. For C++ the list includes these types, plus Microsoft Foundation Classes (MFC) and Active Template Library (ATL) projects. If you click each icon, a brief description appears. We will be working with the Windows application, console application, and ASP .NET web application project types. We will create each type so you can become familiar with them.

Creating a Console Project

A console application is a command-line application. It does not have any UI built in. Console applications are useful for performing background processing where you do not need or want the overhead of a Windows graphical user interface (GUI). Some uses for this include posting large numbers of transactions to a database, producing character-based reports, and running batch-jobs during off hours using a scheduling program.

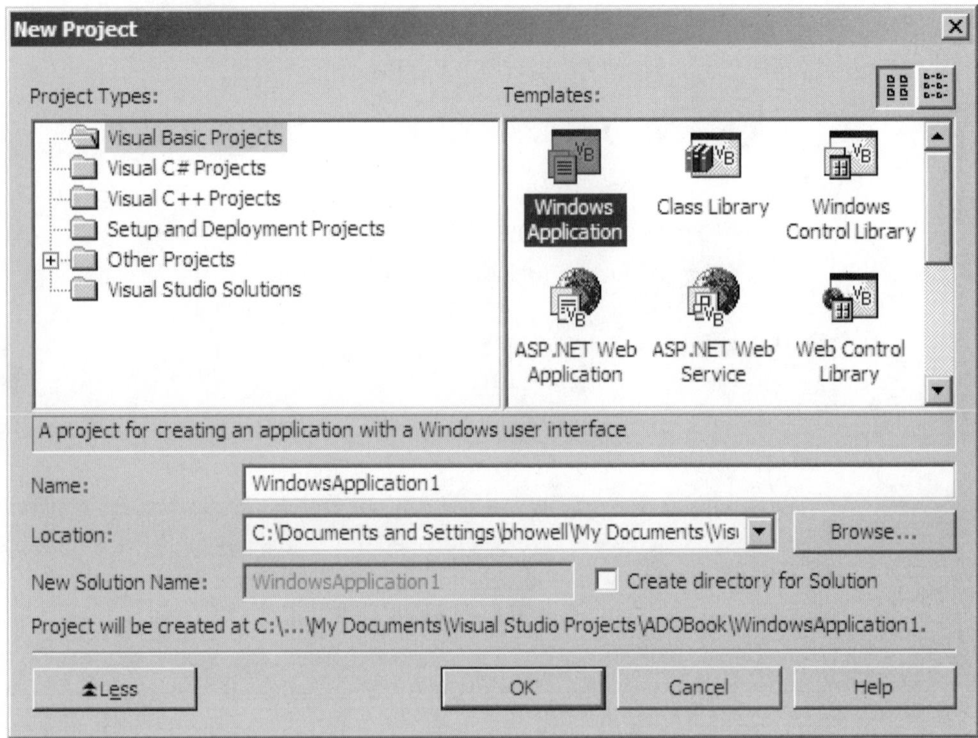

FIGURE 3.3 The New Project dialog.

To create a console application, choose the Console Application project template. Change the name of the project to ADOBook03-01 as in Figure 3.5 and click OK.

Visual Studio will create an empty console application with one code module. The code module will contain a procedure template for `Sub Main()`. This is the entry point for our application. Let's add one line of code to the `Main` procedure. Since this is our first application, we'll use the old "Hello World" standby.

```
Module Module1

Sub Main()
    Console.WriteLine("Hello World")
End Sub

End Module
```

FIGURE 3.4 More project templates.

Now let's compile our program. Select Build ADOBook03-01 from the Build menu (Figure 3.6).

You will see the output window roll out and the display of the status of the compile. When the compile is finished, it will display any error statistics. Assuming all went well, we can run our little program. To do this, open a console window. Do not use the standard console icon that comes with Windows. If you look in the Start menu, under Microsoft Visual Studio .NET Tools you will see a Visual Studio .NET Command Prompt entry. This is just like a regular command prompt except that it sets up the environment for executing .NET applications. You may want to create a shortcut to this on your desktop or command bar for easy access. You may also want to create a shortcut so that the command prompt starts up in the Visual Studio Project folder so you can easily navigate to the folder your executable is in.

Once the command prompt is started, navigate to the folder your program is in. By default, Visual Studio creates the executable in a bin subfolder under your project folder. On my machine the path is:

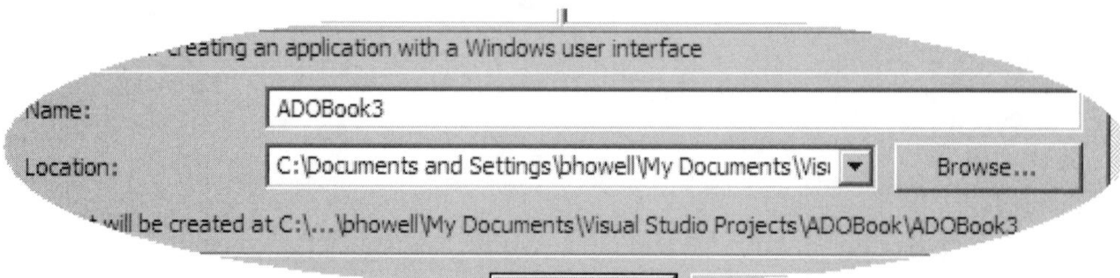

FIGURE 3.5 Changing the project name.

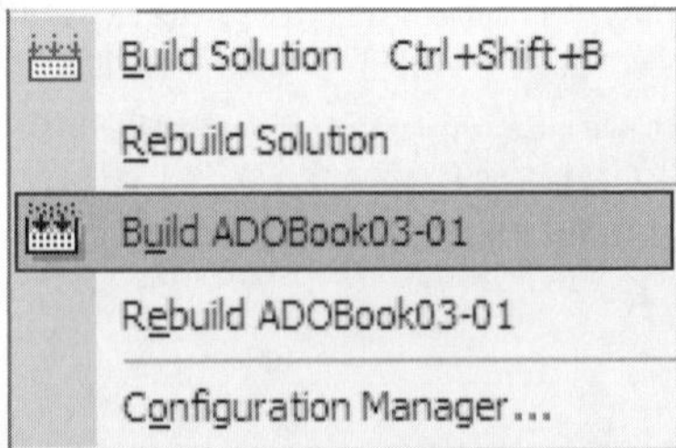

FIGURE 3.6 The Build menu.

```
C:\Documents and Settings\bhowell\My Documents\Visual Studio
Projects\ADOBook\ADOBook03\ADOBook03-01\bin
```

Once you have found the folder, type the name of our little program, ADOBook03-01 and press enter. You should see "Hello World" on the screen and the command prompt should return.

TIP—If you have Display the Full Path in the Address Bar Setting turned on in the folder options of explorer, you can copy the path to the clipboard and then paste it on to the command line in the Command window. Navigate to the bin folder in explorer, select the text in the address bar, and press Ctrl+C to copy it to the clipboard. Then go to the Command window, type `cd` (the change directory command) and a space, then open the System menu, and select Edit|Paste from the menu. The path will be pasted in and the command will execute.

VB 6—The standard module in VB 6 was different than the standard module in VB .NET. VB 6 code modules were in the global namespace. Any public variables or functions declared in a module had application scope. In addition, variables and functions were public by default. VB 6 code modules did not have to be declared or instantiated, and were not reference types. In fact they were not types at all; they were just scope identifiers. Code and data in all modules were created when the program executed and remained in scope until the program terminated. In VB .NET, modules are full reference types. They behave much like classes except they cannot be instantiated or declared and they cannot inherit or be inherited. When I first started with VB .NET, I created my first app much the same way I did in VB 6. I always use `Sub Main` as my startup object. That way I can perform program initialization functions and any security checks before I show my main form. Well, the program started fine except that when I tried to transfer control to my startup form, the whole application terminated. What I discovered was that as soon as the last code in the module finishes executing, the module goes out of scope and terminates. Since my form was declared as a public module-level variable, it also was destroyed. In VB .NET when the last reference to an object is destroyed or goes out of scope, the object is automatically destroyed and all objects contained within it. I had to use the `Application.Run(frm-MainForm)` method to successfully transfer control to my form without ending the program.

Creating a Windows Project

To create a Windows application, click the New Project button and select the Windows application template icon. Change the name of the project to ADOBook03-02. When you are done, the project window should look like the one in Figure 3.7.

As expected, Visual Studio created a blank form and opened its designer window. As you can see in Figure 3.7, Visual Studio added new references to the project. `System.Windows.Forms` is the new Windows Forms class library. This library effectively wraps most of the Windows user API into a .NET class library. The `System.Drawing` library wraps the Graphical Device Interface (GDI+) APIs. Between these two, you have everything you need to create a robust UI.

With the form's designer already open, resize the form and drop a button on it. Change the `Text` property of the form to `Hello,` and change the button's `Text` property to `Say Hello`. Your form should look like what is illustrated in Figure 3.8.

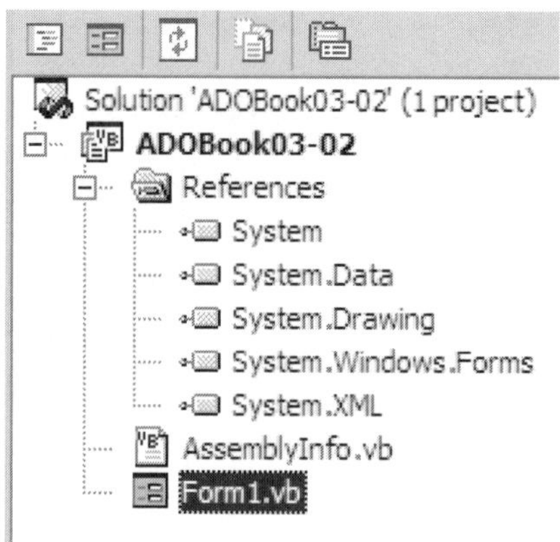

FIGURE 3.7 A Windows Forms project.

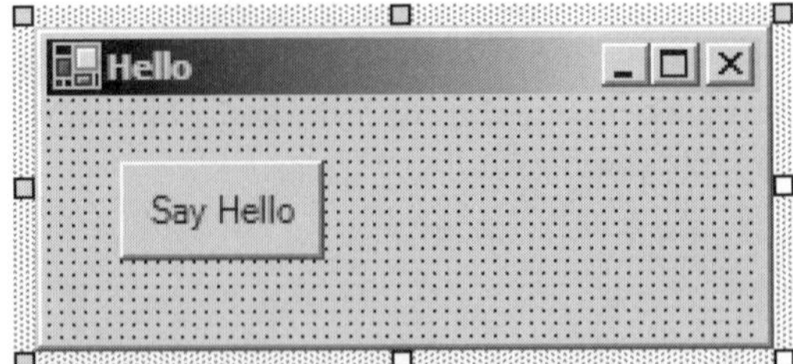

FIGURE 3.8 Hello World form.

Next, double-click the Command button. This will create a function template for the button's click event. Add the following code to the click event:

```
Private Sub Button1_Click(ByVal sender As System.Object, _
ByVal e As System.EventArgs) Handles Button1.Click
    MessageBox.Show("Hello World")
  End Sub
```

Click the Run button to compile and run the program. We do not need the command prompt for this because it is a Windows program. After the program compiles, our window should appear. Click the Say Hello button. A message box should appear. Close the message box. To end the program, close the window.

ASP .NET PROJECTS

Now we get to the point where Visual Studio .NET really shines in comparison to previous versions. Previously, to develop a web application with Visual Studio tools, you had to jump between Visual Interdev, FrontPage, and VB, depending on the type of web application you were building. You used Visual Interdev to build client-side web applications, FrontPage for static pages, and VB to develop web classes and server-side components. Each tool had its strengths and weaknesses. All that is history with Visual Studio.NET. There are no longer separate tools required to develop web applications. The process for developing a server-side web application is now as close as it gets to the process for developing a standard Windows application. Let's create a simple application to demonstrate what we mean.

Before we begin, let's make sure we have all of the requirements in place to create a web application. If you did a full install of Visual Studio.NET Professional or higher you should be all right, but let's make sure.

- You need to have Internet Information Server (IIS) 5.0 installed. This is installed with Windows 2000 or XP Pro. If you are running Windows NT 4.0, you should check the version. Visual Studio should have updated it if it detected that it was out of date.
- The IIS service must be started on Port 80.
- Make sure some other product did not install another web server, such as Apache. On Windows XP, you will not receive an error when two services try to use the same port (80). The first service to start gets the port. On WinNT 4 and 2000, you will receive a message in the event log if another application tries to start on a port already in use. If another product is using Port 80, you will have to stop that service to use IIS. Also, make sure you change the service's startup method to manual.
- IIS needs to be updated with Microsoft ASP.NET files (ASPX) extensions. Again the Visual Studio install should have installed these. To check, open the Management Console (right-click on My Computer and select Manage), expand the Internet Information Services node, expand Web Sites, right-click on Default Web Site, and select Properties. Select the Home Directory tab and then click the Configuration… button on the lower half of the form. You should see something like that shown in Figure 3.9.

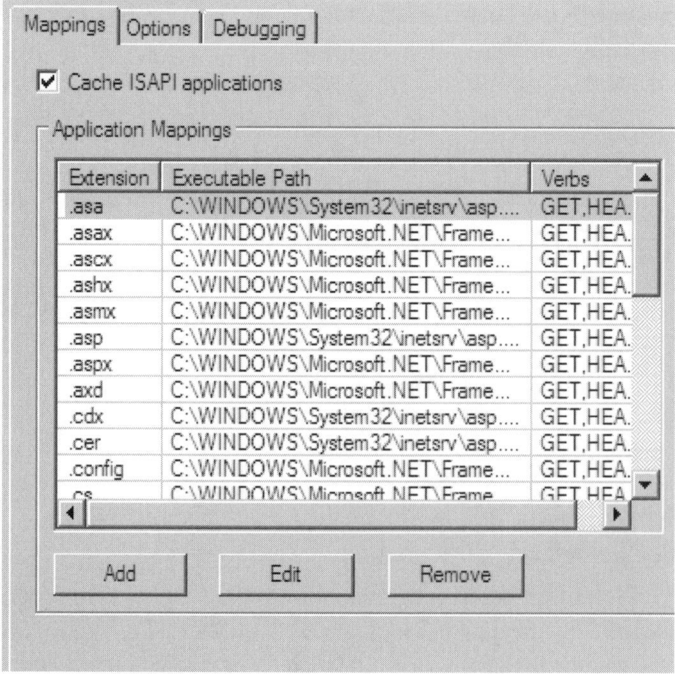

FIGURE 3.9 ISAPI mappings for ASP.NET applications.

Notice all the references to .NET. If you do not see any of these you may have to reconfigure your machine. The Visual Studio Installer should do this for you.

Once you are sure all of the prerequisites are met, you can create your project. Close any projects that are open. Select New Project and when the dialog opens select ASP.NET Web Application. Change the name of the project to ADOBook03-03. and click OK. The first thing different you will notice is that Visual Studio contacts the web site. This is because Visual Studio keeps the project on the IIS server. If this is your local machine the default path is `C:\InetPub\WWWRoot\ADOBook03-03.` If the web site is on a server, then the files are located there. The Project Explorer should look like Figure 3.10, with the References node expanded.

Things to notice:

- References—Notice the reference to System.Web. This library contains all of the classes for building a web application.
- ADOBook03-03.vsdisco—This is the Web Services discovery document. This document is used for Universal Description, Discovery and Integration (UDDI) directory services. These services help users find Web Services and provide a standard for their discovery. It is like a search engine for Web Services.
- Web.config—This document contains application configuration information, in a similar manner to an ini file.

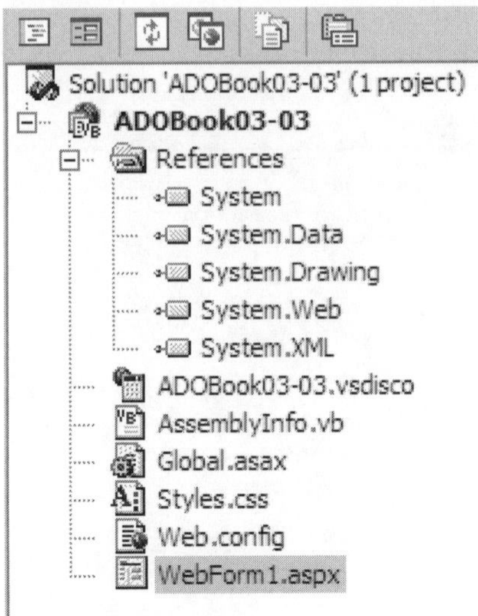

FIGURE 3.10 A new ASP.NET project.

If you open the vsdisco or web.config files, you will see that they are Extensible Markup Language (XML) files. That is after all what Web Services are all about. The saying for .NET is "If you can't tell, assume it's XML!"

Now comes the real neat part. Let's add a button to our new Web Form. Roll out the toolbox. Now, instead of the Windows controls, we see Web Form controls. Drag and drop a button onto the form. By default, the form uses absolute positioning for elements, meaning elements are fixed and cannot move around by themselves when the user resizes the browser window. You can use flow positioning as well. With this mode the elements will repaginate when the user resizes the window. Since we are designing forms, we will stay with absolute positioning. If the user's browser window is too small to contain the full form, scroll bars will appear to let the user expose the rest of the form.

Now let's also add a label to inform our user of the application's purpose. Drop a label control on the form. Change the `text` property of the label to read Say Hello World Application. Change the button's `text` property to read Say Hello. Position the controls as shown in Figure 3.11.

TIP—When designing Web Forms, keep the targeted users in mind. If you have the ability to require a minimum screen resolution (800x600 for example) then you should design your form with this in mind. If you will have no control over your user's machine, then you should design your form to a minimum standard of 640*480 so anyone will have a positive experience. Studies have shown that the user's experience counts most for the success of any application, no matter how elegant the underlying code is.

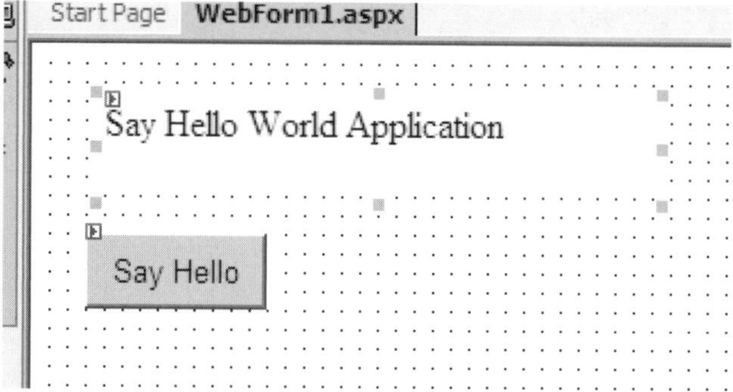

FIGURE 3.11 The top of the Web Form.

Create a Web Form. Change the `pageLayout` property of this form to `FlowLayout`. Now you can type directly on the page. In fact, you have all of the design features of FrontPage right in the IDE! Drop down the style list and select Heading 1. Type Hello World directly on the page. Also, drop another button onto the page. Change its text to Back. Just for fun, click on the HTML tab at the bottom of the design window. You will see that it is pretty normal HTML. ASP.NET applications by default generate standard HTML so the forms will run on any browser.

In WebForm1, double-click the button. A code window will open and a click event procedure will appear. In the body of the click event, enter this code:

```
Me.Response.Redirect("WebForm2.aspx")
```

Now do the same thing with WebForm2 except enter WebForm1 in the line of code. Now comes the good part. Click the Run button. As expected the program compiles, but instead of running as a Windows application a browser window opens and the WebForm1 appears. Pull down the View menu and select Source. Look at the HTML. It is very basic HTML. Click the Say Hello button. WebForm2 appears. Click the Go Back button and WebForm1 reappears. To end the application, close the browser window. All of the processing occurs on the server so the page will render properly in any browser. Just to try this out, I accessed the page from a Linux box I have running the KDE X-Windows environment. It uses a browser called Konquerer. (It's supposed to be a sly dig on Explorer, I think.) It's not Netscape, Internet Explorer (IE), or any well-known browser. The application worked just fine.

OTHER TYPES OF APPLICATIONS

There are several other types of applications you can create. I will describe them in brief here. We will look into some of these in later chapters.

- Class library—This is a group of components you wish to access from other applications. The most typical use for this is a middle-tier business rule layer, but they have other uses as well. The database components are all part of a class library, as are all of the other assemblies in the references of any application. You can also use a class library to build a set of classes to be inherited from.
- Windows control library—This type of project contains Windows user controls. You would use this to build controls to use on Windows Forms.

- ASP.NET Web Service—This is also a middle-tier component but it is designed to be accessed using HTTP protocol. All communication is handled by SOAP and data is transmitted as XML. ASP.NET Web Services can have a web-based client or can have a Windows GUI-based client.
- Web control library—These are groups of controls designed to be used on Web Forms.
- Windows service—This is an application designed to run in the background as a Windows service. Examples of services are SQL Server, IIS service, event logging, and so forth.

THE SERVER EXPLORER

One way to manage database within the IDE is the Server Explorer. In prior versions of VB we had the Data View window. This has evolved into the Server Explorer. We now have access to many of the management functions of each server we have access to. This is dependent upon your privileges on each server. Given the requisite privileges, we can now start and stop services, manage message queues (more on this in a later chapter), and perform other server-related functions. The one item that was left out is access to the IIS management functions. The main use of the Server Explorer from a database programmer's point of view is that it gives us access to SQL Servers on each machine. Through this tool we can create databases, tables, views, stored procedures, triggers, and database diagrams. The tools are fully integrated into the IDE. When you open a table designer, it opens in the workspace. Stored procedure windows are color-coded just like VB code windows.

The SQL Server management tools that are integrated into Visual Studio are intended to manage MSDE (Microsoft Database Engine) databases as well as full SQL Servers. The MSDE databases are functionally equivalent to SQL Server databases except that there is a limit to the number of concurrent logged-in users of about five. After this, performance will degrade. The MSDE is freely distributable and is intended to replace the Jet Database Engine used by Microsoft Access. As such, the intent is for it to be used as a desktop database server. However, you can connect to an MSDE database across a network, provided you have the tools to create the connection.

Most of the other limitations of the MSDE are because the tools provided with the IDE do not give easy access to them. They are still available if you have the right tools. If you have access to a full SQL Server client installation, you can use the Enterprise Manager to manage your MSDE databases.

The Enterprise Manager does not know that it is not a full SQL Server. Some of the things you can do with the Enterprise Manager that you cannot do with the IDE are create logins and users, change database security privileges, customizing the locations of the physical database files, and run the maintenance wizard to create scheduled maintenance tasks such as backups, importing and exporting data, and other tuning and management functions. Since most of these functions call system-stored procedures to work, you can access them that way using the SQL Server query analyzer or with a database project. You could also write some VB utilities to perform these functions. There are also some nice shareware tools like SQLPad (www.sqlpad.com). Another way of managing logins and privileges is with Microsoft Access 2000 or later. If you create an Access Database Project (.adp file), you can have access to the SQL Server Security and Replication services. Since I cannot assume you have access to any of the additional tools beyond those provided by the IDE, we will limit our discussion to those tools.

INSTALLING THE MSDE

The MSDE is not installed by default when you install Visual Studio. The Visual Studio installer merely copies the setup files for MSDE to a directory on your hard drive. Before using the MSDE you must install it. To install the MSDE you must run the setup from there. By default, Visual Studio setup places the files in `C:\Program Files\Microsoft Visual Studio .NET\Setup\MSDE`. If you installed Visual Studio in another location, you will have to look for the files there.

Run the setup program by double-clicking Setup.exe. What you will see is a special install for the MSDE. It is different from the install program for SQL Server 2000. Unless you want to install it to another location (due to disk space limitations), accept all the defaults. If you are using the MSDE, make sure the location you install to has plenty of disk space because you cannot choose an alternate location for the data files, and by default they are placed in a subfolder under where you installed the MSDE.

NOTE—If you already have SQL Server 7.0 or 2000 installed, or have access to a server, you may choose not to install the MSDE. They are functionally equivalent and the MSDE is not necessary. You can still install it if you prefer to work locally or do not wish to use the resources of the server.

CREATING DATABASES

It is very easy to create a database using the Server Explorer. Hover the mouse over the Server Explorer. Expand the node for the server on which you wish to create the database. Expand SQL Servers node. Right-click on the node. Select New Database from the context menu. A Create Database dialog opens (Figure 3.12). Enter the name of the database you wish to create. Keep Use Windows NT Integrated Security selected, unless the server you are connecting to requires SQL Server Security. If so, select it and enter a valid user name and password that allows database creation on this server. If you are using the MSDE, use Windows Integrated Security. Next click OK. This will create the new database.

NOTE—There is no way to drop (delete) the database through the Server Manager.

Enter TestDB in the database name and click OK. The new database will be created. Next we will add tables.

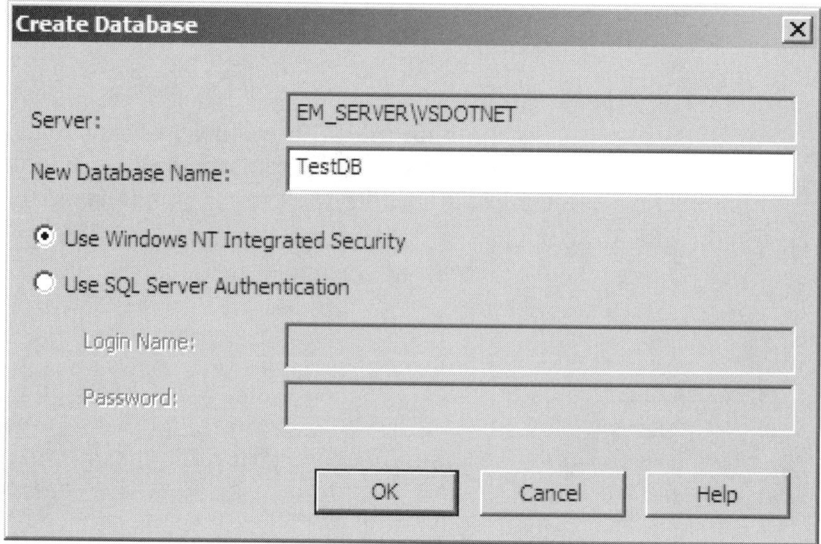

FIGURE 3.12 The Create Database dialog.

Creating and Managing Tables

Tables are the basic building blocks of a database and hold the data that the database stores. Tables are structures that consist of rows and columns, similar to a spreadsheet. Once you have created your database, the next step is to create tables.

To create a table, right-click on the Tables node under the database you just created. You may have to expand it first. Select New Table from the context menu. A table designer window will open in the main workspace. At the top is a grid for entering the column names and base data types. On the bottom are additional attributes for the column. These change depending on the data type of the column in question. If you ever used Microsoft Access to create an Access table, this designer should be very familiar to you. Let's fill in the designer as is indicated in Figure 3.13.

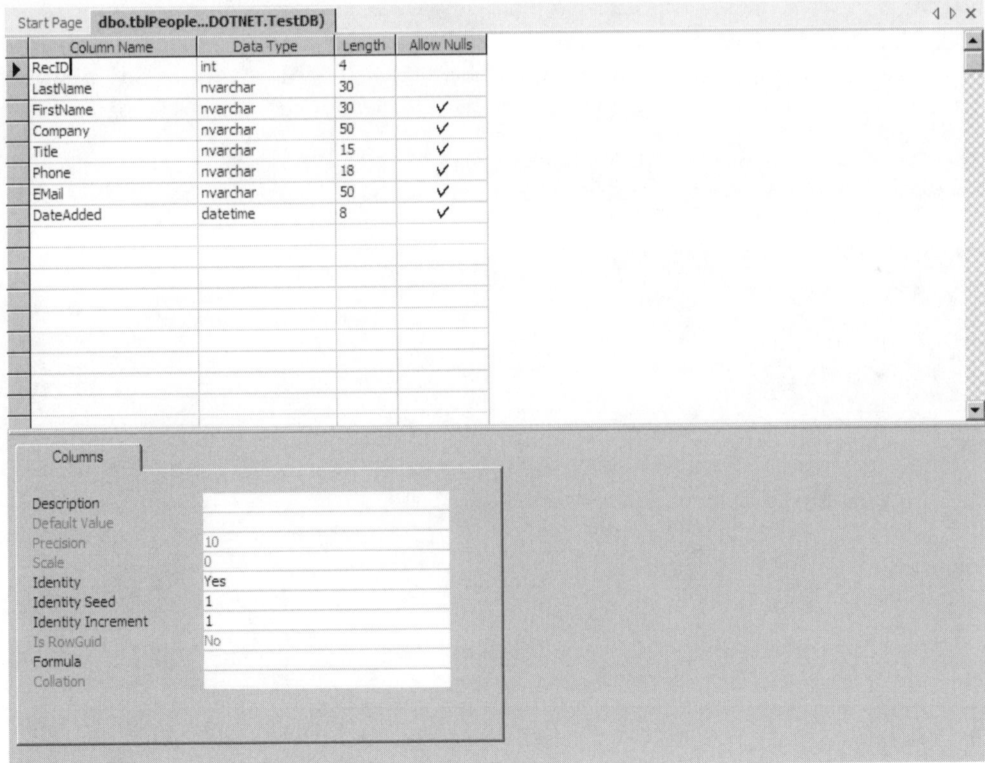

FIGURE 3.13 The table designer.

Adding Columns

When the designer opens, it is blank. You must now add columns to the table. The grid at the top allows you to add columns quickly, and the details appear at the bottom. I usually get the columns in first, then go back and change any defaults in the bottom portion of the screen. You can change the defaults it uses for data types in the Tools/Options dialog, under Database Designers. There are separate entries for SQL Server and Oracle (see Figure 3.14).

The column name can be anything you want. It can even include spaces. If you include spaces in a column name, you must surround it with square brackets when referencing it in a Transact-SQL statement.

TIP—Avoid using spaces in column names. Not all database systems support this and you must remember the square brackets. If you wish to create an SQL Statement that displays meaningful headings in grids and on reports, you can always alias the column name to one that contains spaces, again using the square bracket syntax. Keep column names as short as possible, while retaining the meaning of the data they contain. Avoid long names like AllowUserToLogIn-MultipleTimes. Use something like MultiLogin instead. If you don't, you will be kicking yourself later on when you have to reference this column in code. Also, don't use column names that omit vowels. Other programmers will never figure out what your pattern is and will not be able to understand your schema. If possible, establish a naming standard and stick with it.

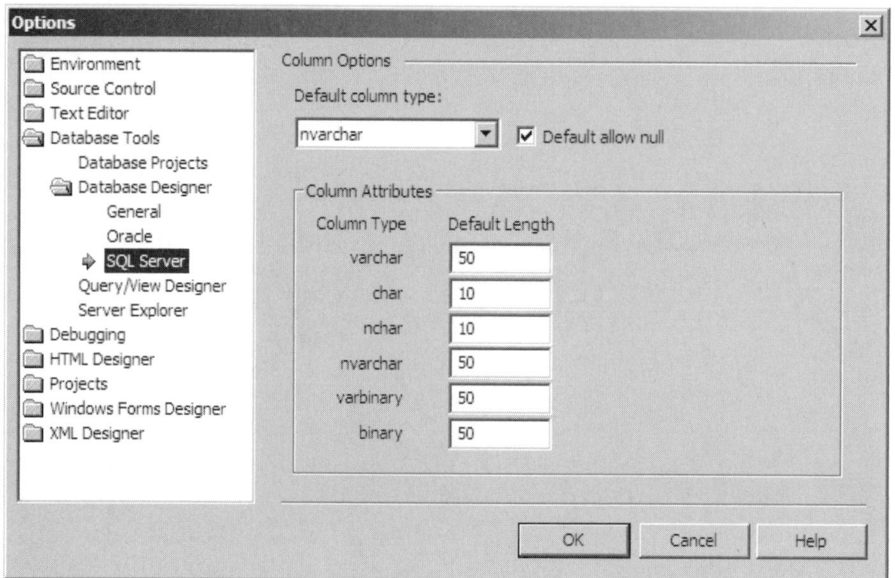

FIGURE 3.14 The Options dialog with Database Designer defaults open.

SQL Server Data Types

The data type dropdown lists all the possible data types for SQL Server. I will list the basic ones here. The others are either variants of these or rarely used.

- NVarChar/VarChar —A variable length string. VarChars can be up to 255 characters, nVarChars can be up to 64 kilobyte (KB) characters in length. We typically use nVarChar. VarChar is there for backward compatibility. The great thing about nVarChar is that it only uses the space needed to store the data. A null column does not take any space.
- Char/nChar—These are fixed-length text fields. If the text length is less than the length of the field, it is padded with nulls (ASCII Zero).
- Int/BigInt/SmallInt/TinyInt—Non-scaled integers. Can hold whole numbers only. The variations set different sizes. Int is 4 bytes, BigInt is 8 bytes, SmallInt is 2 bytes, and TinyInt is 1 byte.
- Bit—Bit fields are true/false only fields. A bit can only have a value of 1 or 0. Bit columns cannot be used in indexes. If you need to index a true/false value, use a Char(1) and define it as 1 or 0.
- Decimal/Numeric—Scaled Integer. Both types mean the same thing. A scaled integer is a whole number plus a fixed number of decimal places. This differs from a floating-point value that is a real number and has no integral value. A scaled integer is an integer with the decimal point arbitrarily moved to the left a set number of places.
- Money—A numeric with the decimal point set at position 4.
- Float/Real—True fractions or real numbers. Used mainly for scientific applications. Do not use reals to store monetary amounts or quantities. Use int or numeric for this. It is possible for two reals with the same apparent value to fail equality tests because they are not really the same number.
- DateTime—And its variations. Holds a date/time value. The variations limit the range of dates accepted.
- Text/nText—A pointer to a large amount of textual data. The size of the text is limited only by disk space.
- Image/nImage/Binary—A pointer to a large amount of binary data, such as a picture or sound image. Similar to text except will accept any binary data. Anything you can imagine can be stored in an Image field. As with text, the size is limited only by disk space.
- TimeStamp—A special field used by the system to record sequential time data.

- UniqueIdentifier —A special value that holds a GUID (globally unique identifier). Used to guarantee row uniqueness.

The length column is available for character and numeric values. It determines the maximum size of the data. For numerics it also determines the scaling factor. The Allow Nulls column determines whether or not null values are allowed in the column.

The lower part of the screen contains attributes of each column beyond the basic data type:

- Description—You may enter a description of the column. It is advisable to use this attribute because it will help when documenting the schema. Put descriptions in when you create the columns; if you have to go back and fill them in, you may find the task daunting.
- Default value—The "default" default value of any column is `Null`. If you have defined the column as allowing nulls, this is okay. If you have defined the column as not allowing nulls, it is always a good idea to define a default value so you can insert rows without remembering which columns don't allow nulls. You can also use a system-stored procedure or function as the default. There is one situation where you MUST define a default value. This is when you append a new column to an existing table and define it as Not Null. Since SQL Server must be able to store some value in the column other than null, you must define a default. It then loads the new column with the default.
- Precision and scale—These two attributes are active only for the numeric or decimal data types. Precision is the maximum number of digits allowed. Scale is the position starting from the right of the decimal point. A scale of zero means no decimal point is allowed.
- Identity, identity seed, and increment—These attributes are active only for integer data types. An identity column is used to uniquely identify the row within the table. By definition, it cannot have any meaning beyond this. You can define identity columns that automatically assign the next incremental value when a new row is inserted into the table. The `Identity` attribute tells SQL Server that you wish this column to be an identity column. `Identity seed` is the number you wish SQL Server to start numbering with. `Increment` is how much you wish SQL Server to add to the previous value when inserting a row. You may only have one identity column per table.
- IsRowGUID—This attribute is active on columns that are defined as `Unique-Identifiers`. If set to true, this tells SQL Server that this column is globally unique for this row. No other row in any database in

the world will have this GUID. When set to true, the function call to NewID is automatically placed in the default value attribute. This function returns a GUID. This property is used mostly for database replication, but you can also use it along with the time stamp data type to perform your own data synchronization between databases.

- Formula—This allows you to specify that a column is the result of a calculation. In this sense, the column is really a pseudocolumn. This is similar to a formula column in a spreadsheet. The calculation may be row-level only. That is, it must reference other columns within the same table and row. No aggregates may be used.
- Collation—On SQL Server 2000 and above only. You can now specify column-level collation. Collation is another word for sorting sequence. This attribute is active on character columns only. If you open the dialog by clicking the ellipsis, you will see that this is primarily used for multi-language support. You can use it to turn off case-sensitivity on certain columns if you wish. My advice is to leave it alone. Too much tampering here can cause confusion later on.

Indexes and Keys Tab

Indexes are data structures built on top of database columns that are used to provide fast access to the data. Indexes may be unique, where every key value must be different for the row it represents, or nonunique, where multiple key values can have the same value for two or more different rows. Every table should have at least one unique index called a primary key. To set up the indexes for a table, click the Indexes button on the toolbar, or select Property Pages from the View menu. Once the Property Pages open, select the Indexes/Keys tab (Figure 3.15).

To create an index, click the New button. The system will create a default index name for you. Next select the first column for the index. You may select as many columns as you need but be aware that the larger the index, the longer it will take to update the table. Index usage should be planned carefully so it provides the most benefit without adding too much overhead.

If you have more than one file group defined, you can choose to place your index in a different data file than the table. In some circumstances this can be beneficial, especially if the data files are on separate physical volumes. Database administrators frequently choose to do this as it can help improve performance. With smaller desktop databases there will only be one file group. Next you must decide if your index will be unique. A unique index can have at most one row with a specific value in the index. Your primary key will be a unique index by default. You can use a nonunique index to speed access to a table using a nonunique entity, such as a last name or city. If all you need to do is make sure that only one row has any particular value, you can use a unique constraint. A constraint is like an index, except it uses hash values instead of the actual key values. By using a hash value, it makes checking for uniqueness very fast. The drawback is that you cannot use a constraint to speed up access to data.

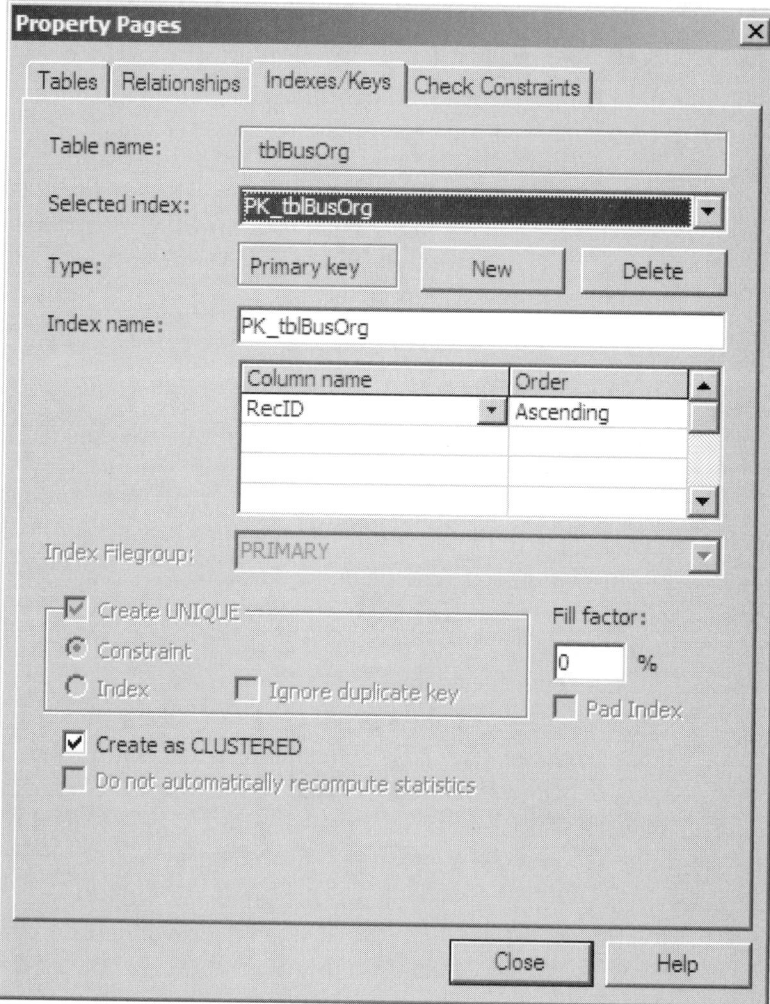

FIGURE 3.15 The Indexes/Keys tab of the Table Property page.

The Ignore Duplicate Key check box tells SQL Server not to abort an `insert` statement if one of the statements would create a duplicate key. This does not mean that the row will be inserted; it just means that SQL Server will not abort the transaction, but issue a warning. Any other statements in the Transact-SQL script will be executed. If you uncheck the check box, SQL Server will issue an error message and abort and roll back the transaction. My advice is to leave it unchecked and handle the error in your program. Otherwise you will never know that a table was not updated properly.

The last item is Create Clustered. This selection can be applied to only one index per table at a time. This causes SQL Server to sort the actual rows according to the sort order of the index. This speeds up sequential access to the data dramatically, but slows down inserting and updating because SQL Server must insert or move the row into the correct position instead of just appending it to the end of the table. The last item, Do Not Automatically Recompute Statistics, should be left unchecked. This has to do with how the Query Optimizer decides how to best access a table when running a query. We will look at this later on, but for now leave it alone. I have never had to touch this selection.

Relationships Tab

As long as we have the Property Pages open, let's look at the Relationships tab. Since we are using a relational database it stands to reason that relationships are what set this type of database apart from others. On this tab we can declare relationships between tables and also enable declarative referential integrity (DRI). It is important to note the difference between these two related concepts.

- *Relations* describe links between tables using foreign keys.
- *Referential integrity* tells SQL Server what to do when a related column is updated or inserted.

Let's look at these in more detail.

Relations and Foreign Keys

Before we can use any DRI we must define the relationships between tables. Two or more tables can be related if they share common attributes. For example, you could have a table that describes a work location and a table that describes employees. In real life, many employees can share the same work location. Suppose we assign a value to identify each work location. We can call it the Location ID. Then if we store the Location ID on each employee record we have a way of linking the employee record to the location record. If we define the Location ID as a unique key on the work location record, we can then define the Location ID on the employee record as a foreign key (see Figure 3.16). This establishes a formal relationship between the two tables.

Note how the foreign key on tblEmp is linked to the primary key on tblLocation. This relationship defines a one-to-many relation. For every location record, there can be many employee records. In such a relation, the key on the *one* side of the relation must be unique. You may have a compound index, as long as the index is unique. It does not have to be the primary key, as long as it is unique. On the *many* side of the relationship, the foreign key is defined on the Location ID column. If no index exists on the foreign key, SQL Server defines a nonunique index for the purpose of creating the link.

Types of Relations

There are basically three types of relations:

- One-to-one —There is no more than one record in Table A for every record in Table B. Depending on referential integrity settings, there may be no records in Table A for a record in Table B or no records in Table B for a record in Table A.
- One-to-many—For every record in Table A, there are zero or more records in Table B with the same foreign key.
- Many-to-many—For every record in Table A, there are zero or more records in Table B with the same foreign key, and for every record in Table B, there can be zero or more records in Table A.

Whether there can be zero records on the many side of a one-to-many or many-to-many relation depends on how the referential integrity settings are defined.

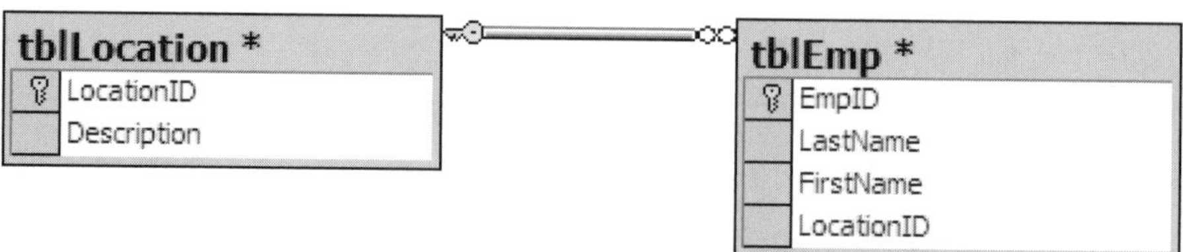

FIGURE 3.16 Relation defined between Location and Employee tables.

Referential Integrity

Now that we've seen how to define a relationship between tables, let's look at the DRI. We defined referential integrity as the rules used by SQL Server when inserting or updating rows in tables with defined relationships. The settings for DRI are at the lower portion of the Property Pages as in Figure 3.17.

- Check existing data on creation—This option tells SQL Server to validate all the DRI rules when the new relation is saved initially. Be careful with this because on very large tables this could take some time.
- Enforce relationship for replication—This tells SQL Server to enforce the relation when replicating data. Unless you will be using replication, this is of no concern to you. If you are using replication, you may want to turn this off if you define a relationship after a table that is in. With this off, SQL Server will not check DRI rules when synchronizing databases.
- Enforce relationship for INSERTs and UPDATEs—This tells SQL Server to check the relationship when inserting or updating rows. If a foreign key is missing or does not match a value in the foreign table, the insert or update will fail and SQL Server will throw an error. If this is unchecked, SQL Server will allow the insert or update with invalid data in the foreign key. If this item is checked, the following two items are enabled.
- Cascade update related fields—If a related field is changed on the one side of a one-to-many relation, all of the related columns on the many side of the relation are automatically updated with the new value. Be careful here because large tables can cause noticeable performance degradation. If the item is unchecked, SQL Server will throw an error if you change the column and the change would break referential integrity.
- Cascade delete related records—If a row is deleted on the one side of a one-to-many relation, all rows in the related table with the same foreign key value will also be deleted. If the item is left unchecked, SQL Server will throw an error if you try to delete a row with related rows on the many side of the relation.

Check existing data on creation
Enforce relationship for replication
Enforce relationship for INSERTs and UPDATEs
Cascade Update Related Fields
Cascade Delete Related Records

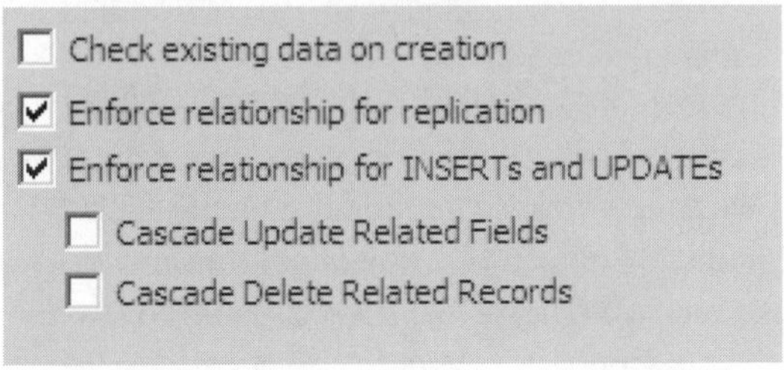

FIGURE 3.17 Referential integrity settings.

Confusion About Nulls—I have met many experienced programmers who struggle with the mathematical concept of null. Simply put, null means "undefined." It does not mean zero, it does not mean a null string, it does not mean ASCII zero. Zero is a valid mathematical value and does not mean undefined, it means zero. A null string is also called a zero-length string and it does not mean undefined, it means a string with no characters. The ASCII value `Null` means an ASCII value of zero, not undefined, as in a `Null`-terminated string or padding with nulls.

What do we mean by undefined? We mean the value is unknown. We do not mean it has no value. We mean we do not know what the value is. Therefore, any database column that is null has an unknown value.

Therefore, given this definition, the result of any operation involving a null is null.

1 + null is null

2X + 3Y * 12 / null is null

"My Name is " & null is null

Another way of saying this is one plus an undefined (or unknown) value is also unknown.

Also note that we do not say "equals null," we say "is null." That is because any equality test between null and any other value will fail by definition. The statement "If X = Null" will always return `false`. As a matter of fact, the statement "If Null = Null" will also always return `false`. In SQL syntax, if we want to test for null we say "Where ColumnX Is Null" or "Where ColumnX Is Not Null." In VB you can use the "IsNull" property of the row's item property: "If X.IsNull Then..."

Check Constraints

Check constraints (see Figure 3.18) are rules that are applied to columns before they can be written to the database. For example, you might specify that a column value must be less than 100 or that a text field cannot contain all spaces.

The constraint expression must return a true or false value and cannot contain aggregate expressions. The constraint in Figure 3.18 causes SQL Server to reject any value that is all spaces in the Contact Name column. The three check boxes have a similar function to the Relations tab.

VIEWS AND THE QUERY DESIGNER

Views and the query designer fit together naturally because you use the query designer to create views. A view is a preconfigured select query that is stored in the database and can be used just like a table. In most cases, views can be updated just like queries. One of the most common uses for views is when creating reports. You do not have to use the query designer to create views.

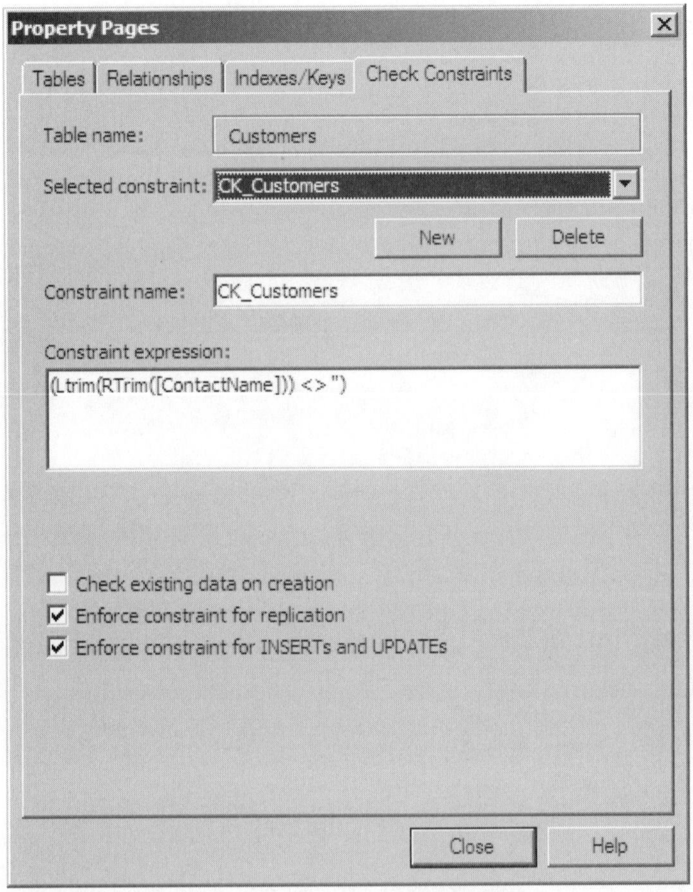

FIGURE 3.18 The Check Constraints tab.

You can also create them using a Transact-SQL script. We will look at that method later when we examine the database project. For now we will use the query designer.

To open the query designer (see Figure 3.19), first we must find the views. Using the Server Explorer, navigate to and expand the Northwind database. Expand the Views tab and select Alphabetical List of Products. To open the view in Design mode, right-click on it and select Design View from the context menu (Figure 3.20).

If you have used the query designer in Microsoft Access this should appear familiar to you. The screen is divided into four panes: Diagram, Show Grid, SQL, and Results

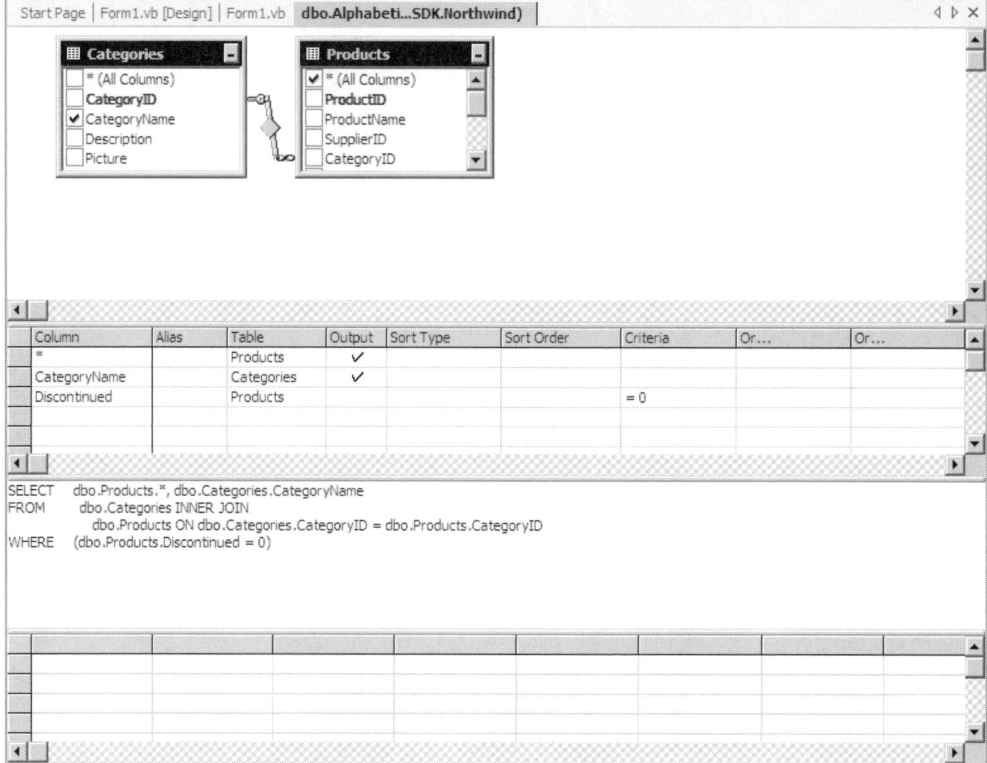

FIGURE 3.19 The query designer.

The Diagram Pane

The Diagram pane is where you add the tables you want to include in your view. There are two ways to add tables:

Drag and drop your table from the Server Explorer. This is the simpler way.

Use the Add Tables dialog. Use this method if you are going to create a complex view using numerous tables. To use the Add Tables dialog, click the Toolbar button.

Next we must define the joins between tables. We do this by dragging a foreign key column to a primary table and dropping it. This is a very impor-

FIGURE 3.20 The Design View button.

tant step. If we do not create a join, we will get a *Cartesian product* when we run the query. A Cartesian product is a result that joins every single row from one table with every single row of another, where the number of rows is equal to the product of the number of rows of both tables. Suppose we have a table with 20,000 rows and another table with 500 rows. The Cartesian product of these would be 10,000,000 rows, not exactly what we desire.

There are three main types of joins:

- Inner —In this type of join, both columns used to join the tables must have values that satisfy the join condition.
- Left or right outer —One table will include all rows, while the other table will contain only rows that satisfy the join condition. If the table on the left side of the join condition is to return all rows, we call it a Left Outer Join. If the table on the right is to return all rows we call it a Right Outer Join. Sometimes we leave out the word outer and say only Left Join or Right Join. When a row is returned that has a missing other side of the join, the columns on the opposite side are filled with nulls.
- Full outer – All rows from both side of the join are included, filling the missing halves with nulls.

If you right-click on the join line, then select Property Pages from the menu, you can see the details of the join (Figure 3.21).

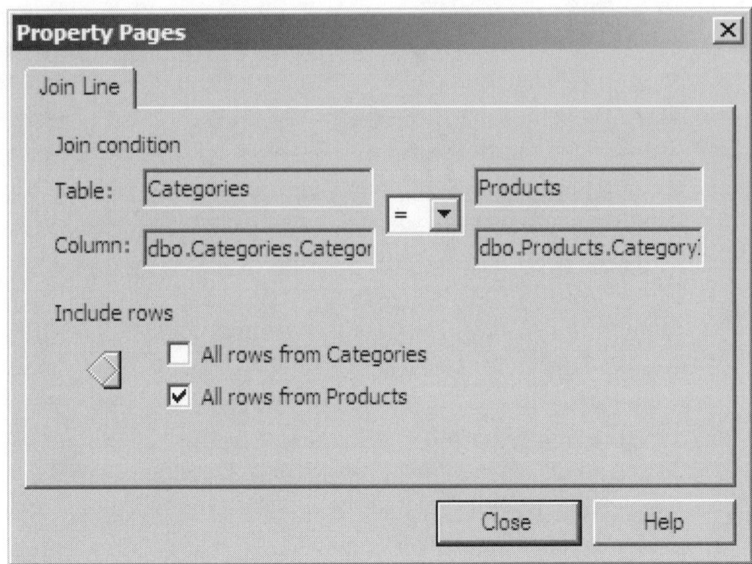

FIGURE 3.21 Join property page.

Show Grid Pane

Next we have to tell SQL Server which columns we want to include in the view. You should only include columns that you will actually need in your output (screen, report, etc.) so that network traffic will be minimized. You can select columns to include two ways. You can check them off in the table diagrams or you can choose them from the drop down lists in the Show pane. The other columns allow you to set the sort order, specify whether or not to output the columns, and specify selection criteria.

SQL Pane

In this pane, the SQL statement being built by the Diagram and Show Grid is displayed. You can also type an SQL statement directly. I find that this is often easier for me. If you know SQL well and are familiar with the database schema you are working with, it is faster to type the statement directly than to click and drag with the mouse. After you've typed the statement, you can check the syntax by clicking the Check Syntax button on the toolbar.

Results Pane

The Results pane displays the data returned by the view. You can use this to test your query before using it in an actual program.

Stored Procedures and Triggers

The stored procedure editor works just like a regular code window. It supports full color-coded syntax. Stored procedures and triggers are written using the Transact-SQL language. Stored procedures are self-contained programs. They can do pretty much anything you want, but usually are used to perform operations on the database that cannot be done using a single SQL statement. A trigger is a special kind of stored procedure that executes when a row is inserted, updated, or deleted from a table.

Transact-SQL language is best left to a book of its own, and there are plenty on the market. The stored procedures we will use will be pretty simple. We will limit ourselves to procedures that fetch data or update the database using parameters.

One interesting thing about the Procedure window is that SQL queries are outlined in blue. If you right-click inside this outline you will see a Design SQL Block entry in the context menu. If you select this item, a Query Design window opens. You can now design your query graphically and when you save the query it will appear in the stored procedure.

DATABASE DIAGRAMS

The database diagram is a way of representing the schema graphically. SQL Server has a built-in diagramming tool. You can create several named diagrams to document your database structure. The diagram is more than a documentation tool. It is an active designer for the database. You can create tables and relations right in the diagram and the database will be updated when the diagram is saved.

DATABASE PROJECTS

Database projects provide another method of manipulating databases. With the database project, you can create scripts and queries to execute on an SQL Server or MSDE database. You can create schema change scripts, or SQL queries. You can also use source code control to manage the scripts. The database project provides similar functionality to the Query Analyzer that comes with the full version of SQL Server. The handy part of using a database project is that now you can include it in your solution and track the various stored procedures and queries that are used by the solution.

VB 6—VB 6 also had a database project. However that type of project was very different. The VB 6 database project was a template for creating a project with a DataEnviroment designer and a DataReport designer precreated. Since VB .NET supports neither of these tools, its database project is used to manage SQL queries and scripts.

You create a database project the same way you create any other new VB project. You can also add one to an existing solution. Select New Project from the File menu, or if you are adding it to an existing solution select Add Project/New Project. When the new project dialog opens, find the template called Database Project. You should find it under the Other Projects node of the tree control (Figure 3.22).

There are two subfolders in the project for storing change scripts and another for queries. It is very important to make the distinction between these scripts and stored procedures. The scripts are saved as disk files and are external to any database. Stored procedures are compiled and saved inside the SQL Server database. When a script is run or debugged, it uses the database connection defined in the project as the default database, but the scripts can be run on any SQL Server database.

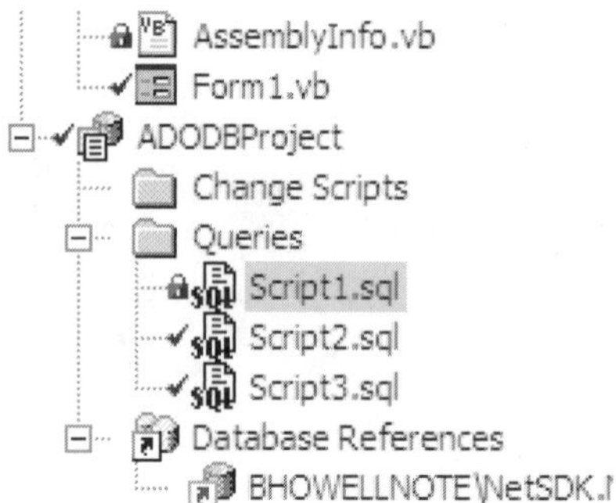

FIGURE 3.22 Solution Explorer view of a database project.

The database project gives you a way of organizing and distributing SQL Server scripts. It also allows them to be included in version control. This is actually a real benefit. If you have ever been involved in a project that has multiple distributed databases and must manage changes between them, you will appreciate the ability to organize your scripts.

When creating a script, there are several templates you can choose from. This is a time saver in that you do not have to create the script from scratch. It also provides a nice header block you can (and should) fill in for documentation purposes.

Running Scripts

You can run your scripts directly in the IDE. If you run a script that outputs data, it will appear in the Output window. This is a great way of validating your output before you use the script in a program.

SUMMARY

We covered much ground so far. We have gotten familiar enough with the Visual Studio IDE to create projects and compile and run them. We looked into the Server Explorer and learned how to manage an MSDE or SQL Server database from within the IDE. We now have enough background to begin looking at the ADO .NET tools in detail. In the next chapter, we will take an in-depth tour of the ADO .NET class library.

CHAPTER 4

The ADO .NET Class Library

ActiveX Data Objects .NET is in some ways a misnomer. It implies that ADO .NET is implemented as an ActiveX object library, the same way as ADO was. In a sense this is true, because like ADO, ADO .NET wraps the OLEDB COM classes. However, unlike ADO, ADO .NET is not itself an ActiveX object library. It is implemented as a collection of .NET classes. ADO .NET also has a high-performance native mode for SQL Server that does not use OLEDB at all! The basis for ADO .NET is XML. Perhaps it should have been called XDO for XML Data Objects. As we dissect the class library, you will see why.

ADO .NET CLASS LIBRARY OVERVIEW

The central class in ADO .NET is the DataSet. While it is tempting to compare the DataSet to the ADO RecordSet object, it is really a different type of object entirely. The ADO .NET DataSet is really a repository for XML data. ADO .NET has more to do with reading and persisting XML data than it does accessing databases. Instead of its primary function being to access databases, its primary function is to access, store, and save XML documents from many different sources. The database is just one of those sources. Data is persisted as World Wide Web Consortium (W3C)–compliant XML, so any consumer complying with the standard, no matter the platform, can use it. The DataSet can be used as a stand-alone object for storing any data you can imagine. It is also designed to be the remoting agent of choice. Since it is designed to read any XML data stream, it uses this method for marshalling data between remote sources and local programs.

The DataSet is composed of a collection of tables, relations, and constraints. Does anyone remember the in-memory database that was supposed to be released with Windows 2000 and then was pulled from the release at the last minute? Well here it is, reincarnated as the DataSet. That's right, the class has all the power you need for an in-memory database, including tables, indexes, foreign keys, and DRI. It can draw its data from a database, or you can use it as a stand-alone in-memory data cache that can be persisted to disk or sent over the network.

The other main classes are for connecting to and running queries on databases. There are two main branches to the class library, the SqlClient classes and the OleDbClient classes. As we said before, SqlClient is optimized for SQL Server 7.0 and later databases. It uses native access and does not require OLEDB. The OleDbClient classes use the OLEDB data providers. They can be used for Oracle, Access, and any other supported database *except ODBC.* There is a special version of the OLEDB ODBC driver available for download from the Microsoft site. More on that later.

Connection Class

The connection classes provide the means to connect to the database. They also manage transactions, and connection pooling. The various parameters for connecting to a database are set via the `ConnectionString` property. In previous versions of ADO, most of the `ConnectionString` values were exposed through properties. For security reasons, ADO .NET only exposes the `ConnectionString`. We will enumerate the details of the various values of the `ConnectionString` in the chapter on the Connection object.

Command Class

The Command class provides methods for storing and executing SQL statements and stored procedures. It has a Parameters collection that is used to pass parameters into and out of stored procedures. The collection can also be used to set the parameters for a parameterized SQL statement. The DataAdapter class contains four Command classes for selecting, updating, inserting, and deleting data. The class can also be used by itself for non-databound access to the database. Of all the ADO .NET classes, the Command class is the closest to the ADO Command class in functionality and remains essentially unchanged as far as properties and methods go. Of course, it is a .NET Framework class and does not use COM at all. It also has some enhancements over the old ADO Command object.

DataReader Class

The DataReader is used to retrieve data. It is used in conjunction with the Command class to execute an SQL Select statement and then access the returned rows. It provides forward-only read-only access to the data. The DataReader is also used by the DataAdapter to pump data into a DataSet when the `Fill` method of the DataAdapter is called. The DataReader provides high-speed access to data. You can use a DataReader to pull data for web pages that are read-only, reports, graphs or any other application that does not require data binding and only displays data.

The DataAdapter Class

The DataAdapter is used to connect DataSets to databases. It is a go-between class. It is comprised of four Command classes and one DataReader class. The DataAdapter is most useful when using data-bound controls in Windows Forms, but it can also be used to provide an easy way to manage the connection between your application and the underlying database tables, views, and stored procedures. Another way of looking at the DataAdapter class is as a way of containing SQL statements and stored procedures for easy programmatic access. All of the SQL needed to maintain a database entity can be contained in a DataAdapter object. The DataAdapter also uses support classes that will create the SQL statements for updating the database from a predefined `Select` statement, and will fill the parameter collections of the Command objects contained in the class. There is also a wizard that helps create the DataAdapter and another wizard that will create a DataSet from the Command objects contained within the DataAdapter.

COMPARISON OF ADO .NET AND ADO 2.X

Since ADO .NET is so different from ADO 2.x (or just ADO), a comparison is a good idea. Those of you who are fluent with ADO will find the transition easier if you have some basis for associating ADO practices with ADO .NET's. For those of you who have never used ADO, it is still worth the time to see how ADO .NET evolved from ADO and why the changes were made. Here we will look at the differences from a programming point of view. Also, just because ADO .NET is the new kid on the block doesn't mean that there are not still applications that would be better served by ADO. Each has its strengths and weaknesses.

Two Different Design Goals

ADO and ADO .NET are fundamentally different because the designers had two different goals in mind when they designed the software. ADO is a descendant of the Data Access Objects (DAO)/Remote Data Object (RDO) models. One goal of the designers of ADO was to combine the two older data access technologies into one homogeneous object model that could be used to access any supported database. The other goal was to reduce dependency on open database connectivity (ODBC), an older database standard and replace it with OLEDB, a COM-based standard for connecting to databases. Because of this, the ADO object model was aligned with the two older technologies, DAO and RDO. ADO is also an inherently connected technology. This means that an open database connection is maintained for the life of any of the RecordSet objects that hold data.

In later versions of ADO (2.1 and later) it was possible to use a disconnected architecture. This was added to support stateless web applications. Most desktop applications continued to use the connected model. In some cases this is because the applications needed the concurrency support and were highly transactional. In other cases it was because that was what the programmer knew how to do.

ADO .NET was designed to support the stateless model by default. It is an inherently *disconnected* architecture. While ADO .NET continues to support the OLEDB COM-based database access standard, the new goal is to eliminate even that. ADO .NET uses the new SOAP object protocol and uses XML as its storage and communications medium. The SqlClient classes that support SQL Server are the example of the direction Microsoft is headed. The plan is for developers to create native ADO .NET class libraries to support their database product. The SqlClient classes do not use OLEDB. It is one of the long-term goals of Microsoft to eliminate COM. If it seems to you that they took a 180-degree turn, you are not imagining things. That is part of the reason for this book.

The ADO Architecture and Practice

With all that said, let's very quickly review the ADO object model. There are three main objects in ADO.

- The Connection object manages database connections and transactions.
- The Command object encapsulates SQL statements and manages access to stored procedures. It contains a Parameters collection to manage passing data into and out of stored procedures.

- The RecordSet object holds the results of SQL queries and implements methods for navigating through the rows and for adding, deleting, and updating rows.

In its native connected mode, when you update the RecordSet, the results are immediately updated in the underlying database as well. If the RecordSet is opened with a dynamic cursor, other user's changes to the database are immediately made available. The RecordSet can also be used as a stand-alone object. It has all of the properties required to connect to and access the database. The practice for using ADO in a typical client/server Windows Desktop application written using Visual Basic 6.0 was:

1. The programmer would create an instance of a Connection object as either a global variable (a public module level variable in a standard module) or as a module-level variable in a class module. Sometimes the class would be compiled into a separate ActiveX component so it could be deployed as a middle-tier component. Other times it would just be a class module in the Desktop application project.
2. As part of the program's initialization sequence, the programmer would prompt the user for security information (user name and password) and then open a connection to the database.
3. The open Connection object would remain open and be used throughout the life of the application to open RecordSets and execute commands. If it were a global variable, it would be referenced directly. If it were a module-level variable in a class module, it would be used by the class, and all database access would be initiated through an instance of the class.
4. When the user closed the program, the connection would be closed and the connection object deinstantiated.

This practice generally worked fine in a local area network (LAN) environment where the server was on the same LAN as the clients. It also worked decently when the server was located across a WAN, depending on traffic and how resource intensive the application in question was. There are some problems with this type of arrangement:

1. This kind of application does not scale up well. Because it holds an open connection throughout its life, the server must allocate resources to the user until the user closes the application. The application generally performs well with a low number of users, but performance deteriorates rapidly as the server's resources and memory utilization exceed certain

limits. The answer is to expand the server. This helps for a while, but every server has its limits.

2. Sloppy programming can easily cause memory and resource leaks that will bring the application and the server to its knees. Programmers must be disciplined enough to remember to release resources when they have finished with them. I have not met many who are. Even when they are, a simple oversight can cause this problem. For example, the failure to close and uninstantiate a RecordSet can be disastrous. This is especially true if the RecordSet is opened many times during the course of the application's life. Also, I've known programmers who think that just setting a RecordSet's variable to nothing without explicitly closing it is good enough, not realizing that the server keeps the cursor alive until the user closes the connection. If this is part of the main processing of the program, the server will get bogged down in short order.
3. The more simultaneous open connections that are required, the more client licenses you need to buy. If you want to use a concurrent licensing model for SQL Server, then you must have enough licenses for each user logged on at the same time. This issue, obviously, is economic, not technical.

Even with these shortcomings, sometimes this type of application architecture is indicated. This is especially true in applications that are highly transactional and require instant data availability. Some of these would include trading systems and banking applications. The users of these applications need to see database updates as they happen. The only way to do this is by maintaining an open connection. These applications require high-performance networks, workstations, and servers. They also require pretty savvy programming techniques. If those are your requirements, ADO may still be the way to go for you. You can use ADO in your VB .NET application. As a matter of fact, with VB .NET's multithreading capability and ADO it is possible to design these extremely high performance applications. Previously C++ would have been the language of choice because these applications usually use multithreading to achieve the performance they require.

ADO .NET Architecture and Practice

ADO .NET is inherently disconnected. This is the exact opposite of ADO. It was designed this way to support the stateless nature of ASP .NET and Web Services. We have already outlined the ADO .NET class library so let's outline the practice for using ADO .NET in a Windows Forms application.

1. Your application will consist of multiple forms. At first glance, you would think that you would create an ADO .NET Connection object in the main class of your application and pass it to your forms as they needed it. However, this turns out to be more work than you need to do. Since connections only need to last as long as the latest call, we really do not need one central Connection object the way we might want in a VB 6 ADO application.
2. In ADO .NET, the best practice is to have each form have its own connection object. This way the forms are entirely encapsulated. What I do is pass the connection string to each form. Once the connection has been validated during the logon sequence, all you need to retain is the formed connection string. If you are worried about holding a password in memory where it could possibly be compromised, you can encrypt the connection string and decrypt it just before setting the property of the Connection object. That way it only exists in a plain-text state for a very short period of time.
3. When you need to populate your bound controls, use the DataAdapter's `Fill` method on the DataSet the controls are bound to. The DataAdapter will open and close connections as needed.
4. When you need to update the database, use the `Update` method of the DataAdapter.
5. When the user closes the program, there is no need to worry about closing database connections because they remain closed until needed.

The process for an ASP .NET web-based application is:

1. Display an ASP .NET Web Form. In this form, there would be fields the user will fill in that will be used to build an SQL query.
2. When the user clicks a button, the program executes a DataAdapter's `Fill` method passing the values from the form that the user entered through the DataAdapter's `SelectCommand` parameters collection.
3. Assuming you have bound controls on the form to the DataSet, when you execute the form's `DataBind` method, it will post the page back to the client with the values from the DataSet in the controls.
4. The user makes changes to the data. When finished, the user clicks another button. Since data binding on an ASP .NET form is display only, you now have to manually assign each value from the form to the parameters of the DataAdapter's `UpdateCommand` parameters collection.

5. You would then call the `UpdateCommand`'s `ExecuteNonQuery` method to update the database.

Why can't I use the same techniques in ASP Windows Forms as I do in Windows Forms? Because the ASP .NET form is stateless. What do we mean by stateless? We will go into this more in the chapter on ASP .NET, but essentially it means that there is no connection between calls to the server. Each time the client calls code in the server, the whole server-side program must reexecute. For this reason, any data generated in one call to the server is lost as soon as the call is completed. This is true of DataSets as well. Therefore, even though you are using bound controls, as soon as the call to the server completes, the underlying DataSet is destroyed. When you make changes and send them back up to the server, there is no DataSet to rebind the controls to. In a Windows Form, the DataSet is continually in existence therefore the form controls can communicate with it whenever they need to.

As we have said, ADO .NET is optimized for web-based stateless applications. However, there are some potential problems with this architecture as well:

1. There is some overhead to authenticating a connection each time the database is accessed. The Connection class uses connection pooling to minimize this effect. For SQL Server it is minimal, but it is still a concern. You can control this programmatically, and if a single form makes several accesses in rapid succession, it would be wise to maintain the open connection until the form is finished. In a Windows Form this is easy, but in an ASP .NET application you must make sure you don't execute rebind too often as there will be a round-trip to the server each time and the connection could be lost between requests. Make sure all of your database access happens during one ASP request. If you don't, you will be opening and closing connections for each database access.
2. You will not be able to see database updates made by other users in real-time. As we said, if you need this kind of real-time availability, then ADO may be a better choice.. This is true of ASP Windows Forms and Windows Forms.
3. This is related to the previous item. You cannot use pessimistic concurrency with ADO .NET. With pessimistic concurrency, each row is locked as soon as the client reads it. The lock is not released until the user moves to another row or until the row is updated. In a highly transactional environment, where you need row-level read locking, you cannot use ADO

.NET. There are other techniques for achieving a similar result, but they would have to be implemented by the programmer.

4. In any client/server application it is always desirable to manage your database queries so that they return reasonable amounts of data. All too often this is not considered when programmers write database access code. They often develop using a test database with a limited number of rows, and then when they try it on the production database they find that their application fails because the query returns millions of rows. ADO would attempt to handle this by using the RecordSet's row caching and delayed fetching to keep in memory only enough rows to display or manipulate. Even so, it could easily bring an application to its knees. With ADO .NET, this is even more important because when you fill a DataSet, ADO .NET must fetch all of the rows returned by the server. If your query returns millions of rows, this could be disastrous. You absolutely *must* manage your database queries so that they return manageable numbers of rows.

ADO .NET is not the answer for all types of applications. ADO is still alive and kicking. If you need high-concurrency and real-time data availability, ADO should still be considered. ADO .NET is best for web applications that use a stateless architecture. It is also indicated when a Windows application does not require real-time access to data. Since most everyday applications do not need high-performance real-time access, ADO .NET should be used since it is very efficient and is designed to work with XML. You could also use a combination of both techniques in your system, using each for its strengths.

Multitier Application Design

This is another one of those buzzwords. What do we mean by multitier architecture and what does it have to do with the ADO .NET class library? Most of us think of a three-tier architecture or a business rules layer when we think of a multitier architecture.

Multitier architecture is an application architecture where the code is divided into logical layers and is spread over multiple software components and multiple physical machines.

Even though some consider multiple-component architecture where the code all resides on one machine as multitier, it is not. Applications written using multiple code modules and DLLs on a single machine have been around for years. They are not usually considered multitier. To be a multitier application, the code must not only be divided into multiple modules, it must be divided logically into layers with each layer performing a specified task. It also implies that the layers are distributed across multiple servers.

The most common forms of multitier applications are web applications. They typically have a presentation layer (the web browser), a middle layer (IIS and the ASP scripts or VB code-behind-forms for ASP .NET) and a database layer (SQL Server, Oracle, and others). In smaller deployments the server-side code (ASP) can run on the same machine as the database. In larger deployments the ASP code would run on its own machine or be spread across several machines for load-balancing purposes.

Simple two-tier Windows client/server applications are another common form, although many of these are being phased out in favor of multiple layers.

Now that we've established what multitier is, what does it have to do with the ADO .NET class library? Well, it turns out that ADO .NET is optimized for multitier applications. In fact, the whole .NET Framework is designed to make multitier architecture easy to design and implement. The separation of the data containers and view managers (the DataSet class) and the actual data access classes (DataAdapter and Connection) is one way ADO .NET makes multitier programming easier that it was in the past. The ability to create XML Web Services is another way.

NOTE—When we say ADO .NET makes multitier design easy, we do not mean simple. It does make it easier than it was in the past using COM+, but it is certainly not an easy task. Multitier design must be undertaken carefully and much thought must be put into any design. Once all that has been done, it is relatively easy to create the components and programs using the .NET Framework.

THE SQLCLIENT AND OLEDBCLIENT CLASSES

One of the design goals of ADO .NET was to phase out reliance on OLEDB, the database access technology based on COM+. Microsoft also realized that there are a large number of OLEDB providers that are well established. To accomplish this goal and retain backward compatibility with OLEDB providers, Microsoft created two branches to the data access classes. The OleDbClient set of classes can use any of the existing OLEDB providers *except the*

ODBC OLEDB provider[1]. The SqlClient set of classes does not use OLEDB. It is a native ADO .NET data access technology. It is Microsoft's goal to see third parties build other database-specific providers. There is already an Oracle client set of classes in beta. There are advantages and disadvantages to both approaches. In this section we will go over the benefits and drawbacks of each set of classes.

The two sets of classes are *roughly* parallel. That means that while the class libraries mostly have counterparts in each client, it is not 100 percent. For example, the SqlClient's SQLPermissions class has a counterpart in OLEDB, but the properties and methods do not fully line up. This makes cross-database platform development difficult, and requires that some intermediate component layer be built that can adapt itself to the underlying database.

One answer would be to exclusively use the OleDbClient classes, but there is a performance price as they are not as efficient as the native SqlClient classes with SQL Server databases. Which set of classes you use depends on your design goals. If you must design for cross-database compatibility, my advice would be to use the OleDbClient classes. Even then, you will have to write some database-specific code. While cross-database compatibility was a consideration some years ago, I think that it is less of an issue now. I remember having to create cross-database systems, only to find that all implementations were on SQL Server. All that extra programming was never used.

The good news is that the two sets of classes merge with the DataSet. The DataSet was designed to be database-neutral. Both sets of client classes send their data to the DataSet for storage and local manipulation so your presentation-layer code can be one single code base. This is an improvement over the past where even the RecordSet would be slightly different for different database systems. Any future ADO .NET client classes (Oracle for example) also must provide data to the DataSet in order to conform to the ADO .NET standard.

Next we will summarize most of the ADO .NET classes, starting with the database access classes and the two clients (SQL and OleDB). We will discuss the classes together. I will note where they are different; otherwise you can assume they are the same. Then we will summarize the DataSet and the classes that it uses. We will discuss these classes and more in further detail in the separate chapters on each.

---

1. There is a special ODBC .NET driver available from *http://msdn.microsoft.com/downloads.*

THE CONNECTION CLASSES

The Connection classes do just as you would think. They contain the information needed to open a database connection. In addition, they are used to manage transaction objects. The five main members of this class are ConnectionString, Open, Close, and BeginTransaction.

The `ConnectionString` Property

The `ConnectionString` property is a concatenation of various elements that tell ADO .NET about the database and server you wish to connect to. A semicolon (;) separates the elements. This is not much different than ADO or ODBC. The connection string definitely traces its heritage back to the ODBC DSN string. Many of the elements are the same. The five main elements of the connection string are:

- OLEDB Provider—The name of the OLEDB provider. This is only needed for the OleDbClient classes. If provided with the SqlClient classes an error will be thrown.
- Server —The domain name or Windows machine name of the server. You can also use an Internet Protocol (IP) address. If the name is registered on a Domain Name System (DNS) server you can use that because it resolves to an IP address. Otherwise you can use the Windows machine name if it is in the same workgroup or Windows domain. For SQL Server you can also map an alias to an IP address or named pipe using the client configuration utility. With Oracle you can use the global database name. Oracle clients need to be set up using the SQLNet configuration utility before you can access them using ADO .NET. As this implies, you need an Oracle client installation and license.
- Database—This is the name of the SQL Server database or the Oracle instance name.
- UserName or UID—This is the login user name.
- Password or PWD—The password for the user.

A typical connection string for SQL Server where the server name is MyServer and the database name is MyDB would look like this for the OleDbClient:

```
Provider=SQLOLEDB.1;Server=MyServer;Database=MyDB;User
ID=Bob;Password=xxxx
```

For the SqlClient:

```
Server=MyServer;Database=MyDB;User ID=Bob;Password=xxxx
```

For an Oracle database located on server UNIX1 with instance name MYOraDB would look like this for the OleDbClient:

```
Provider=MSDAORA.1;Server=UNIX1;Database=MyOraDB;User
ID=Bob;Password=xxxx
```

You cannot use the SqlClient classes to connect to an Oracle database.

The `Open` and `Close` Methods

These do exactly what they sound like. The `Open` method opens a connection to the database specified in the connection string. The `Close` method closes it. You do not have to call the `Open` and `Close` methods explicitly. If you call a DataAdapter's `Fill` method, it will automatically open the connection, execute the SQL or stored procedure, and close the connection. If you open the connection before calling the `Fill` method, the DataAdapter will not close the connection when it is finished.

The `BeginTransaction` Method

ADO .NET handles transactions differently than all previous Microsoft data access technologies. In the past, transactions were not named and they were started on the connection object. You could nest transactions if the underlying database allowed it but the nesting was in the order the transactions where started. This made tracking the transaction scope very difficult, especially if the transactions were started in various procedures throughout the program. The programmer had to make sure the right transactions were in the correct scope. Now, when you begin a transaction, it gets assigned to a transaction object which represents a nesting level. You assign a transaction object to a database operation, such as a command object, and the object will operate at that level. The `Commit` and `Rollback` methods are now in the transaction class.

The Command Class

This class is used to execute commands against the database. The command can be an SQL statement, a stored procedure, or the name of a table or view. The Command class contains a collection of parameter objects for use in passing values to a stored procedure or SQL statement. The class also contains its own connection object. You can pass in an already created connection object or you can create one directly in the Command class. Either way, the Command class only holds a reference to a connection object so there are no excess connections that will be opened to the server.

There are three different kinds of commands that can be executed by the Command class. These commands are executed by calling one of four execute methods:

- `ExecuteReader`—Returns data to the client as rows. This would typically be an SQL select statement or a stored procedure that contains one or more select statements. This method returns a DataReader object that can be used to fill a DataTable object or used directly for printing reports and so forth.
- `ExecuteNonQuery`—Executes a command that changes the data in the database, such as an update, delete, or insert statement, or a stored procedure that contains one or more of these statements. This method returns an integer that is the number of rows affected by the query.
- `ExecuteScalar`—This method only returns a single value. This kind of query returns a count of rows or a calculated value.
- `ExecuteXMLReader` —(SqlClient classes only) Obtains data from an SQL Server 2000 database using an XML stream. Returns an XML Reader object.

The DataReader Class

The DataReader class is used to get the results of a select query as a stream of data from the server. The `Read` method of the DataReader is used to load a row at a time of data into a buffer. The columns in the row are accessed using the ordinal index of the column. You can also obtain schema information using the `GetSchemaTable` method. This method returns a DataTable object containing the column information. This information can then be used to create a DataTable to hold the rows returned by the query. The DataReader class can only move forward through the data stream because it opens a forward-only cursor on the server. This is the most efficient way of accessing data.

The XMLReader Class

Similar to the DataReader, the XMLReader gets data from a SQL Server 2000 database, but in XML format. This is useful for accessing SQL Server via HTTP if it is behind a secure firewall. This class can only be used with the SqlClient on SQL Server 2000 databases. In addition, you must format your SQL query using the For XML clause.

THE DATAADAPTER CLASS

The DataAdapter class contains four Command objects and some methods for populating and updating DataSets from the commands. Essentially, the DataAdapter is a worker class that holds the four Command objects and has the ability to execute the commands and send the results to a DataSet. The DataAdapter knows how to build update, insert, and delete statements from the context of the `Select` statement provided by the programmer. It also knows how to generate parameter lists. To do this it uses a helper class called the SQLCommandBuilder.

The Fill Method

The `Fill` method causes the DataAdapter to execute the Command object in the `SelectCommand` property, generate a DataReader object to obtain the results, then pump the results into a DataTable in a DataSet. This is a real time-saver in that the programmer has to execute only one method. The same results could be obtained by using discrete Command, DataReader and DataTable objects, but Microsoft made it easy by doing the work for you.

The FillSchema Method

Similar to the `Fill` method, the `FillSchema` method fills the DataTable's Columns collection, but it does not retrieve any data from the database. This is useful for creating a typed DataSet at design time without wasting resources to retrieve data.

The Update Method

The `Update` method will take any changes made to a DataSet and post them back to the database. The method uses the UpdateCommand, InsertCommand, and DeleteCommand to do this. The DataAdapter knows how to interrogate the DataSet for what changes to make. In one method, it determines which rows to update, insert, or delete. The `Update` method uses optimistic concurrency to ensure that multiple users' updates do not interfere with each other.

THE DATASET CLASS

The DataSet is the heart of ADO .NET. The DataSet is essentially a collection of DataTable objects; in turn each object contains a collection of DataColumn and DataRow objects. The DataSet also contains a Relations collection, which can be used to define relations between DataTable objects. There is a Constraints collection, which can be used to define unique keys and data validation rules. There are also DataView objects that work hand-in-hand with the DataSet. These objects can be used to define filters, sort orders, and display attributes in a given DataTable. You can change from one DataView to another and instantly change the way data is presented to the user. The DataView is part of the data binding mechanism in ADO .NET.

The DataTable Class

The DataTable is just what it sounds like. It is a collection of rows and columns. When we discuss the DataSet, we are really discussing the DataTable, because that is where most of the action takes place. The approach Microsoft took this time around is a bit different than in past versions of ADO and other data access technologies. In the past, the object used for holding table data was the RecordSet. The RecordSet had a collection of columns or fields. These contained the metadata that described each column. The rows were not represented as a collection, and only one row at a time could be accessed. There was the concept of the current row. You used methods like `MoveNext` and `MovePrevious` to change the current record pointer. The only way to access multiple rows at a time was to clone the RecordSet. Additionally, there was an edit buffer that was used when the user wanted to make changes to the data. There was also an insert buffer used to add rows to the RecordSet. In most cases, when a row was changed, as soon as the user moved to another row, the data was updated to the database. The database update was automatic and was the default behavior. You could also programmatically force an update using the `Update` method of the RecordSet object. The RecordSet mostly relied on the error handling in the underlying database system to validate data. It did very little error checking without a round-trip to the server.

By contrast, the ADO .NET DataTable is organized differently. It also has a Columns collection that contains metadata describing the data in the table. Instead of the current row and row pointer method used in the past, the

DataTable rows are represented as a true collection. This means there is no longer any concept of the current row. The rows are accessed via a numerical index. The nice thing about this is that all rows are always available. The bad thing is that it's up to the programmer to make sure you are updating not only the correct column, but also the correct row. Luckily, when you bind the DataTable to controls on a form, the form keeps track of the current row though its BindingContext class. If you are not using a form, then you must track the row index yourself. One bad thing is that there is no way to obtain the index of a row from the row itself.

This is annoying when you are using a `For Each x In DataTable1.Rows` construct. You must maintain your own loop counter. In this case, a `For I = 0 to DataTable1.Rows.Count - 1` construct would be a better choice.

The Rows collection is also only loosely connected to the Columns collection. In prior versions of ADO, you accessed the value of a column by positioning the row pointer to the desired row, then accessing the `Value` property of the field object. To get the value at a given row and column of the DataTable, you must reference the Rows collection by row index and column index, much like an array. To read the data, this creates a rather arcane-looking line of code:

```
Dim x as String

x = DataSet1.Tables(0).Rows(3)("LastName")
```

This would return the value in the fourth row (the Rows collection is zero-based, like all .NET collections) in the LastName column. Thankfully, the designers of ADO .NET allowed the row items to be indexed by the column name or it would make no sense at all. The previous snippet uses a shorthand form. The full form follows:

```
x = DataSet1.Tables(0).Rows(3).Items("LastName").Item
```

The Items collection is the default property for the Rows collection, so it can be omitted. To get other information about the column, you have to reference the Columns collection. To get the data type of the column, the syntax is as follows:

```
Dim x as String

x = DataSet1.Tables(0).Columns.Items("LastName").DataType().ToString
```

I admit to having a less-than-easy time adapting to the new way of doing things. This is one of the problems I've had with highly object-oriented languages. Sometimes the syntax gets really arcane and confusing because everything is wrapped in collections and objects. To me the old ADO syntax was much easier to understand:

```
X = RecordSet1("LastName").Value
Y = RecordSet1("LastName").Type
```

Perhaps a combination of the two, where you could use the current record concept or access directly by row and column index would be a good compromise. I can see the advantages of directly accessing rows. You don't have the overhead of looping through the data until you find the correct row. However, usually you don't know which row you want by its ordinal position. The only way to find it would be to loop through the collection testing conditions, so I don't see what's gained except an arcane syntax. Well, maybe they'll clean it up with the next revision.

The DataRelation Class

Objects can be used to create a parent/child relationship between `DataTables` in a `DataSet`. While `DataRelations` appear similar to join-type relationships in databases, they do not create a join. A join creates a third entity that is the flat representation of the two tables. The `DataRelation` simply defines the relationship between two tables as a parent/child structure. Are you wondering what the difference is? The difference is in the way the child rows are accessed.

Say we have an order header table and a line item table. The order number relates the two tables. In order to get the rows in the line item table that match the header record, you would call the `GetChildRows` method of the row in the header record, passing as a parameter the `DataRelation` object that defines the relationship to the line item table. The method returns an array of child (line item) records that match the condition in the relation. The array, in case you were wondering, is an array of `DataRow` objects.

The DataView Class

The `DataView` class is the enabler of data binding on the `DataSet`'s part. Each `DataTable` has a default `DataView` that is created automatically. Controls on forms are actually bound to the `DataTable`'s default `DataView`. You can create additional `DataView` objects as needed. You can use

DataViews to predefine things like sort orders and filters. They are especially useful when combined with the DataGrid control. Another great use for the DataView is to control security access levels. The DataView's AllowEdit, AllowDelete, and AllowAdd properties can be used to control access to data based on which user is logged on.

SUMMARY

We've taken the quick tour of the ADO .NET classes. This chapter was intended to give you an overview of what to expect in the next chapters, where we'll dive in and crunch through all the properties, methods, and some of the more obscure classes. We deliberately left out too many programming examples in this chapter. We intended it to be a quick read-through so you would be familiar with where we are headed. This is like studying a road map prior to taking a trip, so you have a rough idea of what to expect. Now we are ready to begin the trip. First stop: the Connection class.

CHAPTER 5

Connecting to Databases

The first step in working with a database in ADO .NET is to connect to the database using either the SQL Client or the OleDb Client classes and an OLE DB provider. This chapter is all about how you make that connection. As stated previously, there are two Connection classes, one for the SQL Client and one for the OleDb Client. Each class has roughly parallel sets of properties, methods, and events. The OleDbConnection class is slightly more interesting than the SqlConnection class because it supports more database providers. The SqlConnection class is SQL Server-specific, and because of this, many provider-specific settings are built into it. We will discuss both providers together, and where there are differences I will note them. There is a third set of classes for connecting using ODBC data sources.[1] These must be downloaded separately from Microsoft and are not part of Visual Studio. The ODBC classes are useful for connecting to older versions of databases not supported by OLEDB and also many of the older ISAM style databases such as dBase and Paradox.

USING THE CONNECTION CLASS

There are two ways to use the Connection classes. In either way, you first have to create an instance of the class. The first way of creating an instance is to drag and drop the component onto your form, user control, or component class. The other way is to programmatically declare a variable of the SqlConnection or OleDbConnection type. Both of these methods do effectively the

1. These are in beta as of the date of this writing.

same thing. The advantage to using the Component Model is that you can design your component visually. If you create it programmatically, then you will have to do all the work in code yourself.

VB6—Many VB6 programmers did not like using drop-in toolbox components because in VB6 you often had to sacrifice flexibility in favor of ease of use. With VB .NET this is no longer the case. I would recommend using the Component model as much as possible. It not only saves time, but the generated code conforms to a good coding standard. You can also use features like dynamic properties (where property values are automatically saved to disk in XML format) when you use the Component model. Moreover, you can use your own components as drop-in tools if they are built using the Component model. You don't sacrifice any flexibility at all when using the .NET Component model.

Since most of the properties of the Connection classes are read-only, we will be concentrating on the `ConnectionString` property and its various elements. It is through the connection string that the class is configured. The open and close methods take no parameters in ADO.Net so there really isn't much to say about them. Later on we will cover the `BeginTransaction` method and the SqlTransaction class.

We will be doing hands-on work in this chapter so it's time to fire up the Visual Studio IDE. Let's look at the first scenario. You want to add an SqlConnection object to a Windows Form. First let's create an empty Windows application. Name the application ADOBook05-01. Leave the form named Form1. We'll be using it as a platform for demonstrating the Connection class.

The easiest way to do this is to drag and drop an SqlConnection object onto the form. Roll out the toolbox if it's not already displayed. Click the Data tab. You will see a variety of data components. Drag the SqlConnection icon and drop it anywhere on the form. You should end up with the results in Figure 5.1.

We've mentioned this in a previous chapter, but I mention it again for reinforcement. Notice how the component did not create a visual image on the form itself; instead the image appears in a separate pane below the form. In previous versions of VB, we had controls that were invisible at runtime. They really had no visual interface and were code components, but VB6 did not have a Component model like VB .NET. The only way to create code-only components was to create an OCX control and force the programmer to host it on a form or other container. This is no longer the case with VB .NET and the Component model. The Component model was built just for allowing nonvisual components to be treated the same way as visual ones.

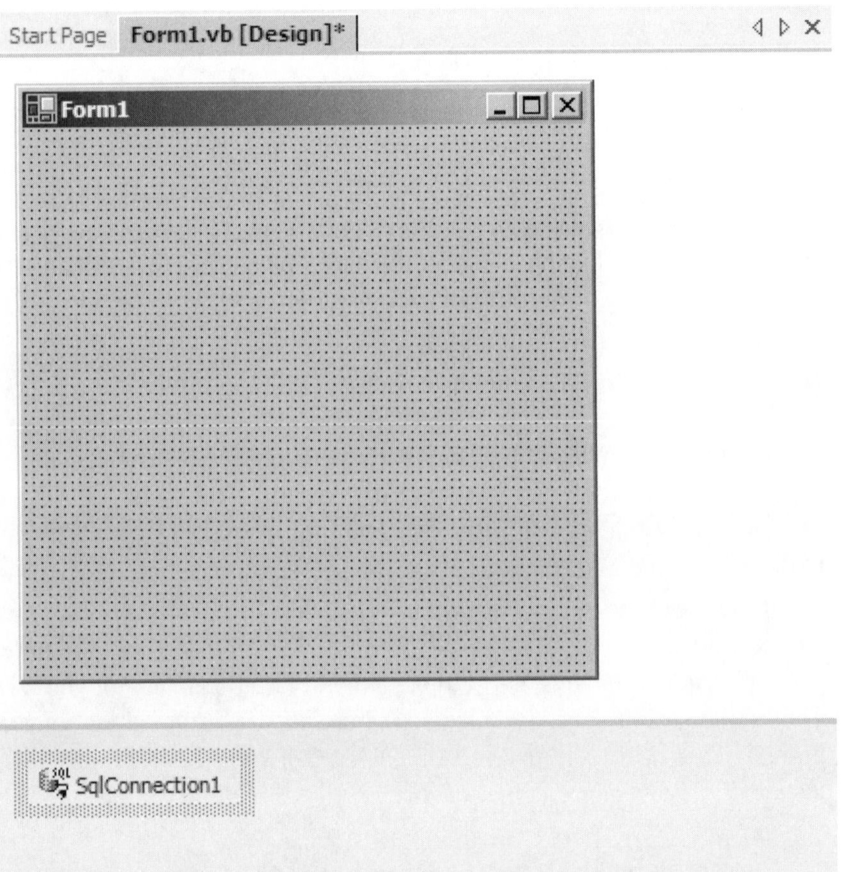

FIGURE 5.1 An empty form with an SqlConnection object.

Look at the Properties window in Figure 5.2.

Notice there are only three properties that you can change: the name of the component, its scope modifier, and the Connection string. Unlike in previous versions of ADO, the individual Connection properties are read-only this time around. The Connection string is used to provide the object with the information it needs to access the database.

When you want to provide the Connection string, you can just type the full syntax of the string into the `ConnectionString` property, but this is a computer after all. There is a visual way of creating the Connection string. Click on the `ConnectionString` property. A drop-down Arrow button appears. Click this button. Your display should look like Figure 5.3.

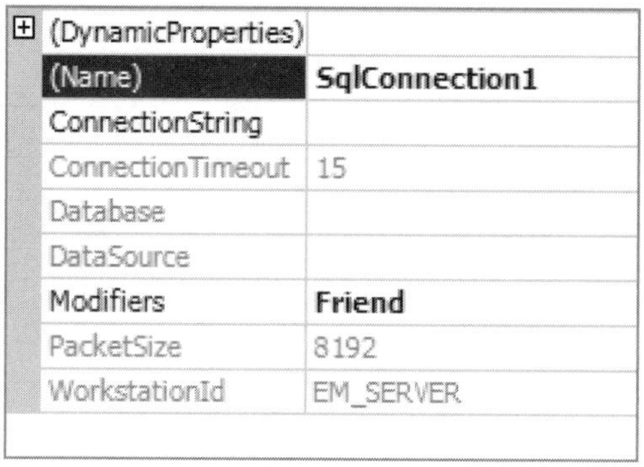

(DynamicProperties)	
(Name)	SqlConnection1
ConnectionString	
ConnectionTimeout	15
Database	
DataSource	
Modifiers	Friend
PacketSize	8192
WorkstationId	EM_SERVER

FIGURE 5.2 The SqlConnection object's properties.

What you see in the drop-down list are the connections you have defined in the Server Explorer, plus one entry for creating a connection. Click the entry for a new connection. The ADO Data Link Properties page appears as in Figure 5.4.

If this looks familiar, it is the same Data Link dialog that you would get with the old version of ADO as well. The Connection object uses the information provided from this dialog to build the Connection string for you. The Connection page is preselected for you. Since we are using the SqlConnection class there is no need to select a provider; SQL Server is presumed. Let's look at the three required entries on this screen.

1. Select or enter a server name.—You can enter a Windows machine name, a DNS name, a WINS name, or an IP address (assuming you are connecting using TCP/IP protocol). If you are using named pipes, you must use a Windows or WINS name. If you use a Windows machine name, the

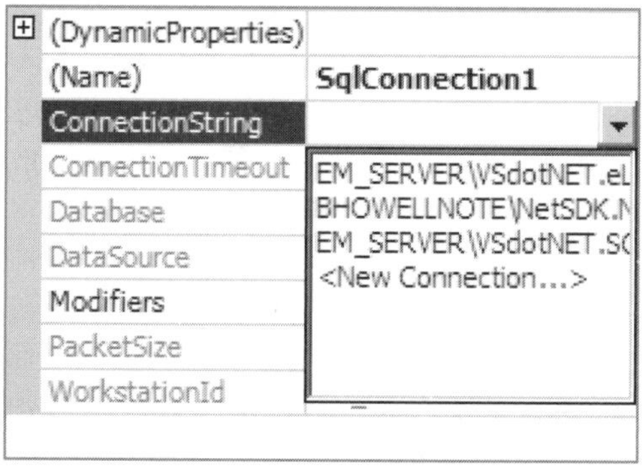

(DynamicProperties)	
(Name)	SqlConnection1
ConnectionString	
ConnectionTimeout	EM_SERVER\VSdotNET.eL
Database	BHOWELLNOTE\NetSDK.N
DataSource	EM_SERVER\VSdotNET.SQ
Modifiers	<New Connection...>
PacketSize	
WorkstationId	

FIGURE 5.3 The `ConnectionString` property with the drop-down open.

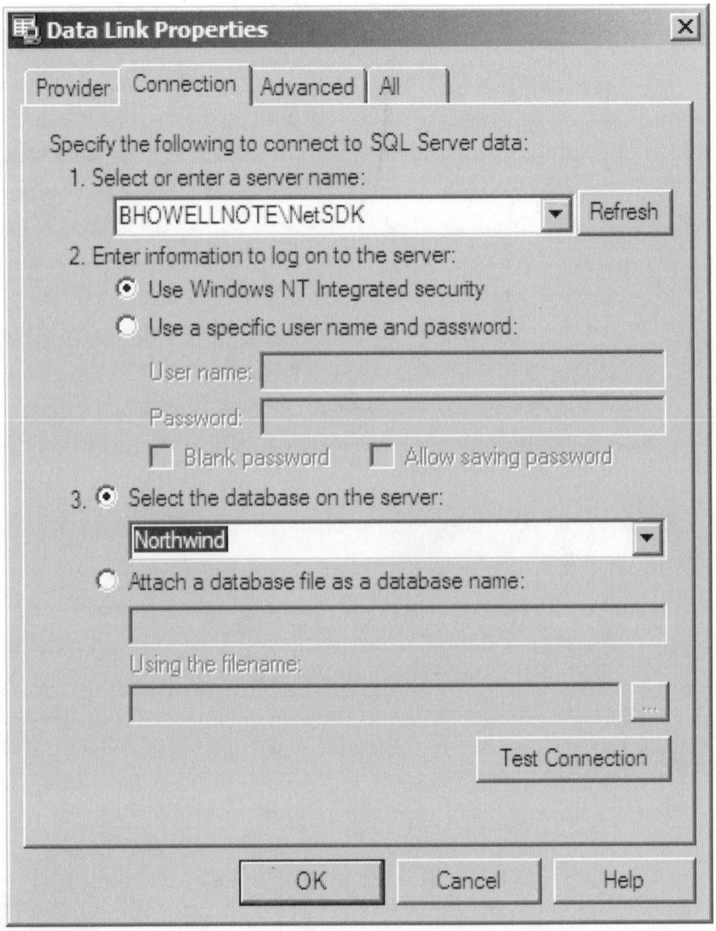

FIGURE 5.4 The Data Link Properties page.

machine must be in the same Windows domain or workgroup as your machine. In a Windows 2000 network with Active Directory, you can also use a machine in a trusted domain by qualifying the domain, with the typical Domain\MachineName format. The drop-down list will only show SQL Servers that are in the same domain or workgroup. If you typically work with an SQL Server that is in a remote domain, and you know its address, you can create an alias using the client network utility. When you create an alias, you tell the SQL Server client software to associate an alias name (that you make up) with an IP address or machine name. The alias is only valid on the local machine. The alias name will then appear in the drop down as well.

2. Enter information to log on to the server.—You have two choices here, depending on how your administrators have set up your server. If you are

using the MSDE[2] locally, you should select Use Windows NT Integrated Security as this is the only way to connect. When you install the MSDE, it configures it to use integrated security. With this method, SQL Server uses Windows NT/2000/XP user accounts and just adds them to SQL Server automatically with full privileges. If your server requires a user name and password, then select Use a Specific User Name and Password. If you check Allow Saving Password the password will be visible in the Connection string that is generated. This may be acceptable when designing your application, as you will not have to enter the password each time you use a database object. It may represent a security flaw when the application is distributed because the password may be able to be retrieved by a programmer using a hex editor. If you select this option, remember to unselect it before creating your release build. My advice is to leave it unselected.

3. You can then enter the information in the text boxes as shown in Figure 5.5.
4. ConnectionStringSelect the database on the server.—This setting is for selecting the default database. If you leave this out, you may have to qualify any object names (tables, stored procedures, views, etc.) with the database name when designing queries. Unless you absolutely need to do this, I advise selecting the database name you wish to use. I can't think of

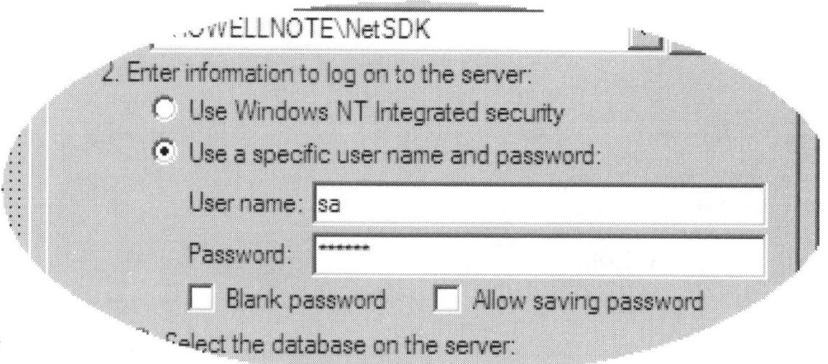

FIGURE 5.5 Using a specific user name and password to log on.

2. In case you skipped Chapter 1, the MSDE is the Microsoft Database Engine, a desktop implementation of SQL Server 2000 that is freely redistributable and intended to replace the MS Access Jet engine.

any reason to leave this blank. Even if you want to select the database programmatically at runtime, there are better ways to do that.

5. Attach a database file as a database name. You can use this selection instead of supplying a database name. When you use this option, you are going to supply a file name that is the name of an SQL Server database file. This is an interesting option because it allows you to copy databases by simply copying the data file that contains the database. This option is only available for SQL Server 7 and above. You can specify a data file (.mdf) file, formerly called a device file, and attach it to an existing database with a given database name.

When you click OK, the Connection string is formatted and placed in the `ConnectionString` property. If you want to see some of the other Connection string settings, click the Advanced tab prior to closing the dialog. On this page, you can edit any of the Connection string settings that are valid for SQL Server as in Figure 5.6. Note that there is no error checking here. You will not know if there is an error in the Connection string until you try to open the database, either explicitly by executing the `Open` method or implicitly by executing the `Fill` or `Update` method of a data adapter that references the Connection object. If the Connection string has a parsing error, the SqlConnection class will throw an error of type ArgumentException. You can trap the error by Catching the exception type with structured exception handling.

Even though we used the SqlConnection class in our example, the same process is used for the OleDbConnection class as well. The only difference is that you must also select an OLEDB provider before filling in the Connection tab. Next we will look at the providers in detail.

THE SQL SERVER DATA PROVIDER

Of course we first look at the flagship, SQL Server provider. A typical Connection string SQL Server looks like this:

```
provider=SQLOLEDB;data source=EM_SERVER\VSdotNET;initial
catalog=eLandBill;password=svcslave;persist security info=true;user
id=sa;workstation id=EM_SERVER;packet size=4096
```

Application Name	
Auto Translate	True
Connect Timeout	
Current Language	
Data Source	EM_SERVER\VSdotNET
Extended Properties	
General Timeout	0
Initial Catalog	Northwind
Initial File Name	
Integrated Security	
Locale Identifier	1033
Network Address	
Network Library	
Packet Size	4096
Password	*****
Persist Security Info	True
Replication server name c...	
Tag with column collation ...	False
Use Encryption for Data	False
Use Procedure for Prepare	1
User ID	sa
Workstation ID	EM_SERVER

FIGURE 5.6 The Advanced tab for SQL Server.

Note that if we were using the SqlConnection class the `Provider=SQLOLEDB` element would not be used. Also if an element (or property) is missing it will use the default setting. We've already gone over most of these settings (when we looked at the Data Link Properties page). Just for completeness, I'll summarize them again here:

1. Provider—This is the name of the OLEDB data provider, in this case SQLOLEDB is the name of SQL Server provider.
2. Data source or server—The name of the database server. You can use the Windows machine name, an IP address, a DNS name, an SQL Server alias, or a WINS name.
3. Initial catalog or database—The name of the database on the server you specified. This is optional but if omitted all references to SQL Server objects must be fully qualified with the database name.

4. User ID—SQL Server login name of the user if you are not using Windows NT integrated security.
5. Password—SQL Server password of the user if you are not using Windows NT integrated security.

The rest of the elements are defined next. These are SQL Server–specific parameters.

1. Workstation ID—The Windows name of the client machine. The Connection class provides this element for you. It can be used to identify who is logged on when viewing SQL Server process information through the Enterprise Manager.
2. Persist security information—If true, allows the password to be visible in the Connection string. The ADO .NET Connection classes do not return the password in the Connection string if this value is set to false. The default is false.
3. Packet size—This is the size of each block of data sent from the server back to the client. The default, 4096, should be fine in 99.99999 percent of the cases. In my view, this setting is a holdover from the days of slow networks when tuning the packet size could have a meaningful effect on performance. With today's fast networks, there is no perceptible effect on performance.
4. Integrated security—Formerly called Trusted_Connection. Indicates the User Authentication mode. This can be set to yes or no. The default value is no. If this property is set to yes, then SQLOLEDB uses Microsoft Windows NT Authentication mode to authorize user access to the SQL Server database specified by the `Data Source` and `Initial Catalog` property values. If this property is set to no, SQLOLEDB uses Mixed mode to authorize user access to SQL Server database. SQL Server login and password are specified in the `User ID` and `Password` properties. If using Windows NT Authentication mode you do not provide a user ID and password.
5. Current language—Indicates a SQL Server language name. Identifies the language used for system message selection and formatting. The language must be installed on SQL Server, otherwise opening the Connection will fail.
6. Network address—Indicates the network address of SQL Server specified by the `Data Source` property. This is only available when the connection is open.

7. Network library—Indicates the name of the network library (.dll) used to communicate with SQL Server. The name should not include the path or the .dll file name extension. The default is provided by SQL Server client configuration. You can use this property to force SQL Server client to use a certain protocol to connect.
8. Use procedure for prepare—Determines whether SQL Server creates temporary stored procedures when commands are prepared.
9. Autotranslate—Indicates whether OEM/ANSI characters are converted. This property can be set to true or false. The default value is true. If this property is set to true, SQLOLEDB performs OEM/ANSI character conversion when multibyte character strings are retrieved from, or sent to, SQL Server. If this property is set to false, SQLOLEDB does not perform OEM/ANSI character conversion on multibyte character string data.
10. Application name—Indicates the client application name. This property is useful for determining who is logged on when viewing the process display in the Enterprise Manager. The Connection class sends this to the server automatically so there is no need to manually set this property. If you do, it will override the setting that the Connection class would have provided.
11. Connect timeout—The amount of time in seconds that the client waits for a Connection response from the server. The default is 30 seconds. If you are using a slow network or are connecting to a very busy server, you may want to increase this value. A value of zero tells the client to wait indefinitely (not a good idea).
12. Use encryption for data—Tells SQL Server to encrypt data before sending it back to the client. To use this property, SQL Server must have encryption enabled. If it does not, an exception will be thrown on an open attempt. This is not supported when using MSDE.

THE ORACLE DATA PROVIDER

The Microsoft OLEDB provider for Oracle databases can be used to connect to Oracle 7 and higher databases. A typical Connection string for Oracle looks like this:

```
Provider=MSDAORA.1;Password=MANAGER;User ID=SYSTEM;Data Source=ORACLEDB
```

This Connection string uses the default user and password that comes with the Oracle release. There really isn't much to say about the Oracle provider. Since the Oracle client architecture is radically different than SQL Server's, most of the tuning and such is done via other methods that are beyond the scope of this book.

For the Oracle provider, the `Data Source` property must reference a valid Oracle security identifier (SID), which you must set up using the Oracle Net Manager. The SID then resolves everything else.

Before you can access an Oracle database, you must have installed the Oracle client software for the version of Oracle you are using.

THE MICROSOFT ACCESS (JET) DATABASE PROVIDER

The Microsoft OLEDB provider for Jet Databases (4.0) has another complex Connection string. Just look at this sample from the Northwind sample database.

```
Provider=Microsoft.Jet.OLEDB.4.0;Password="";User ID=Admin;Data
Source=C:\Program Files\Microsoft
Office\Office\Samples\Northwind.mdb;Mode=Share Deny None;Extended
Properties="";Jet OLEDB:System database="";Jet OLEDB:Registry
Path="";Jet OLEDB:Database Password="";Jet OLEDB:Engine Type=5;Jet
OLEDB:Database Locking Mode=1;Jet OLEDB:Global Partial Bulk Ops=2;Jet
OLEDB:Global Bulk Transactions=1;Jet OLEDB:New Database Password="";Jet
OLEDB:Create System Database=false;Jet OLEDB:Encrypt Database=false;Jet
OLEDB:Don't Copy Locale on Compact=false;Jet OLEDB:Compact Without
Replica Repair=false;Jet OLEDB:SFP=false
```

If you are at all familiar with Microsoft Access, then you will see a parallel with the Access command-line startup options. There are just too many properties to go over completely. I will list them and give a brief meaning but it will be up to you to use the Access documentation for the full explanation.

1. Provider—The name of the OLE DB provider—Microsoft.Jet.OLEDB.4.0. This provider will open all databases up to Access XP. It was written for the Access 2000 format, but works with the XP format as well. (I believe they are the same.) There is also a provider for the Access 97 database format named Microsoft.Jet.OLEDB.3.51. It is similar but has fewer properties. I'm sure they will open Access 95 format (3.0) as well. I haven't tested if any of these can be used with the old 16-bit versions of Jet (1.0 and 2.0) databases that were written for Windows 3.1.
2. User ID and password—These mean what they are. Jet databases can be configured to be secure or open. By default they are open. Even when

they are open, they still use a default user ID of `Admin` with a blank password. In order for a Jet database to be secure, you must also specify a workgroup database name.

3. Data source—For Jet databases this is the path to the .mdb file.
4. Jet.OLEDB:System database—This is the name of the Workgroup database. Normally this defaults to system.mda. If you are opening a secure Jet database you will have to supply the path to the system database (.mdw file) that you created.
5. Jet OLEDB:Engine type—The version of the database engine you are using.
6. Jet OLEDB:Locking mode—Setting for how to control concurrency. The choices are page locking or row locking. Row locking is the default.
7. Jet OLEDB:Registry path—An option alternate registry path for Jet to get its settings from. When writing Access applications, often it is desirable to have your secured application use one set of settings, while ad-hoc Access use by the user is not affected. This setting will point Jet to an alternate location than the default for getting its start up settings.

The other settings are either not implemented or esoteric. In most cases, all you need are the four main ones (provider, Data Source, user ID, and password). When opening a secured database you also need the path to the system database (.mdw file).

Connection Pooling

Connection pooling is the process by which the Connection classes conserve resources by maintaining a pool of open connections from the workstation to the server. As an example, suppose we have an application that opens a connection, retrieves data, and closes the connection. Then, a second later it wants to open the connection again. The Connection class will reuse the first connection. This is true as long as the Connection strings are identical. It will do this even from different applications as long as the Connection strings are identical. You can force the Connection class to release any pooled connections by called the `ReleaseObjectPool` method of the OleDbConnection class. All current connections must first be closed and then you must wait for the garbage collector to come around, but at least you have some control over when to release the connection. The SqlConnection class manages Connection pooling for you and there is no need to programmatically release connections.

Determining the State of a Connection

One of the new features of the Connection classes is the implicit open. This means that the Connection class will open a database connection when it is needed. It is not necessary in most cases to call the `Open` method before attempting a database access. When the database operation is complete, the Connection class will close the connection. At any point in your program, you have no way of knowing whether or not the connection is open. The Connection classes provide a property for this purpose, called the `State` property. You can test the `State` property to see if the connection is open. The `State` property can have value corresponding to the `System.Data.ConnectionState` enumeration:

- Closed—The connection is currently closed.
- Open—The connection is currently open.
- Connecting—The Connection object has sent the Connection string to the server, but the server has not yet responded.
- Executing—A Command object is executing a command using this connection.
- Fetching—A Data Reader is using this connection to get a stream of data from the server.
- Broken—The connection was severed unexpectedly, either by the server or due to a system exception.

CONNECTION CLASS EVENTS

The ADO .NET approach to events is a complete reversal of the ADO approach. ADO had events for each step of the process: `WillConnect`, `Connected`, `AlmostConnected`. (Just kidding about that last one; but it did have too many events.) The ADO .NET people went in the opposite direction. The ADO .NET Connection classes have only two events. Actually, all of the .Net framework is light on events. Instead of different events, the ADO .NET designers use different EventArgs object types to pass more specific information about why the event was fired. The Connection classes are no different.

The StateChanged Event

The StateChanged event fires whenever the Connection object's `State` property changes. If you need to know the exact moment a connection is established, you can use this event. It passes an EventArgs object of type StateChangeEventArgs. This object has two properties: `CurrentState` and `OriginalState`. These each have a value of type `System.Data.ConnectionState`. You can test these properties and take action based on their values.

We can create a simple application to demonstrate this. Let's use our ADOBook05-01 project. Add two command buttons to the form and one list box. Your form should look like Figure 5.7.

You should already have an OleDbConnection object on the form. If not, drop one on now. Let's set it up to connect to the Northwind database. Drop down the list for the `ConnectionString` property on the properties window. Either select an existing connection or create one. If you create one, fill in the Properties page as illustrated in Figure 5.8.

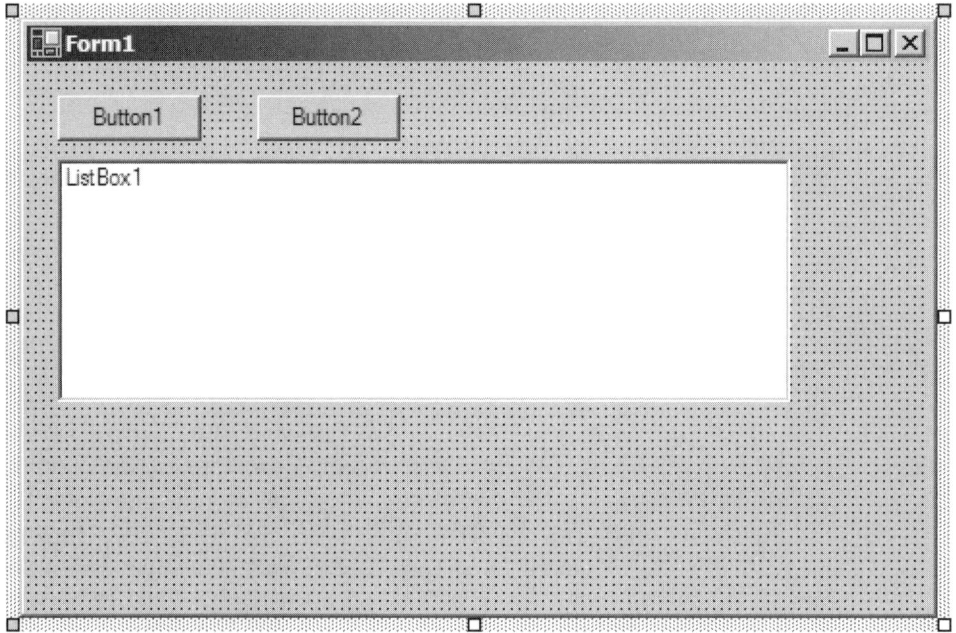

FIGURE 5.7 Form for demonstrating the StateChanged event.

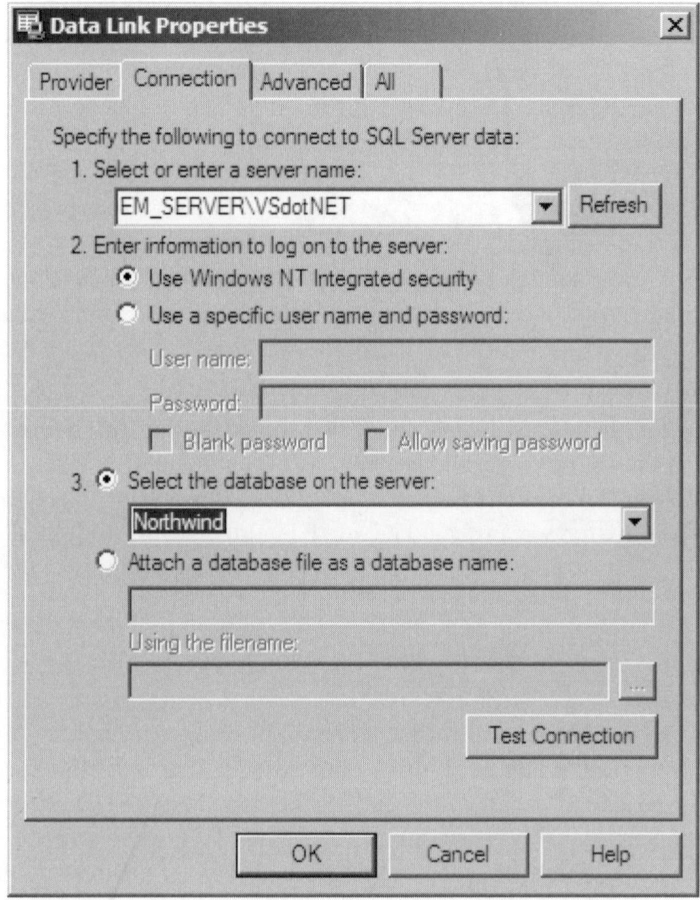

FIGURE 5.8 Data Link Properties with Northwind selected.

Of course you would substitute the name of your server. Next, double-click the first button (Button1). The code window opens and a click event procedure has been created for you. Add the following code to the procedure.

```
Private Sub Button1_Click(ByVal sender As System.Object, _
  ByVal e As System.EventArgs) Handles Button1.Click
    OleDbConnection1.Open()
End Sub
```

In the Button2 click event, add the following code:

```
Private Sub Button2_Click(ByVal sender As System.Object, _
  ByVal e As System.EventArgs) Handles Button2.Click
    OleDbConnection1.Close()
End Sub
```

Next create the StateChanged event for the Connection object. To do this, drop down the Class Name list (on the left) and select the OleDbConnection1 object. Then drop down the Method list on the right and select the StateChanged event. The IDE will create an event procedure for you. Place the following code in the event procedure:

```
Private Sub OleDbConnection1_StateChange(ByVal sender As Object, ByVal
e As System.Data.StateChangeEventArgs) _
Handles OleDbConnection1.StateChange
         ListBox1.Items.Add("Original State = " &
e.OriginalState.ToString & ", Current State = " _
 & e.CurrentState.ToString)
     End Sub
```

When we run the program, this should display the state of the connection in the list box. Run the program. Click Button1. This opens the connection. Then click Button2. This closes the connection. After you have clicked both buttons, the screen should look like Figure 5.9.

Save this project as ADOBook05-01 if you have not already done so. This is its index on the CD.

The InfoMessage Event

The InfoMessage event fires when a message with low severity is returned from the data source. Low severity messages are those that do not result in an exception. For Microsoft SQL Server, this includes error messages with a severity of 10 or less. For other providers this is system-dependent.

The InfoMessage event passes an EventArgs object of type `OleDbInfoMessageEventArgs`. It has the following properties:

- ErrorCode—The ANSI SQL compliant error code of the message.
- Errors—A collection of OleDbError objects sent from the source.
- Message—The full text of the message sent from the server. In case of multiple messages, the first one in the collection is sent in this property. You should iterate through the Errors collection for other messages.
- Source—The name of the object that caused the message.

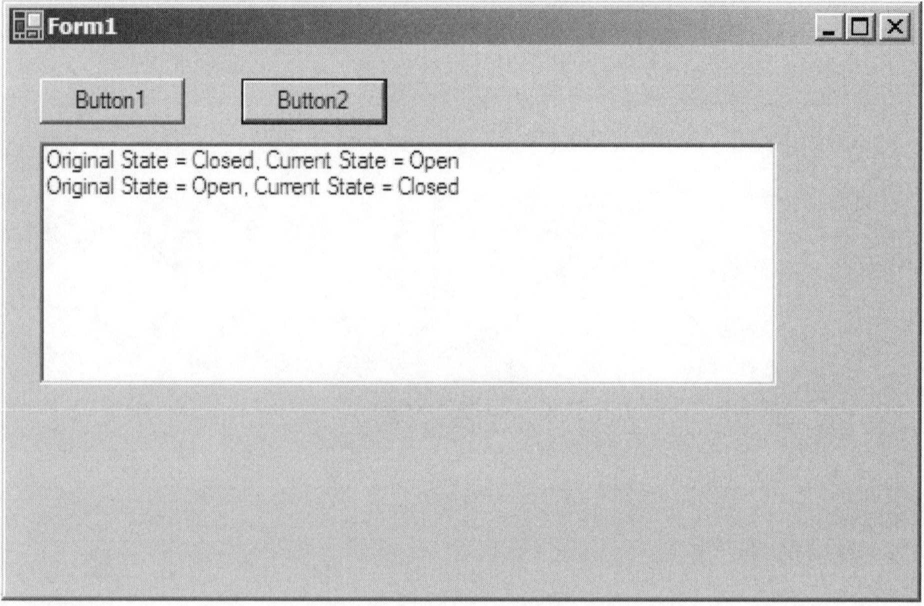

FIGURE 5.9 StateChanged event demonstration.

USING TRANSACTIONS—THE TRANSACTION CLASS

Transactions are the other operations that are handled partially by the Connection class. They are handled partially because in this version of ADO .NET, you only start transactions using the Connection class. Once a transaction is started, you keep it in a Transaction class object. The Transaction object is then used to commit or roll back the transactions.

Since we are using SQL Server for our database of preference, we will use SQL Client classes to demonstrate transactions. Create a project and name it ADOBook05-02. Alternatively, you can get the project from the CD if you don't want to key in the code.

Add a grid control and five buttons to the form. Dock the grid to the top of the form. Name the form frmTRX. Label the buttons as in Figure 5.10.

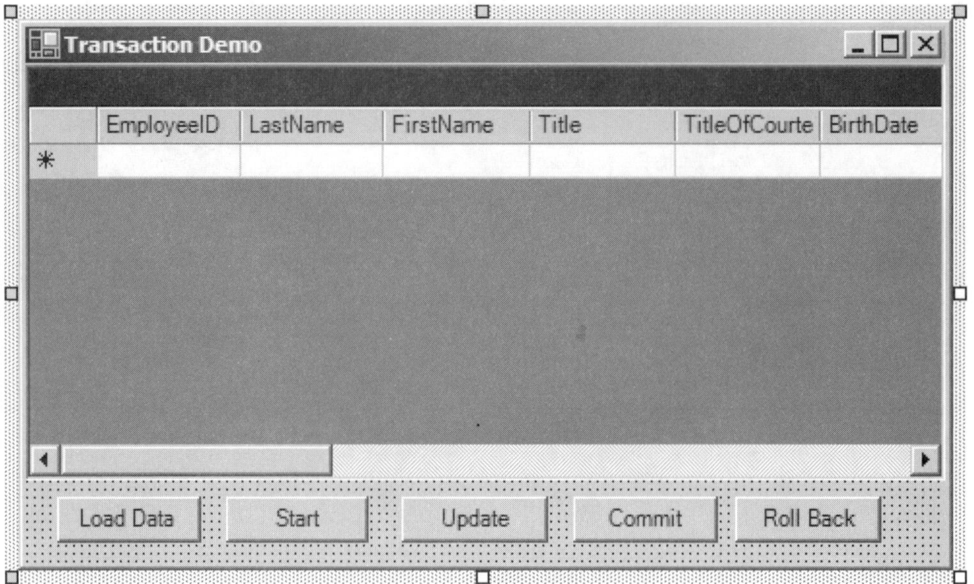

FIGURE 5.10 Completed Transaction demo form.

Drag a SqlDataAdapter and drop it on the form. When the configuration wizard opens, select the Northwind database from the list of connections as in Figure 5.11.

When you click next you will choose SQL Statements as the query type. The next page asks you to create the `Select` statement. Either type in the statement or use the Query Builder tool to create it. I would use the tool as it avoids errors. When you have finished, the wizard should look like Figure 5.12.

Click the Finish button. Now you have configured the Data Adapter. Next, right-click on the DataAdapter and select Generate Dataset… The Generate Dataset dialog will open. Everything should be preselected for you. Just make sure that Add this Dataset to the Designer is checked as in Figure 5.13.

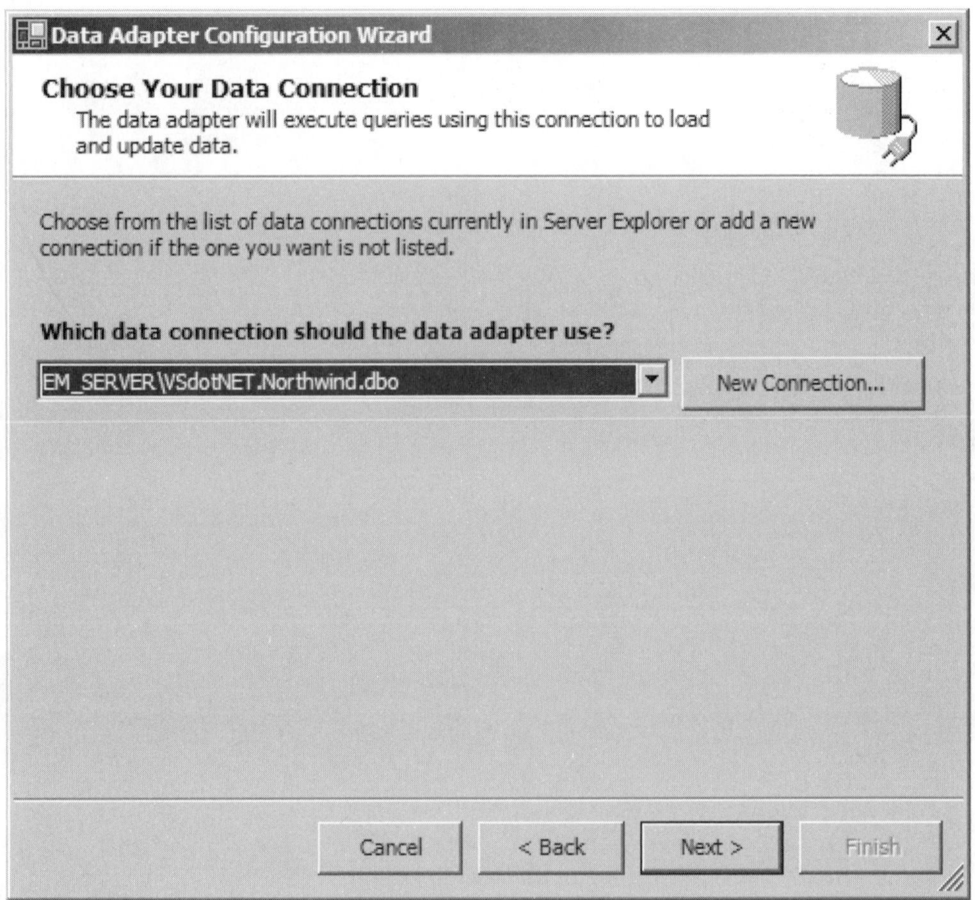

FIGURE 5.11 The Data Adapter Configuration Wizard.

Now select the datagrid on the form. Scroll the Properties window until you see the `DataSource` property. Drop down the arrow. Select the DataSet we just created, named DataSet11 as in Figure 5.14.

Now select Employees as the `DataMember` property using a similar approach. The grid's columns should now populate with the columns of the Employees table. We now have the basic layout of the form done. Now we have to add code to make it all work.

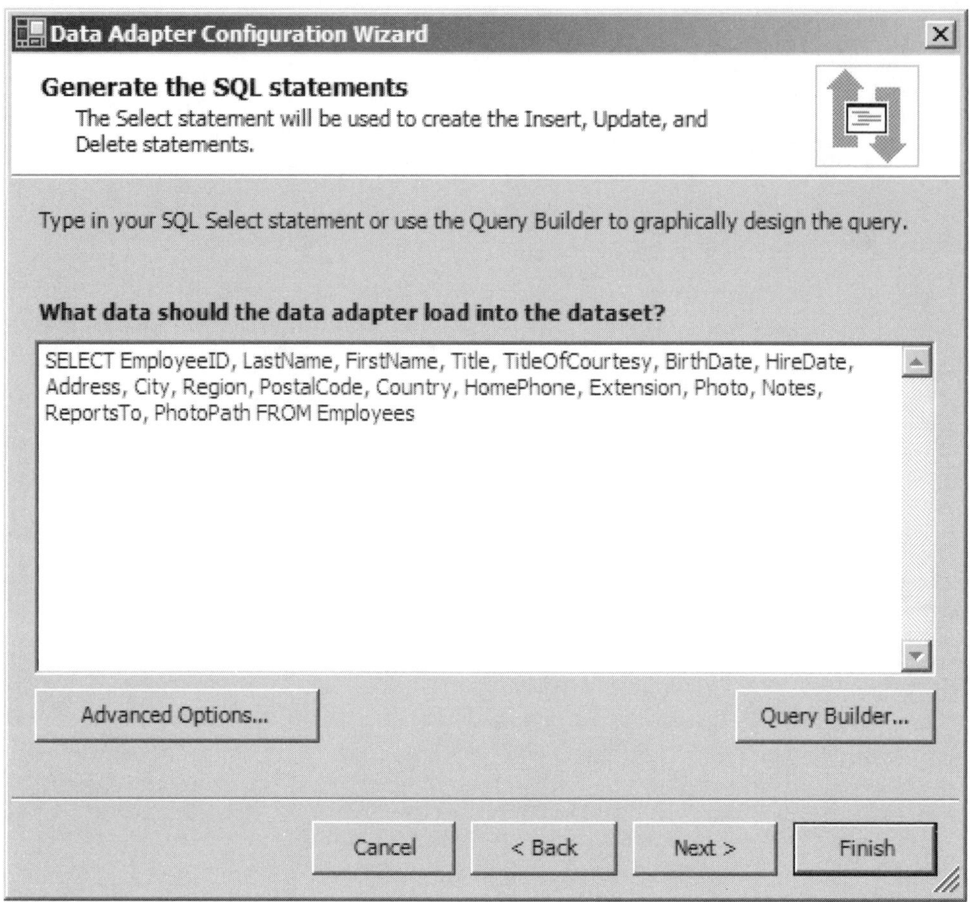

FIGURE 5.12 The Configuration Wizard with the `Select` statement.

First, let's make sure we can get data. In the Button1 click event, place this code:

```
    Private Sub Button1_Click(ByVal sender As System.Object, _
             ByVal e As System.EventArgs) Handles Button1.Click
If SqlConnection1.State = ConnectionState.Closed Then
             SqlConnection1.Open()
         End If
      SqlDataAdapter1.Fill(DataSet11, "Employees")
End Sub
```

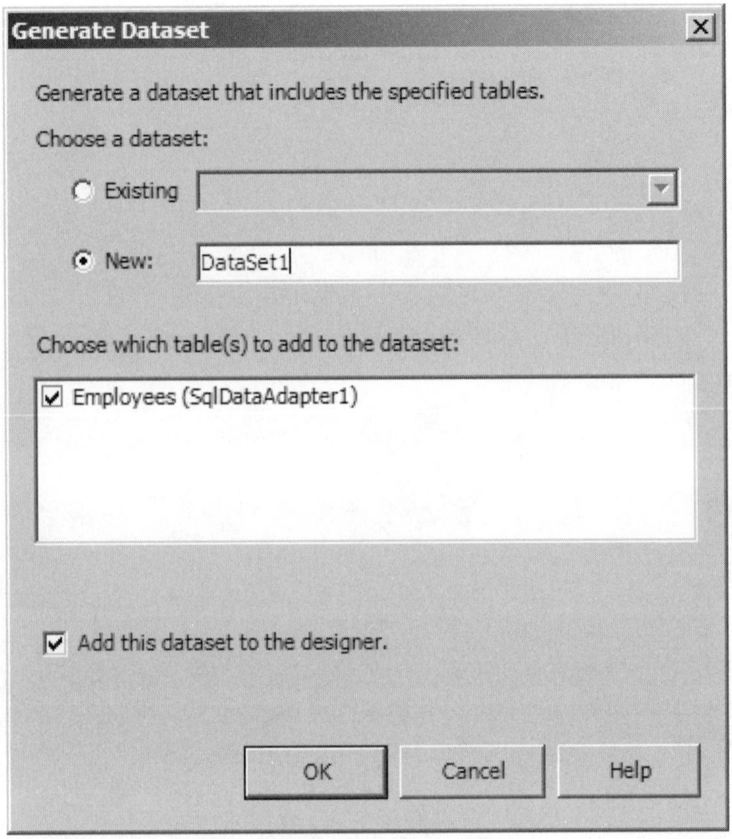

FIGURE 5.13 The Generate Dataset dialog.

We'll go back and analyze the code later. Compile and run the program. When you click the Load Data button (Button1) the grid should fill with data as in Figure 5.15.

Next, let's fill in the code for the Update button, Button3. This button takes any changes to the DataSet made by editing the grid and updates the database with them.

```
    Private Sub Button3_Click(ByVal sender As System.Object, _
ByVal e As System.EventArgs) Handles Button3.Click
         Try
If DataSet11.HasChanges Then
                    Me.BindingContext.Item(DataSet11, _
"Employees").EndCurrentEdit()
                    SqlDataAdapter1.Update(DataSet11)
```

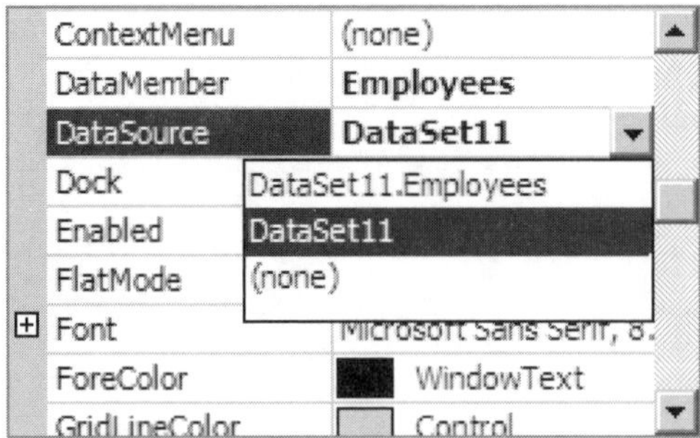

FIGURE 5.14 Selecting the DataSet11 as the grid's DataSource.

```
                DataSet11.AcceptChanges()
            End If
Catch errobj As Exception
            MsgBox(errobj.Message)
        End Try
    End Sub
```

Again, we'll analyze the code later. Let's compile and run the program again. This time make a few changes to the grid. Click the Update button. Now close the application and run it again. The changes should still show. If we had made the changes and not clicked Update, no changes would have been written to the database.

Transaction Demo

EmployeeID	LastName	FirstName	Title	TitleOfCourte	BirthDat
1	Davolio	Nancy	Sales Repres	Ms.	12/8/194
2	Fuller	Andrew	Vice Presiden	Dr.	2/19/195
3	Leverling	Janet	Sales Repres	Ms.	8/30/196
4	Peacock	Margaret	Sales Repres	Mrs.	9/19/193
5	Buchanan	Steven	Sales Manag	Mr.	3/4/1955
6	Suyama	Michael	Sales Repres	Mr.	7/2/1963
7	King	Robert	Sales Repres	Mr.	5/29/196
8	Callahan	Laura	Inside Sales	Ms.	1/9/1958
9	Dodsworth	Anne	Sales Repres	Ms.	1/27/196

Load Data | Start | Update | Commit | Roll Back

FIGURE 5.15 Transaction demo with data.

Now we will begin to add the code to manage the transactions. First let's look at the SqlTransaction class. Besides the `Commt` and `RollBack` methods, there is one other method and a property.

The IsolationLevel Property

The `IsolationLevel` property is used to set the isolation level of a transaction. Isolation level is to transactions what row locking is to an individual update. It controls how much the current transaction affects other transactions and other users of the database. Isolation levels are a feature of the underlying database system. SQL Server and Jet (MS Access) supports the isolation levels described later. Other database systems may or may not support these levels. Some databases do not support transactions at all.

The following section, from the *OLE DB Programmer's Reference*, describes isolation levels very well. Since I couldn't do any better myself, I decided to include its description.

Transaction isolation levels are a measure of the extent to which changes made outside a transaction are visible to that transaction. In particular, transaction isolation levels are defined by the presence or absence of the following phenomena:

- **Dirty read**—A dirty read occurs when a transaction reads data that has not yet been committed. For example, suppose transaction 1 changes a row. Transaction 2 reads the changed row before transaction 1 commits the change. If transaction 1 aborts the change, transaction 2 will have read data that is considered to have never existed.
- **Nonrepeatable read**—A nonrepeatable read occurs when a transaction reads the same row twice but gets different data each time. For example, suppose transaction 1 reads a row. Transaction 2 changes or deletes that row and commits this change or deletion. If transaction 1 attempts to reread the row, it retrieves different row values or discovers that the row has been deleted.
- **Phantom**—A phantom is a row that matches the search criteria but is not initially seen. For example, suppose transaction 1 reads a set of rows that satisfy some search criteria. Transaction 2 inserts a new row that matches the search criteria for transaction 1. If transaction 1 reexecutes the statement that read the rows, it gets a different set of rows.

According to these phenomena, the **isolation** levels defined by OLE DB are as follows:

- **Read Uncommitted** (also called **Browse**)—A transaction operating at the Read Uncommitted level can see uncommitted changes made by other transactions. At this level of isolation, dirty reads, nonrepeatable reads, and phantoms are all possible.
- **Read Committed** (also called **Cursor Stability**)—A transaction operating at the Read Committed level cannot see changes made by other transactions until those transactions are committed. At this level of isolation, dirty reads are not possible but nonrepeatable reads and phantoms are possible.
- **Repeatable Read**—A transaction operating at the Repeatable Read level is guaranteed not to see any changes made by other transactions in values it has already read. At this level of isolation, dirty reads and nonrepeatable reads are not possible but phantoms are possible.
- **Serializable** (also called **Isolated**)—A transaction operating at the Serializable level guarantees that all concurrent transactions interact only in ways that produce the same effect as if each transaction were entirely executed one after the other. At this isolation level, dirty reads, nonrepeatable reads, and phantoms are not possible.

ADO .NET adds two more levels:

- Chaos—This means that the current transaction cannot override any transaction with a higher isolation level.
- Unspecified—The current isolation level cannot be determined.

The default isolation level is ReadCommitted. This is consistent with optimistic concurrency. If changes are made to rows that other users have changed since they were read, an error will be thrown.

When using transactions, it is necessary to maintain an open connection to the server during the course of the transaction (from `BeginTransaction` through `Commit` or `Rollback`). If you close the connection before the transaction is complete, you will lose isolation. For this reason, we will be explicitly opening and closing the connection in the demonstration.

Just as a reminder, the SqlTransaction object is declared at the module level as follows:

```
Private sqlTRX As SqlClient.SqlTransaction
```

In the click event for Button2, place the following code:

```
Private Sub Button2_Click(ByVal sender As System.Object, _
ByVal e As System.EventArgs) Handles Button2.Click
     Try
If SqlConnection1.State = ConnectionState.Closed Then
              SqlConnection1.Open()
          End If
          sqlTRX = _
SqlConnection1.BeginTransaction(IsolationLevel.Serializable)
          SqlDataAdapter1.SelectCommand.Transaction = sqlTRX
SqlDataAdapter1.InsertCommand.Transaction = sqlTRX
          SqlDataAdapter1.DeleteCommand.Transaction = sqlTRX
          SqlDataAdapter1.UpdateCommand.Transaction = sqlTRX
     Catch erroobj as Exception
          Msgbox(errobj.Message)
     End Try
End Sub
```

Change the code in the Button1 click event procedure to look like this:

```
     Try
          Button2_Click(Button2, New System.EventArgs())
          DataSet11.Tables("Employees").Clear()
          SqlDataAdapter1.Fill(DataSet11, "Employees")
     Catch errobj As Exception
          MsgBox(errobj.Message)
     End Try
```

This way we eliminate the redundant code that opens the connection and starts the transaction. Notice in the Button2 click event that we overrode the default and made the transaction isolation level serializable. In order to demonstrate transactions, we need two programs operating on the same data. Otherwise, the demonstration would be incomplete. The whole purpose of transactions is to ensure data integrity across multiple operations and among concurrent users. In our case, we will be running both users on the same machine. Since they are separate processes running in separate transactions, the effect is the same as if they were running on different client workstations.

The code to commit and roll back transactions is pretty straightforward:

```
     Private Sub Button4_Click(ByVal sender As System.Object, ByVal e As
System.EventArgs) Handles Button4.Click
       Try
              sqlTRX.Commit()
```

```
        Catch errobj As Exception
            MsgBox(errobj.Message)
        End Try
    End Sub

      Private Sub Button5_Click(ByVal sender As System.Object, ByVal e As
System.EventArgs) Handles Button5.Click
        Try
            sqlTRX.Rollback()
        Catch errobj As Exception
            MsgBox(errobj.Message)
        End Try
    End Sub
```

Note that once a transaction has been terminated (by calling `Commit` or `Rollback`), the transaction object is no longer valid and cannot be reused. A new SqlTransaction object must be created by calling the `BeginTransaction` method of the SqlConnection object again. Of course, the same object variable can be reused.

Before we demonstrate concurrency by firing up two instances of the application, let's test it by itself just to make sure it all works as expected. First, run the application. Click the Load Data button. This will populate the grid control. It will also begin a transaction. The application should again appear as in Figure 5.15.

Make changes to the grid. Now click the Update button. This updates the database, but we have a pending transaction open. Click the Roll Back button. Now click the Load Data button again to refresh the data. Notice that the changes have disappeared. Click the Start button. This will begin a new transaction. Add a new row to the grid and delete an old one. Click Roll Back and Load Data. The row you added should be gone and the deleted row should return. Click Start again. Add a new row and click Commit and Load Data. This time the row you added is retained.

Let's add one more feature to our demo program. We will add radio buttons so we can control the isolation level of our transactions without recompiling the program. Add two more command buttons to the form. Label one Refresh. We want to be able to refresh the data without starting a new transaction. Label the other Close. This will close the connection and clear any locks without actually closing the program. Add a group box (formerly called a frame) to the form. You will have to resize the form and rearrange some of the buttons. Add five radio buttons to the group box. The form should look like Figure 5.16.

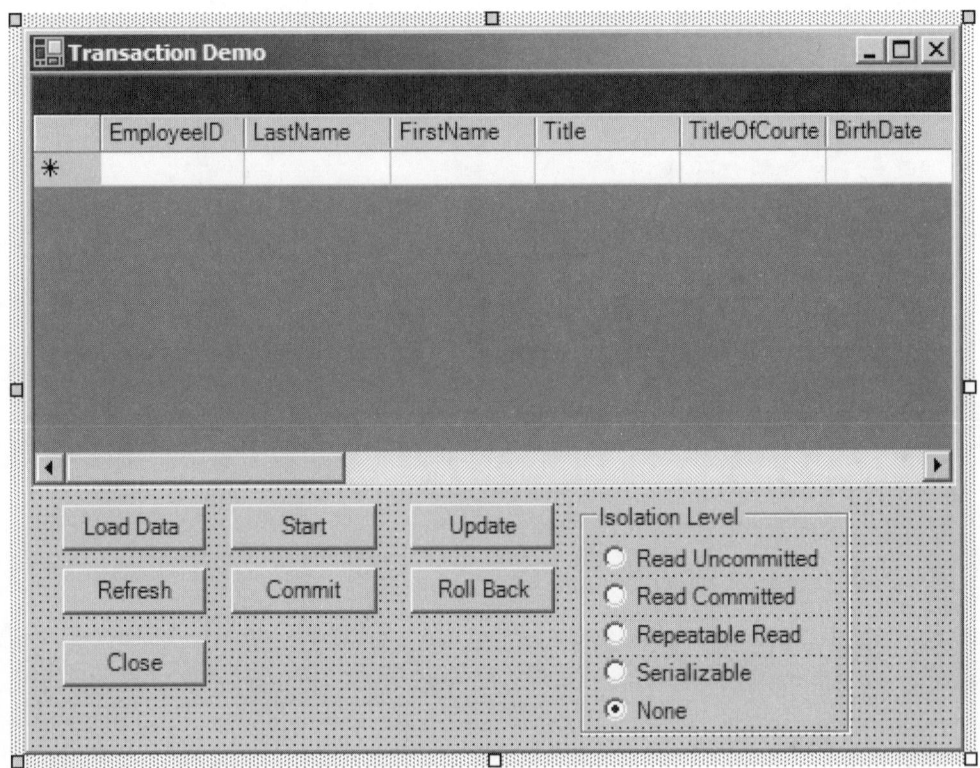

FIGURE 5.16 Form with radio buttons added.

Name the five buttons, rdRU, rdRC, rdRR, rdSerial, and rdNone respectively. Add the following code to the Button2 click event:

```
Private Sub Button2_Click(ByVal sender As System.Object, _
ByVal e As System.EventArgs) Handles Button2.Click
  Try
    If SqlConnection1.State = ConnectionState.Closed Then
          SqlConnection1.Open()
    End If
    If rdRR.Checked Then
    sqlTRX =
SqlConnection1.BeginTransaction(IsolationLevel.RepeatableRead)
    ElseIf rdRU.checked Then
    sqlTRX =
SqlConnection1.BeginTransaction(IsolationLevel.ReadUncommitted)
    ElseIf rdRC.Checked Then
    sqlTRX =
```

```
SqlConnection1.BeginTransaction(IsolationLevel.ReadCommitted)
        ElseIf rdSerial.Checked Then
        sqlTRX =
SqlConnection1.BeginTransaction(IsolationLevel.Serializable)
        Else
            SqlTrx = Nothing
        End If
        SqlDataAdapter1.SelectCommand.Transaction = sqlTRX
        SqlDataAdapter1.InsertCommand.Transaction = sqlTRX
        SqlDataAdapter1.DeleteCommand.Transaction = sqlTRX
        SqlDataAdapter1.UpdateCommand.Transaction = sqlTRX
    Catch errobj As Exception
        MsgBox(errobj.Message)
    End Try
End Sub
```

In the Button7 (Refresh) click event place the following code:

```
    Private Sub Button7_Click(ByVal sender As System.Object, _
ByVal e As System.EventArgs) Handles Button7.Click
        Try
            DataSet11.Tables("Employees").Clear()
            DataGrid1.CaptionText = "Reading Data"
            SqlDataAdapter1.Fill(DataSet11, "Employees")
        Catch errobj As Exception
            MsgBox(errobj.Message)
        End Try
        If Not sqlTRX Is Nothing Then
            DataGrid1.CaptionText = "Transaction Pending Type: " &
sqlTRX.IsolationLevel.ToString
        Else
            DataGrid1.CaptionText = "Ready - No Trx"
        End If
    End Sub
```

Change the Button1 click event to call this procedure:

```
    Private Sub Button1_Click(ByVal sender As System.Object, _
ByVal e As System.EventArgs) Handles Button1.Click
        Try
          Button2_Click(Button2, New System.EventArgs())
          Button7_Click(Button7, New System.EventArgs())
        Catch errobj As Exception
          MsgBox(errobj.Message)
        End Try
    End Sub
```

Compile the program. The isolation level can only be set when the transaction is first started. There is an `IsolationLevel` property but it is read-only.

We have shown that the transactions work for grouping multiple database operations and making them all be accepted or rejected. The real power with transactions though is the ability to tune how concurrent updates are handled. This is why we use isolation levels. Make sure the latest version of the code is compiled. To do the concurrency test, we will have to run two instances of the program. To do this we will use the executables instead of running from the IDE.

The executables are created in a folder named "bin" directly below the folder containing the source files. Navigate there using Windows Explorer and run two instances of the program. Next, we will demonstrate each of the isolation levels.

Read Uncommitted

With this level, you should be able to see other user's uncommitted updates. Let's try it and see. In one instance of the program, select the Read Uncommitted radio button. Do the same for the second instance. In the first instance, click Load Data. Then do the same for the second instance. We have started a transaction in the first instance, but we have not yet attempted to change data. That's okay because we are demonstrating that we can see uncommitted changes made by the second instance. Now change a row in the second instance and click Update, but do not click Commit. In the second instance, click Refresh. You should be able to see the uncommitted changes made by the second instance.

I'm not sure why a programmer would want to do such a thing as view the uncommitted updates of another user. The whole purpose of not committing until all operations are complete is just so other users will not see any partially updated data that could be misinterpreted. The old example of the bank transaction where money is moved from one account to another comes to mind. Why would you want anyone to chance reading data where the money had been deducted from one account but not added to the other? It makes no sense. Suppose the first transaction was rolled back? Now you would see data that doesn't even exist! The only possibility I can think of is where you have two transactions open in the same user session and you want one to be able to see the uncommitted transactions of the other. There are better ways of accomplishing this. The danger of using transactions that way is that *all other users* also see the uncommitted data. Sound advice is to use this level sparingly, if at all. If anyone wants to suggest valid reasons for using this level, send them to bob@emanageservice.com.

Read Committed

The Read Committed isolation level gives you a little more safety. When you use this level, you cannot see uncommitted updates by other transactions. Let's use our demo program again. If you closed them, fire up two more instances or just click both Close buttons to clear them. On the one on the left, click the Read Committed radio button. On the one on the right, select the Serialized radio button. Click both Load Data buttons. This starts a transaction and populates the grid. In the grid on the right, change some data and then click the Update button. Do *not* click the Commit or Rollback buttons. Now, in the grid on the left, click Refresh. Notice you do not see the changes made in the right-hand grid.

Now let's get dangerous. We have a change in a pending transaction in the right-hand grid. What happens if we change the same data in the left-hand grid? Let's try it! Change something in the left grid that you changed in the right grid, but don't make the same change. Use some other name of random string. This way we will see which changes were accepted. Now click Update on the left-hand grid. Hmm, it seems to have locked up. Wait out the 30-second command timeout. Eventually, an error dialog pops up saying that the timeout has expired and a red-circled exclamation point appears on the grid. It won't do the update because the other grid's pending transaction has the row locked. Click the Commit button on the right-hand grid and now click the Update button again on the left-hand grid. Now the update will be accepted. Click the Commit button on the left-hand grid. Now click both Refresh buttons. You should see the last changes updated which are those from the left-hand grid.

For the next demonstrations, set the command timeout for the four command objects in the Data Adapter to five seconds. This will shorten the wait time.

Read Repeatable

The Read Repeatable isolation level ensures that once a transaction is started, the same set of selection criteria (the same `where` clause in a `Select` statement) will return the same number of rows and the same values in the columns. This is useful for reports and other analytical processing that requires a consistent view of the data, unaffected by other's changes.

We will need to make a slight change in the program to make this demonstration work. Remember we said that Read Repeatable would return the same records using the same selection criteria? We need to add a feature to our program so that we can use a `where` clause in our `Select` statement. To do this, first add a text box to the form. Next, we'll make the text box multiline. Go to the Property window. Scroll down until you find the `MultiLine` property. Change its value to `true`. Scroll down further and find the `ScrollBars` property. Select `Vertical`. This adds a vertical scroll bar to the text box. Now you will be able to resize the text box vertically. Your revised form should appear as in Figure 5.17.

Next, we'll have to change the code to accommodate the `where` clause. In the code window, open the object list (left-hand combo box). Select Base Class Events. In the procedure box (on the right) scroll down until you find the Load event and select it. A load event procedure will be created. Create a module-level variable called `strSQL`. In the event procedure, assign the value of the `SqlDataAdapter1.SelectCommand.CommandText` to the variable `strSQL`.

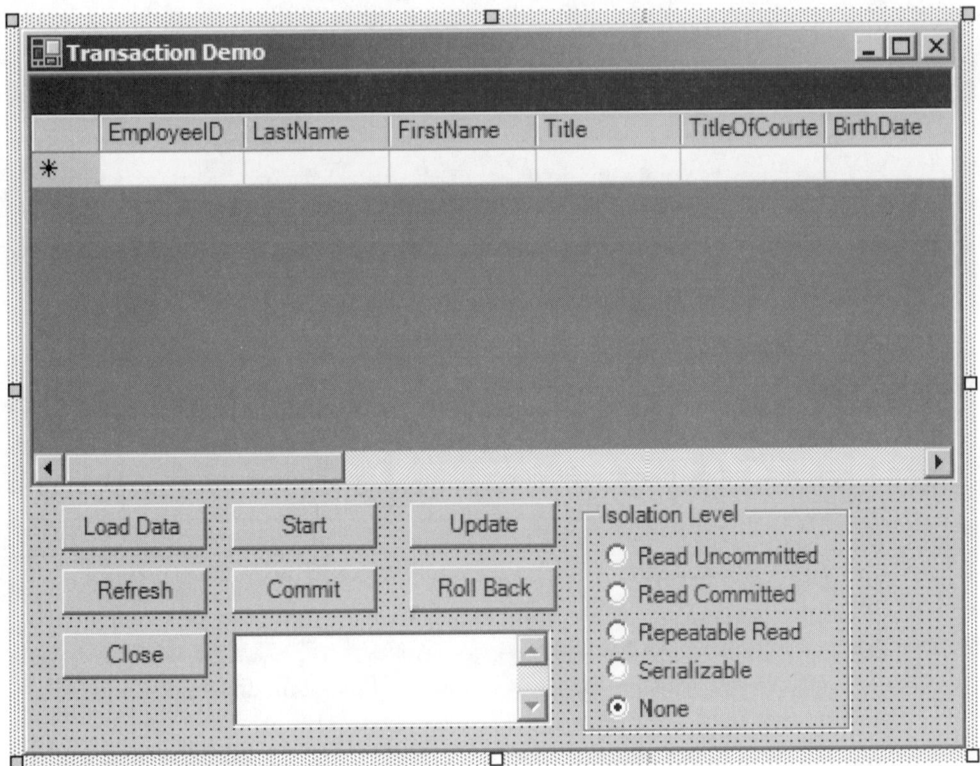

FIGURE 5.17 Revised form with text box for `where` clause.

```
  Private Sub frmTRX_Load(ByVal sender As Object, _
ByVal e As System.EventArgs) Handles MyBase.Load
        strSQL = SqlDataAdapter1.SelectCommand.CommandText
  End Sub
```

This preserves the original `Select` statement so we can change the `where` clause freely. In the Refresh button's click event, concatenate the value of the text box to the end of the stored `Select` statement. It is the line in bold in the example.

```
Private Sub Button7_Click(ByVal sender As System.Object, _
ByVal e As System.EventArgs) Handles Button7.Click
    Try
        DataSet11.Tables("Employees").Clear()
        SqlDataAdapter1.SelectCommand.CommandText() = Trim(strSQL & "
" & TextBox1.Text)
        DataGrid1.CaptionText = "Reading Data"
        SqlDataAdapter1.Fill(DataSet11, "Employees")
    Catch errobj As Exception
        MsgBox(errobj.Message)
    End Try
    If Not sqlTRX Is Nothing Then
        DataGrid1.CaptionText = "Transaction Pending Type: " &
sqlTRX.IsolationLevel.ToString
    Else
      DataGrid1.CaptionText = "Ready - No Trx"
    End If
End Sub
```

Now we're ready to demonstrate the Read Repeatable isolation level. Start up two new instances of the executable. Arrange them left and right as we did before. In the left-hand grid, select Read Repeatable isolation level. In the right-hand grid, select None. In the left-hand grid, type the `where` clause `Where Title Like 'Sales%'`. This will cause SQL Server to return only rows that have Sales as the first five characters of the title. Leave the right-hand grid `where` clause blank.

Now load the data in both grids. Add a row to the right-hand grid. Make sure the row satisfies the `where` clause by including the words Sales Rep in the title field. Now refresh the left-hand grid. The new row appears. Notice that Read Repeatable does not mean that new rows, known as phantoms, will still be omitted. Now delete the new row from the right-hand grid and click Update. Refresh the left-hand grid. The deleted row still appears. This is what is meant by repeatable read. As long as the same transaction is pending, you will never lose any rows.

You may gain new rows, however. What happens if we change the existing data? Try changing a row that appears in the left-hand grid in the right-hand grid. Click Update. The prompt says that it's updating but it appears to lock up. This is because the Read Repeatable transaction in the other grid has the row locked. In fact, all of the rows that were read inside the transaction are locked. Now click the Roll Back button in the left-hand grid. Suddenly the update in the right-hand grid completes. The two lower isolation levels will allow changes to be made to data inside the transaction from other users. They do not lock the rows. The Read Repeatable and Serializable levels put write locks on the rows that are inside the transaction. The Serializable level also puts a read lock on any row that has been updated but not committed.

TIP—I have found that an understanding of record locking and transaction isolation levels is among the weakest areas of knowledge of many Visual Basic programmers. For some reason, maybe it's the rogue nature of many programmers, they seem to write code as if the user of their program is the only person on the network. Unless pressed they almost never do any concurrency testing. This leads to much consternation later in the life cycle as users experience seeming lock ups and other problems. A good understanding of record locking and isolation levels is mandatory for anyone creating all but the simplest programs.

Serializable

This level is to be used where data integrity is the highest priority. This level puts read locks on updated rows within the transaction. To demonstrate this, open two instances of the demo program. Select Serializable isolation level for both grids. Use the same selection criteria (`Where title like 'Sales%'`) in the left-hand grid. Make a change to one of the rows in the left-hand grid and click Update. Now try refreshing the rows in the right-hand grid. You will appear to lock up as the locked row is encountered. Click Commit in the left-hand grid and the refresh command will complete in the right-hand grid.

There are innumerable possible combinations to try out with this demonstration, but we don't have the space to cover them all. If you are working on a program and want to test possible concurrency issues, you can easily modify this program to try different scenarios.

Using Save Points

Save points are named places within a transaction to where a series of updates can be partially rolled back. During the progress of a complex series of operations, it may be desirable to be able to roll back partial transactions and then retry the segment that failed without reexecuting the entire transaction. Save points provide this ability. The programmer can set a save point by calling the `Save` method of the Transaction object and providing a unique name that can later be used in a `rollback` method call.

Some Practical Advice

There are a number of items to mention, learned from experience:

- Do not start a transaction at the beginning of an interactive editing session. You don't have any control over how long a user might take to complete the session. The user may even start the transaction and then go to lunch or finish up for the day leaving rows locked indefinitely that others may need to access.
- Do not use transactions as an undo mechanism. Although it is possible to use them for this, it again locks rows for long periods that others may need. This can be the cause of apparent lock ups and other problems.
- Keep transactions short. Make sure the scope is as narrow as possible and have an exception mechanism in case the transaction encounters data locked by other users. It is best to use short command timeout values inside transactions so users are not frustrated by apparent lock ups.
- Remember the purpose of transactions: to make sure all of the operations inside either succeed or fail. Thus, it is best to use rollback as an exception process. If any part of the transaction fails, roll it back, wait a short amount of time (milliseconds), then retry the series of operations since the transaction was started or since the last save point. Only after all operations within the transaction have succeeded should it be committed.
- If after a certain number of retries the transaction cannot be completed, advise the user and provide a way to save the data temporarily (as an XML document, for example) so the user can come back later and try to save it again.

SUMMARY

We have examined the Connection classes in detail. We have learned the various ways to connect to databases. We have learned the finer points of Connection strings. We have examined transactions in depth. Now it is time to look at how we access the data in the database one we have made our connection. We shall do this by examining SqlDataAdapter class and their related classes, the SqlCommand class, and the SqlCommandBuilder class. Forward ho!

CHAPTER 6

ADO .NET DataAdapters

DataAdapters are the interface components that sit between the DataSet and the database. They contain the commands necessary to read data and optionally update the database with changes made to the DataSet. There are also some helper classes that make our programming lives easier. They do this by creating the `Update` statements from the `Select` statement we provided, and by fetching parameter lists for stored procedures from the database. So far, we have only seen how to connect to a database. Now we will actually get data and do updates.

THE DATAADAPTER CLASSES

Like the Connection classes, there are separate DataAdapter classes for the OleDbClient and the SqlClient. We will be using the SqlClient versions for our demonstrations. All of what we learn applies to the OleDbClient versions as well except where noted. At the heart of the DataAdapter is the Command class. For you ADO veterans this is similar to the ADO Command object and has similar properties and methods. The big difference is that the ADO .NET Command class does not send its output to a `RecordSet` object. It uses another object, called a DataReader, to send a stream of data into a DataTable object, which usually resides inside a DataSet, although it does not have to. There are also separate methods for executing update queries that do not return data, such as `Insert`, `Update`, or `Delete` statements.

THE DATAADAPTER CONFIGURATION WIZARD

The easiest way to create a DataAdapter is to simply drag one from the toolbox and drop it onto a form or other container. As a learning exercise, let's do this, and dissect the results.

Creating the Demo Project

First, create a Windows Forms project. Name the project ADOBook06-01. If you don't want to follow along with the steps, place a data grid on the form, and set the `Dock` property to `Fill`. Next, place a Panel on the form and dock it to the bottom. The grid should fill the top of the form outside the panel. If it does not, right-click on the grid and select Bring to Front. This should fix the problem. Place three buttons on the panel and set the `Text` property as in Figure 6.1. Finally, place a label and a text box on the form.

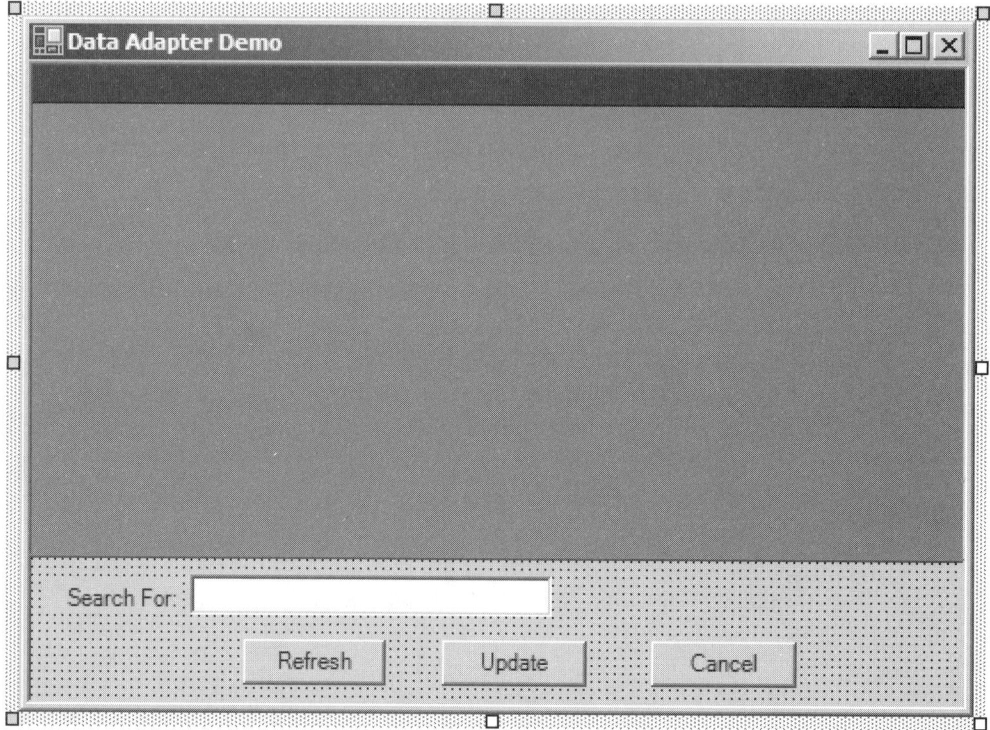

FIGURE 6.1 Roughed-out Data Adapter Demo form.

This will be used for a partial string to use in queries. Your form should look like Figure 6.1. We'll use this form for our examples in this chapter.

The DataAdapter

When you drag and drop a DataAdapter for either client (SQL or OLEDB), the DataAdapter Configuration wizard opens automatically. First, you must choose a connection. You may either select a predefined connection you have created in the Server Explorer, or create one. See Figure 6.2.

Whichever connection you choose here will become the connection the four Command objects will use. Once you've chosen your connection click

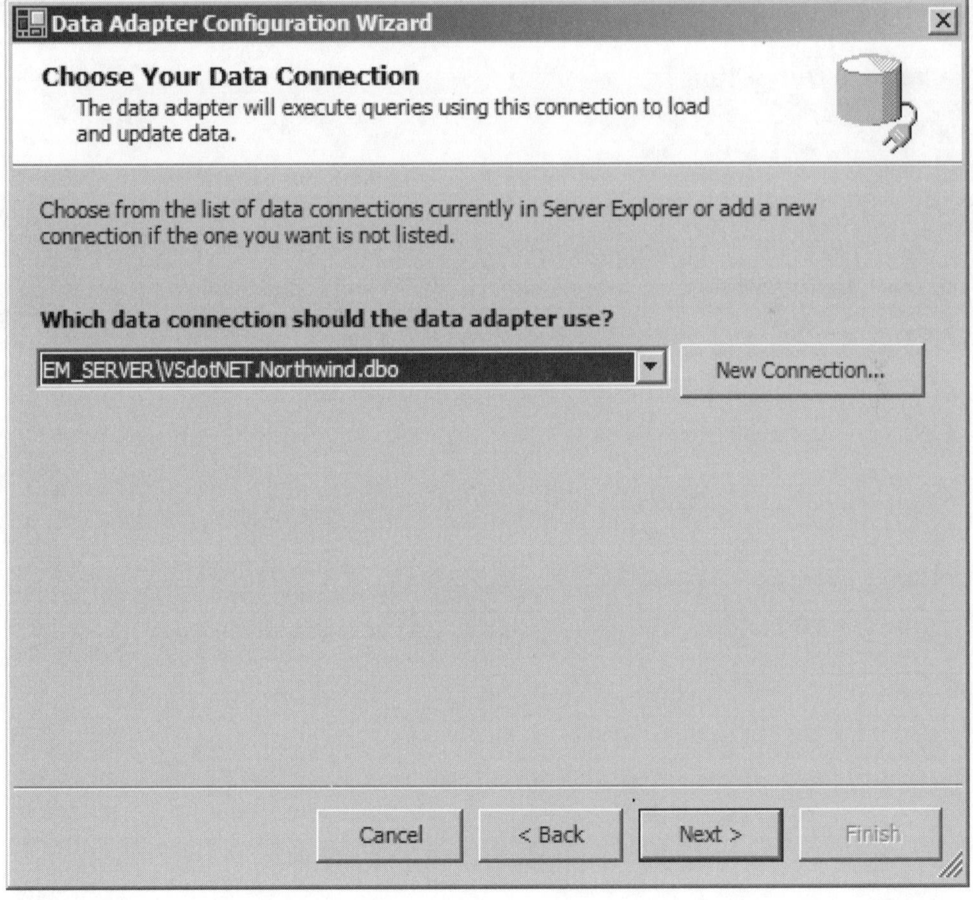

FIGURE 6.2 The Choose Data Connection page.

Next. On the next page, you will choose how the DataAdapter will get its data and how it will update the database. The choices are SQL statements or stored procedures, as in Figure 6.3.

We will go through each of these choices. The three choices are:

- SQL statements—With this choice, the DataAdapter uses SQL statements to do all its work. You will enter a `Select` statement, then the DataAdapter will generate the `Insert`, `Update`, and `Delete` statements for you.
- Create stored procedures—You enter an SQL `Select` statement and the DataAdapter will generate four new stored procedures that will be used to access the database.

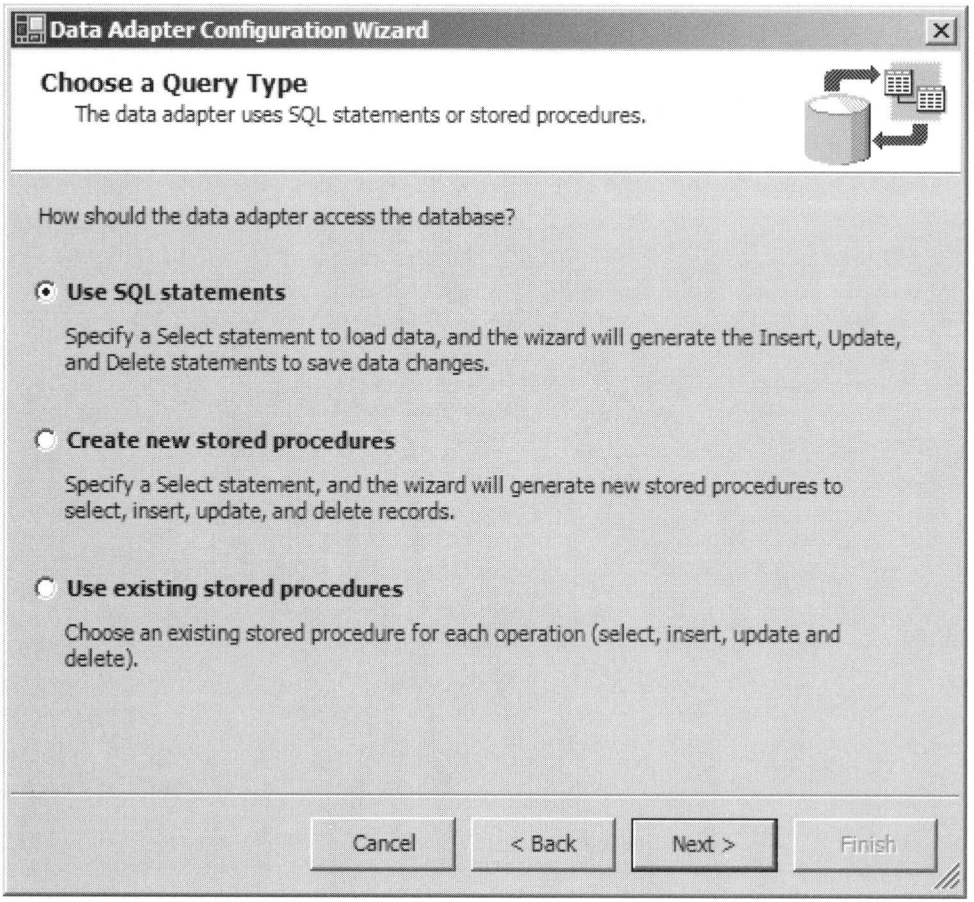

FIGURE 6.3 Choose Query Type page.

- Use existing stored procedures—You will have to tell the DataAdapter which existing procedures to use. This is useful in certain security-sensitive industries (such as banking) which do not allow direct access to tables.

SQL Statements

Select the SQL statements option and click Next. The next page that opens allows you to key in an SQL `Select` statement or you can use the Query Builder to create the statement graphically (illustrated in Figure 6.3). Figure 6.4 shows the SQL statements page.

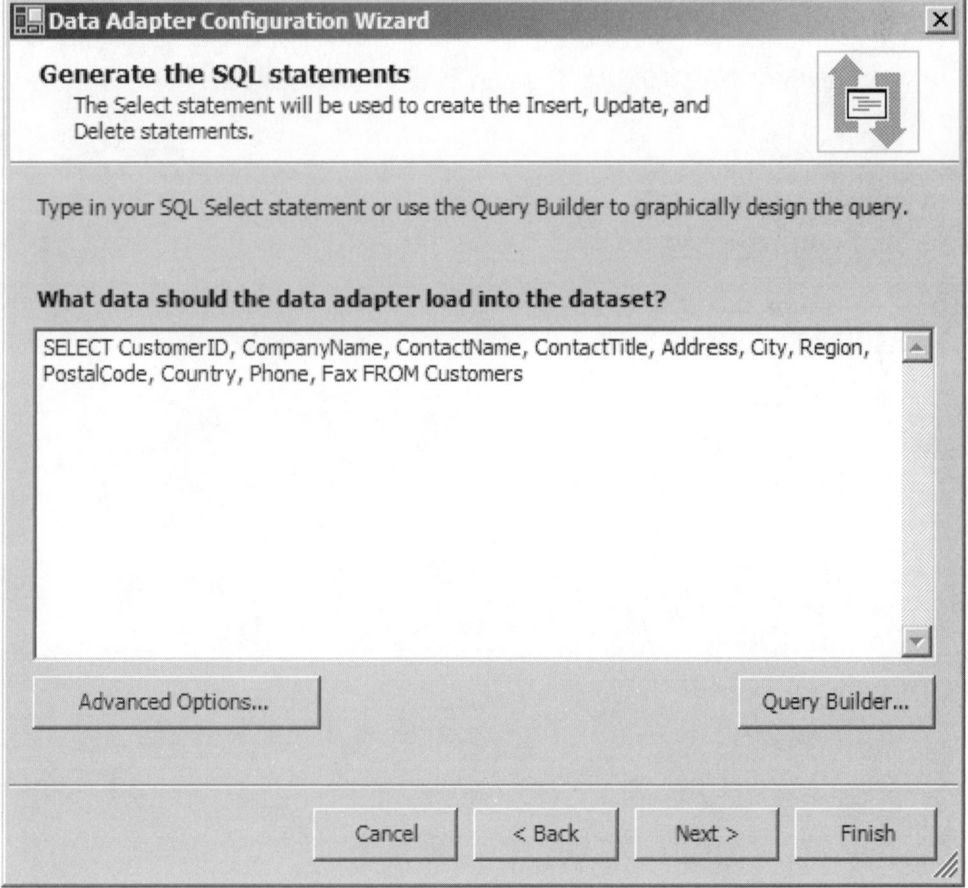

FIGURE 6.4 The SQL statements page.

To use the Query Builder, click the button. Any SQL that is already entered will be parsed and the Query Builder will be filled in for you. If there is no statement, an empty Query Builder screen will open. The Query Builder with the SQL statement shown in Figure 6.4 loaded looks as in Figure 6.5.

THE QUERY BUILDER

The Query Builder consists of four panes. The functions of the Query Builder are accessed via context menus, since the builder is running as a modal form.

The builder can also be accessed other ways nonmodally, such as for designing views. When it is displayed nonmodally, a toolbar appears with the functions accessible from there.

The top pane is the diagram pane. Here you can see your tables and joins represented graphically. The context menu for the diagram pane appears as in Figure 6.6.

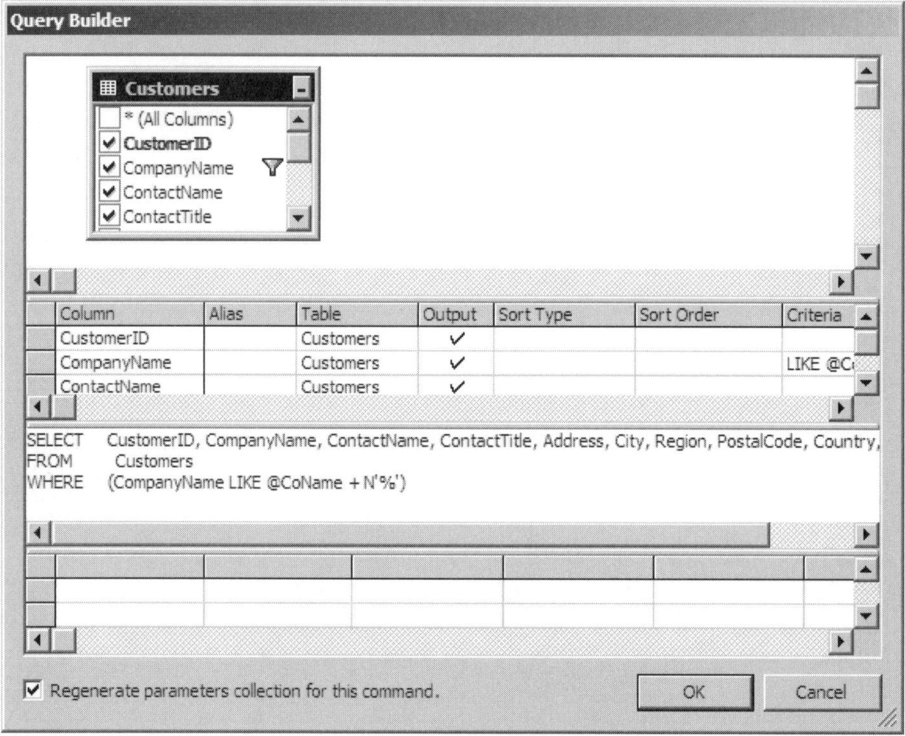

FIGURE 6.5 The Query Builder with the Select statement loaded.

FIGURE 6.6 Diagram pane context menu.

You can access the context menu by clicking the right mouse button over the diagram pane, but, of course, you already knew that! The menu functions are:

- Run—You can run most queries to test them. Do not run queries that make changes to data, as you will not be able to reverse them. For select queries, the output appears in the output pane on the bottom of the designer.
- Add Table...—Opens the Add Table dialog, shown in Figure 6.7. You may choose from tables, views, or functions that return data. Note that you may add the same table more than once to create a self-join. The system automatically creates an alias for the subsequent instances. You may add tables by clicking the Add button or by double-clicking the table or view name. You can change the group by options and select aggregate functions and other options. You don't want to use Group By because it may render the query read-only and the DataAdapter may not be able to create the other three update queries from it. If all you needed were to read the data, then this would be acceptable. Some types of Group By queries are acceptable and it will be able to create the `Update` statements from them.
- Select All—Selects the SQL statement.
- Group By—Selecting this option changes the query into a Group By query (see Figure 6.8). These queries are useful for summarizing data.
- Change Type—This option allows you to change the query type from select to other types, such as insert or update. You really don't want to do

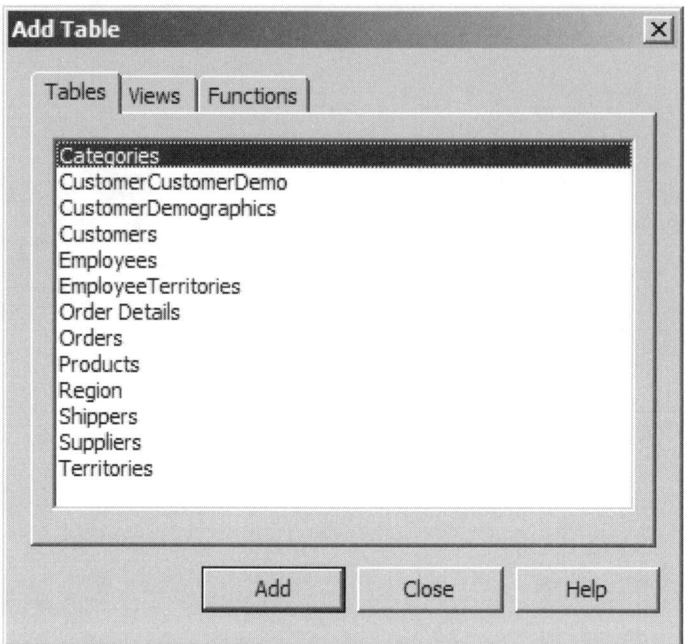

FIGURE 6.7 The Add Table dialog.

this at this point because you want to use a select query that returns data. See Figure 6.9.

- Show Panes, Hide Pane—Turns the display of the four panes of the query builder on or off.
- Verify SQL Syntax—When the cursor is over the SQL Text pane this option appears. It allows you to have SQL Server check the syntax of the query. This is useful for validating that a query will compile before using it inside a program. Also, if you type in a query manually this will cause SQL Server to parse the query and fill in the diagram pane for you.
- Navigation Items—These items appear when you are over the Results pane and the query has been run. They allow the typical next, previous, and so forth. This is self-explanatory.

The Advanced options (see Figure 6.10) button allows you to customize how the wizard will create the `Update`, `Insert`, and `Delete` statements. (Why do they insist on calling anything that requires an additional dialog box "advanced"? Which "nonadvanced" users are going to be configuring a DataAdapter?) The dialog is shown in Figure 6.10.

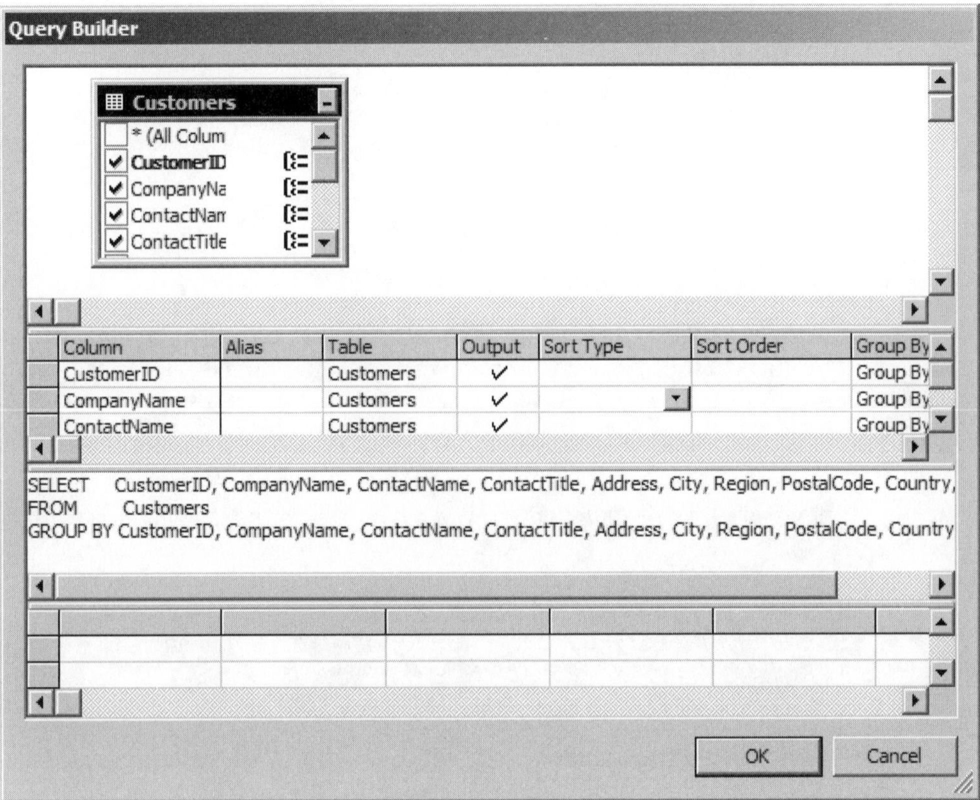

FIGURE 6.8 Query Builder with Group By selected.

By default, the Adapter will create `Insert`, `Update`, and `Delete` SQL statements based on the `Select` statement you provided. If you intend the DataAdapter to read data only, you can save some overhead by not creating the SQL statements. To do this, clear the first check box. This will also disable the other two check boxes, as they have no meaning if you are only reading from the database.

CONCURRENCY MANAGEMENT

The second check box, Use Optimistic Concurrency, determines how the wizard will create the `Insert` and `Update` SQL statements. ADO .NET does not fully rely on SQL Server (or other database system) record locking to implement concurrency. For those who may not be used to working in

FIGURE 6.9 The Change Type submenu.

multiuser environments, concurrency is the way a database system handles conflicts between users. For example, user A reads some data. User B reads the same data. What happens when users A and B make changes and try to update the data at the same time? The way a database system handles these situations is called concurrency management. Most systems use some combination of row locking and row versioning to manage concurrency. Row

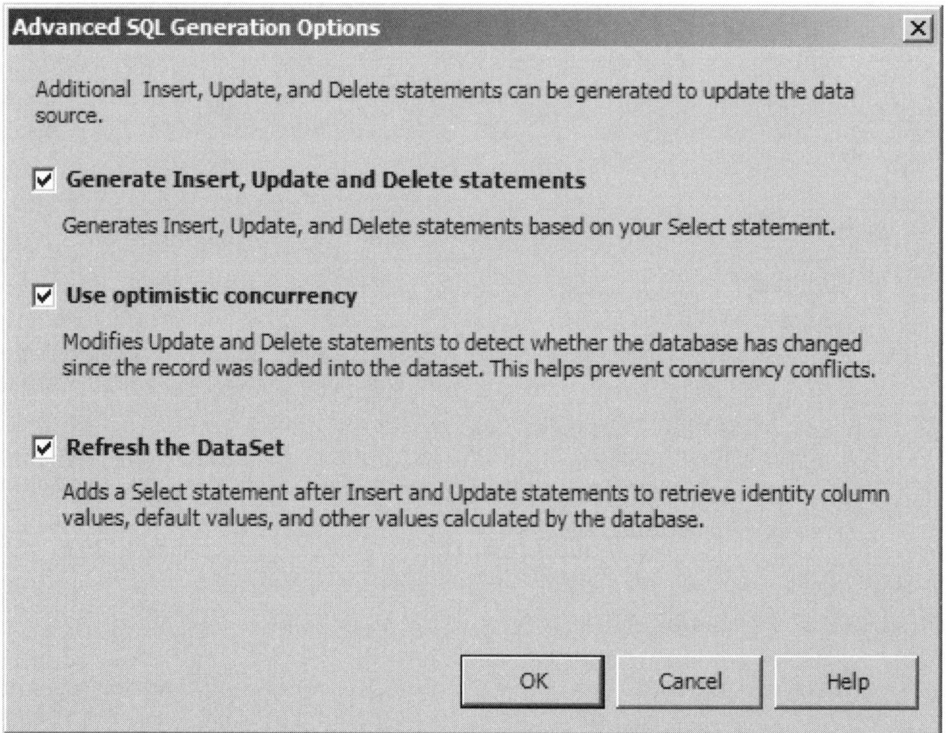

FIGURE 6.10 The Advanced SQL Generation Options dialog.

locking is the oldest way of managing concurrency. Also called pessimistic concurrency, row locking places a logical lock on the data when the first user reads it. Typically, the user can place a read lock or a write lock on the row. A read lock gives the first user exclusive access to the row. No other user can read the same row until the first user releases the lock. With a write lock, other users can read the row, but they cannot update the row until the first user releases the lock. The problem with this is that if the second user updates the row, the first user's updates are overwritten. This is known as the-last-one-wins rule.

With optimistic concurrency, the row is never locked when it is read. Instead, row versioning is used to determine if any changes have been made to the row since it was last read by user A. If user B changed the record after user A read it, the row version would change and user A would know that the record changed. The row is only locked when the update begins, and it is released immediately after the update is complete. This minimizes the time any one row is actually locked. The theory behind optimistic concurrency is based on the statistical probability that any given row is normally read many more times than it is updated, and that the odds of any two users updating the same row at almost the same time is relatively low. The downside of optimistic concurrency is that it requires the row to be read a second time just before it is updated. This read is required to check the row version. This will cause a slight increase in network traffic.

As a general best practice, use optimistic concurrency when updates are relatively infrequent. This would include almost all online interactive applications, including Windows GUI and web applications. Pessimistic concurrency is better used for batch type operations where there is no user interaction because performance is usually better. Since batch jobs run fast, the time any given row is locked is usually minimized and the system doesn't have to read the row twice for each update. The caveat here is that ADO .NET does not support pessimistic concurrency. You can use other techniques to achieve similar results. Stored procedures and dynamic SQL statements both achieve high performance for batch jobs.

Now that we understand general concurrency management, we can look at how ADO .NET handles it. ADO .NET uses a combination of row locking (on servers that support it) and row versioning. The row versioning it uses is implemented in code in the DataSet and the DataAdapter. The DataSet does its part by storing both the original row values, which are never changed, and the current row values, which may change programmatically due to a user editing a bound control. We will look at this later on in the chapter on DataSets. The DataAdapter does its part by creating `Insert`, `Update`, and

`Delete` statements that use each value in the original `select` clause in the `where` clause of the query. This way, if any data changed since the row was read, the `where` clause will fail and the data will not be updated. The DataAdapter uses the original values stored in the DataSet as parameters for the `where` clause, and the changed (or current) values in the DataSet as the parameters used in the update (set clauses for `Update` statements and value lists for `Insert` statements) clauses of the SQL statements.

When I first saw this, I was confused by why it was using all of the columns in the original `Select` statement as `where` clause parameters. I thought that this must be very inefficient. Would I have to index all the columns in each table? I was partially right. It can be very inefficient on a poorly designed database. As long as there is a unique key included in the `select` clause, it should be okay. I have not done any testing on this. As a standard practice, I always include a primary key in my tables that is not dependent on the data in the row. I use an identity column with autoincrement as my primary key on all my tables. That way, I always have a unique row identifier. I always include this key in my `select` clauses. There are other ways of checking row versions. You could use a time stamp column, which gets updated automatically each time a row is changed. You could then use this column to make your comparison. It seems that this would be more efficient than checking each column value. For the purposes of this book, we'll stick with the way the DataAdapter handles it.

In a minute we'll dissect the SQL statements the DataAdapter generates using our sample application. First, let's look at the last check box, Refresh the DataSet. What this does is place a copy of the `Select` statement used to create the update queries immediately after the respective `Insert` or `Update` statement. This `Select` statement is then called to cause an automatic refresh of any DataSet that is referenced in the call to the DataAdapter's `Update` method. This is another area with which to be very careful. You could generate a lot of network traffic if you are refreshing large DataTables each time a single row is updated. It has always been a best practice to keep your returned row counts as low as possible. This has never been truer than with ADO .NET.

THE SELECT COMMAND

First, let's look at the `Select` statement. In order to do this, we must complete the wizard. Click to close the Advanced SQL Generation Options dialog. Then click the Finish button on the main Wizard window. This wizard will close. Now we can use the Property window to examine how the wizard created the DataAdapter. Don't worry, we can run the wizard repeatedly to correct any problems or just to regenerate the Data Adapter. The wizard remembers the existing configuration and allows you to update it at any time. To get to the SQL `Select` statement we created in the wizard, we have to scroll down the Property window until we see the `SelectCommand` property. Expand it by clicking the Plus button. Your window should look like Figure 6.11.

To view the `Select` statement, select the `CommandText` property. Next, click the ellipsis button that appears. This will open the familiar query designer we saw previously. In the SQL pane, the `Select` statement will appear.

```
SELECT CustomerID, CompanyName, ContactName, ContactTitle, Address,
City, Region, PostalCode, Country, Phone, Fax
FROM Customers
WHERE (CompanyName LIKE @CoName + N'%')
```

We're selecting certain columns from the Customers table. We are also allowing the user to select rows based on the `where` clause. In case you are not that familiar with SQL, this statement says, "Give me the following columns from all rows in the Customers table where the CompanyName starts with the parameter (@CoName) provided."

I included the `where` clause just for some complexity so you can see how the DataAdapter handles it. By including the "at" sign (@) in front of the parameter name, the DataAdapter will automatically create a parameter object for the placeholder. The data type of the parameter is determined by the data type of the column on the left of the operator. We can see the param-

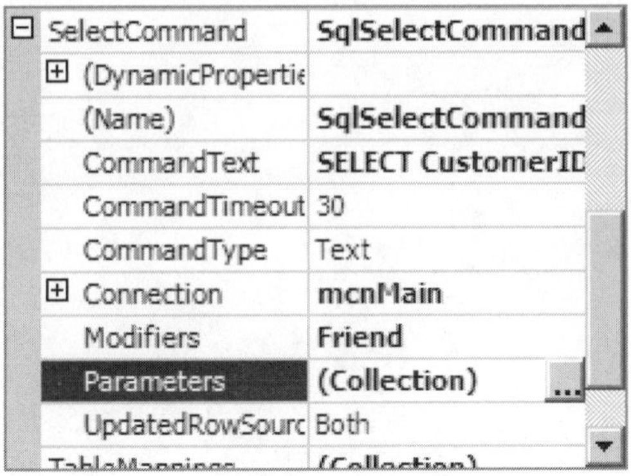

SelectCommand	SqlSelectCommand
(DynamicPropertie	
(Name)	SqlSelectCommand
CommandText	SELECT CustomerID
CommandTimeout	30
CommandType	Text
Connection	mcnMain
Modifiers	Friend
Parameters	(Collection)
UpdatedRowSourc	Both
TableMappings	(Collection)

FIGURE 6.11 The SelectCommand of the DataAdapter.

eter that was created by viewing the Parameter collection. To do this, close the query designer and go to the Property window. Find and select the `Parameters` property of the SelectCommand. (See Figure 6.12.) When you click the ellipsis button, the Property collection form opens.

The editor shown in Figure 6.12 is a typical collection editor. It appears any place that a collection can be edited visually at design time. The items in the collection are listed by name in the list at the left. The details of each item appear in the property pane on the right. This is an improvement over the VB 6 Property pages. With this new editor, you can just scroll through the list of items and the properties appear automatically on the right. We will look at the

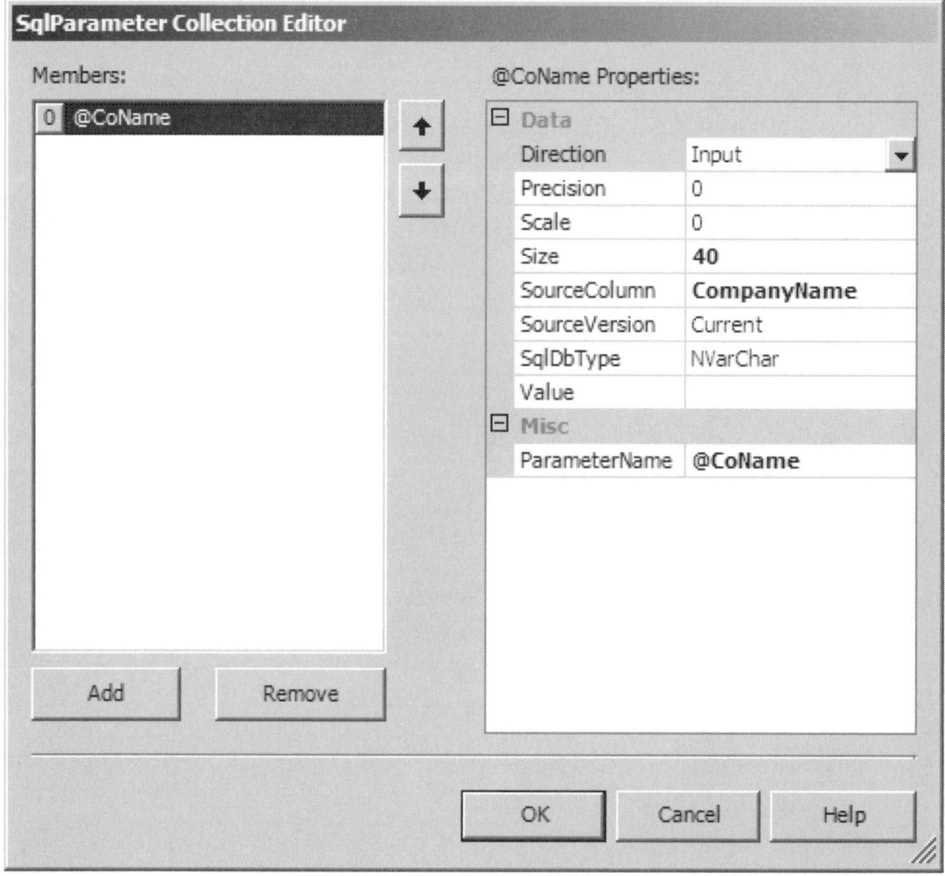

FIGURE 6.12 The Parameter collection editor.

parameter properties in detail when we examine the Property class. Right now, we just wanted to see what the wizard did with the parameter we included in the SQL statement.

The Update Command

The `Update` statement is the most interesting of the statements generated by the wizard. It contains the parameters required to support optimistic concurrency. To see the statement, go to the Property window and find the `UpdateCommand` property. Just as with the `SelectCommand`, the `UpdateCommand` is an SqlCommand object. Click the plus box to expand it and then find the `CommandText` property. When you click the ellipsis button, a query designer opens just as with the `Select` statement.

```
UPDATE    Customers
SET       CustomerID = @CustomerID, CompanyName = @CompanyName,
ContactName = @ContactName, ContactTitle = @ContactTitle, Address =
@Address, City = @City, Region = @Region, PostalCode = @PostalCode,
Country = @Country, Phone = @Phone, Fax = @Fax
WHERE     (CustomerID = @Original_CustomerID) AND (Address =
@Original_Address OR @Original_Address IS NULL AND Address IS NULL) AND
(City = @Original_City OR @Original_City IS NULL AND City IS NULL) AND
(CompanyName = @Original_CompanyName) AND (ContactName =
@Original_ContactName OR @Original_ContactName IS NULL AND ContactName
IS NULL) AND (ContactTitle = @Original_ContactTitle OR
@Original_ContactTitle IS NULL AND ContactTitle IS NULL) AND (Country =
@Original_Country OR @Original_Country IS NULL AND Country IS NULL) AND
(Fax = @Original_Fax OR @Original_Fax IS NULL AND Fax IS NULL) AND
(Phone = @Original_Phone OR @Original_Phone IS NULL AND Phone IS NULL)
AND (PostalCode = @Original_PostalCode OR
@Original_PostalCode IS NULL AND PostalCode IS NULL) AND (Region =
@Original_Region OR @Original_Region IS NULL AND Region IS NULL);

SELECT    CustomerID, CompanyName, ContactName, ContactTitle, Address,
City, Region, PostalCode, Country, Phone, Fax
FROM        Customers
WHERE     (CustomerID = @CustomerID)
```

The bold SQL keywords are to aid readability. What happened to our simple `Select` statement? Because we selected Optimistic Concurrency and Refresh the DataSet, the statement got a lot more complicated. If we take a look at the Parameter collection we will see that there are two versions of each parameter, one for the main parameter, and one with the word Original prepended to it (see Figure 6.13).

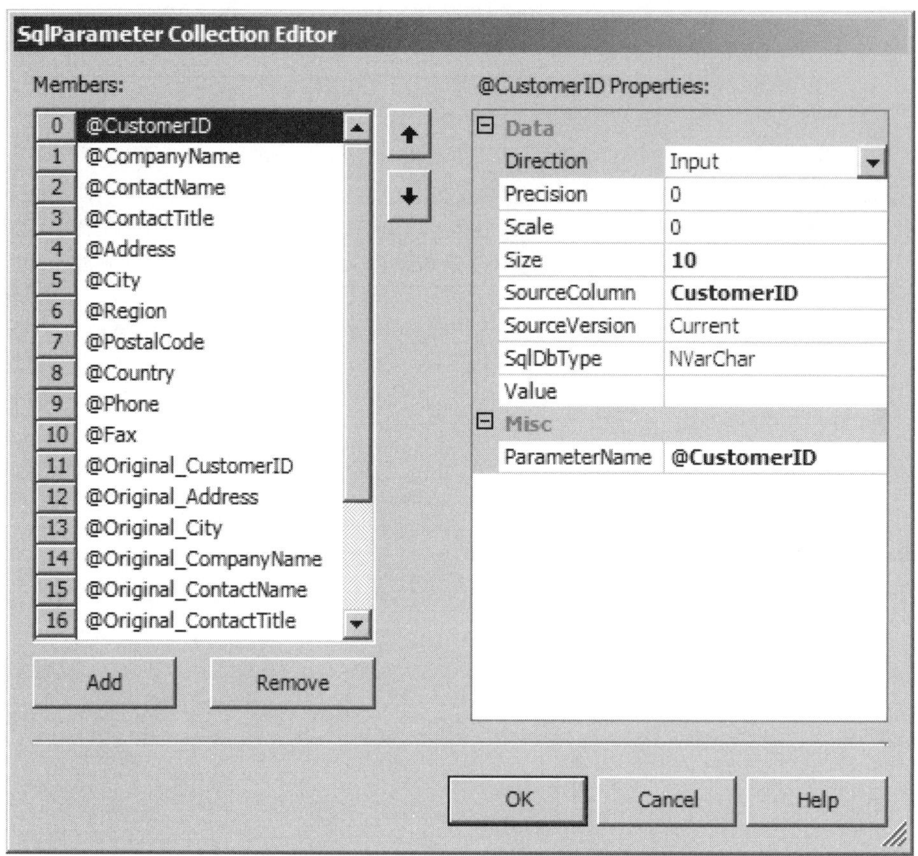

FIGURE 6.13 Parameter collection of Update command.

What this query is doing is using the `where` clause to determine if the original data has changed since the time it was read. If it has changed, the query updates nothing (because the `where` clause fails) and the DataAdapter will throw an error. If the data has not changed, the `Update` statement succeeds in changing the data. Take special note that this relies on the DataSet keeping track of the original values of all of the rows involved. Also, keep in mind that the `Update` method of the DataAdapter tries to execute *all* of the pending changes in the DataSet, including deletes and inserts. It's so easy to think only in terms of one row at a time. Normally, if one of the `Update`, `Insert`, or `Delete` statements fails, the DataAdapter stops processing the operation. The operations that completed successfully are permament but any operation that failed would obviously not be complete. You can adjust this behavior by setting the `ContinueUpdateOnError` property to true. If you do this, then the DataAdapter will merrily go on until it is out of updates.

Let's look at what happens if we uncheck the Use Optimistic Concurrency option. Rerun the DataAdapter Configuration wizard. You can do this from the designer by right-clicking on the DataAdapter and selecting Configure DataAdapter.... When you get to the Select query screen, click the Advanced Options button. Uncheck the two options as shown in Figure 6.14.

After clicking OK, click through the rest of the wizard screens. Now let's find the `UpdateCommand` property again and open the query designer. The SQL statement is quite a bit simpler than before.

```
UPDATE    Customers
SET       CustomerID = @CustomerID, CompanyName = @CompanyName,
ContactName = @ContactName, ContactTitle = @ContactTitle, Address =
@Address, City = @City, Region = @Region, PostalCode = @PostalCode,
Country = @Country, Phone = @Phone, Fax = @Fax
WHERE     (CustomerID = @Original_CustomerID)
```

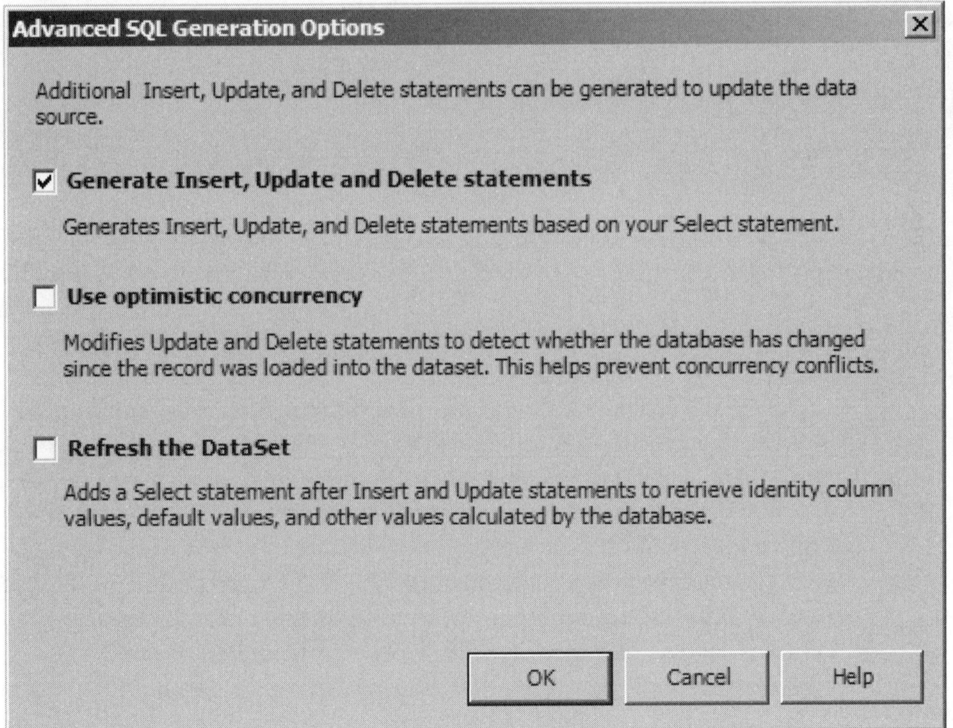

FIGURE 6.14 Advanced options with concurrency and refresh unchecked.

This probably looks a little more like you would think it should. What are the consequences of this form of the statement? There is no checking to see if the data has changed. What this means is that the last one to update wins. I don't like either method of handling the concurrency problem. Without the optimistic concurrency check box selected, users could chaotically overwrite each other's updates. With it checked, the system would act as if the row no longer existed if another user updated it after the first user read it. This is not the case. The row still exists; it has merely been changed.

The best process would be to reread the row, then compare each column value in the recently read row to each original value. If no column values have changed, then update the row. If any column values did change, then you could issue a message and allow the user to take appropriate action. Of course, you would do all of this inside a stored procedure and a transaction. This way you get to use pessimistic concurrency for the duration of the update. This prevents any other user from accessing the row being operated on until your update is complete. Since it is happening inside a stored procedure or a transaction, it should complete very fast, not keeping the row locked for too long. We'll demonstrate this technique later in the chapter.

THE INSERT AND DELETE COMMANDS

Let's look at the `Insert` and `Delete` statements the DataAdapter created. The `Insert` statement is the same whether or not we choose optimistic concurrency. Since we are adding a new row, we don't have to worry about anyone else changing the row since it will not have existed yet. The only possible issue here is that someone else tries to add a row with a nonunique unique key. In this case, the server will abort the operation and the DataAdapter will simply throw an error.

There is a concurrency issue with the `Delete` statement beyond another user deleting the row before you do. What if another user made changes to the row that makes it undesirable to delete due to business rules or some other reason? For example, what if a table had a column which, if true, indicates that the row should not be deleted. If another user set the value to true after you read the row, you would be able to delete the row because to you, the value would still be false. For this reason we need optimistic concurrency on deletions. Here is the `Delete` statement with concurrency checked.

```
DELETE FROM Customers
WHERE     (CustomerID = @Original_CustomerID) AND (Address =
@Original_Address OR @Original_Address IS NULL AND Address IS NULL) AND
(City = @Original_City OR @Original_City IS NULL AND City IS NULL) AND
```

```
(CompanyName = @Original_CompanyName) AND (ContactName =
@Original_ContactName OR @Original_ContactName IS NULL AND ContactName
IS NULL) AND (ContactTitle = @Original_ContactTitle OR
@Original_ContactTitle IS NULL AND ContactTitle IS NULL) AND (Country =
@Original_Country OR @Original_Country IS NULL AND Country IS NULL) AND
(Fax = @Original_Fax OR @Original_Fax IS NULL AND Fax IS NULL) AND
(Phone = @Original_Phone OR @Original_Phone IS NULL AND Phone IS NULL)
AND (PostalCode = @Original_PostalCode OR
@Original_PostalCode IS NULL AND PostalCode IS NULL) AND (Region =
@Original_Region OR @Original_Region IS NULL AND Region IS NULL)
```

The `where` clause used here is the same as the `where` clause for the `Update` statement. If we turn off concurrency, we get this statement:

```
DELETE FROM Customers
WHERE      (CustomerID = @Original_CustomerID)
```

If there are no restrictions on deleting rows from the table, this would probably do fine. The other issue is referential integrity. If there are rules or foreign keys on this table that prohibit the row's deletion, they will be handled by the database system. The DataAdapter will throw an error if referential integrity rules are violated.

Just for completeness, let's look at the `Insert` statement:

```
INSERT INTO Customers
          (CustomerID, CompanyName, ContactName, ContactTitle, Address,
City, Region, PostalCode, Country, Phone, Fax)
VALUES      (@CustomerID, @CompanyName, @ContactName, @ContactTitle,
@Address, @City, @Region, @PostalCode, @Country, @Phone, @Fax)
```

As we said, we don't have to be concerned over concurrency with the `Insert` statement, so it's just a normal SQL statement.

Using Stored Procedures

At the beginning of this discussion, around Figure 6.3, we saw that there were two other options for the query type. We have looked at SQL statements. Now, let's look at stored procedures. If we start at Figure 6.3 and select New Stored Procedures, we get another page after clicking Next twice. The first click is still the `Select` statement. Even though we want to use stored procedures, the wizard still needs a basis for building the stored procedures so we must still give it a `Select` statement. After entering the `Select` statement, we get the page in Figure 6.15.

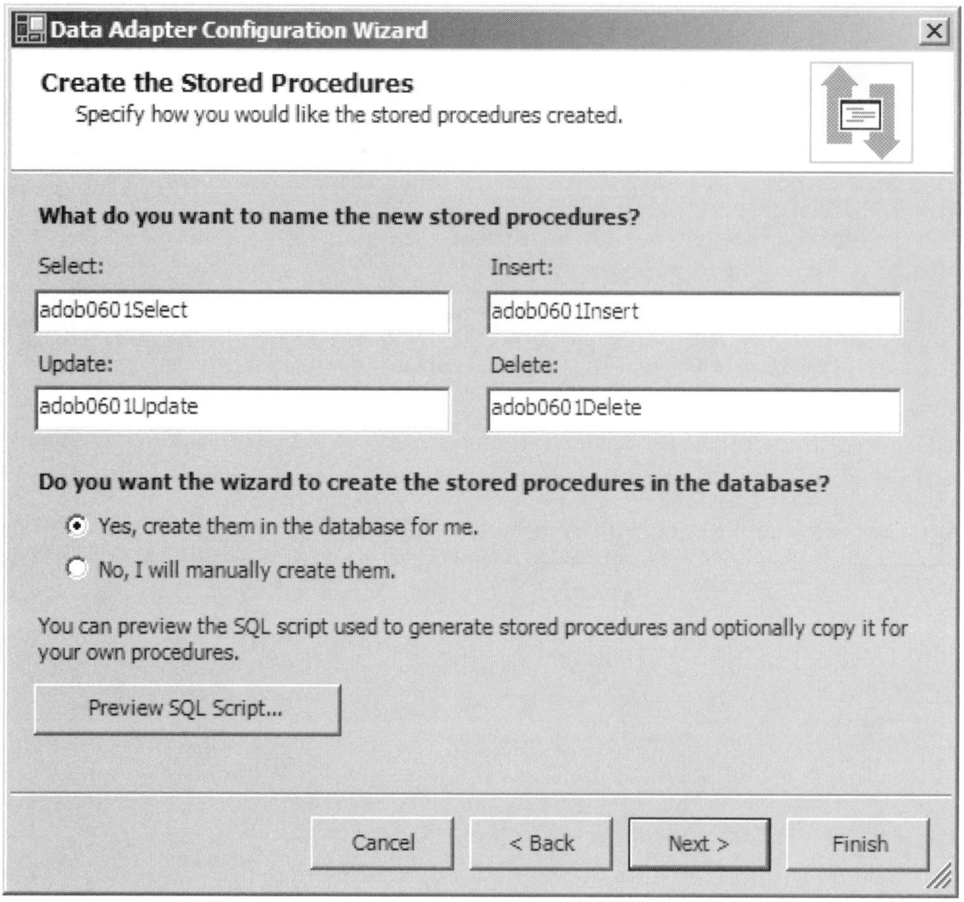

FIGURE 6.15 The Create Stored Procedures page.

The four TextBoxes allow you to name your stored procedures. You should use meaningful names that conform to some naming convention. As per Microsoft standards, avoid using the sp_ prefix as this is reserved for system-stored procedures. A good practice is to use some form of your company initials or an acronym for the application you are building as a prefix. That way you can be reasonably assured your stored procedures won't interfere with another vendor's applications. Let's use adob0601 as our prefix.

There are a couple of options. You can have the wizard create the stored procedures for you, or you can create them manually later on. Either way, the wizard uses a script that it generates to create the stored procedures. If you click the Preview SQL Script… button, another window opens showing the generated script as in Figure 6.16. You can save the script using the Save As... button or cut and paste it into a text editor to run later. You can then customize the script if needed.

If you scroll down through the script, you will see that the procedures simply wrap the same SQL statements we generated directly. The advantage to using stored procedures is that you can reuse the same procedures with DataAdapters elsewhere in your project. You can also include the scripts in your project and put them under source control so you can use them to recreate the procedures in another database.

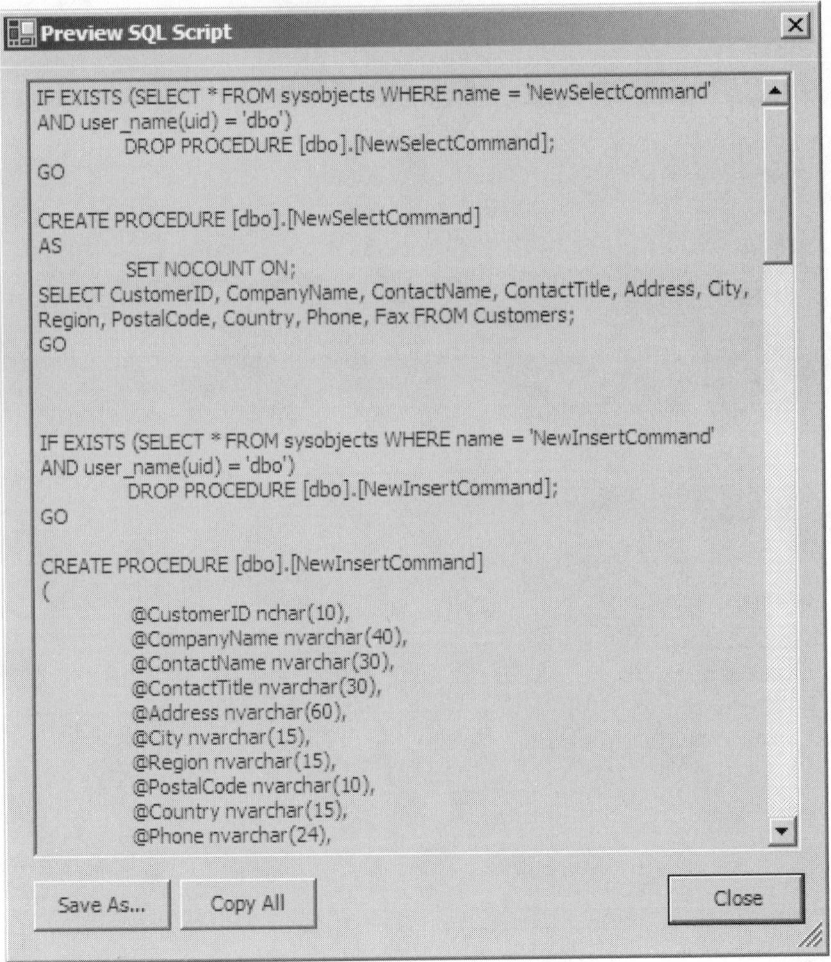


```
IF EXISTS (SELECT * FROM sysobjects WHERE name = 'NewSelectCommand'
AND user_name(uid) = 'dbo')
        DROP PROCEDURE [dbo].[NewSelectCommand];
GO

CREATE PROCEDURE [dbo].[NewSelectCommand]
AS
        SET NOCOUNT ON;
SELECT CustomerID, CompanyName, ContactName, ContactTitle, Address, City,
Region, PostalCode, Country, Phone, Fax FROM Customers;
GO



IF EXISTS (SELECT * FROM sysobjects WHERE name = 'NewInsertCommand'
AND user_name(uid) = 'dbo')
        DROP PROCEDURE [dbo].[NewInsertCommand];
GO

CREATE PROCEDURE [dbo].[NewInsertCommand]
(
        @CustomerID nchar(10),
        @CompanyName nvarchar(40),
        @ContactName nvarchar(30),
        @ContactTitle nvarchar(30),
        @Address nvarchar(60),
        @City nvarchar(15),
        @Region nvarchar(15),
        @PostalCode nvarchar(10),
        @Country nvarchar(15),
        @Phone nvarchar(24),
```

FIGURE 6.16 Preview SQL Script window.

Using Existing Stored Procedures

The third option is to use existing stored procedures. When you select this option, you have the opportunity to supply your own stored procedure names. The wizard will attempt to populate the Parameter collection from the stored procedure, as in Figure 6.17.

The `Select` and `Insert` commands have been completed. The `Update` command is ready to select from the drop down in Figure 6.18.

Once you have selected your procedures, the rest of the pages are the same as for the other options. If the procedures you choose do not support optimistic concurrency, you may get a warning to that effect. If this is of no

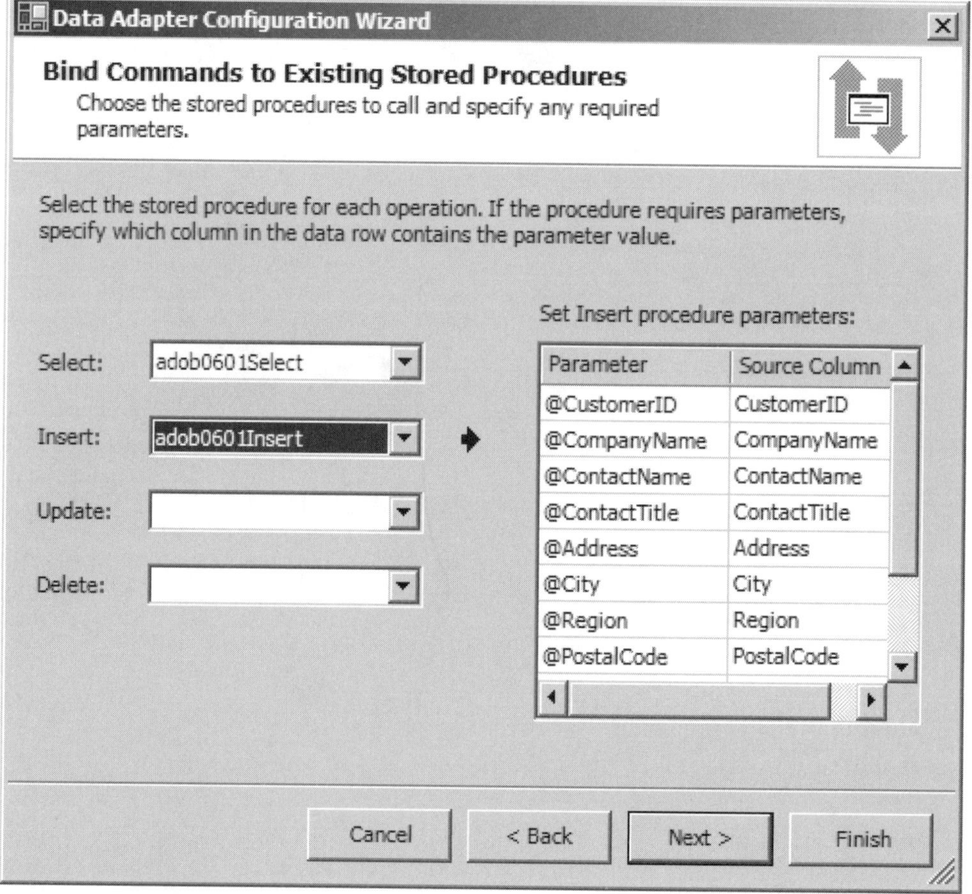

FIGURE 6.17 Existing Stored Procedures page.

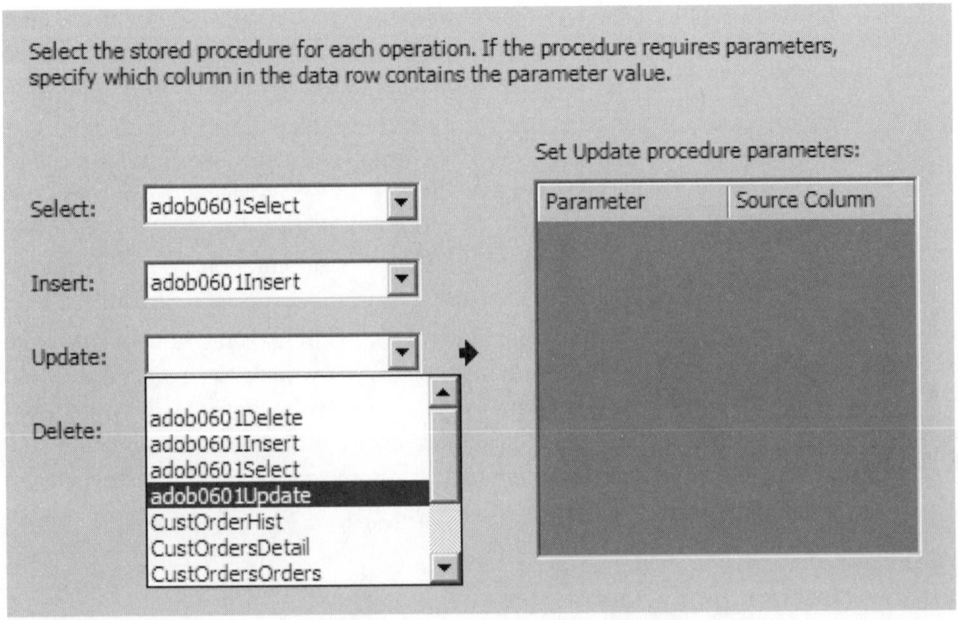

FIGURE 6.18 Selecting the procedure name from the drop down.

concern to you, you may ignore the warning. If you desire optimistic concurrency, you must make sure your stored procedures pass the original values as well as the new values.

We have now seen how to use the wizard to configure the DataAdapter. In the next section, we will configure one entirely in code for you pure programmers who shun wizards and other automated tools. If you are in the latter group, look at the new tools in Visual Studio .NET. They are more sophisticated than their predecessors and can at least give you a place to start, which you can customize later. In this employment environment, anything that saves some time is worth looking at. But for you purists…

PROGRAMMATICALLY CONFIGURING A DATAADAPTER USING THE COMMANDBUILDER

Sometimes, you cannot know at design time exactly how your Data Adapter will be configured. The configuration might depend on user input or data in another table. You may want to use dynamic SQL where you build your statements at runtime instead of using replaceable parameters. This is especially useful in a query generator search screen where you do not know in advance what the user wants to search for.

Create a Windows Forms project called ADOBook06-02. (Or get it from the web site.) If you want to work along, use the starter project, otherwise you can just follow along. We'll be using the same interface as the last project, so you can make a copy of it and delete the DataAdapter and Connection object. So far, we have not run any of these projects; we're using them only to demonstrate the DataAdapter configuration. We will run the project before the end of the chapter.

The secret to configuring a DataAdapter is in knowing how to create the four Command objects that it contains. As we have seen, the Command object contains the SQL statements or stored procedure call syntax, and also contains a Connection object and the Parameter collection for passing values into and out of stored procedures or replaceable parameters in an SQL statement.

Declaring the DataAdapter

There are two ways to declare the DataAdapter. We've already used one of the ways, which is to just drag one from the toolbox and drop it onto your form. You can then cancel out of the wizard to have an unconfigured DataAdapter in your project. If your host object uses the Component model (forms do), you can use this method. You will then have access to the properties in the Property window and the events will appear in the event drop down in the code window. This is halfway between using the wizard and manually configuring the DataAdapter. You can still use the Property window to set SQL statements or stored procedures, and the DataAdapter will generate the Parameter collection for you. However, this is not what we want to demonstrate, is it? We will use the real programmer's way of creating a DataAdapter, by declaring it in code.

We will declare our DataAdapter as a module-level variable. That way we have access to it throughout our form. We also need a Connection object, so let's declare them now.

```
Private mCN As New SqlClient.SqlConnection()
Private mDA As New SqlClient.SqlDataAdapter()
```

I like to keep my variable names simple for these demos, and I'm sure you'll thank me for that. If this were a production application I would have named the objects a little more descriptively. In order to make the application work, we need one more object. We need to declare a DataSet object as well so we can display data in the grid.

```
Private mDS As New DataSet()
```

Initializing the DataAdapter

The next question is: Where do we initialize the objects? In VB 6 there would be no issue here. We would do it in the Form_Load event. In VB .NET, we also have a Load event. We could initialize the objects there. But the Load event is really there for backward compatibility. In a true object-oriented language, we would use the class constructor. To find the default constructor, expand the region titled Windows Form Designer generated code. Right at the beginning you will find `Sub New()`. This is the default constructor. Place the initialization code in the constructor, after the call to `InitializeComponent()`. When you are finished, the constructor should look like this: (Our code is in bold.)

```
Public Sub New()
    MyBase.New()

    'This call is required by the Windows Form Designer.
    InitializeComponent()

    'Add any initialization after the InitializeComponent() call
    Dim cmdSel As New SqlClient.SqlCommand()

Try
    mCN.ConnectionString =
"Server=em_server\vsdotnet;Database=Northwind;Integrated Security=SSPI"
    cmdSel.Connection = mCN
    cmdSel.CommandType = CommandType.Text
    cmdSel.CommandText = "select * from Customers"
    mDA.SelectCommand = cmdSel
Catch errobj As Exception
    MsgBox(errobj.Message)
End Try

End Sub
```

Let's go through it line by line.

The first line of code assigns the Connection String to the SqlConnection object. Note that the Connection String will vary depending on the name of your server or machine. We discussed the `ConnectionString` property values at length in the last chapter.

The next line assigns the Connection object to the `Connection` property of the SqlCommand object. We must create this object ourselves. It is declared at the beginning of our code block. We will describe all of the properties of the Command object later on in the chapter.

Next we assign the `CommandType` property of the Command object. There are three possible values for this property: `CommandType.Text`, `CommandType.StoredProcedure`, and `CommandType.TableDirect`. Since we will be using a SQL statement we are going to use `CommandType.Text`. This property helps the Command object parse the value in the `CommandText` property. Next we assign the SQL statement to the `CommandText` property. Finally, we assign the Command object to the DataAdapter's `SelectCommand` property. That's it for a simple configuration. We have not yet created commands for updating the database. We will do this in the next phase of the demonstration. As we shall see, there are two ways to do this. Of course we can create then manually as we did with the `SelectCommand`. There is also a way to have the DataAdapter create them automatically using a helper class.

That's it as far as initialization goes at this stage. We'll look into some more complex scenarios later on.

Making it Work

To get the program working, we need to do one more thing. We need to program the click event for the Refresh button to load and display the data. To do this, place this code in the click event:

```
   Private Sub btnRefresh_Click(ByVal sender As System.Object, ByVal e
As System.EventArgs) Handles btnRefresh.Click
        Try
            mDA.Fill(mDS)
            DataGrid1.DataSource = mDS.Tables(0)
        Catch errobj As Exception
            MsgBox(errobj.Message)
        End Try
   End Sub
```

In this code snippet the DataAdapter fills the DataSet with the output of the `Select` statement. Then the data grid's `Data Source` property is set to the first member of the DataSet's Tables collection. Now let's run the project. If all was done correctly, you should see the screen in Figure 6.19 when you click the Refresh button.

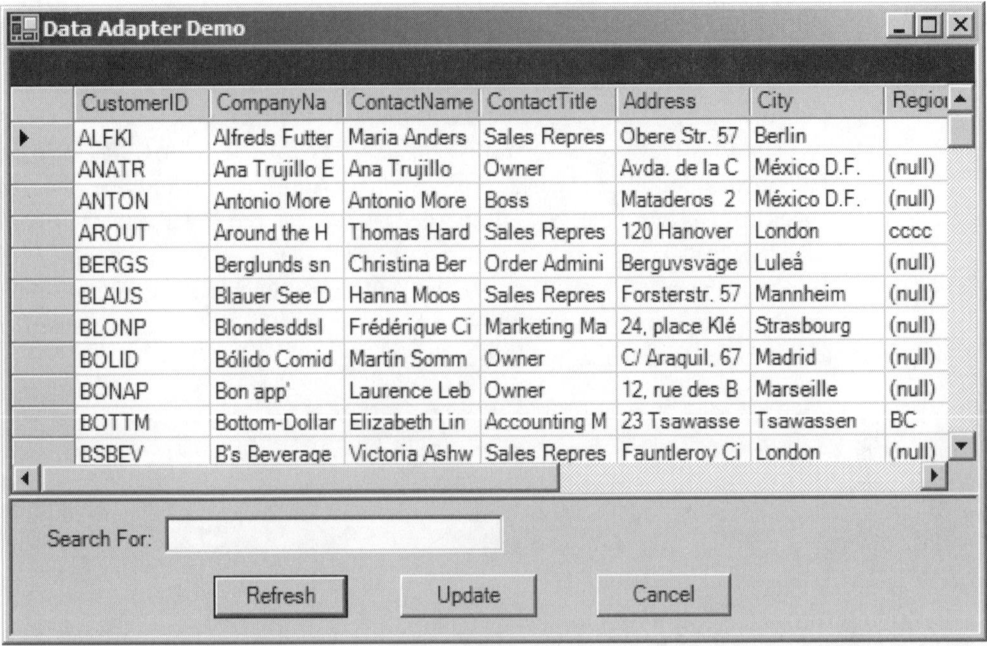

FIGURE 6.19 Data Adapter Demo with data loaded.

Updating the Database

Up to now we have only loaded data into the grid. The next step is to add code that will enable us to update the data back to the database. As we said before there are two ways to do this: by typing an SQL statement into the Command object or by using the `CommandBuilder` class to generate the SQL statements. The latter will also generate the Parameter collections for those SQL statements. Unless you really need to generate your own SQL statements the preferred method would be use the `CommandBuilder` object. This way all the parameters required for optimistic concurrency will be generated for you. Creating the SQL statements manually requires that you be aware of whether the parameters to create are current values or original values. When you use the `CommandBuilder`, the object automatically determines this for you.

Displaying the Generated SQL

Now let's modify our user interface to display the generated SQL statements for us. To do this we will add another panel and four text boxes. When we are done our interface will look like the example in Figure 6.20.

The four text boxes should be named TextBox1, TextBox2, TextBox3, and TextBox4. The check box labeled AutoGen should be named CheckBox1. This check box, if checked, will cause the DataAdapter to generate the `Insert`, `Update`, and `Delete` statements. If it is left unchecked, the DataAdapter will not generate the statements automatically but we may type them into the text boxes. We will now modify the code to cause the DataAdapter to generate the SQL statements.

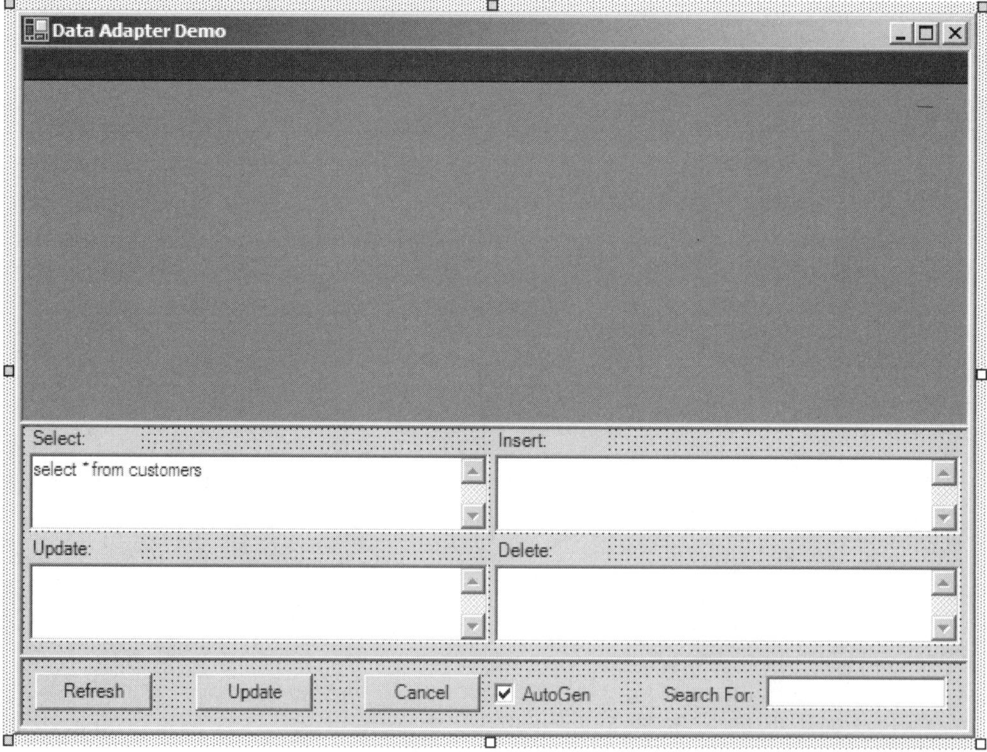

FIGURE 6.20 Modified Data Adapter Demo with SQL display.

Adding the CommandBuilder

The first thing we must do is add an SQL `CommandBuilder` object to the form. We will do this at the same place we declared the DataAdapter and DataSet object. We must also remove the SQL statement we assigned to the SQL command object of the DataAdapter in the initialization code. First let's get the declaration for the SQL `CommandBuilder`. Find the point in the code where the DataAdapter and DataSet are declared. Add the following line immediately after those declarations:

```
Private mDB As New SqlClient.SqlCommandBuilder()
```

This will declare our `CommandBuilder` object. Next expand the hidden region of Windows generated code and remove the assignment of the SQL statement to the Select Command's `CommandText` property. When you were finished the constructor should look like this:

```
Public Sub New()
    MyBase.New()

    'This call is required by the Windows Form Designer.
    InitializeComponent()

    'Add any initialization after the InitializeComponent() call
    Dim cmdSel As New SqlClient.SqlCommand()

    Try
        mCN.ConnectionString =
"Server=em_server\vsdotnet;Database=Northwind;Integrated Security=SSPI"
        cmdSel.Connection = mCN
        cmdSel.CommandType = CommandType.Text
        mDA.SelectCommand = cmdSel
    Catch errobj As Exception
        MsgBox(errobj.Message)
    End Try

End Sub
```

Generating the SQL

Next we will modify the Refresh button's click event procedure to generate the SQL statements programmatically. The way the `CommandBuilder` works is that you assign it the DataAdapter as a property and then you retrieve the three Update command objects (`Insert`, `Update`, `Delete`) via three methods called `GetInsertCommand`, `GetUpdateCommand`, and `GetDeleteCommand`. I believe it creates the update SQL statements at the moment you assign the Data Adapter to the `CommandBuilder` object. This assumes of course that you have already assigned the `Select` command a valid `Select` statement. Now let's take a look at the modified click event of the Refresh button:

```
    Private Sub btnRefresh_Click(ByVal sender As System.Object, _
ByVal e As System.EventArgs) Handles btnRefresh.Click
        Try
            If TextBox1.Text = "" Then Exit Sub
            If mDS.Tables.Count > 0 Then
                mDS.Clear()
            End If
            mDA.SelectCommand.CommandText = TextBox1.Text
            If CheckBox1.Checked Then
                mDB.DataAdapter = mDA
                mDA.UpdateCommand = mDB.GetUpdateCommand()
                mDA.InsertCommand = mDB.GetInsertCommand()
                mDA.DeleteCommand = mDB.GetDeleteCommand()
                TextBox1.Text = mDA.SelectCommand.CommandText
                TextBox2.Text = mDA.UpdateCommand.CommandText
                TextBox3.Text = mDA.InsertCommand.CommandText
                TextBox4.Text = mDA.DeleteCommand.CommandText
            End If
            mDA.Fill(mDS)
            DataGrid1.DataSource = mDS.Tables(0)
        Catch errobj As Exception
            MsgBox(errobj.Message)
        End Try
    End Sub
```

As you can see the code got considerably more complicated. However, even though it is more complicated than before it is still quite a bit simpler than creating the commands manually by parsing the `Select` statement. Essentially the `CommandBuilder` creates the commands and we just have to retrieve them into the appropriate places in the DataAdapter. We included the four text boxes so we can see the kinds of commands it creates. Otherwise we would have to break the code and examine the commands in the immediate window. This makes it a little easier for us.

When we run the project we'll see the SQL statements appear in the four text boxes. This will happen when we click the Refresh button. Let's run it now. If you did everything correctly your screen should look like Figure 6.21 after clicking the Refresh button. If it doesn't work, remember to check your `ConnectionString` property of the SqlConnection object. Make sure you have the correct user name and password and you are pointing to the correct server.

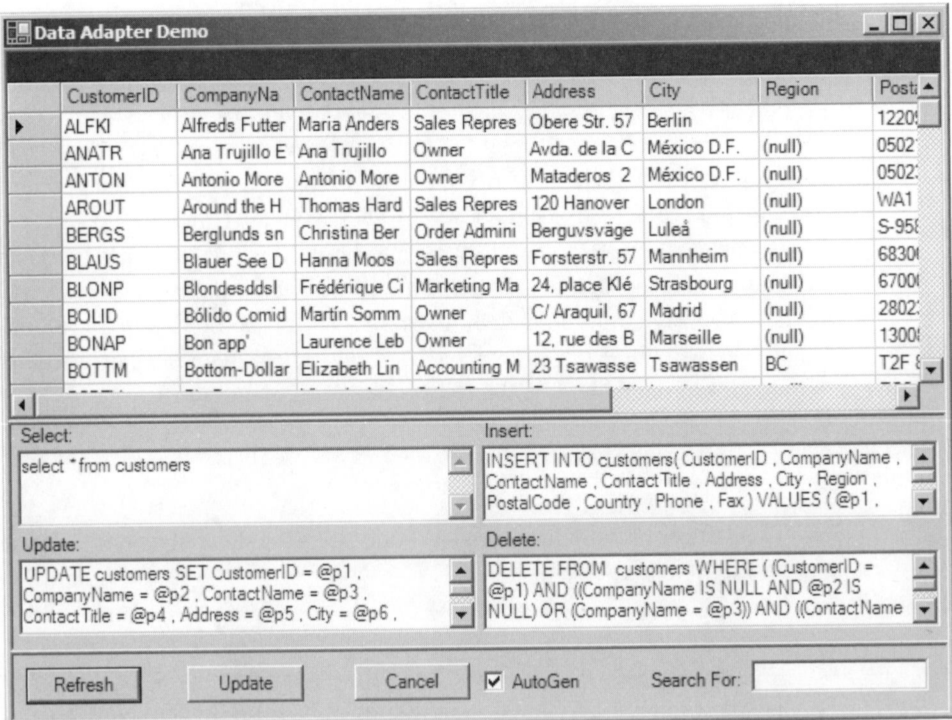

FIGURE 6.21 The modified screen after the refresh button is clicked.

To see the complete SQL command scroll down using the scroll bars. Notice that the parameters have generic names P1, P2, and so forth. One would think it could derive the parameter names from the field names but it doesn't. If we make a change in the grid, say to the Contact title, and then click the Update button we will see that the data gets changed in the database. Using this method the programmer does not have to concern himself with the details of creating the SQL statements. Also he does not have to worry about assigning parameters values during updates. The Data Adapter will handle this for you. If you choose to create your `Update` statements manually, you will have to manually assign each parameter to its value, since the Data Adapter has no way of associating the parameter values with the field values. However, if you set up your parameter lists properly you can control the association so that the Data Adapter knows which parameters belong to which columns.

Programmatically Configuring the DataAdapter Using Your Own Code

To prepare for this project, create a Windows Forms project and call it ADOBook06-03. You can copy the form file from the previous project into this project. We will then modify the code in the new project. You can also download the code from the book's web site if you don't want to type it in.

In our next exercise we will look into how to manually set up the Data Adapter so that the `Update` statement will work automatically and we will not have to assign our parameters manually. In order to do this in a less confusing way we will use a simpler `Select` statement that does not select all of the fields in the table. Use the following `Select` statement:

```
Select CustomerID, CompanyName, ContactName, ContactTitle  from
customers Where CompanyName Like @CoName + '%'
```

This statement will allow us to test our `Update` statements and also use a parameter to retrieve data.

Using Dynamic Properties

Before we continue, let's look at an interesting feature of the .NET framework. The feature is called dynamic properties. It is similar to the use of initialization files in previous versions of Visual Basic. Instead of the initialization file format it uses an XML format. The data is stored in this file when you set the property in the Property window. There are also programmatic ways to retrieve the data. The method is similar to the `GetPrivateProfileString` Windows API calls but much simpler to use.

The name of the file, app.config, is stored in the same folder as the program by default. We can set any property of any control to be a dynamic property. You can do this by using the dynamic properties entry in the Property window. To make a property dynamic, first select the Control on the form designer. Then scroll the dynamic properties entry into view in the Property window and click the plus box. An ellipsis button will appear next to `Advanced` property. Clicking the ellipsis button opens the Dynamic Properties dialog box. It appears as in Figure 6.22.

When we start entering code for the program we will see how to retrieve the property values from the app.config file. This will save us a lot of time reentering SQL statements. Now let's get back to the task at hand. We'll have

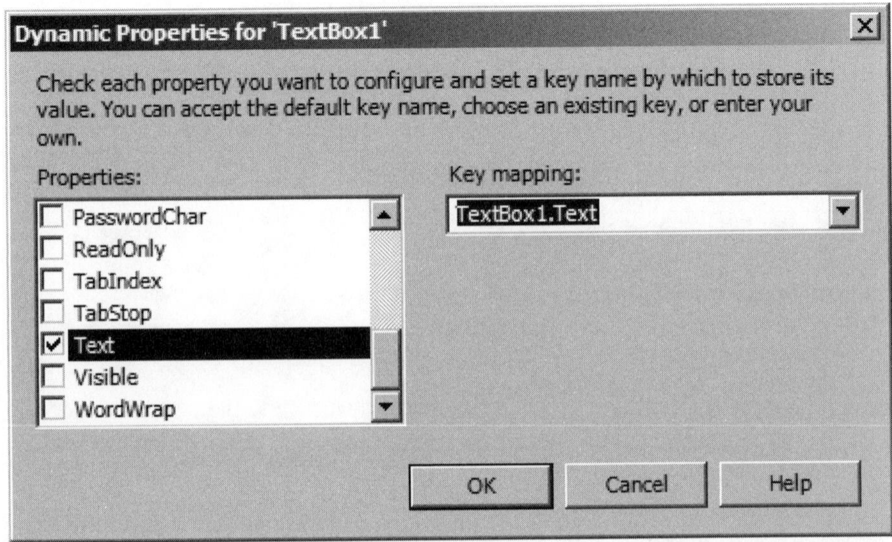

FIGURE 6.22 The Dynamic Properties dialog.

to make changes to the Refresh button's click event. We will show you the changes now and explain them line by line later. Here is the new Refresh button's click event:

```
Private Sub btnRefresh_Click(ByVal sender As System.Object, _
ByVal e As System.EventArgs) Handles btnRefresh.Click
  Dim cmdSelect As New SqlClient.SqlCommand()
  Dim cmdInsert As New SqlClient.SqlCommand()
  Dim cmdUpdate As New SqlClient.SqlCommand()
  Dim cmdDelete As New SqlClient.SqlCommand()
  Dim prm As New SqlClient.SqlParameter()

  Try
    If TextBox1.Text = "" Then Exit Sub
    If mDS.Tables.Count > 0 Then
      mDS.Clear()
    End If
    cmdSelect.Connection = mCN
    mDA.SelectCommand = cmdSelect
    mDA.SelectCommand.CommandText = TextBox1.Text
    prm.ParameterName = "@CoName"
    prm.DbType = DbType.String
    mDA.SelectCommand.Parameters.Add(prm)
    mDA.SelectCommand.Parameters("@CoName").Value = txtSearch.Text
    mDA.InsertCommand = cmdInsert
```

```
        mDA.UpdateCommand = cmdUpdate
        mDA.DeleteCommand = cmdDelete
        mDA.SelectCommand.CommandText = TextBox1.Text
        mDA.InsertCommand.CommandText = TextBox2.Text
        mDA.UpdateCommand.CommandText = TextBox3.Text
        mDA.DeleteCommand.CommandText = TextBox4.Text
        mDA.Fill(mDS)
        DataGrid1.DataSource = mDS.Tables(0)
    Catch errobj As Exception
        MsgBox(errobj.Message)
    End Try
End Sub
```

The code is not yet complete. We still have to add the code to create the `Insert`, `Update`, and `Delete` statements. The code as it stands will just get the data from the database and load it into the grid. We did this with a couple of lines of code when we configured the DataAdapter using the wizard. Now it will take considerably more lines because we have to do everything ourselves. The first thing we have to do is manually create the Command objects to load into the four Command properties of the DataAdapter. So we create and call them `cmdSelect`, `cmdInsert`, `cmdUpdate`, and `cmdDelete`. Further down in the code we assign these objects to the `Command` properties of the DataAdapter.

Reading Data

Let's first look at the code to read the data from the database. The first thing we have to do is assign the Select command a Connection object. Next we assign the Select command `CommandText` property to the value of TextBox1. Next we assign the Command object to the DataAdapter's `SelectCommand` property.

Next we must manually create a parameter to pass into the SQL statement. We declared a Parameter object in the declaration section of the procedure. Now we must assign the name of the parameter to the `ParameterName` property of the Parameter object. Then we must add the parameter to the Select command's Parameters collection. The last thing we have to do with the parameter is assign it the value of the text box that contains the search field. The next seven lines will be made clear when we add the code to create the `Update` statements. Right now the project is ready to run. So let's run it and see the results. Your screen should look like Figure 6.23.

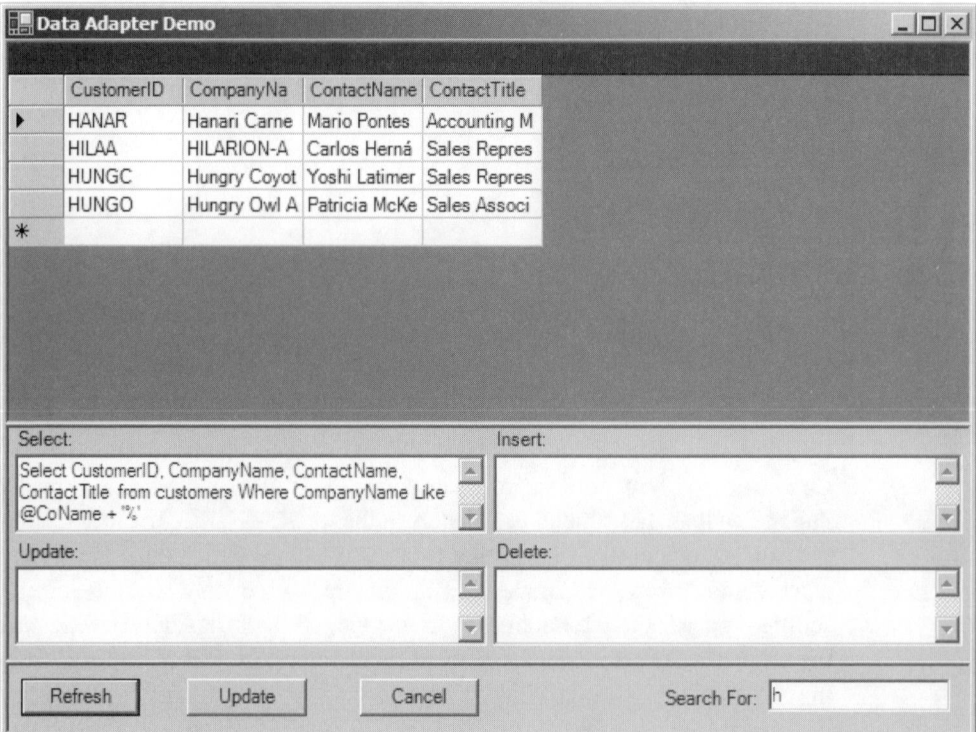

FIGURE 6.23 The demo screen with a custom select statement.

Notice that we searched for *H* which means to give me all records that have a company name starting with *H*. By default searches are case insensitive. Creating the `Select` statement is the easy part. The other three statements are a little more difficult.

Creating the `Update` Statement

The most difficult statement is `Update`. In order for the DataAdapter to work properly, the Parameter collection must be created carefully. We must be sure to create two parameters for each column in the `Select` statement so that we can employ optimistic concurrency. We can create the `Update` statements manually and create our own parameter list, or we can create a procedure to parse the `Select` statement and create the parameters for us. First let's do it by manually creating our own parameter collection. Before we can create a parameter list we must create the update SQL statements:

```
Update   Customers
Set      CustomerID = @CustomerID,
CompanyName = @CompanyName,
ContactName = @ContactName,
ContactTitle = @ContactTitle
Where    CustomerID = @Original_CustomerID And
         CompanyName = @Original_CompanyName And
         ContactName = @Original_ContactName And
         ContactTitle = @Original_ContactTitle
```

The statement itself is pretty simple. The `Set` clause uses the first set of parameters to assign the new values to the columns. In the `where` clause we use the other set of parameters (prefixed by `Original_`). These parameters will be used to pass the original unchanged values of the columns into the `Update` statement. If you look back at the `Update` statement created by the `CommandBuilder` object, you will notice that it does a lot of checking for nulls as well as the value in parameters in the `where` clause. In order to simplify the statement we will not check for the nulls, we will assume the parameters are not `Null`. This makes it a little easier to see what we're doing. By setting properties in the Parameter objects we tell the DataAdapter which are the original values and which are the current values. Note that just by declaring the parameters in the SQL statement does not automatically create the Parameter collection. We still must do this manually in code. For now we will create the parameters using hard-coded statements. In a bit, we will create a procedure to parse the update SQL statement and create a parameter list for it. Let's look at the code to create the Parameter collection for our SQL statement.

Since we are creating the Command object ourselves, we will need a variable to hold the Command object while we configure it. We will also need a variable to hold a Parameter object while we configure it. Unlike in the last demonstration, we will not declare the variables as `New`. This is because we will need to create multiple instances of each object. Therefore we need to create the objects as we need them. Also, since the code to initialize the DataAdapter is now considerably more complicated, let's move the code into its own separate subprocedure. The next section contains the new procedure. We will go through it line by line so you understand what it is doing. The procedure appears to be quite long but it repeats itself for each Parameter object, so the code is really not as complicated as it looks.

To backtrack, here is the SQL statement for the `Insert`.

```
Insert Into Customers (CustomerID, CompanyName, ContactName,
ContactTitle)
Values (@CustomerID, @CompanyName, @ContactName, @ContactTitle)
```

And here is the code for the `Delete` statement.

```
Delete From Customers
Where CustomerID = @Original_CustomerID And CompanyName =
@Original_CompanyName And ContactName = @Original_ContactName And
ContactTitle = @Original_ContactTitle
```

The Code to Create the Commands

These SQL statements should be placed in TextBox3 and TextBox4 respectively. Since we have created dynamic properties from the `Text` property, the SQL statements will be saved in the app.config file.

```
Private Sub InitDA()
    Dim cmd As SqlClient.SqlCommand
    Dim prm As SqlClient.SqlParameter

    Try
      mCN.ConnectionString =
"Server=em_server\vsdotnet;Database=Northwind;Integrated Security=SSPI"
      cmd = New SqlClient.SqlCommand()
      cmd.Connection = mCN
      cmd.CommandText = TextBox1.Text
      mDA.SelectCommand = cmd
      prm = New SqlClient.SqlParameter()
      prm.ParameterName = "@CoName"
      prm.DbType = DbType.String
      mDA.SelectCommand.Parameters.Add(prm)

      ' UPDATE COMMAND
      ' First assign the SQL statement
      cmd = New SqlClient.SqlCommand()
      cmd.CommandText = TextBox2.Text
      cmd.Connection = mCN

      ' Customer ID Parameter
      prm = New SqlClient.SqlParameter()
      prm.ParameterName = "@CustomerID"
      prm.DbType = DbType.String
      prm.SourceVersion = DataRowVersion.Current
      prm.SourceColumn = "CustomerID"
      cmd.Parameters.Add(prm)

      ' Company Name Parameter
      prm = New SqlClient.SqlParameter()
      prm.ParameterName = "@CompanyName"
```

```
prm.DbType = DbType.String
prm.SourceVersion = DataRowVersion.Current
prm.SourceColumn = "CompanyName"
cmd.Parameters.Add(prm)

' Contact Name Parameter
prm = New SqlClient.SqlParameter()
prm.ParameterName = "@ContactName"
prm.DbType = DbType.String
prm.SourceVersion = DataRowVersion.Current
prm.SourceColumn = "ContactName"
cmd.Parameters.Add(prm)

' Contact Title Parameter
prm = New SqlClient.SqlParameter()
prm.ParameterName = "@ContactTitle"
prm.DbType = DbType.String
prm.SourceVersion = DataRowVersion.Current
prm.SourceColumn = "ContactTitle"
cmd.Parameters.Add(prm)

' Customer ID Parameter
prm = New SqlClient.SqlParameter()
prm.ParameterName = "@Original_CustomerID"
prm.DbType = DbType.String
prm.SourceVersion = DataRowVersion.Original
prm.SourceColumn = "CustomerID"
cmd.Parameters.Add(prm)

' Company Name Parameter
prm = New SqlClient.SqlParameter()
prm.ParameterName = "@Original_CompanyName"
prm.DbType = DbType.String
prm.SourceVersion = DataRowVersion.Original
prm.SourceColumn = "CompanyName"
cmd.Parameters.Add(prm)

' Contact Name Parameter
prm = New SqlClient.SqlParameter()
prm.ParameterName = "@Original_ContactName"
prm.DbType = DbType.String
prm.SourceVersion = DataRowVersion.Original
prm.SourceColumn = "ContactName"
cmd.Parameters.Add(prm)
```

```
' Contact Title Parameter
prm = New SqlClient.SqlParameter()
prm.ParameterName = "@Original_ContactTitle"
prm.DbType = DbType.String
prm.SourceVersion = DataRowVersion.Original
prm.SourceColumn = "ContactTitle"
cmd.Parameters.Add(prm)

mDA.UpdateCommand = cmd

' INSERT COMMAND
' First assign the SQL statement
cmd = New SqlClient.SqlCommand()
cmd.CommandText = TextBox3.Text
cmd.Connection = mCN

' Customer ID Parameter
prm = New SqlClient.SqlParameter()
prm.ParameterName = "@CustomerID"
prm.DbType = DbType.String
prm.SourceVersion = DataRowVersion.Current
prm.SourceColumn = "CustomerID"
cmd.Parameters.Add(prm)

' Company Name Parameter
prm = New SqlClient.SqlParameter()
prm.ParameterName = "@CompanyName"
prm.DbType = DbType.String
prm.SourceVersion = DataRowVersion.Current
prm.SourceColumn = "CompanyName"
cmd.Parameters.Add(prm)

' Contact Name Parameter
prm = New SqlClient.SqlParameter()
prm.ParameterName = "@ContactName"
prm.DbType = DbType.String
prm.SourceVersion = DataRowVersion.Current
prm.SourceColumn = "ContactName"
cmd.Parameters.Add(prm)

' Contact Title Parameter
prm = New SqlClient.SqlParameter()
prm.ParameterName = "@ContactTitle"
prm.DbType = DbType.String
prm.SourceVersion = DataRowVersion.Current
prm.SourceColumn = "ContactTitle"
cmd.Parameters.Add(prm)
```

```
        mDA.InsertCommand = cmd

        ' DELETE COMMAND
        ' First assign the SQL statement
        cmd = New SqlClient.SqlCommand()
        cmd.CommandText = TextBox4.Text
        cmd.Connection = mCN

        ' Customer ID Parameter
        prm = New SqlClient.SqlParameter()
        prm.ParameterName = "@Original_CustomerID"
        prm.DbType = DbType.String
        prm.SourceVersion = DataRowVersion.Original
        prm.SourceColumn = "CustomerID"
        cmd.Parameters.Add(prm)

        ' Company Name Parameter
        prm = New SqlClient.SqlParameter()
        prm.ParameterName = "@Original_CompanyName"
        prm.DbType = DbType.String
        prm.SourceVersion = DataRowVersion.Original
        prm.SourceColumn = "CompanyName"
        cmd.Parameters.Add(prm)

        ' Contact Name Parameter
        prm = New SqlClient.SqlParameter()
        prm.ParameterName = "@Original_ContactName"
        prm.DbType = DbType.String
        prm.SourceVersion = DataRowVersion.Original
        prm.SourceColumn = "ContactName"
        cmd.Parameters.Add(prm)

        ' Contact Title Parameter
        prm = New SqlClient.SqlParameter()
        prm.ParameterName = "@Original_ContactTitle"
        prm.DbType = DbType.String
        prm.SourceVersion = DataRowVersion.Original
        prm.SourceColumn = "ContactTitle"
        cmd.Parameters.Add(prm)

        mDA.DeleteCommand = cmd
      Catch errobj As Exception
        MsgBox(errobj.Message & vbCrLf & errobj.StackTrace)
      End Try
    End Sub
```

As you can see, there are basically two snippets of code in this procedure. One creates the Command object and the other creates each Parameter object. The Command object snippet is self-explanatory. A new instance of an SQL Command class is assigned to the `cmd` variable. Then we assign the Connection object to the Command object's `Connection` property. Lastly, we assign the `Text` property of the appropriate text box containing the SQL statement to the `CommandText` property of the Command object.

The parameter creation snippet is a little more involved but not that difficult to understand. First we create an instance of a Parameter object and assign it to the `prm` variable. Then we assign the name of the parameter to the Parameter object's `ParameterName` property. It is important to get the name of the parameter correct because this is how it associates the parameter to the parameter placeholder in the SQL statement. Then we assign the data type of parameter to the Parameter objects `DBType` property. All of our properties happen to be strings, but they could be any type in the DBType enumeration. Some types require additional properties to be set, such as the size, scale, and so forth. The `DBType` property returns a data type that is compatible across all the CLR languages (Visual Basic, C#). There is another enumeration, `SQLDBType`, which returns native SQL Server types. If you are an SQL guru, you may want to use these instead as they may be more familiar. The caveat is that now your code will be SQL Server specific. Next we must tell the Property object whether our property is an original value or a current value. This property is there primarily to support interaction with the DataSet. Original values are used in the `where` clauses. Current values are used to pass the new values in the data set that the user has changed. Otherwise there's no real difference between the two types of parameters. The `SourceColumn` property is used to associate the parameter with a column in the table. Again this is to support interaction with the DataSet.

The `Update` SQL statement uses both parameter types to support updating and optimistic concurrency. The `Insert` statement does not need original values since there are none. Therefore it only uses current values. The converse is true of the `Delete` statement. There are no current values, just original values.

Now that we've manually created our parameters the long way let's run the project to verify that it works. When we run the project, the screen should look like Figure 6.24 after we click the Refresh button.

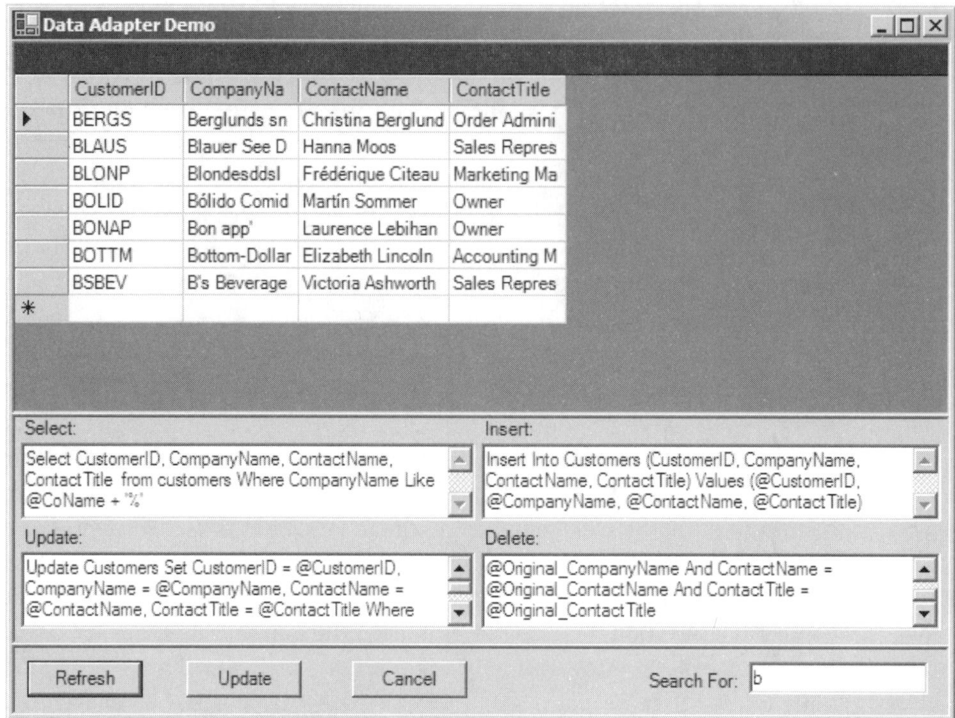

FIGURE 6.24 The demo with manually entered SQL statements.

To test the application, try changing one of the fields. Then click the Update button. Change the search for text box to another letter and click Refresh. Then change it back to *b* and click Refresh. Your change should have persisted. Now add a new row to the grid. Make sure the customer ID's unique and begins with B. Type anything else you want in the other four columns. Click the Update button. Now repeat the exercise, changing the search for text box to another letter. Click Refresh, then change it back, and click Refresh again. You should still see your new row. Now delete the row you just added by selecting the row and hitting the delete key. Click the Update button again. If you refresh the grid again your row should remain deleted.

PARSING YOUR SQL STATEMENT–A BETTER WAY

Now that we've seen the program work with manually creating the SQL statements let's look at a quick procedure to parse the SQL statement and create the parameters for us. Of course you could use the CommandBuilder object, but that would be too easy—we are programmers after all.

To prepare for this project, create a new Windows Forms project and call it ADOBook06-04. You can copy the form file from the previous project into this project. We will then modify the code in the new project. You can also download the code from the book's web site if you don't want to type it in.

As it turns out, SQL statements are well formed and have a very predictable pattern. This makes parsing them relatively easy. If you remember your computer science compiler course, you remember that parsing a string can be a complex process. First you have to tokenize it, converting the text into numerical values that can be used in a look-up table. Then there is usually some mapping of all identifiers to another table. From there on it gets even more complicated depending on whether you are building a compiler or an interpreter. Thankfully, SQL statements are considerably easier to parse. We are not dealing with a sequential set of instructions. The SQL statement is usually just one line. Our parser will be somewhat simplified. We do not have to parse the Select statement. We only have to parse the Update statements (Insert, Update, and Delete). We will use the following sequence of steps:

- Remove all white space from the string. This includes carriage return-line feed pairs, tabs, and multiple space characters. Multiple space characters will be replaced by a single space. Tabs will also be replaced by a single space.
- The string will then be converted to all lower case. This will avoid issues with case sensitivity.
- We will then determine whether we are dealing with an Insert, Update, or Delete statement. Each of these have different, but very predictable, formats.

The SQL Parser Code

Let's take a look at the code and see what it does. Again the code block is lengthy, but it is still worthwhile to look through.

```
    ' This procedure creates the parameters for a Data Adapter command
object.
    Private Sub CreateParameters(ByVal strSQLIn As String, ByRef cmd As
SqlClient.SqlCommand)
        Dim strClauses As String
        Dim strSetsList() As String
        Dim strWhereList() As String
        Dim strAssigns() As String
```

```
    Dim strWhere As String
    Dim strSets As String
    Dim strColList As String
    Dim strValList As String
    Dim strInsCols() As String
    Dim strInsVals() As String
    Dim i As Integer
    Dim prm As SqlClient.SqlParameter
    Dim strSQL As String

    Try
      ' If it's blank, skip the whole thing.
      If strSQLIn = "" Then Exit Sub
      ' Strips extra white space from string
      strSQL = StripWhite(strSQLIn)
      ' First we convert the SQL statement to lower case to eliminate
      ' casing issues.
      strSQL = strSQL.ToLower
      Select Case strSQL.Substring(0, 6)
        Case "update"
          strClauses = Split(strSQL, "set ")(1)
          strSets = Split(strClauses, "where ")(0)
          strSetsList = Split(strSets, ", ")
          For i = strSetsList.GetLowerBound(0) To
strSetsList.GetUpperBound(0)
            strAssigns = strSetsList(i).Split(" ")
            prm = New SqlClient.SqlParameter()
            prm.ParameterName = strAssigns(2).Trim
            prm.SourceVersion = DataRowVersion.Current
            prm.SourceColumn = strAssigns(0).Trim
            cmd.Parameters.Add(prm)
          Next
          strWhere = Split(strSQL, "where ")(1)
          strWhereList = Split(strWhere, " and ")
          For i = strWhereList.GetLowerBound(0) To
strWhereList.GetUpperBound(0)
            strAssigns = strWhereList(i).Split(" = ")
            prm = New SqlClient.SqlParameter()
            prm.ParameterName = strAssigns(2).Trim
            prm.SourceVersion = DataRowVersion.Original
            prm.SourceColumn = strAssigns(0).Trim
            cmd.Parameters.Add(prm)
          Next
        Case "insert"
          strColList = Split(strSQL, "(")(1)
          strColList = Split(strColList, ")")(0)
          strValList = Split(strSQL, "values (")(1)
```

```
          strValList = Split(strValList, ")")(0)
          strInsCols = Split(strColList, ", ")
          strInsVals = Split(strValList, ", ")
          For i = strInsCols.GetLowerBound(0) To
strInsCols.GetUpperBound(0)
            prm = New SqlClient.SqlParameter()
            prm.ParameterName = strInsVals(i).Trim
            prm.SourceVersion = DataRowVersion.Current
            prm.SourceColumn = strInsCols(i).Trim
            cmd.Parameters.Add(prm)
          Next
        Case "delete"
          strWhere = Split(strSQL, "where ")(1)
          strWhereList = Split(strWhere, " and ")
          For i = strWhereList.GetLowerBound(0) To
strWhereList.GetUpperBound(0)
            strAssigns = strWhereList(i).Split(" = ")
            prm = New SqlClient.SqlParameter()
            prm.ParameterName = strAssigns(2).Trim
            prm.SourceVersion = DataRowVersion.Original
            prm.SourceColumn = strAssigns(0).Trim
            cmd.Parameters.Add(prm)
          Next
      End Select
    Catch errobj As Exception
      MsgBox(errobj.Message & vbCrLf & errobj.StackTrace)
    End Try
  End Sub
```

In a normal parser, you would use two pointers to feed a text stream into the parser. Since our SQL commands are short, we will just loop through strings ignoring multiple spaces.

In this code example we first call `StripWhite` to strip the white space from the command. Then we check the first six characters of the string to see what we're dealing with. This makes it easier to work with. The `Select` … case block then processes the statements based on whether they are `Update`, `Insert`, or `Delete` statements. To parse the statements I use the Visual Basic Split function. Why not use the `Split` method of the String class? I did try this, but the delimiter in the `Split` method is limited to one character. The Split function, on the other hand, allows the delimiter to be a substring. I do not know why Microsoft did not bring the same functionality forward with the String class. For you .NET purists, this may seem like a throwback to VB 6. I am very pragmatic, I use what works best. Sometimes the older functions have better functionality than the new `Class` methods. When that is the case I will always use the older function.

StripWhite Function

Here is the function to strip white space from the file:

```
Private Function StripWhite(ByVal strIN As String) As String
  Dim i, j As Integer
  Dim strOut As String

  Try
    If strIN = "" Then Exit Function
    ' Strip out any embedded cr-lf's
    strIN = strIN.Replace(vbCrLf, " ")
    ' Strip out any embedded tabs
    strIN = strIN.Replace(vbTab, " ")
    Do Until i > strIN.Length - 1
      If strIN.Substring(i, 1) = " " Then
        strOut = strOut & " "
        j = i + 1
        Do Until j > strIN.Length - 1 Or strIN.Substring(j, 1) <> " "
          j += 1
        Loop
        i = j - 1
      Else
        strOut = strOut & strIN.Substring(i, 1)
      End If
      i += 1
    Loop
    Return strOut
  Catch errobj As Exception
    MsgBox(errobj.Message & vbCrLf & errobj.StackTrace)
  End Try
End Function
```

To test the application use the same procedure we used before. Load some data, make some changes, and update the database. Repeat this process for each of the `Insert`, `Update`, and `Delete` functions. Keep using the Refresh button to make sure your changes were properly updated in the database.

SUMMARY

In the end, it seems as if it's just easier to use the `CommandBuilder`. There may be cases where this is not possible. At any rate, I hope this exercise helps to show what goes on internally in the DataAdapter object. Perhaps you will find some of these procedures useful in your own applications. Feel free to use them but remember they will probably need to be tested more thoroughly than what I have done.

In the next chapter we will look at the DataSet in detail. Since the DataSet is really the heart of ADO .NET, we will spend a lot of time in this chapter.

CHAPTER 7

The ADO .NET DataSet

The ADO .NET DataSet is the soul of ADO .NET. At first glance, it may seem as though the DataSet fills the same position in ADO .NET as the RecordSet did in ADO. Although the two objects seem similar, the DataSet is an entirely different kind of object. It is designed to read, store, and process XML data. So then what exactly is XML? We've been using the term rather freely, but we have yet to really explain what it is. You do not have to know XML per se to use ADO .NET. However, at this point in our adventure it would be a good idea to look at XML and exactly what it is.

WHAT IS XML

XML is not really a technology; it is a standard like Hypertext Markup Language (HTML). Most of us are familiar with HTML by now. Its primary use is to tell a web browser how to format a page visually. It contains tags for changing fonts, placing pictures, changing paragraphs styles, and so forth.

XML, on the other hand, contains tags for defining and transferring data. It is less about the visual display and more about describing data. The ability for XML to be extended by the users without prior approval of a standards body is what makes XML unique over HTML. In order to change HTML you must submit your request to the standards body (W3C) and wait for approval. XML's ability to extend itself is built into its standard. Industries can define their own tags and properties that will enable standardized data formatting within their area. Just as HTML has cascading style sheets, XML has XSL, or Extensible Stylesheet Language. Since we are working specifically with

DataSets we will also need to understand a little bit of the XML Schema Definition (XSD).

We will not attempt a full discourse on XML here. We will go over the basics as it pertains to ADO .NET. Essentially this involves understanding the XSD file and the XML file. The two files ending in the respective extensions (.xsd and .xml) go together. The XSD file describes the data in the XML file. The XSD file contains metadata, which is data that describes other data. When you generate a DataSet using the wizard or create it manually by entering your schema information through the Property window, what you're actually generating is an XSD file. The following is a sample XSD file for the Customers table in the Northwind database:

```
<?xml version="1.0" standalone="yes"?>
<xs:schema id="DataSet1" targetNamespace="http://www.tempuri.org/
DataSet1.xsd" xmlns:mstns="http://www.tempuri.org/DataSet1.xsd"
xmlns="http://www.tempuri.org/DataSet1.xsd" xmlns:xs="http://
www.w3.org/2001/XMLSchema" xmlns:msdata="urn:schemas-microsoft-com:xml-
msdata" attributeFormDefault="qualified" elementFormDefa_u108
?t="qualified">
  <xs:element name="DataSet1" msdata:IsDataSet="True">
    <xs:complexType>
      <xs:choice maxOccurs="unbounded">
        <xs:element name="Customers">
          <xs:complexType>
            <xs:sequence>
            _u32 ?<xs:element name="CustomerID" type="xs:string" />
            _u32 ?<xs:element name="CompanyName" type="xs:string" />
            _u32 ?<xs:element name="ContactName" type="xs:string"
minOccurs="0" />
            _u32 ?<xs:element name="ContactTitle" type="xs:string"
minOccurs="0" />
            _u32 ?<xs:element name="Address" type="xs:string"
minOccurs="0" />
           _u32 ?<xs:element name="City" type="xs:string" minOccurs="0"
/>
            _u32 ?<xs:element name="Region" type="xs:string"
minOccurs="0" />
            _u32 ?<xs:element name="PostalCode" type="xs:string"
minOccurs="0" />
            _u32 ?<xs:element name="Country" type="xs:string"
minOccurs="0" />
            _u32 ?<xs:element name="Phone" type="xs:string"
minOccurs="0" />
           _u32 ?<xs:element name="Fax" type="xs:string" minOccurs="0"
/>
```

```
          </xs:sequence>
        </xs:complexType>
      </xs:element>
    </xs:choice>
  </xs:complexType>
  <xs:unique name="Constraint1" msdata:PrimaryKey="True">
    <xs:selector xpath=".//mstns:Customers" />
    <xs:field xpath="mstns:CustomerID" />
  </xs:unique>
 </xs:element>
</xs:schema>
```

This sample is from a demo application which we will create shortly. Only one line of code in the program was required to create this file. As you can see, the file consists of tags and end tags similar to HTML. There are headers, elements, and attributes just like in HTML. The difference is the tags describe data as opposed to describing a visual layout. This file, the XML schema, only describes the data; it does not contain the data. The XML file that goes along with it contains the data. Each element in the XSD file describes the data block in the XML file. For example, in the XSD file you see CustomerID described as a String type, and when you look in the XML file you will see a corresponding tag called CustomerID followed by the data. Let's look at the first few lines of the XML file and you will see what we mean.

```
<?xml version="1.0" standalone="yes" ?>
- <DataSet1 xmlns="http://www.tempuri.org/DataSet1.xsd">
- <Customers>
  <CustomerID>ALFKI</CustomerID>
  <CompanyName>Alfreds Futterkiste</CompanyName>
  <ContactName>Maria Anders</ContactName>
  <ContactTitle>Sales Representative</ContactTitle>
  <Address>Obere Str. 57</Address>
  <City>Berlin</City>
  <Region />
  <PostalCode>12209</PostalCode>
  <Country>Germany</Country>
  <Phone>030-0074321</Phone>
  <Fax>030-0076545</Fax>
  </Customers>
- <Customers>
  <CustomerID>ANATR</CustomerID>
  <CompanyName>Ana Trujillo Emparedados y helados</CompanyName>
  <ContactName>Ana Trujillo</ContactName>
  <ContactTitle>Owner</ContactTitle>
```

```
<Address>Avda. de la Constitución 2222</Address>
<City>México D.F.</City>
<PostalCode>05021</PostalCode>
<Country>Mexico</Country>
<Phone>(5) 555-4729</Phone>
<Fax>(5) 555-3745</Fax>
</Customers>

     - <Customers>
```

Notice how the XML file makes no attempt to describe the data within it. That is the job of the XSD file. The URL in the second line of the XML file points to the XSD file that contains the schema definition. If that file cannot be found, the system will not be able to parse the XML file properly. The good thing is the file does not have to be on your own system. Since it is a URL it can be on any system reachable over the Internet. This is a big advantage. By keeping the XSD files in a central repository anyone with a network connection to the repository can parse the XML file. The whole XML architecture depends on this capability. If we had to distribute XSD files to everyone who needs them we would not have gained anything over previous technologies.

XSL is to XML what cascading style sheets are to HTML. XSL is generally applied to XML to format the output so that it is understandable to an end user. For the purposes of ADO .NET, we will not be using XSL directly too much. For ADO .NET of interest are the XML file and the XSD file. If you want to know more about XSL there are numerous in-depth books on this subject.

When looking at the XSD file the two main things we're concerned about are elements and attributes. If you look back at the sample XSD file, you'll see that there are lots of tag types. The element tag and its attributes are the primary structure we need to look at. You can see that the element tag has as attributes the name and the data type. This is not the best example because all the data types are strings. How does it know what data types are allowed? Look at the second line of the file. There are a number of arcane tags pointing to URLs. Scroll to the right and find this tag: `xmlns:xs`. Notice that it points to the URL of the W3C. The next attribute defines the name of the document that defines the standard for the DataSet: `xmlns:msdata="urn:schemas-microsoft-com:xml-msdata`. This is a very exciting technology because it allows us to centrally define new extensions (thereby the prefix extensible) to the language for our own purposes. We are not limited to the structure defined by someone else. As long as your customer, your client, or whoever can find the XSD document on the

Web, he or she can understand any file you send. It doesn't even have to be a Windows system, it could be Linux or UNIX. Contrast this with the "old days" when you would have to send arcane and lengthy specifications to whomever you were going to send your data. It was then up to their programmers to write some kind of conversion program to transform it into the format they would need.

There are hundreds, perhaps thousands, of XSD specifications on the Web. Fortunately for us we are only interested in the one that involves DataSets. I hope this look at XML in general took some of the mystery out of the technological mumbo jumbo.

AN OVERVIEW OF THE DATASET

Now let's look at the DataSet class. As we've said, the DataSet class is primarily used to read store and write XML data. It cannot access the database directly. In the previous chapter we examined the DataAdapter and showed how it is used to feed data into the DataSet. We did this from the perspective of the DataAdapter. Now we will do it from the perspective of the DataSet.

We said earlier that you do not have to know anything about XML to use the DataSet, but it does help. If we do nothing more than use the DataSet programmatically as an in-memory data cache for database tables we'll never have to touch XML again. But this is only part of the power of the DataSet. If we want to use the full power of the DataSet we must also learn how to read and write XML directly without using a database. The beauty of this is that even to do this you really do not need to know all the XML tags and details.

The DataSet class is primarily a collection of DataTable objects. It also contains a Relations collection. The DataTable objects contain the definition of the data and the data itself. The DataTable is similar to a table in SQL Server database. It contains rows, columns, and constraints. Instead of using native database data types for the columns, it uses the standardized XSD document data types defined by Microsoft. This way we do not have to be concerned about whether we are using Oracle, SQL Server, Access, or some other database. Once the data is stored in the DataSet all of the data types are standardized. This makes writing one single code base for many different database back ends much easier. All you need is a different interface layer for each database feeding a common DataSet.

The DataTable

As we said the DataTable is a collection of rows and columns similar to a database table. The DataTable itself is a collection of collections. There is a Rows collection and the Columns collection. The Columns collection corresponds to the XSD document and contains metadata describing the table. The Rows collection corresponds to the XML document and contains the actual data. But take a look at how the DataTable is represented visually by the XML editor (Figure 7.1).

Figure 7.2 shows how this same data looks when viewed through the DataSet Properties page.

The Properties page displays the same view of the data without the XML context. You can edit the data only through the XML view because this is a typed DataSet. If it weren't, you could edit the metadata through the Properties page as well. We will explain the difference between a typed and untyped DataSet a little later. Right now we're dealing with a typed DataSet. The short explanation is that the DataSet was subclassed when we declared it through the wizard. This will be covered in detail later in the chapter.

To begin our demonstration let's create a new Windows Form project. Name it ADOBook07-01. Drag and drop the DataAdapter onto the form.

E	Customers	(Customers)
E	CustomerID	string
E	CompanyName	string
E	ContactName	string
E	ContactTitle	string
E	Address	string
E	City	string
E	Region	string
E	PostalCode	string
E	Country	string
E	Phone	string
E	Fax	string

FIGURE 7.1 The XML editor showing the DataTable.

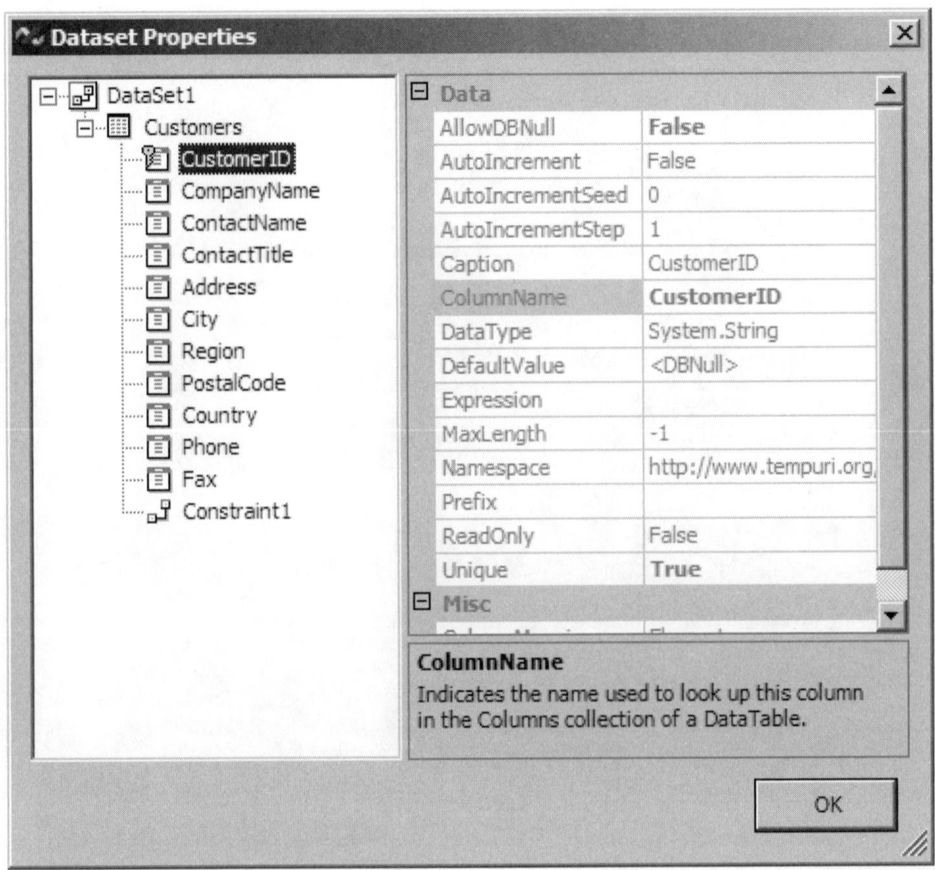

FIGURE 7.2 The DataTable viewed via the Properties page.

When the wizard starts, select the Northwind database. In the SQL Builder select the Customers table. You know how this works, so finish the builder. Next, right-click on the DataAdapter and select Generate DataSet. You should see the dialog box in Figure 7.3.

Clicking the OK button generates a typed DataSet with the Customers table already created. It will also add the DataSet to the designer. That's about as easy as it gets with DataSets. What this did was use the information in the DataAdapter to create an inherited class named DataSet1. Then the wizard created an instance of a DataSet class called DataSet11 of type DataSet1. I know it sounds confusing but I will clear it up later. You can use this wizard over and over to make changes to existing DataSets by adding new tables from new DataAdapters.

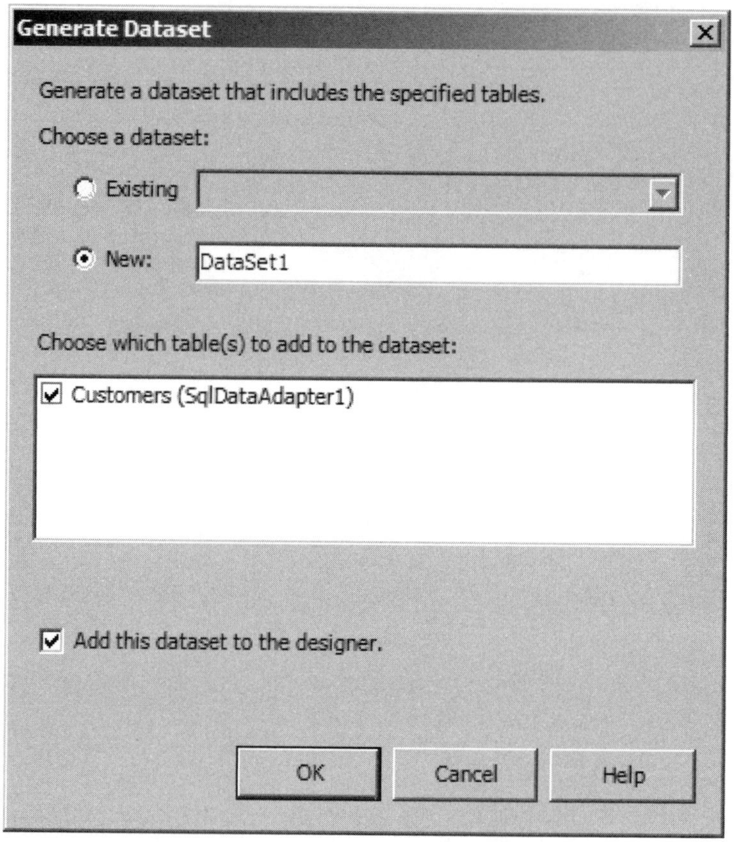

FIGURE 7.3 The Generate DataSet dialog.

TYPED AND UNTYPED DATASETS

As promised, we will explain the difference between typed and untyped DataSets. Another way of saying typed and untyped is to say strongly typed and weakly typed, terminology I prefer because it more aptly describes what is going on. The terms are used interchangeably in Microsoft documentation.

Basically:

- Typed (strongly typed) means the programming language strictly enforces data types. Visual Basic is an example of a strongly typed language.
- Untyped (weakly typed) means you can assign any variable to any other variable. C is an example of a weakly typed language.

In C you can pretty much assign any variable to any other variable without the compiler complaining, no matter the data types of the variables.

For example, C does not complain if you assign a char to an int. Visual Basic normally requires that the data types be compatible when they are assigned. If you try to assign the string variable to a numeric variable the compiler will usually complain. However, Visual Basic is normally not strictly typed. Strict typing means that you can only assign the string to a string and a numeric to another numeric of equal or greater scale. In Visual Basic you can turn on strict typing with an `Option` statement.

When we talk about a strongly typed DataSet, we are talking about something a little different. A strongly typed DataSet is a class that derives from a DataSet. It inherits all the properties, methods, and events of the DataSet class, plus it adds its own so that we can access its members by name instead of just by index.

Suppose a typed DataSet has a table named Customers. We can access the Customers table by a property called `Customers` instead of by the Tables collection. The advantage of this is that the Customers table already has all of the column objects and row objects defined. Check out this snippet of code:

```
Dim cust As DataSet1.CustomersDataTable
Dim myrow As DataSet1.CustomersRow
Dim str1, str2 As String

cust = DataSet11.Customers()
myrow = DataSet11.Customers.Rows(0)
str1 = myrow.Address
str2 = cust.AddressColumn.Caption
```

Notice how we're able to address the tables and rows by name. This is similar to early and late binding in COM. Since the `Customers DataTable` property is derived from the DataTable, we can assign it to a variable that is declared as a DataTable or as the more restrictive type of Customers DataTable.

When we create a strongly typed DataSet, the wizard generates a new class derived from the DataSet class and by default names it DataSet1. It then looks at the results of the queries in the Data Adapter and creates DataTable objects and classes. It then creates properties and methods for manipulating the classes directly. You can see the VB module it generates if you click the Show All Files button in the Project Explorer.

Underneath the XSD file for the DataSet will be the VB module. You can open this and look at the code, but do not modify it because this will confuse the system. If you have an XSD file from another source you can generate your VB module using a command-line utility. This utility parses the XSD file and creates the DataSet class for you. You can also do this programmatically using the emitter classes but this is beyond the scope of this book. This utility is appropriately called xsd.exe and the simple invocation is xsd <xsd file name>. You can use it to generate VB code or C# code via command-line switches (execute xsd.exe /? to view all of the available options).

Let's create a screen similar to the screen we had in the previous project. This screen should contain a grid control, three buttons, and the search text box. In addition place two additional text boxes and another button on the next row. The form should look like Figure 7.4.

You can use the same form as we did in the previous chapter; just copy it into the new directory and edit your project. Make sure you set the startup project to be the new project, and then set the startup form to be the new form. We will use the Show button to demonstrate a little bit of what we've been talking about with typed DataSets. Copy the following code into your project.

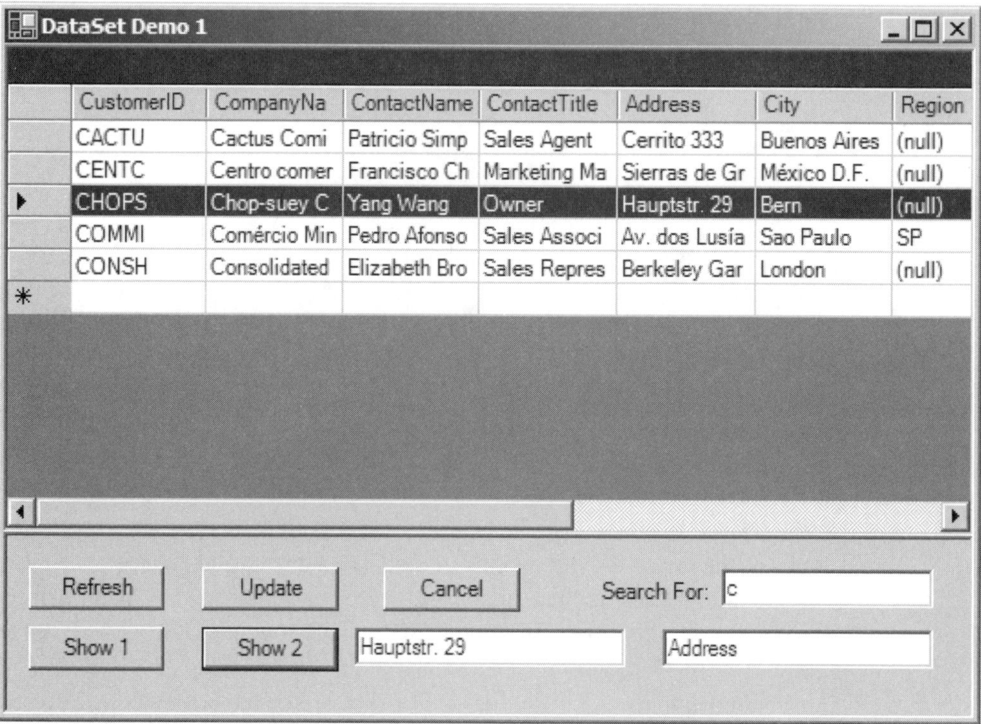

FIGURE 7.4 The DataSet demo form.

```
    Private Sub btnRefresh_Click(ByVal sender As System.Object, ByVal
e As System.EventArgs) Handles btnRefresh.Click
        Dim mDS As ADOBook07_01.DataSet1

        Try
            mDS = DataSet11
            If mDS.Tables.Count > 0 Then
                mDS.Clear()
            End If

            SqlDataAdapter1.SelectCommand.Parameters("@CoName").Value =
txtSearch.Text
            SqlDataAdapter1.Fill(mDS)
            DataGrid1.DataSource = mDS.Tables(0)
        Catch errobj As Exception
            MsgBox(errobj.Message & vbCrLf & errobj.StackTrace)
        End Try

    End Sub

    Private Sub Button1_Click(ByVal sender As System.Object, ByVal e
As System.EventArgs) Handles Button1.Click
        Dim cust As DataSet1.CustomersDataTable
        Dim rows As DataSet1.CustomersRow
        Dim i As Integer

        cust = DataSet11.Customers()
        i = Me.BindingContext(DataSet11.Customers).Position
        rows = DataSet11.Customers.Rows(i)
        TextBox1.Text = rows.Address
        TextBox2.Text = cust.AddressColumn.Caption
    End Sub
```

Pay special attention to the Button1_Click event. Notice how we reference the objects in the DataSet by name. It makes the code much more readable than using arcane indices. When you click the button, the current value of the address column should appear in the text box. You can navigate through the grid control and you will always get the value of the current row. We will explain DataTable navigation in depth later.

Now let's have a look at the untyped version of the same code.

```
    Private Sub Button2_Click(ByVal sender As System.Object, ByVal e
As System.EventArgs) Handles Button2.Click
        Dim i As Integer

        i = Me.BindingContext(DataSet11.Tables(0)).Position
```

```
    TextBox1.Text = DataSet11.Tables(0).Rows(i)("Address")
    TextBox2.Text = DataSet11.Tables(0).Columns("Address").Caption
End Sub
```

Notice how we can access all the properties via the indexes instead of the names. This can be useful when you do not know in advance what your SQL statement will look like. An ad hoc Query Builder would be an example of where this would be very useful.

`DataSet` Properties and Methods

The DataSet contains methods that operate on the DataSet as a whole. The two `Collection` properties, `Tables` and `Relations`, reference the DataTable collection and Relation collection. The following are other methods worth noting:

- `ReadXML` and `WriteXML`—These methods read and write XML text to and from disk files. `ReadXML` can also be used to read XML from a string source.
- `ReadXMLSchema` and `WriteXMLSchema`—These methods read and write XSD schema text to and from disk files. `ReadXMLSchema` can also be used to read XSD text from a string source.
- `GetXML` and `GetXMLSchema`—Methods which a programmer can use to retrieve the XML text into a string variable.
- `InferXMLSchema`—Will try to create a schema from data read from a file. For example, a comma-separated values file can infer a schema where each value is a column.
- `Clear`—Clears out the data in the tables but does not clear the schema information.
- `EnforceConstraints`—When loading data through one of the `ReadXML` methods, tells the DataSet to enforce or ignore constraints such as primary keys or relations.
- `Clone`—Copies the schema information only (no data) from an existing DataSet to a new DataSet.
- `Copy`—Copies the schema and data from an existing DataSet to a new DataSet.
- `AcceptChanges`, `RejectChanges`—Tells the DataSet to either accept or cancel any changes that were made since the last call to Accept or Cancel changes.
- `HasChanges`—Returns True if any data in any table in the DataSet has changed since the last call to Accept or Cancel changes.
- `GetChanges`— Returns another DataSet object with only those rows and tables that have changed.

Some Examples

Let's look at some code examples. These examples will demonstrate the XML `Related` methods. We will modify our DataSet demonstration project. Change the `Text` property of Button2 to read XML. Create another button and change its `Text` property to read Schema. Delete the text box named TextBox2. Set the properties of TextBox1 so that multiline is True and scroll bars are set to both. You will also have to change the `wordwrap` property to False. When you're finished your form should look like Figure 7.5.

Now let's update click events for the two buttons. Place the following code in the Button2_Click event. Erase any code that was already there.

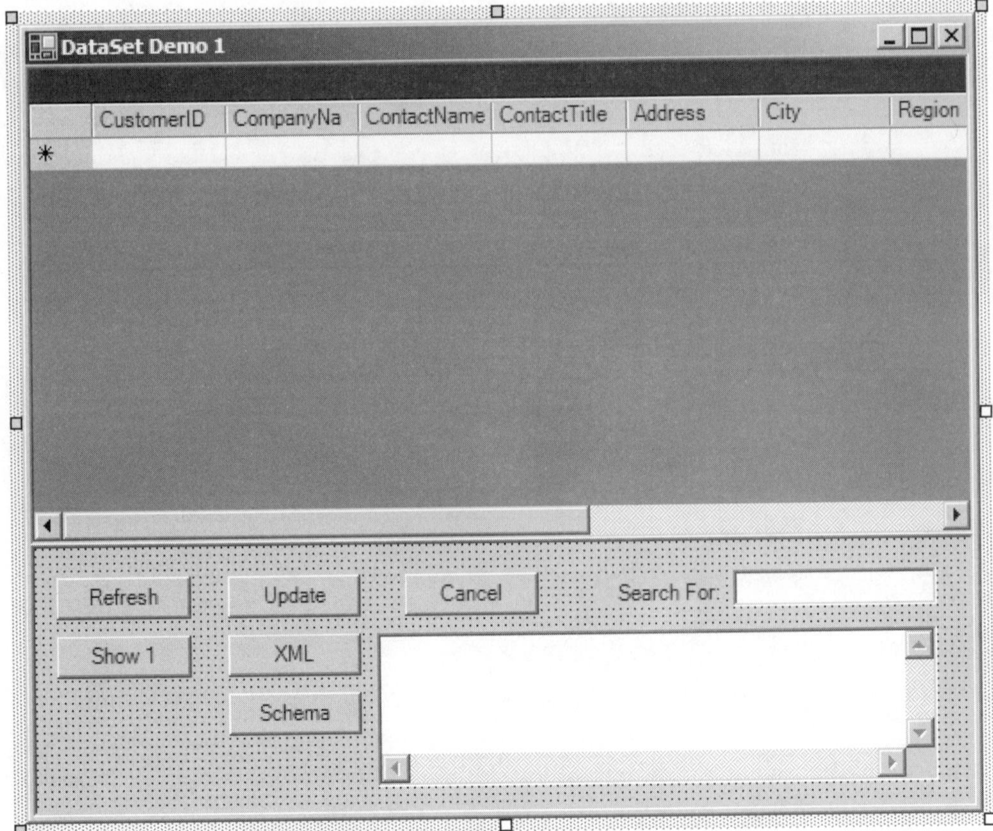

FIGURE 7.5 The modified DataSet demo form.

```
    Private Sub Button2_Click(ByVal sender As System.Object, ByVal e
As System.EventArgs) Handles Button2.Click
        TextBox1.Text = DataSet11.GetXml
    End Sub
```

Place the following code in the Button3_Click event. Erase any code that was already there.

```
    Private Sub Button3_Click(ByVal sender As System.Object, ByVal e
As System.EventArgs) Handles Button3.Click
        TextBox1.Text = DataSet11.GetXmlSchema
    End Sub
```

Now when you run the project, if you click the XML button you'll see the XML text appear in the text box. Likewise, if you click the Schema button you'll see the XSD appear in the text box. Your project should look like Figure 7.6 if you have clicked the Schema button.

Now let's see how to read and write XML data to and from a disk file. Let's modify our form again. This time we will use the XML button to write the data and the Schema button to read the data. We will make the Show button into a Clear button so that we can erase the data in a DataSet and reload it from disk without shutting down and restarting the program. Make your form look like Figure 7.7.

Now let's add two common dialog controls to the form. Add one Save File dialog, and add another File Open dialog. These can be found in the Windows Forms tab of the toolbox.

VB 6—VB 6 veterans should remember the common dialog control. This control served as a template for all of the styles of common dialog. Besides the File Open and Save As versions, there are also color choosers, printer choosers, and font choosers. These were handled by a method call in the VB 6 version of the control. In the .NET version, there are separate components for each type of dialog.

Change the code in the buttons' click events to look like the following.

```
    Private Sub Button1_Click(ByVal sender As System.Object, ByVal e
As System.EventArgs) Handles Button1.Click
        DataSet11.Clear()
    End Sub

    Private Sub Button2_Click(ByVal sender As System.Object, ByVal e
As System.EventArgs) Handles Button2.Click
        Dim strFile As String

        Try
```

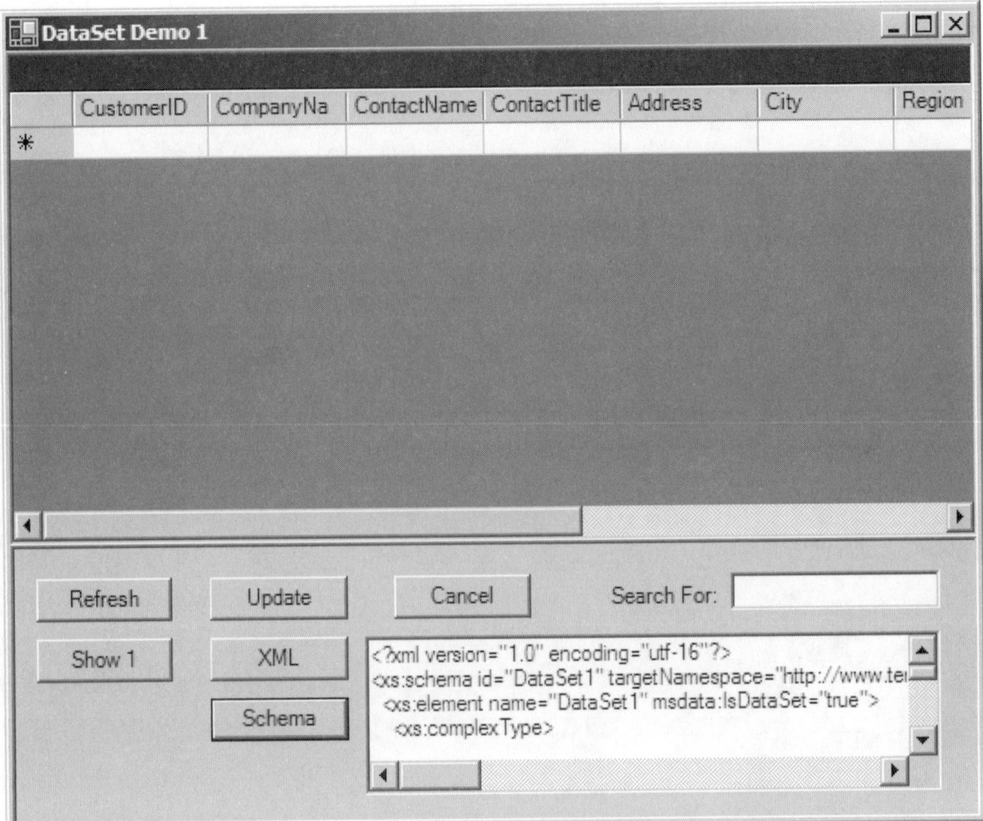

FIGURE 7.6 The demo with the XSD displayed.

```
            SaveFileDialog1.ShowDialog()
            strFile = SaveFileDialog1.FileName
            If strFile = "" Then Exit Sub
            DataSet11.WriteXml(strFile)
        Catch errobj As Exception
            MsgBox(errobj.Message)
        End Try
    End Sub

    Private Sub Button3_Click(ByVal sender As System.Object, ByVal e
As System.EventArgs) Handles Button3.Click
        Dim strFile As String

        Try
            OpenFileDialog1.ShowDialog()
```

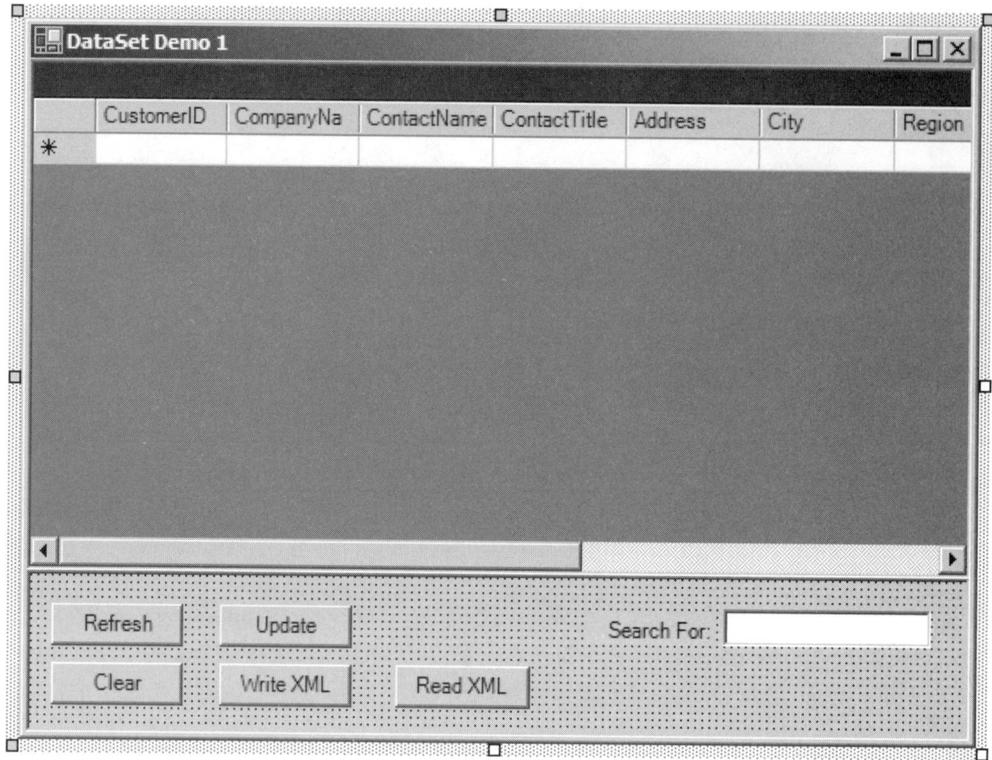

FIGURE 7.7 The revised form for reading and writing XML.

```
      strFile = OpenFileDialog1.FileName
      If strFile = "" Then Exit Sub
      DataSet11.ReadXml(strFile)
      DataSet11.AcceptChanges()
    Catch errobj As Exception
      MsgBox(errobj.Message)
    End Try
  End Sub
```

With this code, the program will prompt the user for a file name using a common dialog display. Then the program will save the contents of the DataSet to the file or read the contents of the file back into the DataSet. When we read the file back into the DataSet the grid control will automatically be populated with the contents of the file. Note the presence of the call to the `AcceptChanges` method. This is necessary when reading XML from a file because all rows are marked as added. If you call the `Update` method of the DataAdapter you will get duplicate key errors returned.

There are some things to take note of. If you sort the grid by clicking on a column heading, it has no effect on the order of records in the XML file. Likewise for any sorts or filters you place on the default DataView of the DataTable. (We will look at the DataView later on.) If you want to limit the output of the XML methods, you must change the SQL query that read the data from the database.

THE DATATABLE CLASS

If the DataSet is the heart of ADO .NET, then the DataTable class is the heart of the DataSet. The DataSet object is essentially a collection of DataTable objects. To understand the DataSet is to understand the DataTable. The DataTable class is itself a collection of DataColumn and DataRow objects. The DataColumn class defines the metadata for the DataTable. Each DataColumn object contains properties that define each column in the table. These properties will be the name, data type, size, and other properties that define the column. The DataRow class contains the values of each column by row. The DataRow class is the element of the DataRowCollection. This is a departure from previous versions of ADO where there was a concept of the current row and you navigated the RecordSet using methods such as `MoveNext` and `MovePrevious`. With ADO .NET, all rows are available at all times. You can use an indexing variable to access the rows, or you can use an enumerator using the For Each ... Next construct.

`DataTable` Properties and Methods

The following methods and properties are defined at the table level. Some are also defined at the DataSet level. When they are invoked at the DataSet level they apply to all of the DataTable objects in the DataSet. When they are invoked at the DataTable level, they only apply to the DataTable they are invoked on.

- Child and parent relations—Collections of Relation objects that point to another table with either a one-to-many relationship to the current table (child) or a many-to-one relationship to the current table (parent). These have to do with master-detail structures. We will look at this later in the chapter.
- Constraints—A collection of constraint objects. There are two kinds of constraint classes—unique and foreign key. A unique constraint is used to guarantee that no two rows in a table have the same value in the col-

umns referenced in the unique constraint. A foreign key constraint is used to determine what happens to a row on the right side of the constraint when a row on the left side is changed. Possibilities include cascaded deletes and updates, and referential integrity violations. For example, you cannot delete a parent row if there are any child rows.

- `DefaultView`—Returns a DataView object that has the default view settings (sorts, filters, and so forth) of the DataTable.
- `AcceptChanges`, `RejectChanges`—Tells the DataTable to either accept or cancel any changes that were made since the last call to Accept or Cancel changes.
- `HasChanges`—Returns True if any data in the DataTable has changed since the last call to Accept or Cancel changes.
- `GetChanges`—Returns a copy of the DataTable with only those rows that have changed since the last call to Accept or Cancel changes.
- `HasErrors`—Returns True if any rows in the table have unresolved errors.
- `GetErrors`—Returns an array of DataRow objects that contain errors.
- `BeginLoadData`—Turns off index building and constraint checking. This is useful if you are loading a large amount of data into the DataTable and you want to increase performance.
- `EndLoadData`—Restores indexing and constraint checking after data is loaded. Be sure to check `HasErrors` for any errors generated and `GetErrors` to edit and fix them.

DataTable Notifications (Events)

The DataTable also provides the following notifications:

- ColumnChanging, ColumnChanged—Fires when a column is going to change and a column has successfully changed.
- RowChanging, RowChanged—Fires when a row is going to change or has successfully changed.
- RowDeleting, RowDeleted—Fires when a row will be deleted or is successfully deleted.

To receive these events, you must declare a variable of type DataTable and assign the DataTable from the DataSet to it. You must use the `WithEvents` keyword in the declaration. You can also wire the events to procedures programmatically without declaring a variable like so:

```
AddHandler DataSet11.Customers.RowChanged, AddressOf mDT_RowChanged
```

Where mDT_RowChanged has this declaration:

```
        Private Sub mDT_RowChanged(ByVal sender As Object, ByVal e As
System.Data.DataRowChangeEventArgs)
            MsgBox("Row Changed")
        End Sub
```

The contents of the procedure in the example are irrelevant.

THE DATACOLUMN CLASS

The DataColumn class is used to store the metadata about each column. Metadata is information that describes the data in the table. This class includes properties such as the data type, column name, and data size. Each DataTable contains a collection of DataColumn objects (an instance of DataColumnCollection) accessible through the `Columns` property.

The Columns Collection

The DataColumnCollection class has properties and methods of its own for managing the collection of columns it contains. These include the `Count` property, and methods for adding/deleting members of the collection. Let's look at some of the properties and methods.

- `Count`—The number of items in the collection.
- `Item`— Returns the DataColumn object at the specified index. The index can be numeric or a string that is the column name.
- `IsReadOnly`—If True means that you can not modify the collection. This is always the case when using typed DataSets. Untyped DataSets column collections can be manipulated in code, typed cannot. By testing this property, you can avoid runtime errors
- `Add`—Adds a DataColumn object to the collection. You can build your DataColumn using a variable and then add it, or you can supply parameters to the method such as name, data type, and so forth. Returns a reference to the DataColumn object just created.
- `AddRange`—Adds a range of DataColumn objects passed as an array.
- `CanRemove`—Returns True if a DataColumn can be removed.
- `Clear`—Clears the collection. Does not work on typed DataSets as the collection is read-only.
- `Remove`, `RemoveAt`—Removes a column with the specified column name (`Remove`) or with the specified index (`RemoveAt`).
- `IndexOf`—Returns the numerical index of the column with the specified name.

`DataColumn` Properties and Methods

The following properties and methods apply to the DataColumn class itself. Not all properties and methods are listed, just the more commonly used ones.

- `AllowDBNull`—Whether to allow the column to have the null value.
- `AutoIncrement`—Indicates that this column will increment its value automatically when new rows are added.
- `AutoIncrementSeed`—Starting number to increment.
- `AutoIncrementStep`—Sets the increment to use when generating the value of the column.
- `Caption`—The caption of the column. This can be used as a field label on a form or report.
- `ColumnName`—The name of the column.
- `DataType`—Returns a type object that contains the data type of the column. To get a string representation of the type you must use its `ToString` method. To assign a data type to the property, you must use the `GetType` method of the System.Type class.
- `DefaultValue`—The value to use when creating new rows if no value is supplied for the column.
- `Expression`—Enables calculations to be performed on columns. More on this later in the chapter.
- `MaxLength`—The maximum length of a text column.
- `Unique`—Indicates whether the values in each row in the table must be unique.

The DataRow Class

The DataRow class is used to hold each row of data in the table. The correspondent collection, the DataRowCollection, is used to hold all of the DataRows in the DataSet. Since I have the rows available in a standard collection, there is no need to navigate the table using methods such as `Move Next`, `Previous`, and so forth as with the old RecordSet object. You can either use an indexing variable and the for loop to navigate the rows or you can use an enumerator with the For … Each … Next construct. Each DataRow is an object itself with its own properties and methods. Let's look at them now.

`DataRowCollection` Properties and Methods

The following methods are on the DataRowCollection class which is returned from the `Rows` property of the DataTable class:

- `Count`—The number of rows in the collection.
- `Add`—Adds a new row to the collection.
- `Clear`—Removes all of the rows from the DataTable. This method effectively deletes all of the data in the table.
- `Contains`—This function is very handy. The program passes it an array of values and it returns True if any of the values are contained in the primary key of the table. This is very useful if you just want to determine if any rows contain a value or set of values. Sometimes this is all you need to determine if data exists.
- `Delete`—Marks the row as deleted. This is different from `Remove/RemoveAt` because when a row is marked as deleted, it is not actually removed from the collection. The `Update` method of the DataAdapter can then be used to propagate the deletions back to the database. If you remove a row, it is gone. The `Update` method will not work.
- `Find`—This is the equivalent of a direct look up. The programmer passes this function a value and it returns the row that contains that value as its primary key. The function accepts an array of values for multiple-column primary keys.
- `InsertAt`—This method inserts an already formed row into the collection at a specified location.
- `Remove`—Removes an existing row from the collection. The caveat about this function is that it requires that you pass it a Row object. See the `Delete` method for comments
- `RemoveAt`—Removes the row at the specified index from the collection. See the `Delete` method for comments.

DataRow Class Properties and Methods

The DataRow class has the following properties and methods.

- `HasErrors`—Gets a value that tells whether there is an error in the row.
- `Item, ItemArray`—Returns the value of a column in the row, or returns an array of values of all of the columns in the row. The `Item` property can be retrieved using either an index or a text key that corresponds to the column name.
- `RowState`—Gets a value that tells whether or not the row is being edited.
- `AcceptChanges, RejectChanges`—Accepts or rejects changes made to the row since a last call to Accept or Reject changes.

- `BeginEdit`—Places the row into a state where changes can be made to it.
- `CancelEdit`—Cancels any edits made to the row and returns it to the state it was in before the user called `BeginEdit`.
- `EndEdit`—Ends the edit of the row and makes the changes permanent.
- `GetChildRows`—Gets any child rows in a master-detail relationship. Each row in a master table may have many rows in the child table. When navigating the DataTable it is important to refresh the child rows each time you reference a new master row.
- `GetParentRows`—Returns the parent row of a child row in a master-detail relationship.
- `GetColumnsInError`—Returns an array of columns with associated errors.
- `HasVersion`—Returns True if any column in the row has changes in it.
- `IsNull`—Returns True if the column in a row has the `Null` value.
- `SetNull`—Sets a column in a row to the `Null` value. You cannot assign the null value to a column as you could in Visual Basic 6. You must use this method instead.

The DataView Class

The DataView class is what we call a helper class. It isn't really necessary for normal functionality, but it helps us perform certain functions that would be difficult other ways. The two most useful features of the class are its ability to sort and filter the rows in a DataTable. The other properties that are useful are `AllowEdit`, `AllowNew`, and `AllowDelete`. You can use the DataView class as a security control object, by creating DataViews with different access rights and then assigning them based on the user's rights. Here are the common properties and methods of the DataView class.

- `AllowEdit`, `AllowNew`, `AllowDelete`—These properties are useful for security control. When the DataView is a flight to the DataTable and these properties are set, the user will only be allowed to perform the functions indicated.
- `ApplyDefaultSort`—When set to True this property removes any sort that has been placed on the DataView and reverts to the default sort order.
- `Count`—Returns the number of rows after the `RowStateFilter` and `RowFilter` has been applied.
- `RowFilter`—This property determines which rows appear after a filter is applied. The filter can be any Boolean expression. The filter is similar

to what you find in the `where` clause of an SQL statement. The difference between this property and the `Find` method on the DataRowCollection is that this property only limits the rows that are visible through the DataView. It does not change the underlying DataTable in any way.

- `RowStateFilter`—The `RowState` indicates whether the row is in Edit mode, being added, and so forth. The `RowStateFilter` is useful for filtering rows based on the RowState value.
- `Sort`–This function accepts a comma-separated values list of fields to sort by. This is passed as a string and is similar to an SQL `Order By` clause. As with an `Order By` clause you can also use the DESC (descending) and ASC (ascending) modifiers.
- `AddNew`—Adds a new blank DataRowView object to the DataView. The DataRowView object that is returned is empty. The DataRowView class provides a customized view of each DataRow.
- `Delete`—Deletes a row from the DataView.
- `Find`, `FindRows`—Finds a row or rows by its specified sort key value.

Now that we're familiar with the properties and methods of the DataSet and its associated classes, let's look at examples of how to use the classes.

TYPED DATASETS

Typed DataSets are the easiest to demonstrate. We've already seen how to use these in previous chapters but for completeness let's quickly go over a demo. Let's use a version of the demo we've already created. To create a typed DataSet we use the Create DataSet wizard that is available when right-clicking the DataAdapter. When we create a typed DataSet using the wizard, the DataSet wizard gets its information from the DataAdapter. It then uses this information to generate a class based on the schema it retrieves from the database. Once the class is generated, the wizard then creates a DataSet that is an instance of the class. We will not go through this demonstration step by step because we've done this numerous times. Let's use our existing project, ADOBook07-01, and look at what we've done.

Describing the creation of a typed DataSet in detail is not easy. For this reason we will use some diagrams to explain the process. As we have said, a typed DataSet is based on a subclassed DataSet. In other words, the system creates a class inherited from the DataSet class. The new class has methods and properties that are customized based on the metadata provided by the DataAdapter. The new DataSet is then created as an instance of this new class. Once you see it laid out it is really easy to understand, and actually quite cool! Let's look at the block diagram in Figure 7.8.

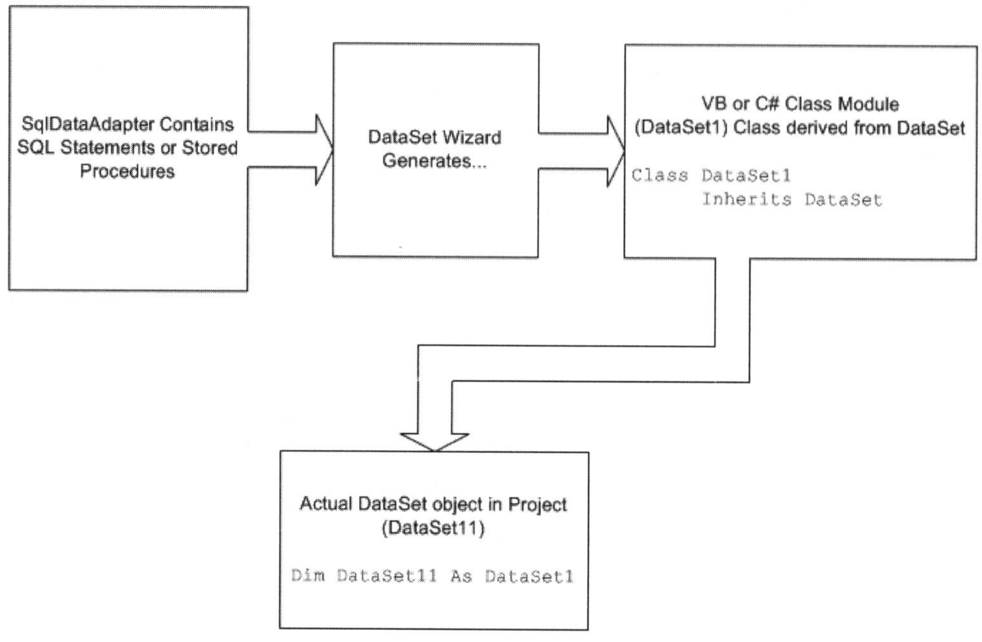

FIGURE 7.8 Typed DataSet creation process.

Figure 7.8 assumes we are using the default DataSet names. You will want to use more descriptive names in your projects. We can see the class module generated by the wizard if we click the Show All Files button in the Project Explorer. The file is located under the DataSet1.xsd file node in the tree (see Figure 7.9).

You can open this file and look at it, but don't make any changes. Mostly what it does is make properties out of the various DataTable objects and their columns. We've already seen the benefits of how it makes our code more readable and easier to document. Besides this there is a slight performance gain as the compiler can use early binding to resolve addresses of members.

Design Considerations

There are some design options to consider when using typed DataSets, and, admittedly ADO .NET can be confusing. There are three ways to approach application design using the DataSet:

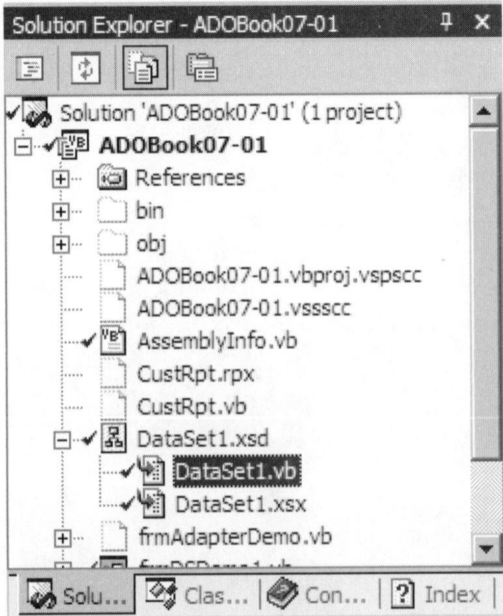

FIGURE 7.9 Project Explorer with Show All Files selected.

1. Use untyped DataSets and do all your configuring in code.
2. Use all typed DataSets and use one DataSet per table.
3. Design your DataSets around your processes and use them as entities that define logical units of database access methods.

All of these methods can be misused or overused. Let's look at each and see when or when not to use each approach.

Untyped DataSets

In general, untyped DataSets should only be used in situations where there is no way to know in advance what database access method will be required. A good example of this would be in an ad-hoc query generator where you have no way of knowing at design time what the user will want to access. Another good example is a report generator. This is similar to the query generator problem except that the output is sent to the printer and it probably has more formatting options.

Another place the untyped DataSet is very useful is when you are not using a database at all. It is entirely acceptable to use a DataSet to enter and store information in a disk file. You may wish to create an application in which a user enters data into a form. The data is them saved to a disk file and emailed to another location. At the other location the data is then read back in from the file and updated to a database. Even in this situation, however, it is more desirable to use a typed DataSet. We'll see how to make a typed DataSet from a user-defined DataTable later in this chapter.

Generally, I would not recommend using the untyped DataSet too often. There is a school of thought that disdains design-time anything. This camp wants to do everything in code at runtime. This usually makes for a system that is difficult if not impossible to debug and maintain. The opposite end of the thought spectrum is that anything that can be done using the tools provided is better than writing the code yourself. This tends to create code that conforms to a lowest common denominator syndrome, where the system is neither creative nor very useful.

I prefer a pragmatic middle-ground approach. Use the tools if they help speed things along, but don't become so reliant upon them that you forget how everything works.

The concept of one DataSet per table is a throwback to ADO and the RecordSet. This may be easier to conceptualize for the VB 6 programmer making the transition to .NET, but it is also very shortsighted. What you are saying is that you really don't want to learn the new technology; you want to stay with what is comfortable. Then why develop in .NET at all? Just stay with VB 6 and ADO. The whole point of the DataSet is to be able to create objects that do so much more than the old RecordSet. If you are going to use the technology, you should be willing to invest the time to learn it so you can put it to its best use. So that's my opinion on that approach.

There may be times where only one table is needed in a DataSet. If this is the case then by all means use one table. Don't feel that you must use multiple tables just because I said so.

So with that said, my recommended approach is to design your database access objects with your processes in mind. The one negative with this approach is that sometimes you end up with too many objects in your class structure and many of them can be redundant. That's all right when initially designing your system. It's not such a bad thing to design your classes and objects with complete encapsulation in mind. That is, each team member can feel free to create his own classes or objects to gain access to the needed data. Later on, after the code is unit-tested, it can be integrated into the main system and the classes can be refactored to promote code reuse and the other more esoteric goals of an object-oriented design. I am a strong proponent of regular refactoring to streamline the design and improve performance.

Refactoring—There is a philosophy of code development methodologies called Agile Methods or Extreme Programming. If you want to know more about these methods you can visit *www.agilealliance.com*. I will not go into detail about these but they all contain a provision for regular refactoring of code. Essentially what this means is that you review your code and try to streamline it as much as possible. Just as in algebra, we can often simplify our code. When we simplify a math formula, we essentially make it easier to read and require less computation to arrive at the answer. Refactoring code has the same effect. Besides making it easier to read, we can often make the code easier for the computer to process. Needless to say, this will make the program execute faster and more efficiently.

UNTYPED DATASETS

Now that we have expounded all the reasons to not use them, let's look at how to create an untyped DataSet. There are two types of untyped DataSets. The first type is the kind we have been discussing up until now, the DataSet that is configured at runtime. The other type is the kind that is configured manually, without using a DataAdapter. This kind of untyped DataSet is created using the design-time properties and methods of the DataSet itself. One of the reasons for using this type of DataSet is when you are not using data from a database. You could be creating an organized, table-style DataSet from user data entry, or you may not have connectivity to a database and you want the user to enter data to be updated to the database later.

Adding Tables at Design Time

You can add tables to the DataSet at design time using the Tables collection. This is accessible in the Property window. Note that this is only available with untyped DataSets. Before we create our untyped DataSet, let's start a new Windows Forms project and call it ADOBook07-02. Name the form frmDataSet2. Name the class and the file the same thing. Next, add a DataSet to the project by dragging one from the toolbox. Select Untyped DataSet in the DataSet wizard. Now we will set up the DataSet with an address book table.

To access the Tables collection visually, click on the ellipsis button next to its entry in the Properties window (see Figure 7.10).

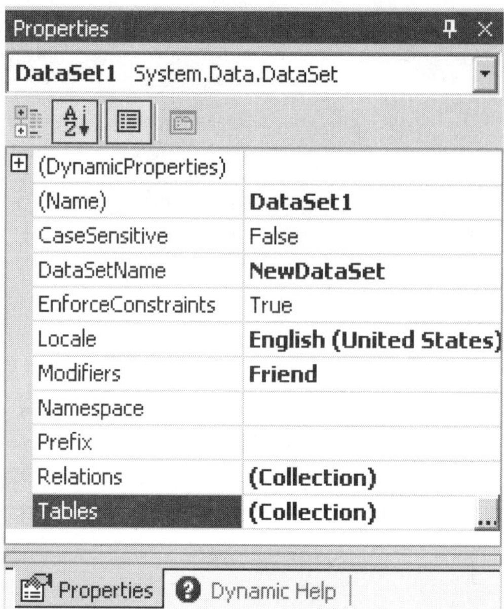

FIGURE 7.10 The Tables collection in the Properties window.

This opens the visual collection designer. This designer is used to visually manipulate many collections in the .NET Framework, not just ADO .NET. The designer allows you to add and edit collections. Let's look at the blank Tables collection in Figure 7.11.

To add a table to the collection, click the Add button. A new empty table will be added called Table1. You may change the name of the table by editing the `TableName` property. Let's call our table AddressBook. To add columns to the table, click the Columns collection ellipsis button in the property pane of the collection editor, as in Figure 7.12.

Let's keep our address book simple by including only the name, address, phone number, age, and birth date. Add the columns so your editor looks like Figure 7.13.

Make sure you make the Age column an int16 data type and the BirthDate column the DateTime data type. We want to do this so not all the columns are strings. This way we can see what the XML looks like for data types other than string (see Figure 7.14).

Now let's add our friendly grid control to the form and a panel. We'll make our form similar to the last project. Now add three buttons to the panel control. When you have finished, your form should look like Figure 7.15.

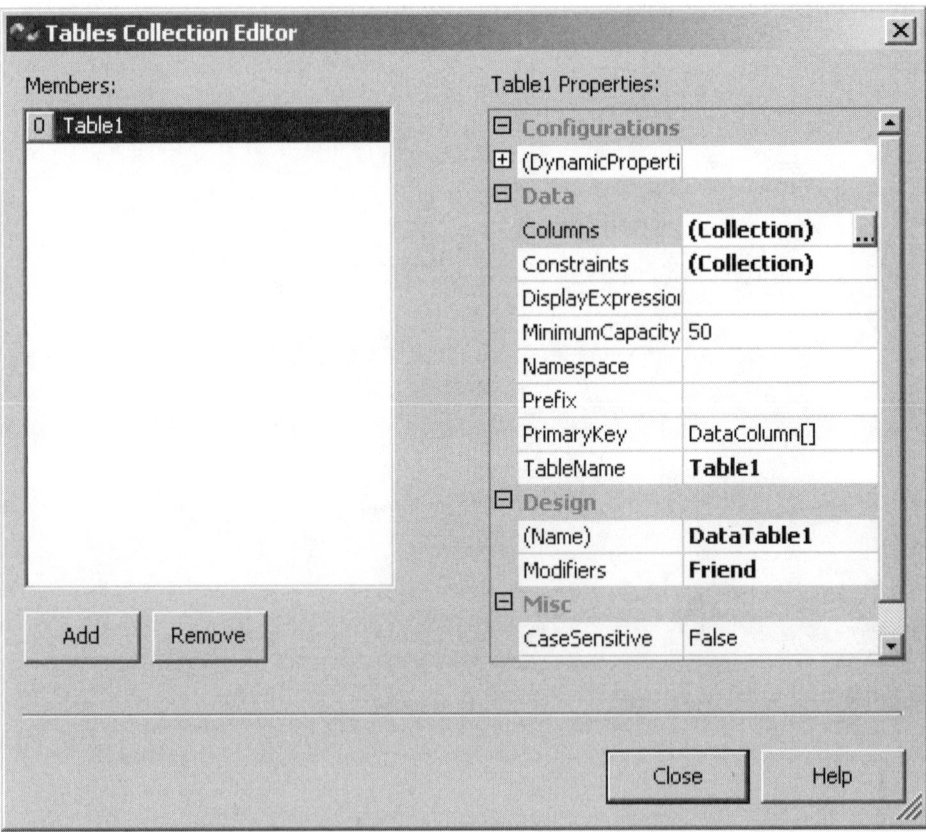

FIGURE 7.11 The collection editor.

Make sure you set the `DataSource` property of the grid control to DataSet1.addressbook. This way the columns of the grid will populate themselves. If you have not already dragged the OpenFileDialog and SaveFileDialog objects to the form, do so now. Now let's add the following code to the button click event procedures:

```
    Private Sub Button1_Click(ByVal sender As System.Object, ByVal e As
System.EventArgs) Handles Button1.Click
        Dim strFile As String

        Try
            SaveFileDialog1.DefaultExt = "xml"
            SaveFileDialog1.Filter = "XML Files|*.xml|All Files|*.*"
            SaveFileDialog1.ShowDialog()
```

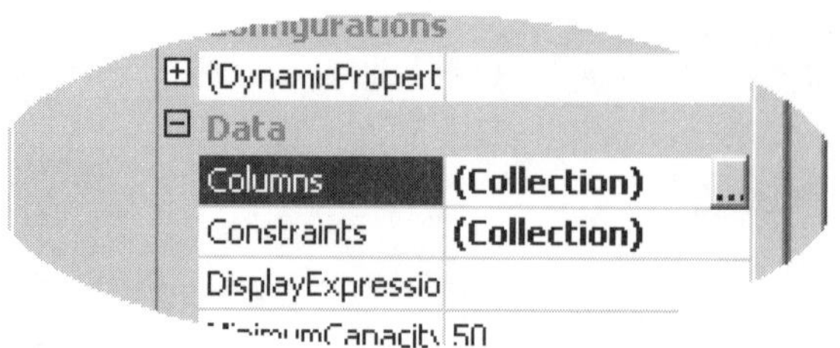

FIGURE 7.12 Accessing the Columns collection.

```
            strFile = SaveFileDialog1.FileName
            If strFile = "" Then Exit Sub
            DataSet1.WriteXml(strFile)
        Catch errobj As Exception
            MsgBox(errobj.Message)
        End Try
    End Sub
```

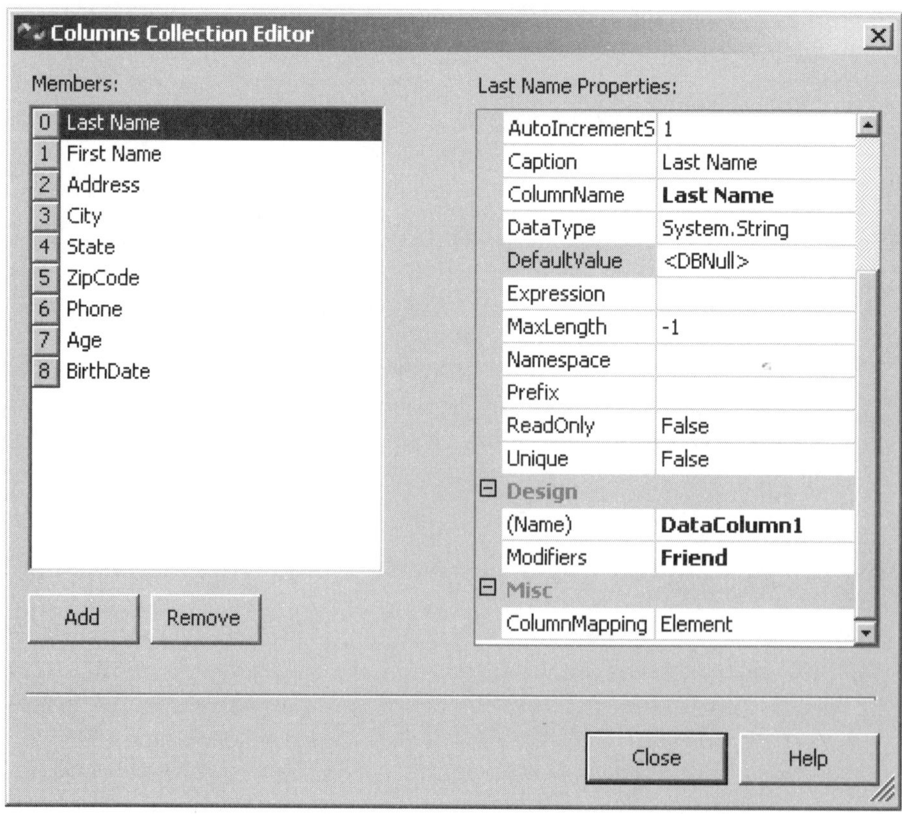

FIGURE 7.13 The Columns collection.

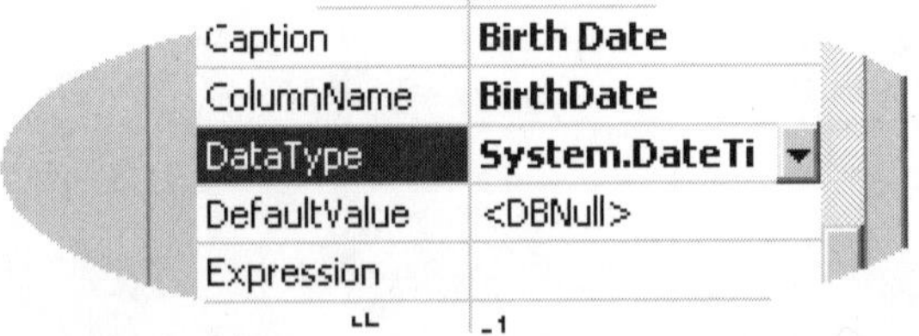

FIGURE 7.14 Selecting a different data type.

```
    Private Sub Button2_Click(ByVal sender As System.Object, ByVal e As
System.EventArgs) Handles Button2.Click
        Dim strFile As String

        Try
            OpenFileDialog1.ShowDialog()
            strFile = OpenFileDialog1.FileName
            If strFile = "" Then Exit Sub
            DataSet1.ReadXml(strFile)
            DataSet1.AcceptChanges()
        Catch errobj As Exception
            MsgBox(errobj.Message)
        End Try
    End Sub

    Private Sub Button3_Click(ByVal sender As System.Object, ByVal e As
System.EventArgs) Handles Button3.Click
        Dim strFile As String

        Try
            SaveFileDialog1.DefaultExt = "xsd"
            SaveFileDialog1.Filter = "XSD Files|*.xsd|All Files|*.*"
            SaveFileDialog1.ShowDialog()
            strFile = SaveFileDialog1.FileName
            If strFile = "" Then Exit Sub
            DataSet1.WriteXmlSchema(strFile)
        Catch errobj As Exception
            MsgBox(errobj.Message)
        End Try
    End Sub
```

Notice that we've added some code to save the XML schema to a file as well. We will see what this will be used for a little later on. Right now, let's run the program. Type some data into one or two rows of the grid control. Now click the Save XML button. A File Save dialog should open. Type in a file name and click OK. Now let's go to Windows Explorer and open the file. If you double-click the file, it should open in Internet Explorer, but you can open it in Notepad as well. You can see the file is XML text:

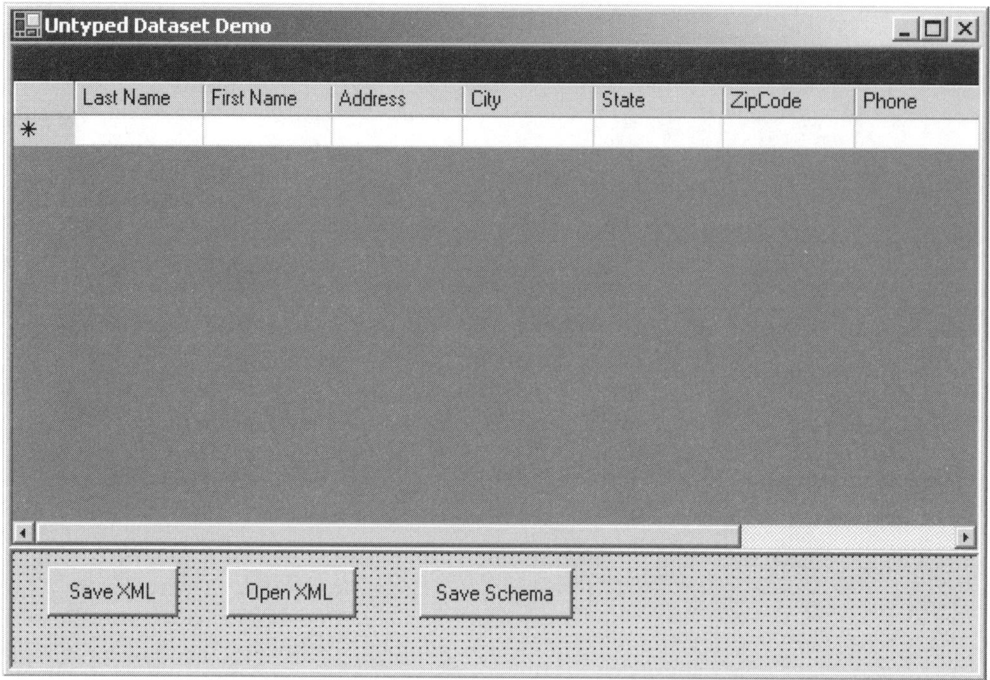

FIGURE 7.15 Untyped DataSet demo form.

```
<?xml version="1.0" standalone="yes"?>
<DSAddr>
  <AddressBook>
    <Last_x0020_Name>Howell</Last_x0020_Name>
    <First_x0020_Name>Bob</First_x0020_Name>
    <Address>3 Robin Lane</Address>
    <City>Farmingdale</City>
    <State>NY</State>
    <ZipCode>11735</ZipCode>
    <Phone>555-1212</Phone>
    <Age>49</Age>
    <BirthDate>1952-11-12T00:00:00.0000000-05:00</BirthDate>
  </AddressBook>
</DSAddr>
```

Notice that there is no indication of the data type of the column in the file. Also notice the interesting way it saves the Birth Date column, paying particular attention to the last characters after the minus sign. This represents the time zone. All you have to do to convert to Universal Time Coordinate

(UTC) is parse the time zone out and then do a dateadd function on it, reversing the sign. Then from UTC you can convert it to any local time zone you want as long as you know the offset from UTC.

This still does nothing to support the data types of the original columns. The only thing that would happen if you tried to load an alpha into a numeric column is a type mismatch error. If we loaded our XML file into a blank DataSet, it would create all string columns. So how do we save the schema data so we can ensure that our DataSet has the correct column definitions? Use a typed DataSet. We mentioned at the beginning of the chapter that there is a command-line tool that can be used to generate a class module from an XSD file. We know we have a way to save the schema to an XSD file. Once we have the XSD file we can then use the tool to create a class module. We can then import the class into our project and use it to create a typed DataSet.

To create the XSD file, run the project and click the Save Schema button. When prompted, enter a file name. Now close the program. Start a command prompt and navigate to the directory where your XSD file is located. To generate the VB DataSet, use the following command line:

```
C:\Documents and Settings\bhowell\My Documents\Visual Studio
Projects\ADOBook\AD
OBook07-02\bin>xsd AddrBook.xsd /d /l:vb
Microsoft (R) Xml Schemas/DataTypes support utility
[Microsoft (R) .NET Framework, Version 1.0.3705.0]
Copyright (C) Microsoft Corporation 1998-2001. All rights reserved.

Writing file 'C:\Documents and Settings\bhowell\My Documents\Visual
Studio Proje
cts\ADOBook\ADOBook07-02\bin\AddrBook.vb'.

C:\Documents and Settings\bhowell\My Documents\Visual Studio
Projects\ADOBook\AD
OBook07-02\bin>
```

There are several options for this utility. The /d tells it to generate a DataSet. The other option, /c, tells it to generate a class file. The class file is not a DataSet, it is a generic class file that you can use in lieu of a DataSet if you do not need the features of one. The /l:vb switch tells it to generate Visual Basic code. The default is C#. You cannot generate C++ code at this time.

Once you have your DataSet class generated, you can include it in your project. Once you have done so, before you do anything else, you must compile the project. This is so the data type of the new DataSet class gets included in the compiled project and you can create instances of it. Then delete the existing DataSet. Now drag a new DataSet from the toolbox. When you drop the DataSet, the wizard will open. Select Typed DataSet and use the default entry, which should be the DataSet class we just created. It will create a DataSet called AddrBook1. Now you must reset the `DataSource` property of the data grid to this new DataSet. Once you have done all of this, you can test the program by loading the existing XML data back into the program. If all went well, the data should appear back in the grid.

MASTER-DETAIL RELATIONS IN THE DATASET

Up until now we have only discussed simple DataSets with one table. We have done this to keep our examples simple for the purpose of demonstrating the XML roots of the DataSet. This belies the power of the DataSet. The true power lies in its ability to define multiple tables and to define relationships between them. In ADO, you could accomplish this with the data-shaping commands and the multidimensional ADO objects. If any of you ever tried to do this, you were up against an arcane language invented by a computer scientist from hell. I never used it and I am not afraid of arcane languages. I just didn't have the time to learn the weird syntax. Doing the same thing in ADO .NET is not nearly as mystifying. If you've ever created a master-detail table structure in Microsoft Access or SQL Server you already know how to do this.

We will use the Customers, Orders, and Order Details tables in the Northwind database to demonstrate how to create a master-detail form. We will keep it simple at first by using a grid control. The grid control has some very nice features for visually presenting master-detail data without having to write very much code. Once we demonstrate this using the grid, we will create a more complex form and show how to use some code to make the data even more presentable.

The first step in creating our form is to create the visual design. We will use our familiar paradigm for starters. If you wish you can copy the form from the previous project and rename it. Set up your form with the grid and add one more button to enable us to read the data from the database. Next, add three SqlDataAdapters. When you add the first DataAdapter, the wizard will also add a Connection object as well. Make sure you select the Northwind database. Each DataAdapter should support accessing one of the three tables, Customer, Orders, and Order Details. These tables have a natural master-detail hierarchy to them. When you get to the point in the wizard where it asks you to supply the `Select` statement, use the Query Builder to create a standard select for each of the three tables. Don't use the Select * From Customers syntax. Select each column separately.

After the DataAdapters are configured, let's create our DataSet. We will be using a typed DataSet. It is possible to use an untyped one and set everything up in code, but by using a typed DataSet we enable the code to be reused in other applications and it makes the demonstration easier to understand. Drag a DataSet from the toolbox onto the component area. The wizard should open. Select Typed DataSet and change the name of the DataSet to dsOrders. Make sure all three tables are checked in the list and click OK. See Figure 7.16.

Now we must create the relationships between the tables. The DataSet cannot inherit the relations from the database as of this release. Maybe it will

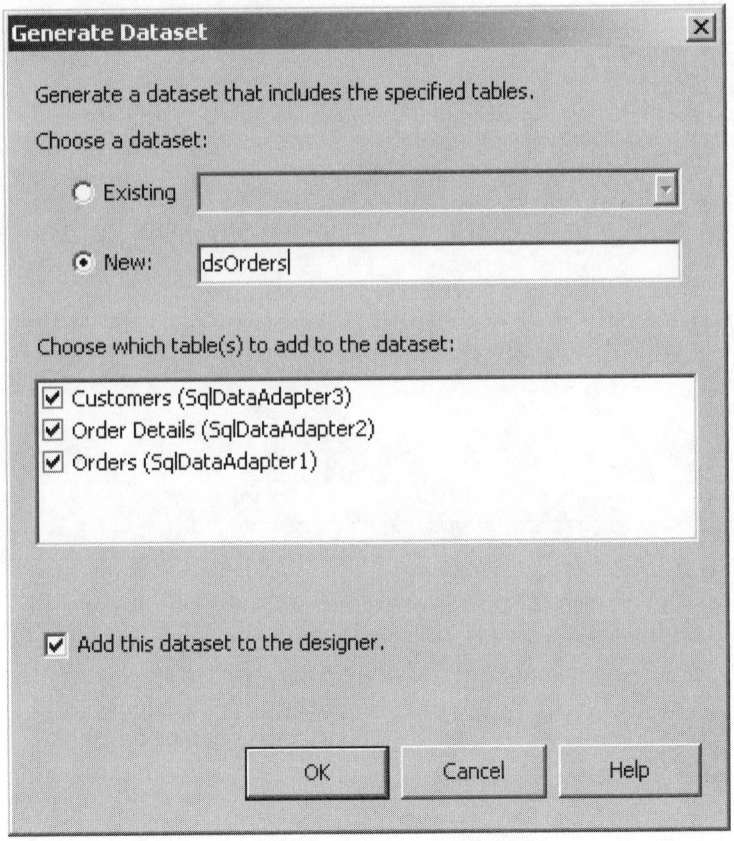

FIGURE 7.16 Generating a multitable DataSet.

be a future enhancement, but for now we have to create them manually. Right-click on dsOrders1 and select View Schema. This will open a database diagram of the DataSet. You should see the three tables laid out for you. To create the relation, drag the column from the parent table across to the child table and drop it on the corresponding column. For the CustomersOrders relation you will drag the CustomerID from the Customers table and drop it on the CustomerID in the Orders table. When you drop the column, the Edit Relation dialog opens (see Figure 7.17).

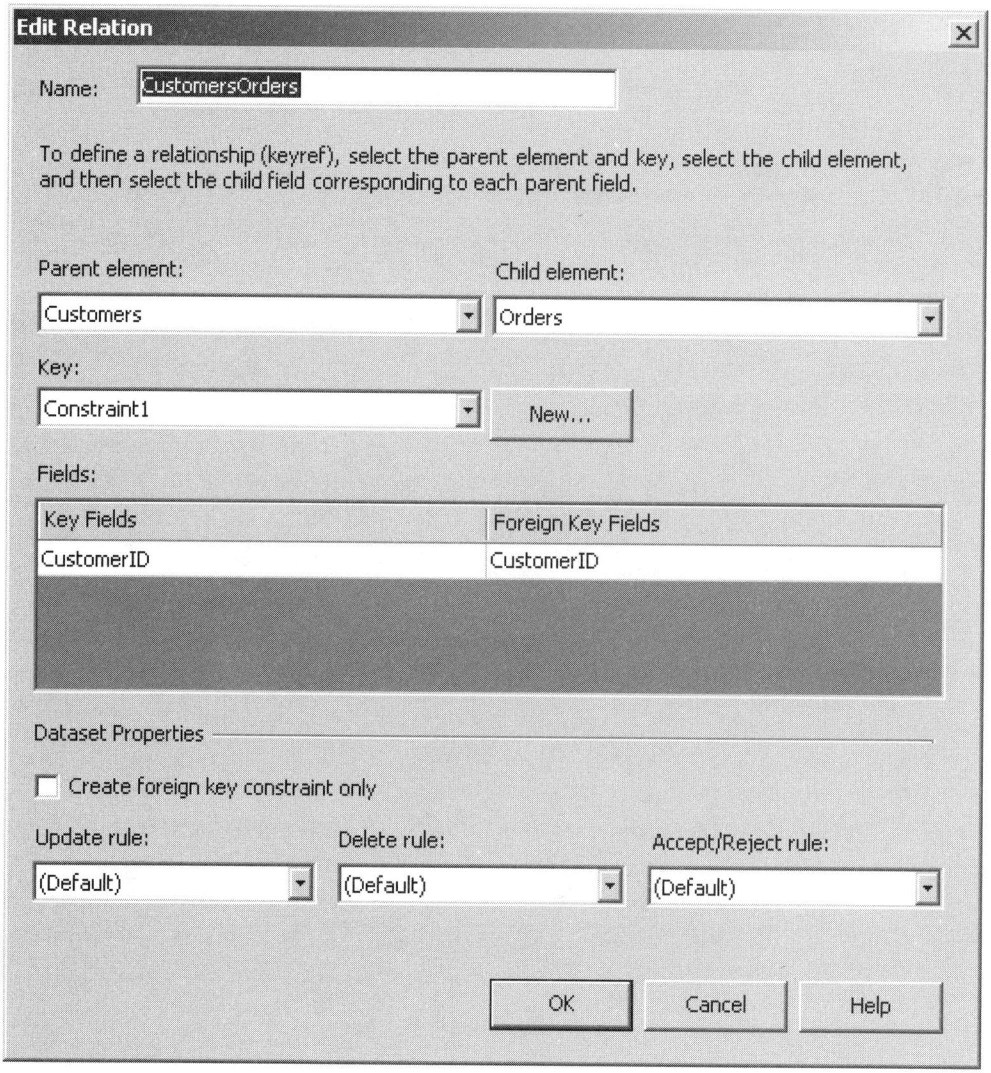

FIGURE 7.17 The Edit Relation dialog.

Make sure you drag the column the correct direction. If you drag it from Orders to Customers you will get a different relationship. Repeat this process for the Orders-Order Detail relation. This time drag the OrderID from the Orders table to the Order Detail table. When you have finished, your diagram should look something like Figure 7.18. We call this an Entity-Relationship or E-R diagram.

Once we have created our DataSet, we can bind it to the grid control. Set the `DataSource` property of the grid control to dsOrders1. Next, set the `DataMember` property to the Customers table. By setting the `DataMember` property, we are telling the grid control which table to display initially. Now we have to create some code to read the database and populate the DataSet. Add this code to the Button4_Click event procedure:

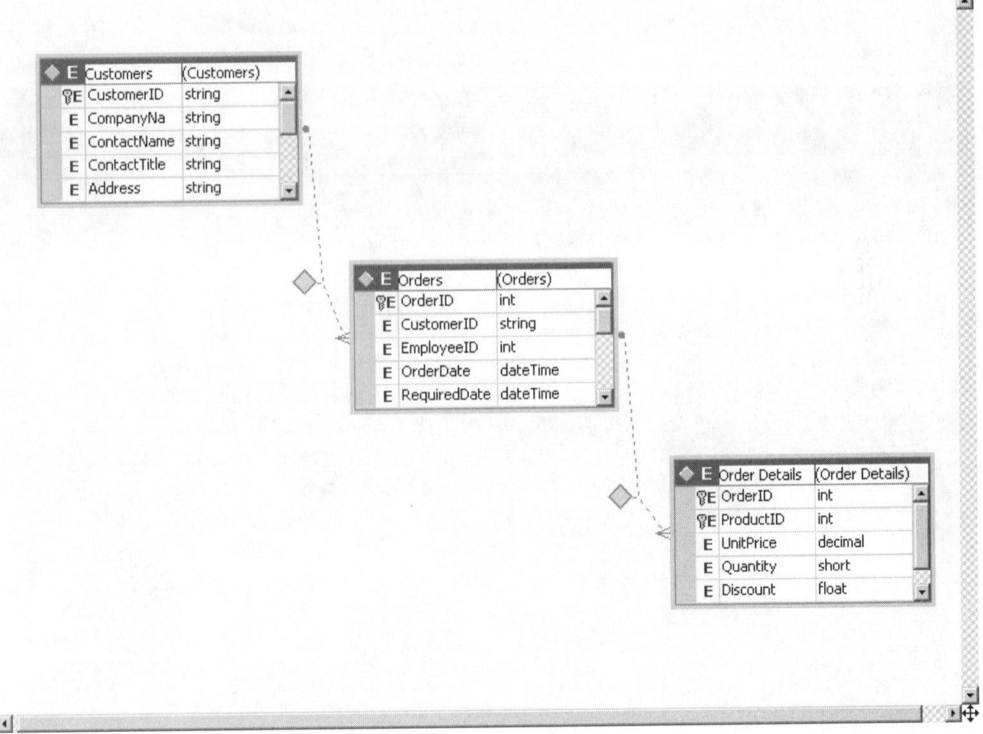

FIGURE 7.18 E-R diagram of dsOrders1.

```
    Private Sub Button4_Click(ByVal sender As System.Object, ByVal e As
System.EventArgs) Handles Button4.Click
        Try
            SqlDataAdapter1.Fill(DsOrders1.Customers)
            SqlDataAdapter2.Fill(DsOrders1.Orders)
            SqlDataAdapter3.Fill(DsOrders1.Order_Details)
        Catch errobj As Exception
            MsgBox(errobj.Message)
        End Try
    End Sub
```

We should now be ready to run the project. When the screen opens, click the Read Data button. The grid should populate with the contents of the Customers table as in Figure 7.19.

The only things different are the plus boxes in the indicator column. In a tree control, this means that we can expand the node. It means the same thing with the grid. If we click one of the plus boxes, we will have the option of drilling down through the levels of detail (see Figure 7.20).

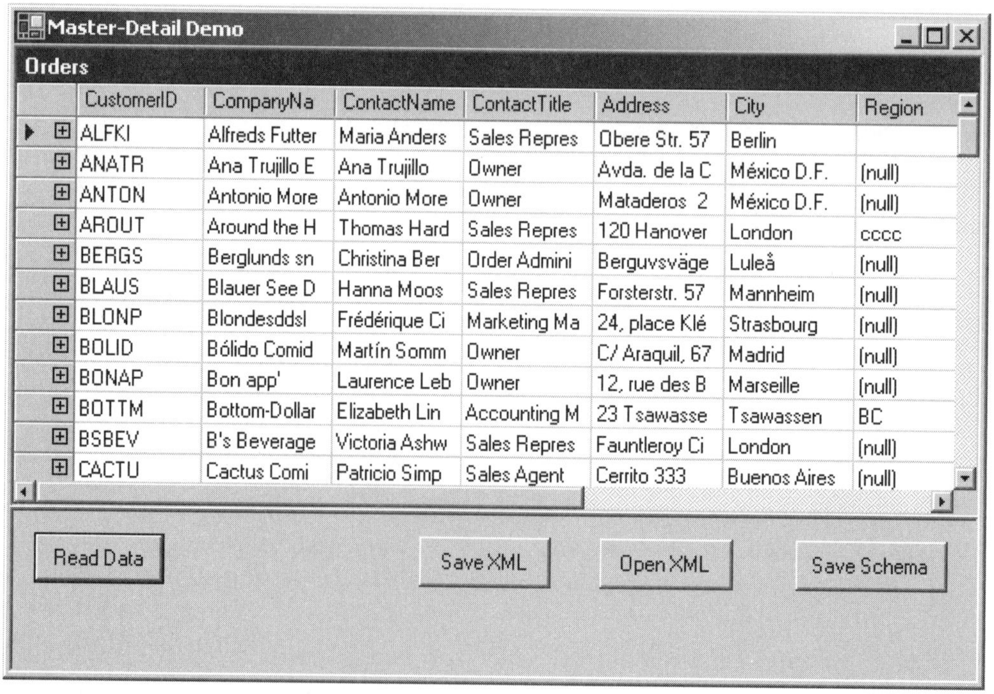

Master-Detail Demo

Orders

CustomerID	CompanyNa	ContactName	ContactTitle	Address	City	Region
ALFKI	Alfreds Futter	Maria Anders	Sales Repres	Obere Str. 57	Berlin	
ANATR	Ana Trujillo E	Ana Trujillo	Owner	Avda. de la C	México D.F.	(null)
ANTON	Antonio More	Antonio More	Owner	Mataderos 2	México D.F.	(null)
AROUT	Around the H	Thomas Hard	Sales Repres	120 Hanover	London	cccc
BERGS	Berglunds sn	Christina Ber	Order Admini	Berguvsväge	Luleå	(null)
BLAUS	Blauer See D	Hanna Moos	Sales Repres	Forsterstr. 57	Mannheim	(null)
BLONP	Blondesddsl	Frédérique Ci	Marketing Ma	24, place Klé	Strasbourg	(null)
BOLID	Bólido Comid	Martín Somm	Owner	C/ Araquil, 67	Madrid	(null)
BONAP	Bon app'	Laurence Leb	Owner	12, rue des B	Marseille	(null)
BOTTM	Bottom-Dollar	Elizabeth Lin	Accounting M	23 Tsawasse	Tsawassen	BC
BSBEV	B's Beverage	Victoria Ashw	Sales Repres	Fauntleroy Ci	London	(null)
CACTU	Cactus Comi	Patricio Simp	Sales Agent	Cerrito 333	Buenos Aires	(null)

Read Data | Save XML | Open XML | Save Schema

FIGURE 7.19 The project populated with data.

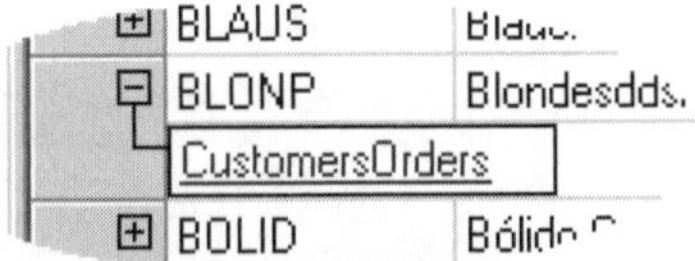

FIGURE 7.20 Plus box clicked.

If we then select the hyperlink (it's not really a hyperlink, it just looks like one), we will now display all the orders for BLONP. The master or parent row moves to the header of the grid as in Figure 7.21.

Likewise, we can also drill down to the line items of each order using the same technique. When there are no more levels to drill into, the plus boxes disappear. See Figure 7.22.

Notice that the order header information also now appears in the grid header. You can use the arrows in the header to scroll left and right to reveal the full record. The right arrow in the caption header brings you back up to

Master-Detail Demo

Orders

Customers: CustomerID: BLONP | CompanyName: Blondesddsl père et fils | ContactName: Frédér

OrderID	CustomerID	EmployeeID	OrderDate	RequiredDate	ShippedDate	ShipVia
10265	BLONP	2	07/25/1996	08/22/1996	08/12/1996	1
10297	BLONP	5	09/04/1996	10/16/1996	09/10/1996	2
10360	BLONP	4	11/22/1996	12/20/1996	12/02/1996	3
10436	BLONP	3	02/05/1997	03/05/1997	02/11/1997	2
10449	BLONP	3	02/18/1997	03/18/1997	02/27/1997	2
10559	BLONP	6	06/05/1997	07/03/1997	06/13/1997	1
10566	BLONP	9	06/12/1997	07/10/1997	06/18/1997	1
10584	BLONP	4	06/30/1997	07/28/1997	07/04/1997	1
10628	BLONP	4	08/12/1997	09/09/1997	08/20/1997	3
10679	BLONP	8	09/23/1997	10/21/1997	09/30/1997	3
10826	BLONP	6	01/12/1998	02/09/1998	02/06/1998	1

Read Data | Save XML | Open XML | Save Schema

FIGURE 7.21 Showing the customer's orders.

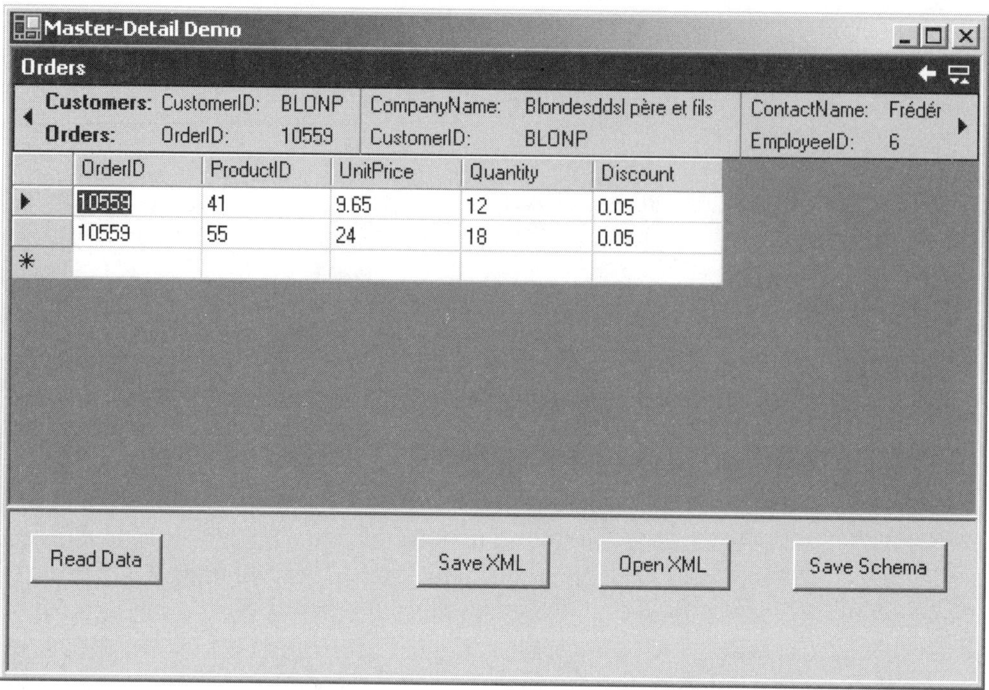

FIGURE 7.22 Showing the order detail.

the next level. The other icon allows you to show and hide the parent row display. Pretty good for writing a minimum of code, wouldn't you say?

Controlling Grid Navigation Programmatically

Next we will create a more sophisticated form so we can demonstrate how to use code to show the details. In our new form, we will display the customer information in a header panel we will create ourselves. Then we will add a Next and a Previous button for the user to navigate through the customers. As the user navigates, the grid control will automatically display the order information for the customer. We can use the same DataSet (dsOrders1) that we have been using. Our new form will appear as in Figure 7.23.

We want to add a new procedure to the form to assist with positioning the data grid. This new procedure will be called SetRowPos and will accept the row position as a parameter.

```
Private Sub SetRowPos(ByVal intPos As Integer)
    DataGrid1.NavigateBack()
```

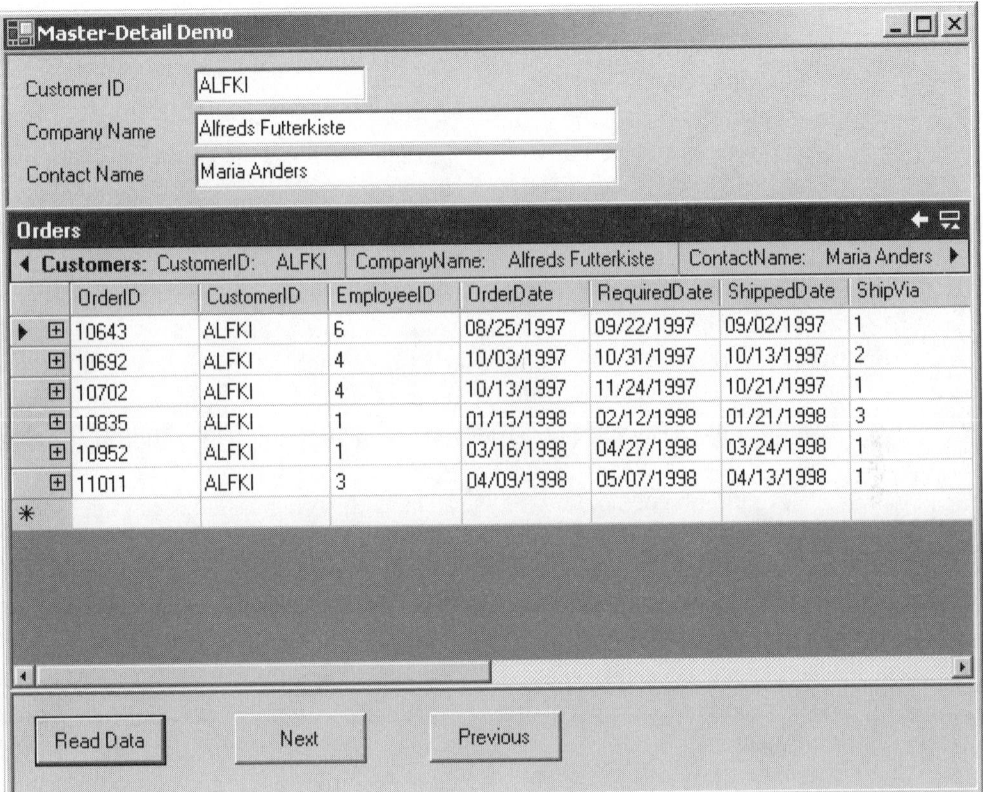

FIGURE 7.23 The form with the new header.

```
        Me.BindingContext(DsOrders1, "Customers").Position = intPos
        DataGrid1.NavigateTo(intPos, "CustomersOrders")
    End Sub
```

All navigation in the grid is relative to the row on which you are currently positioned. The grid does not have any way—that I can tell—of informing the programmer of what level is currently the relation that is displayed on the screen. This would be a nice feature for a future revision.

USING THE DATAVIEW CLASS

Finally we focus on the DataView class. This class is a helper that you can use to customize the behavior of the DataSet. The main functions of interest are sorts and filters, but there are other interesting methods and properties as well. We went through the properties and methods earlier in the chapter. Now let's see how we can use the class to quickly switch attributes of the DataSet which affect its appearance.

Let's create a project called ADOBook03-04. This time, instead of using relations to customize our view of the data, we'll use the DataView class. In a real-world project, we would use a combination of both techniques, along with SQL to optimize performance. For example, we would not typically read all the rows in each table. We would probably use a `where` clause in our `Select` statements to limit the amount of data being transferred over the network. The top level statement would contain a `where` clause that would allow us to limit the results to a subset of the table. The Orders level would then use an `in` clause to limit the order headers to only those that match the results of the Customers query and so on down through the levels of detail. I will demonstrate this later in the chapter.

For the first demo, we will use a DataSet similar to that used in the previous example. The difference this time is that we will eliminate the relations between the tables (for now). We are going to use DataViews to accomplish the same result as the relations did. As with everything in programming, there are always multiple solutions to any problem. That is why we have so much religion in the computer field. Many programmers think their way is the only right way. Please don't be this way with these demonstrations. I am aware that there might be better ways to solve this type of problem. My purpose here is to demonstrate the classes, not necessarily to find the best solution.

This time, we will use two data grid controls so the user does not have to drill down. All of the data will be available all of the time. To save time, we'll look at the finished form, then we will describe how to make it work (see Figure 7.24).

To create the form, place another panel control on the form to hold the two grids. To do this, set the `Dock` property of the existing grid to None. This will allow you to resize it. Temporarily resize it so that it takes up very little space. Now drop your panel on the form. Size the panel so it is a decent size. Next cut and paste the existing grid into the panel so it is a child control of the panel. Now add the new grid. Set the `Dock` property of the new panel to Fill, and set the borderstyle to Fixed 3D. Next set the `Dock` property of the existing grid and the new grid both to Fill. You may have to use a Move To Front command on the existing grid to get them to position properly. I trust that by now you can create the UI without too much coaching. I really want to concentrate on the code.

Next add three DataView objects to the form. You can drag them from the toolbox. The idea behind this project is to automatically populate the

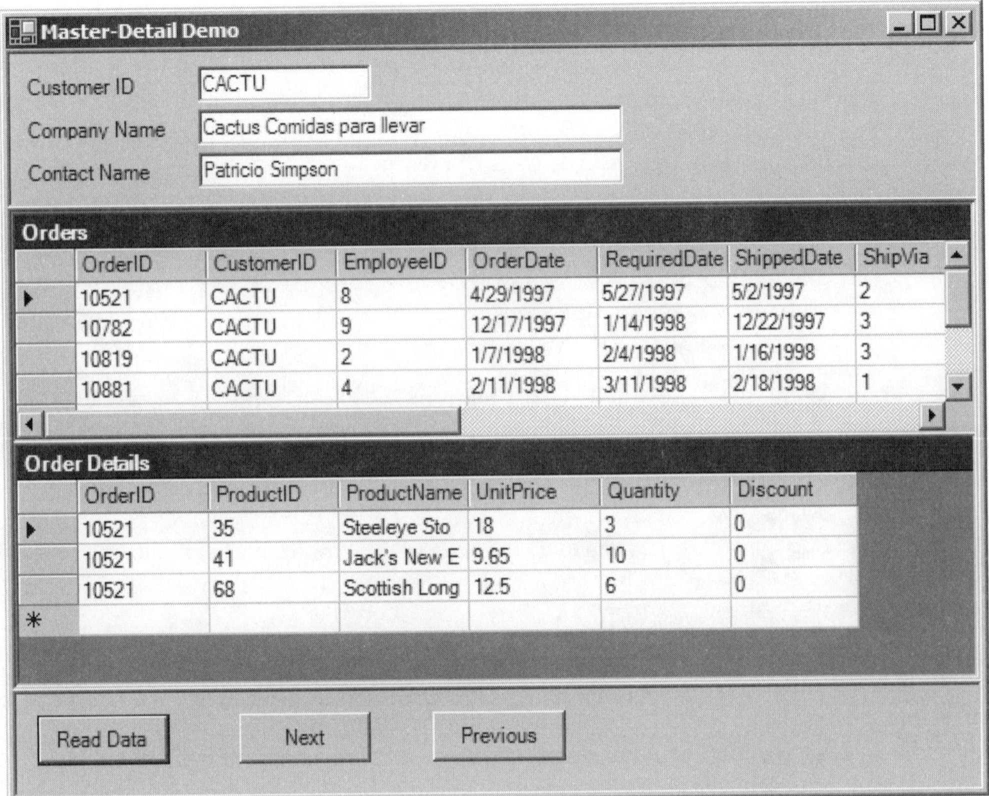

FIGURE 7.24 The project using two grids.

upper grid with the orders for the customer displayed in the header, and then to display the order details in the lower grid for each order as the user navigates the upper grid. The DataView objects will be used to customize the view of the DataSet for each section of the form. We will do this by binding the controls to the DataView objects instead of directly to the DataSet. Yes, DataView is a bindable class that can act as a DataSource.

Create your three DataAdapter objects as we did in the previous chapter. The only thing we will do differently is to create a join in SqlDataAdapter3 so we can display the product name in the lower grid. This just makes it a little friendlier for the user. You can generate your DataSet and call it dsOrders as before. This time we will not create the relations between the tables. Each DataView object will be bound to one of the DataTables in the DataSet. Bind DataView1 to the Customers table, DataView2 to the Orders table, and DataView3 to the Order Details table. Now, change the bindings of the three text boxes in the screen header to bind to DataView1, and then the appropriate column. Do the same for the data grid controls. To complete the project, let's add the following code to the form:

```
    ' This procedure fills the DataSet.
    Private Sub Button4_Click(ByVal sender As System.Object, ByVal e As
System.EventArgs) Handles Button4.Click
        Try
            SqlDataAdapter1.Fill(DsOrders1.Customers)
            SqlDataAdapter2.Fill(DsOrders1.Orders)
            SqlDataAdapter3.Fill(DsOrders1.Order_Details)
            DsOrders1.AcceptChanges()
            SetRowPos(0)
        Catch errobj As Exception
            MsgBox(errobj.Message & vbCrLf & errobj.StackTrace)
        End Try
    End Sub

    ' Move to the next row.
    Private Sub Button1_Click(ByVal sender As System.Object, ByVal e As
System.EventArgs) Handles Button1.Click
        Dim intPos As Integer

        Try
            intPos = Me.BindingContext(DataView1).Position
            intPos += 1
            If intPos > DataView1.Count - 1 Then Exit Sub
            SetRowPos(intPos)
        Catch errobj As Exception
            MsgBox(errobj.Message & vbCrLf & errobj.StackTrace)
        End Try
    End Sub

    ' Moves to the previous row.
    Private Sub Button2_Click(ByVal sender As System.Object, ByVal e As
System.EventArgs) Handles Button2.Click
        Dim intPos As Integer

        Try
            intPos = Me.BindingContext(DataView1).Position
            intPos -= 1
            If intPos < 0 Then Exit Sub
            SetRowPos(intPos)
        Catch errobj As Exception
            MsgBox(errobj.Message & vbCrLf & errobj.StackTrace)
        End Try
    End Sub
```

```
    ' Sets the row filter for the Orders grid.
    Private Sub SetRowPos(ByVal intPos As Integer)
        Dim intOrdPos As Integer

        Me.BindingContext(DataView1).Position = intPos
        DataView2.RowFilter = "CustomerID = '" & Trim(TextBox1.Text) &
"'"
        intOrdPos = DataGrid1.CurrentRowIndex
        SetDetailPos(intOrdPos)
    End Sub

    ' Sets the row filter for the Details grid.
    Private Sub SetDetailPos(ByVal intOrdPos As Integer)
        DataView3.RowFilter = "OrderID = " & DataGrid1.Item(intOrdPos,
0)
    End Sub

    Private Sub DataGrid1_CurrentCellChanged(ByVal sender As Object,
ByVal e As System.EventArgs) Handles DataGrid1.CurrentCellChanged
        SetDetailPos(DataGrid1.CurrentRowIndex)
    End Sub
```

By setting the `RowFilter` property, we immediately change the display in the grid. Isn't that easy? The DataView class is very powerful. When we run the project, each time we move to a new Customer row, the other grids automatically fill with the data for that customer. Likewise, as we navigate through the orders grid, the detail items change. Since we are only applying a filter, there is no round trip to the server required. This makes it perform very efficiently.

Using SQL to Enhance Performance

The last modification we want to make is to optimize performance by limiting the rows returns from the server. We can do this by adding a couple of parameters to the SQL queries in the DataAdapters. Let's modify our form to add one more field to serve as the look-up field. Your form should now look like Figure 7.25.

We will allow our users to use a wildcard search to look up customers by customer ID. We can use SQL to do all of the selecting for us. For SqlDataAdapter1.Selectcommand use the following SQL:

```
SELECT    CustomerID, CompanyName, ContactName, ContactTitle, Address,
City, Region, PostalCode, Country, Phone, Fax
FROM         Customers
WHERE     (CustomerID LIKE @CustID + '%')
```

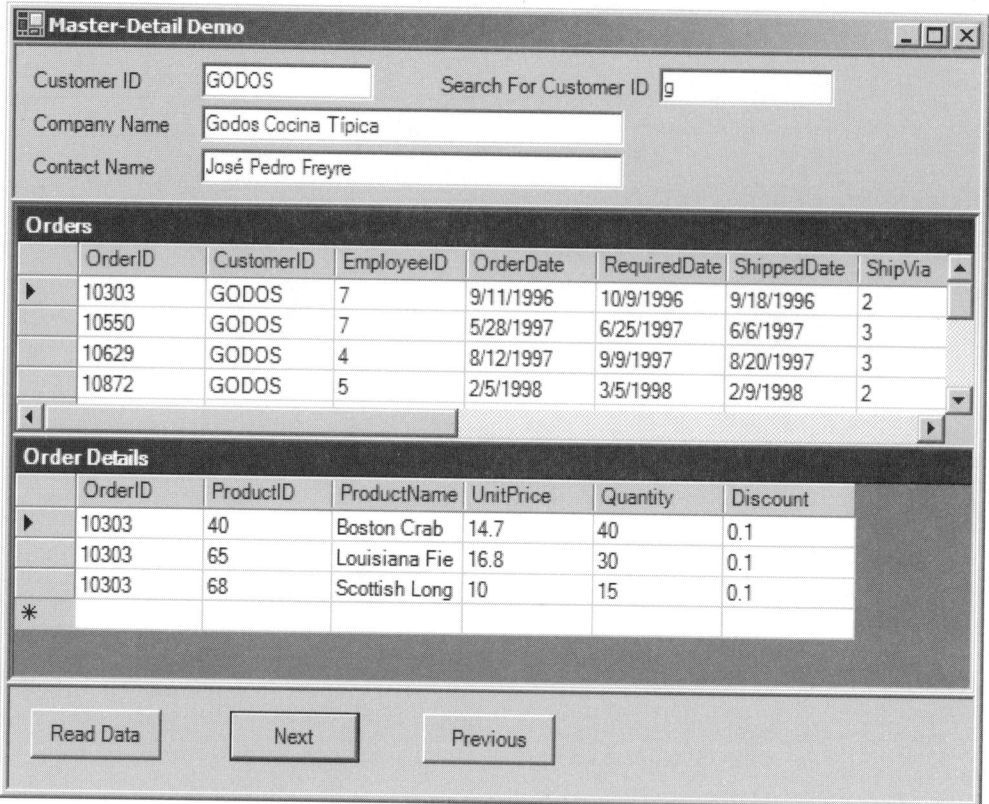

FIGURE 7.25 Form with the search field added.

This will fill the Customers table based on the wildcard provided by the user. Now change the SQL for SqlDataAdapter2 to read:

```
SELECT     OrderID, CustomerID, EmployeeID, OrderDate, RequiredDate,
ShippedDate, ShipVia, Freight, ShipName, ShipAddress, ShipCity,
ShipRegion,
                      ShipPostalCode, ShipCountry
FROM         Orders
WHERE     (CustomerID IN
                          (SELECT     CustomerID
                            FROM         Customers
                            WHERE      CustomerID LIKE @CustID + '%'))
```

Notice that we are using the SQL itself to select the correct rows from the Orders table based on what we found in the Customers table. We will now do a similar thing with the order details:

```
SELECT     [Order Details].OrderID, [Order Details].ProductID, [Order
Details].UnitPrice, [Order Details].Quantity, [Order Details].Discount,
                    Products.ProductName
FROM          [Order Details] INNER JOIN
                    Products ON [Order Details].ProductID =
Products.ProductID
WHERE      ([Order Details].OrderID IN
                         (SELECT     OrderID
                           FROM          Orders
                           WHERE      CustomerID LIKE @CustID + '%'))
```

When we run these queries, we will have all of the rows needed for each table in the DataSet. We then can use the same technique with the DataViews to populate the grid controls. As a matter of fact, only one procedure—the Read Data button click event—needs to be changed.

```
    Private Sub Button4_Click(ByVal sender As System.Object, ByVal e As
System.EventArgs) Handles Button4.Click
        Dim strSearch As String

        Try
            DsOrders1.Clear()
            strSearch = Trim(TextBox4.Text)
           SqlDataAdapter1.SelectCommand.Parameters("@CustID").Value =
strSearch
            SqlDataAdapter1.Fill(DsOrders1.Customers)
           SqlDataAdapter2.SelectCommand.Parameters("@CustID").Value =
strSearch
            SqlDataAdapter2.Fill(DsOrders1.Orders)
           SqlDataAdapter3.SelectCommand.Parameters("@CustID").Value =
strSearch
            SqlDataAdapter3.Fill(DsOrders1.Order_Details)
            DsOrders1.AcceptChanges()
            SetRowPos(0)
        Catch errobj As Exception
            MsgBox(errobj.Message & vbCrLf & errobj.StackTrace)
        End Try
    End Sub
```

Now we have the best of both worlds, the convenience of the DataView class and the efficiency of SQL.

SUMMARY

We have covered the most useful techniques for effectively using the DataSet class. We have seen how to update the database. And we have seen how to use the DataView class to efficiently manage how the data is presented to the user. Next we will look at data binding in the .NET Framework. This version has some significant improvements over previous versions. Let's move forward.

CHAPTER 8

Data Binding in Windows Forms

Data binding is the ability of a set of controls to automatically display data from an underlying DataSource with little or no code provided by the programmer. Data binding is normally connected with visual controls, but it does not have to be. It is possible to bind data to properties of nonvisual components as well. Data binding was introduced by Microsoft in Visual Basic 3.0. Prior to this there were Visual Basic custom controls (VBXs) that could be used to accomplish the same result. When data binding was introduced, it was considered revolutionary. Programmers could now create a fully active data-bound form without writing any code at all. This was an integral part of the rapid application development (RAD) programming methodology. However, many programmers shunned the use of data binding because you also sacrificed a lot of control when you used it. As each new version of Visual Basic was released, more control was given to the programmer using data binding, until now it can be used without sacrificing any control at all. As a matter of fact, now it is actually more desirable to use data binding than not. It simply no longer pays to not use it. Not convinced? Hopefully, by the end of this chapter you will be.

When we talk about data binding in Visual Basic, we are really talking about data binding in the .NET Framework. The framework offers two binding models, one for Windows Forms, and one for Web Forms. The Windows Forms data binding model is two-way. That is, it supports both displaying data in controls and automatically updating the data in the underlying DataSource when the user changes the data in the controls. The Web Forms model is display-only. This has nothing to do with some arbitrary decision made by Microsoft. It is because web-based forms are stateless, and once the page containing the form is served to the client, there is no software behind it to respond to changes and notifications. We will look at both binding methods. Though similar, there are significant differences between them beyond just the display-only issue. In this chapter we will be dealing with Windows Forms. In the next chapter we will look at Web Forms.

DATA BINDING IN WINDOWS FORMS

The most robust data binding is found in Windows Forms. You can bind data to almost any Windows Forms control that displays data. In addition you can bind different columns and even data from different tables to different properties of the same control. The way this is handled is through a property of the form called the `BindingContext`.

THE CURRENCYMANAGER CLASS

The `BindingConText` property of a form returns a CurrencyManager object which inherits from the BindingManagerBase abstract class. The CurrencyManager object manages all the association between the DataTable (the DefaultView of the DataTable to be specific) or other bindable class and the controls they are bound to. Since the data binding functionality is provided by an intermediate object (the CurrencyManager) it provides a lot of flexibility when creating and using bound controls. In previous versions of Visual Basic, the binding mechanism was built into each control. Controls could be bound to one or two DataSources at the most, depending on their function. There were controls that supported data binding, and controls that didn't. Now all controls can support data binding because the binding mechanism has been moved into the helper class. We will study this later in the chapter.

Note that the CurrencyManager class manages the association between bound controls and *one DataTable only* in the underlying DataSource. The DataSource can be a DataView or a DataTable, or even an array. It is very picky about how it identifies the relationship, which is by how the `DataSource` property is set up. For example, if you set up the DataSource to a grid control as DataSet11.Customers, then you must reference it this way when referring to the CurrencyManager. This example assumes that DataSet11 is a data type of DataSet1, which is the class generated during the creation of the typed DataSet. If the DataSource is set up as described, then you would reference the CurrencyManager like this:

```
Me.BindingContext(DataSet11.Customers).Position
```

If you try to use `Me.BindingContext(DataSet1.Tables(0)).Position` (assuming that the first table is Customers) it will not work properly. This is because it references a DataTable object which is higher in the class hierarchy than the Customers class which inherits from it (the DataTable class).

The following will not work either because it still references a DataTable object; i.e., it is late bound:

```
Me.BindingContext(DataSet11, "Customers").Position
```

This will work though because you are coercing the object to the correct type:

```
Me.BindingContext(CType(DataSet11.Tables(0),
DataSet1.Customers.GetType())).Position
```

It seems quirky at first glance, but if you understand OOP it makes sense in that context. At any rate, just make sure you reference the correct data type and you will save yourself many headaches.

`CurrencyManager` Properties and Methods

The following are the properties and methods of interest in the CurrencyManager class.

- `Bindings`—The `Bindings` property returns a BindingsCollection collection of Binding objects. These objects contain references to all the controls bound to the particular BindingContext.
- `Count`—Returns the number of rows in the DataSource.
- `Position`— Returns the row index of the current row that the bound controls are displaying data from.
- `AddNew`—Adds a new row to the underlying data source. This is used mainly to support the DataGrid control. The normal way to add rows is to use the `AddNew` method of the DataView or the `NewRow` method of the DataTable.
- `EndCurrentEdit/CancelCurrentEdit`—`EndCurrentEdit` ends the edit of the current row and moves the data from the edit buffer to the actual row. `CancelCurrentEdit` discards any changes and restores the displayed data to what it was before editing began.
- `Refresh`—This method redisplays all of the data in the bound controls.

- `RemoveAt`—Removes a row from the underlying data source. This is used mainly to support the DataGrid control. The normal way to delete rows is to use the `Remove(At)` method of the DataView or the `Remove(At)` method of the DataTable.
- `SuspendBinding/Resume Binding`—Two methods that allow the temporary suspension and resumption of data binding. You would typically suspend data binding if the user must be allowed to make several edits to data fields before validation occurs (e.g., if one field must be changed in accordance with a second, but where validating the first field would cause the second field to be in error). These are handy methods. I used a similar technique in VB 6 when I had to create my own data binding mechanism to work around shortcomings in the ADO data binding mechanism.
- `CurrentChanged` event—Fires when the bound value of an item changes,
- `ItemChanged`—Fires when an item changes value, by a user edit for example.
- `PositionChanged`—Fires when the CurrencyManager moves to a new row.

THE DATA FORM WIZARD

The Data Form wizard will generate a Windows Form bound to a DataTable in a DataSet. While I would never really use one of these forms in any of my projects, the code they generate can help us understand how data binding works in .NET. The Data Form wizard is quite powerful and while I wouldn't use it to generate forms for a serious application, it could be useful if you needed a quick-and-dirty data entry form. We are going to use it for a different purpose. We will create a form and then analyze the resulting code to see how they work.

The first step is to create a Windows Forms project. Do this now. Call it ADOBook08-01. To invoke the data form wizard, you add a new form to the project. When the template dialog opens, you can select the Data Form Wizard icon, as in Figure 8.1.

Leave the form name as is and click Open. The Data Form Wizard welcome screen appears. Click Next to begin. The first screen is the Select DataSet screen as in Figure 8.2.

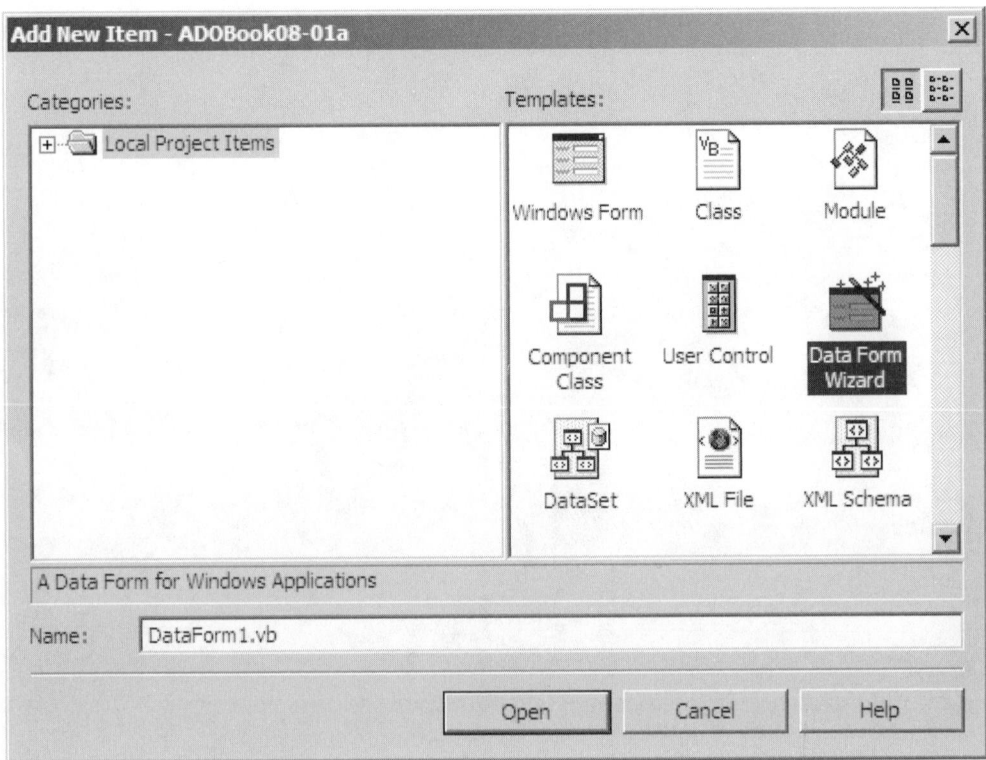

FIGURE 8.1 Selecting the Data Form Wizard.

Tell it to create a DataSet and name it dsMain. When you click Next you will be prompted for a connection. Use our Northwind database connection. The next screen asks you to pick the tables you would like in the DataSet. Move the tables or view from the left pane to the right pane to select them. Use the tables show in Figure 8.3.

Look familiar? Yes, we will use our familiar Customers, Orders, and Order Details tables. You will see why in a minute. The next screen allows us to set up our relations. We set up the relation in the left side of the form, then click the ">" button to move the relation to the right. You can click on the relation in the list to see its details and modify them if needed (see Figure 8.4).

The next screen allows us to select the fields we want displayed on our form (See Figure 8.5).

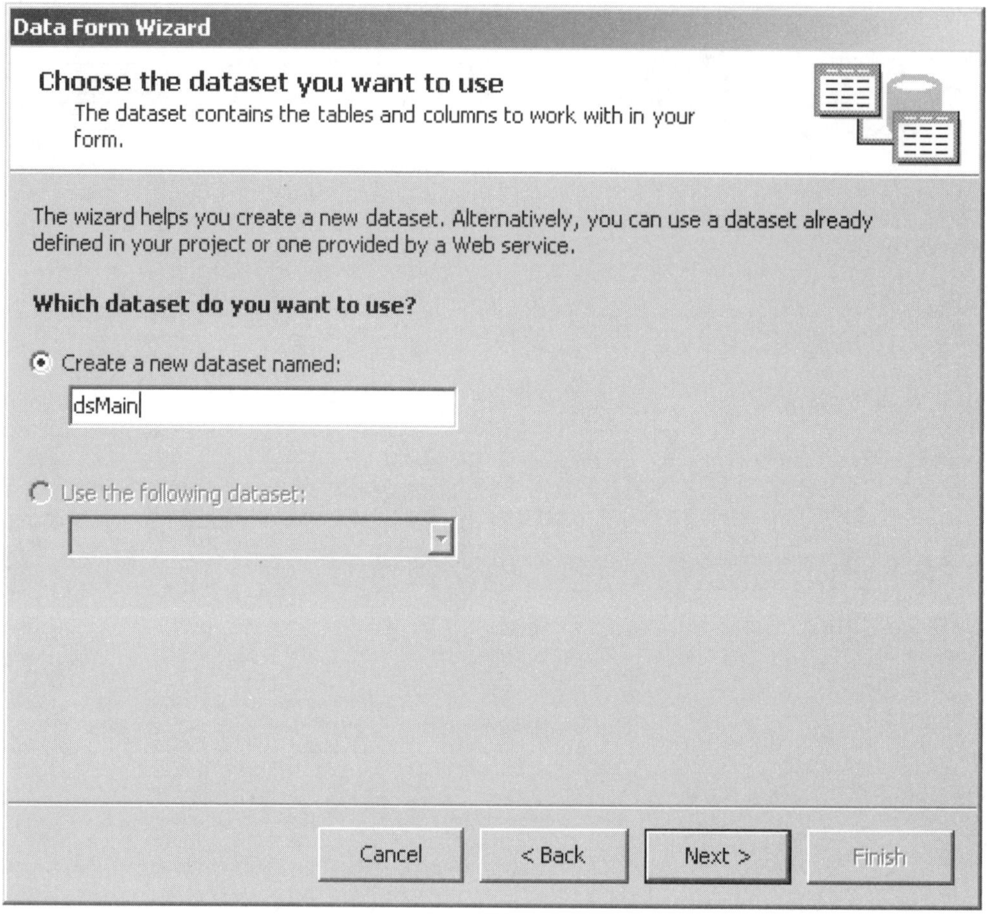

FIGURE 8.2 The Select DataSet screen.

The next screen allows you to control how the data will be displayed on the form, in a grid or as separate fields. Choose separate fields as in Figure 8.6.

When you click Finish the form will be generated. Notice :

- The wizard used the OLEDB versions of the data controls. This is because it must use a lowest common denominator approach since it must be able to use any database server.
- The form had to be resized to be usable. This is probably a bug.
- It only supports two levels of master detail.

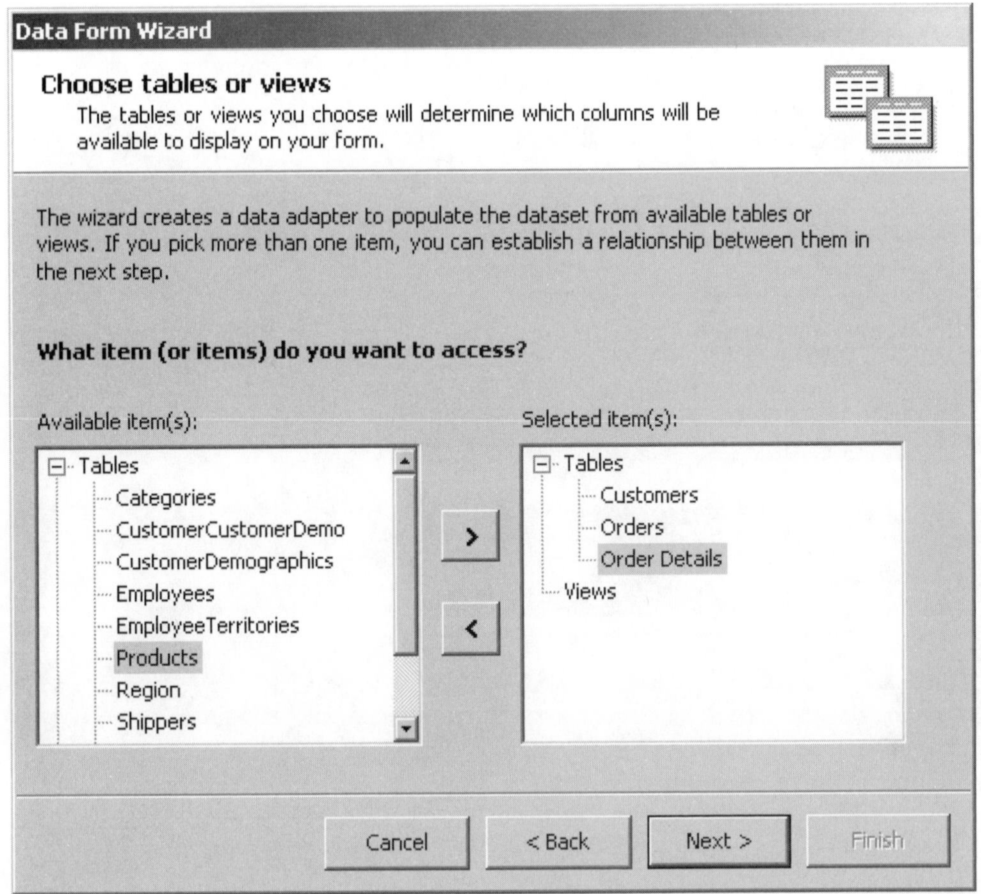

FIGURE 8.3 Selecting the tables.

I deliberately used three levels to show this. You can make a slight modification to the form to drill down into the details. You should already know how to do this, but we will demonstrate soon. Figure 8.7 shows the finished form at runtime.

Remember in the last chapter how we used DataViews to customize the data in the grid? We didn't have to do that. Look at what the Data Form wizard does. It uses a relation as the setting of the `DataMember` property. That's right, the relation itself is bindable. When we do this, we do not have to use any code at all to repopulate the data grid control. So to complete our form, all we have to do is add another grid control and set the `DataMember` property to the correct relation object.

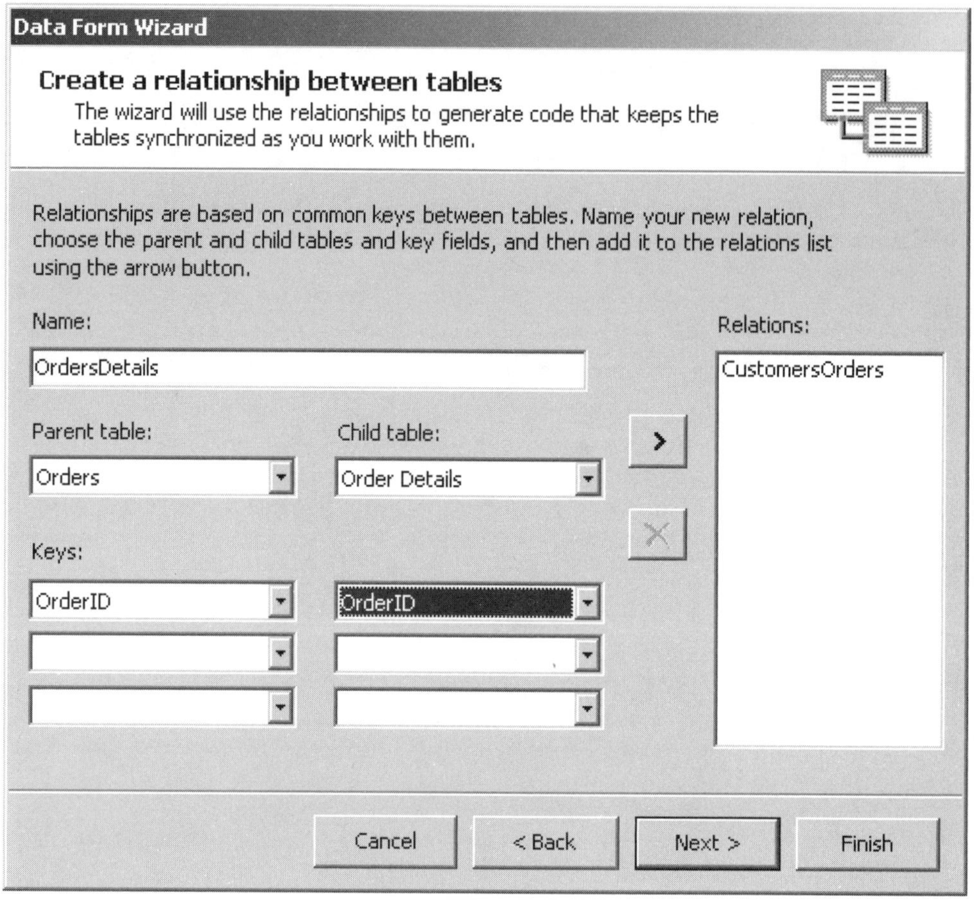

FIGURE 8.4 The Relations screen.

When setting the property, it is important to use the correct value. Set the `DataSource` property to the DataSet. Do not set it to a DataTable. Now we will set the `DataMember` property to the OrdersDetails relation that is nested under the Customers table. Do not use the one under the Orders table (see Figure 8.8).

Now our form will automatically show three levels of detail as before. We didn't have to write any code to support the feature this time. We can already see how powerful the data binding features are in .NET. Now let's look at the generated code to get an idea of what it's doing. We will be concentrating on the data-binding features of the form. We have already covered filling DataSets and updating the database enough times. Figure 8.9 shows the new form with the three levels of detail.

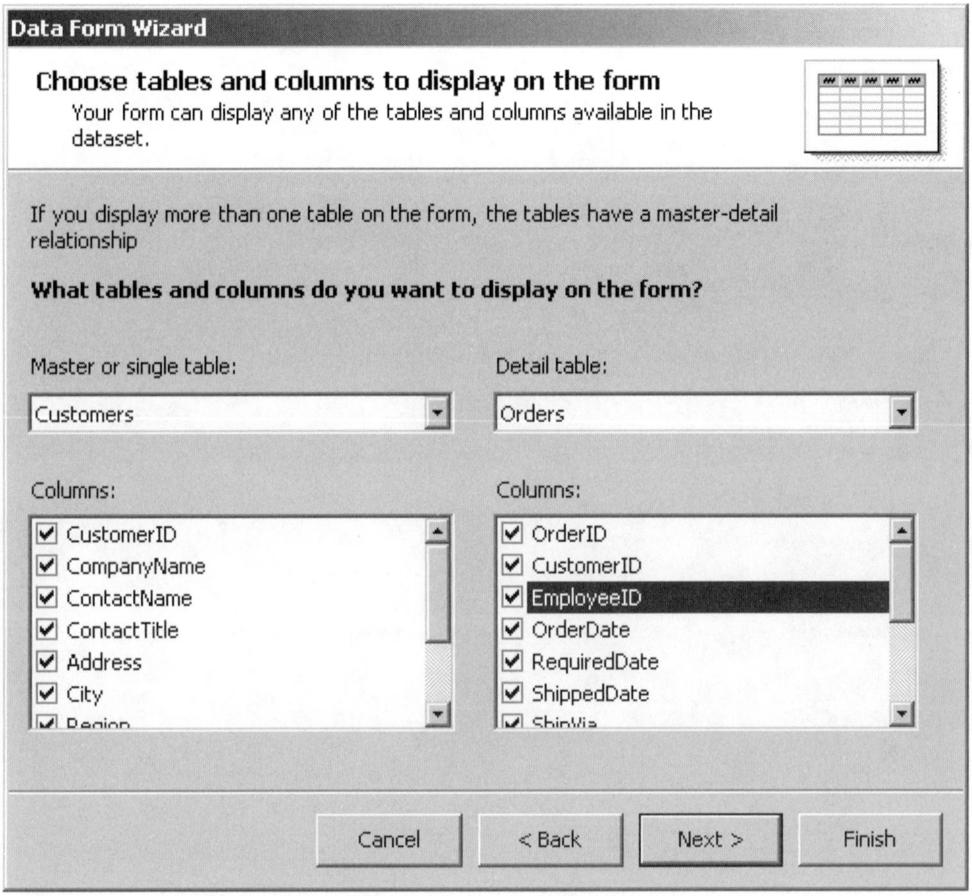

Data Form Wizard

Choose tables and columns to display on the form

Your form can display any of the tables and columns available in the dataset.

If you display more than one table on the form, the tables have a master-detail relationship

What tables and columns do you want to display on the form?

Master or single table: Customers

Detail table: Orders

Columns: CustomerID, CompanyName, ContactName, ContactTitle, Address, City, Region

Columns: OrderID, CustomerID, EmployeeID, OrderDate, RequiredDate, ShippedDate, ShipVia

Cancel | < Back | Next > | Finish

FIGURE 8.5 Select fields to display.

Examining the Code

Next, we will look at the code. We will concentrate on the use of the `BindingConText` property of the form.

VB6—You VB 6 coders will notice that many of the navigation and editing functionality of the RecordSet has been moved into the BindingManager class. Methods to begin and end editing, add new records, and navigate are all now in the BindingManager class.

Before we begin, let me admit that the generated code is not perfect. It does not conform to the coding standards laid out in the Visual Basic documentation and some of the techniques it uses go against recommended tech-

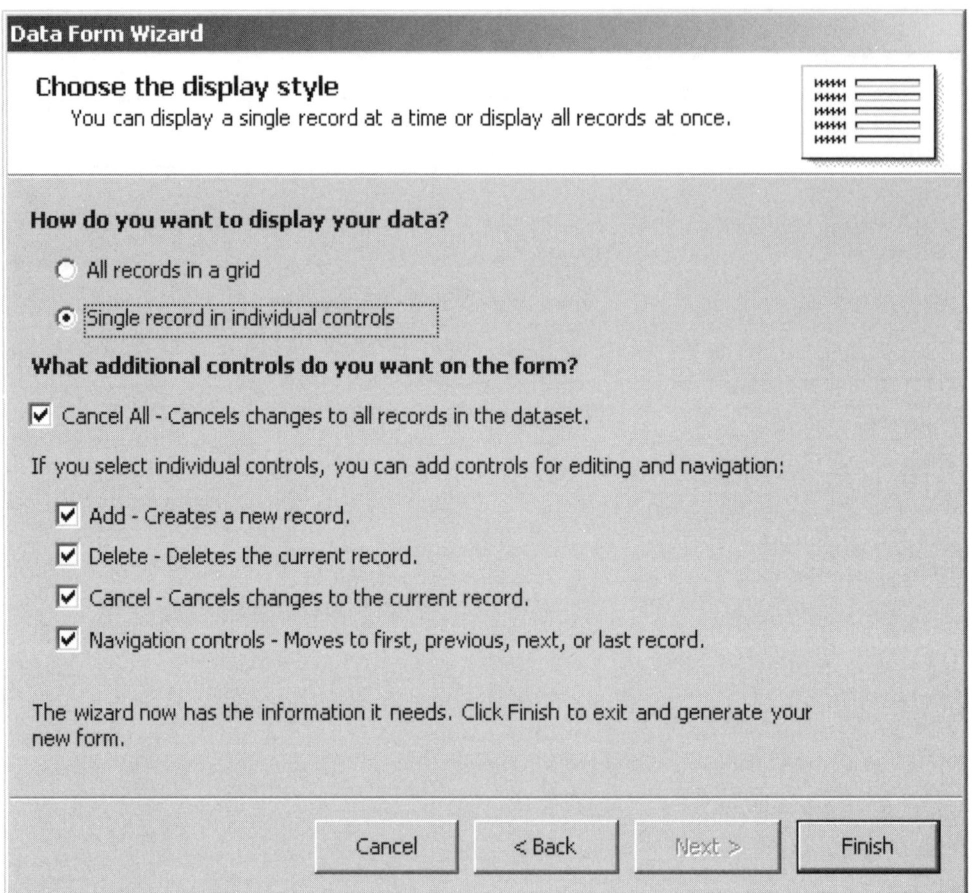

FIGURE 8.6 Selecting the Display format.

niques in the documentation. For example, it uses the BindingContext to delete and add records to the master table, but this is expressly not recommended in the documentation for the CurrencyManager class. I've always had the idealistic notion that generated code should be a shining example of the right way of doing things. Microsoft put all this energy into the code generator, why not make it generate code that at least conforms to the documentation? But my idealism has gotten me in trouble before, so why should this time be any different? But I digress. … Anyway, as a learning tool it can still teach us some things about data binding in the .NET Framework.

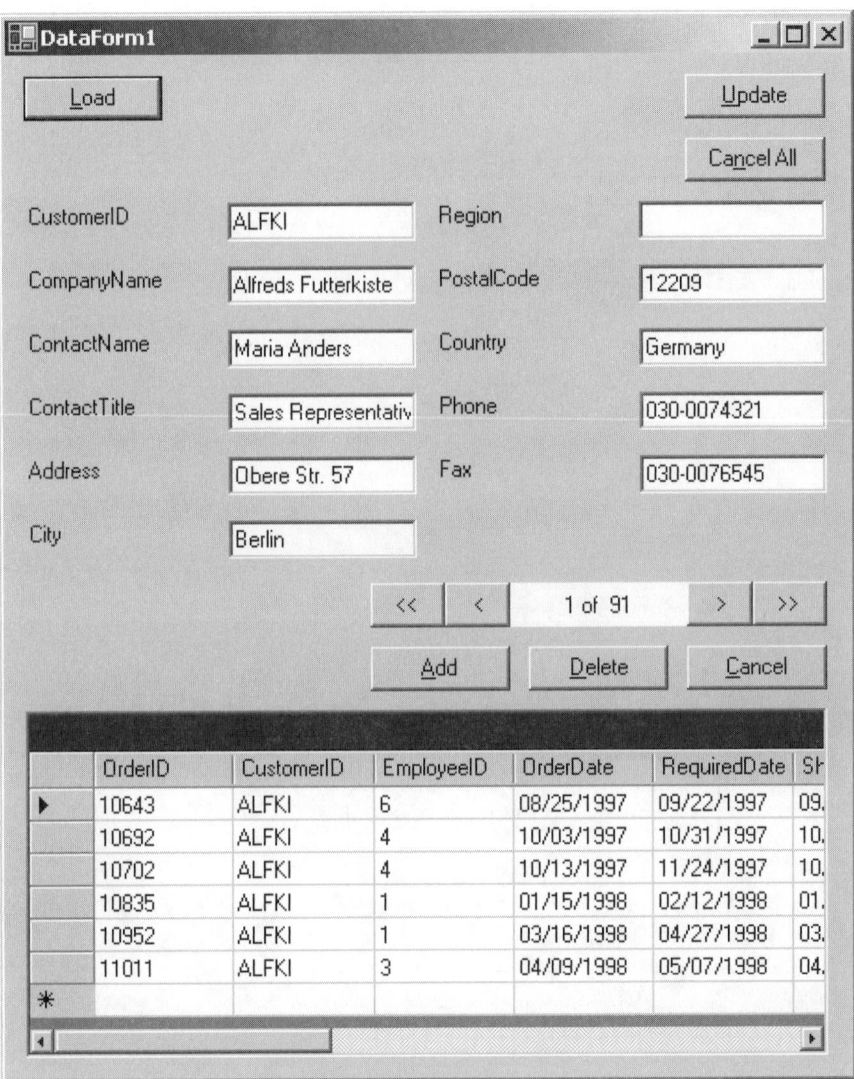

FIGURE 8.7 The wizard-generated form.

Row Navigation

First we will examine how the form does row navigation. The navigation buttons on the form are reminiscent of the old ADO data control, but they are implemented entirely in the code of the form. As with the old control, we have Last, Previous, Next, and First buttons, along with a label area that

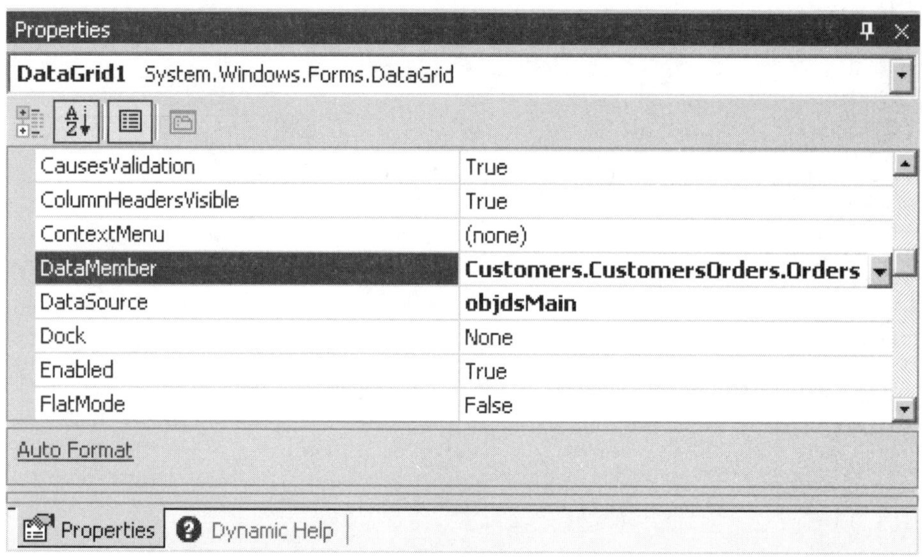

FIGURE 8.8 Selecting the correct relation object.

shows the current and total number of records. The code to implement these functions is quite simple. When you are first learning ADO .NET it often seems difficult to find what were simple functions in ADO. The old RecordSet `Move` methods were like this with me. I was mystified until I discovered the `BindingContext` property. Let's look at the code for the navigation buttons.

```
    Private Sub btnNavFirst_Click(ByVal sender As System.Object, ByVal e
As System.EventArgs) Handles btnNavFirst.Click
        Me.BindingContext(objdsMain, "Customers").Position = 0
        Me.objdsMain_PositionChanged()

    End Sub
    Private Sub btnLast_Click(ByVal sender As System.Object, ByVal e As
System.EventArgs) Handles btnLast.Click
        Me.BindingContext(objdsMain, "Customers").Position =
(Me.objdsMain.Tables("Customers").Rows.Count - 1)
        Me.objdsMain_PositionChanged()

    End Sub
    Private Sub btnNavPrev_Click(ByVal sender As System.Object, ByVal e
As System.EventArgs) Handles btnNavPrev.Click
        Me.BindingContext(objdsMain, "Customers").Position =
(Me.BindingContext(objdsMain, "Customers").Position - 1)
        Me.objdsMain_PositionChanged()
```

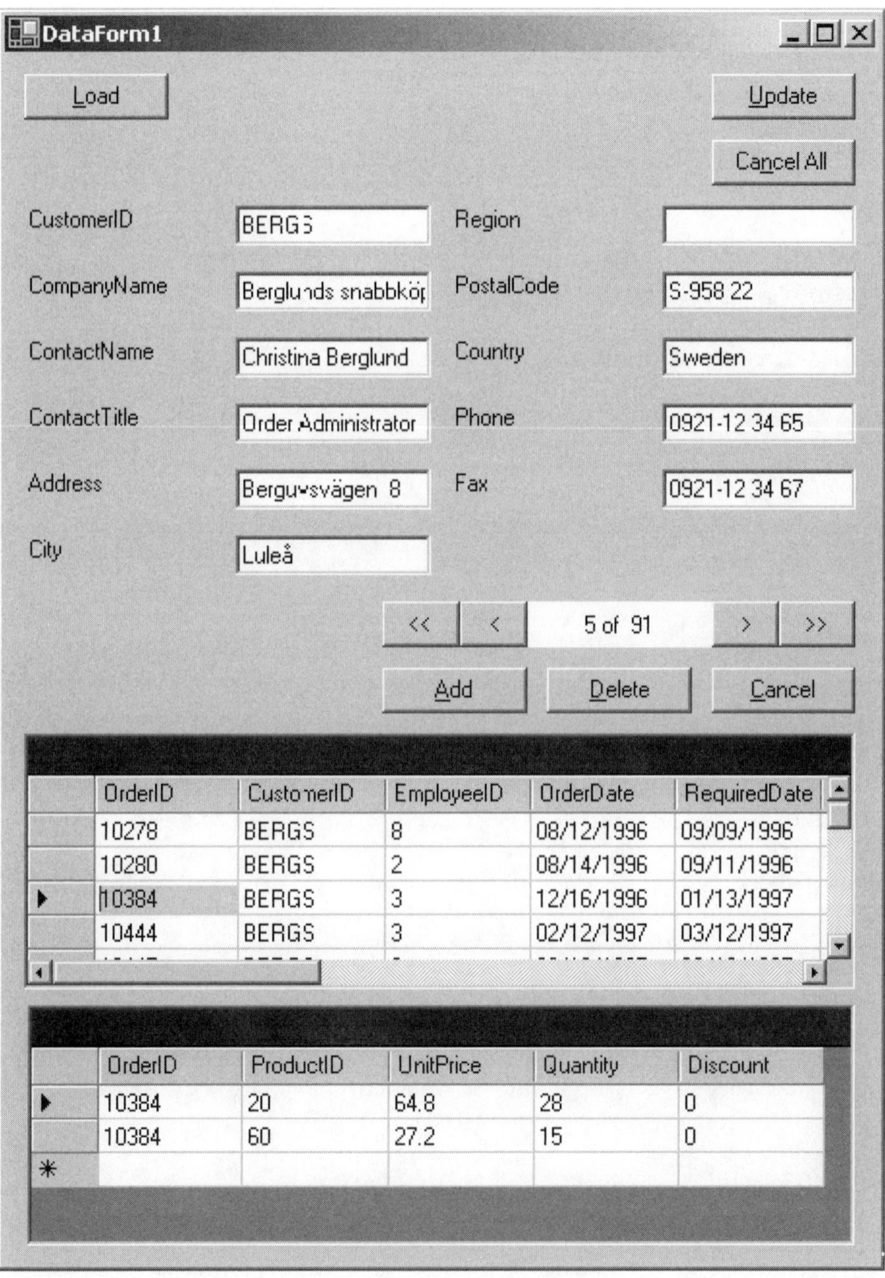

FIGURE 8.9 The form with three levels of detail.

```
    End Sub
    Private Sub btnNavNext_Click(ByVal sender As System.Object, ByVal e
As System.EventArgs) Handles btnNavNext.Click
        Me.BindingContext(objdsMain, "Customers").Position =
(Me.BindingContext(objdsMain, "Customers").Position + 1)
        Me.objdsMain_PositionChanged()

    End Sub
```

There is another procedure we need to see, the objdsMain _PositionChanged procedure. This updates the display.

```
    Private Sub objdsMain_PositionChanged()
        Me.lblNavLocation.Text = (((Me.BindingContext(objdsMain,
"Customers").Position + 1).ToString + " of  ") _
                    + Me.BindingContext(objdsMain,
"Customers").Count.ToString)

    End Sub
```

Here is one of those weird things: The procedure looks like an event procedure, but it isn't. There is no event of the DataSet or the DataTable that fires when the current row is changed because these classes do not have a concept of a current row. It looks almost as if Microsoft took the old ADO data form generator and made some minor changes to make it generate ADO .NET code. Ironically there is an event that can be used for this purpose:

```
    Private Sub dtCustomers_PositionChanged(ByVal sender As Object,
ByVal e As System.EventArgs) Handles dtCustomers.PositionChanged
        Me.lblNavLocation.Text = (((Me.BindingContext(objdsMain,
"Customers").Position + 1).ToString + " of  ") _
                    + Me.BindingContext(objdsMain,
"Customers").Count.ToString)
    End Sub
```

To use this event, you must declare a variable, `dtCustomers`, as a CurrencyManager and assign it to the BindingContext of the Customers table in the DataSet. Make sure you use the `WithEvents` keyword.

```
    Private WithEvents dtCustomers As CurrencyManager
```

Finally, you have to make the assignment. We put the assignment in the constructor so it is executed when the instance of the form class is created.

```
Public Sub New()
    MyBase.New()

    'This call is required by the Windows Form Designer.
    InitializeComponent()

    'Add any initialization after the InitializeComponent() call
    dtCustomers = Me.BindingContext(objdsMain, "Customers")
End Sub
```

To create the event procedure automatically, open the code window and pull down the objects list and select `dtCustomers`, then open the events list and select PositionChanged. You can then copy the code from the other PositionChanged procedure into the correct one. Now delete all the references to the old procedure, as they are no longer needed, and delete the old procedure. You must put a call to the new procedure into the click event for the Load button. This is because it does not fire the PositionChanged event when the data is first loaded.

```
Private Sub btnLoad_Click(ByVal sender As System.Object, ByVal e As
System.EventArgs) Handles btnLoad.Click
    Try
        'Attempt to load the DataSet.
        Me.LoadDataSet()
    Catch eLoad As System.Exception
        'Add your error handling code here.
        'Display error message, if any.
        System.Windows.Forms.MessageBox.Show(eLoad.Message)
    End Try
    dtCustomers_PositionChanged(dtCustomers, New System.EventArgs())

End Sub
```

This initializes the display with the 1 of 91 when the DataSet is first loaded. It's interesting that the mistakes in the Data Form wizard allowed us to learn something about how the framework functions. Now when we run the program, the navigation label is automatically updated. This was one of the things I found difficult when learning ADO .NET. Methods that were all in one place before are now spread all through the class library. It takes some getting used to, but once you get the hang of it, it really is just as easy to use as ADO was, but with more functionality than ever. I like ADO .NET much better that the old ADO now. I would never want to go back.

The navigation buttons themselves do nothing more than increment or decrement the position property of the CurrencyManager. Here is another strange thing. The code that was generated works, but there is an easier way to accomplish the same thing.

```
    Private Sub btnNavPrev_Click(ByVal sender As System.Object, ByVal e
As System.EventArgs) Handles btnNavPrev.Click
        'Me.BindingContext(objdsMain, "Customers").Position =
(Me.BindingContext(objdsMain, "Customers").Position - 1)
        Me.BindingContext(objdsMain, "Customers").Position -= 1

    End Sub
    Private Sub btnNavNext_Click(ByVal sender As System.Object, ByVal e
As System.EventArgs) Handles btnNavNext.Click
        'Me.BindingContext(objdsMain, "Customers").Position =
(Me.BindingContext(objdsMain, "Customers").Position + 1)
        Me.BindingContext(objdsMain, "Customers").Position += 1

    End Sub
```

The commented out code is the generated code. At first glance it seems fine. In older versions of VB this would have to be the way it was done. But we now have unary `add` and `subtract` operators in VB. It's like the developers didn't know about them or something. My version of the line of code does the same thing, but more efficiently. This is a great example of code refactoring. My code is much more efficient because it does not have to access the object's properties twice, which can be relatively expensive because it is late-bound. No error is thrown when you attempt to set the position past the end of the table or before the beginning, so we don't have to worry about that. There are no end-of-file (EOF) or beginning-of-file (BOF) properties, which I found a little annoying at first, but again I was thinking like an ADO programmer. There is no need for these functions because you can just test the position property for greater than the count property minus one or less than zero. Also if you use an enumerator (For … Each … Next construct) to loop though the rows in a DataTable, you will automatically exit the loop when all rows have been processed. There is no longer any need for the Do Until x.EOF … Loop construct.

The Update Process

Now let's look at the code to update the database with any changes. The Update button's click event procedure calls `UpdateDataSet`, which, ironically, updates the database, not the DataSet. The DataSet is updated automatically when the use changes the values on the screen. Let's look at the generated code.

```
    Public Sub UpdateDataSet()
        'Create a new DataSet to hold the changes that have been made to
the main DataSet.
        Dim objDataSetChanges As ADOBook08_01.dsMain = New
ADOBook08_01.dsMain()
        'Stop any current edits.
        Me.BindingContext(objdsMain, "Customers").EndCurrentEdit()
        Me.BindingContext(objdsMain, "Orders").EndCurrentEdit()
        'Get the changes that have been made to the main DataSet.
        objDataSetChanges = CType(objdsMain.GetChanges,
ADOBook08_01.dsMain)
        'Check to see if any changes have been made.
        If (Not (objDataSetChanges) Is Nothing) Then
            Try
                'There are changes that need to be made, so attempt to
update the datasource by
                'calling the update method and passing the DataSet and
any parameters.
                Me.UpdateDataSource(objDataSetChanges)
                objdsMain.Merge(objDataSetChanges)
                objdsMain.AcceptChanges()
            Catch eUpdate As System.Exception
                'Add your error handling code here.
                Throw eUpdate
            End Try
            'Add your code to check the returned DataSet for any errors
that may have been
            'pushed into the row object's error.
        End If

    End Sub
```

The first things to notice are the two lines that end in `EndCurrent-Edit`. These two lines of code formally commit any changes that were made on the screen to the DataSet. Note that there is no `EndCurrentEdit` for the Order Details table. This is strange because other places in the program do refer to the Order Details table. I know the program is supposed to support only one level of detail but it should be consistent. It does fill the table in the load procedure. Let's add one more `EndCurrentEdit` to the procedure so that any changes we make to the details grid get updated as well.

It then does a weird thing to find out if there are any changes to the DataSet. It uses the `GetChanges` method to pull any changes into another DataSet. Then it checks to see if the new DataSet is nothing. Well, yes, that works, but didn't the developers know about the `HasChanges` property? This property returns true if there are any pending changes to the DataSet since the last call to `AcceptChanges` was made. Also, I don't understand why it needs to pull the changes into another DataSet, use this DataSet to update the database, then remerge the changed data back into the original DataSet. This seems very round about when you can just call the `Update` method directly on the main DataSet.

The only thing I can think of is that the developers were thinking the database update code would be located in a remote procedure or a web service, then by capturing only the changes you might minimize network traffic. In this case doing all this logic makes no sense when three lines of code could replace it all. Let's get rid of the old code and use the one line of code technique to simplify things. There is no need to call `AcceptChanges` because it is called automatically by the DataAdapter. We can then get rid of the `UpdateDataSource` procedure altogether. Here is the refactored code. Isn't it easier to understand now?

```
Public Sub UpdateDataSet()
    'Stop any current edits.
    Me.BindingContext(objdsMain, "Customers").EndCurrentEdit()
    Me.BindingContext(objdsMain, "Orders").EndCurrentEdit()
    Me.BindingContext(objdsMain, "Order Details").EndCurrentEdit()
    If objdsMain.HasChanges Then
        Try
            'There are changes that need to be made, so attempt to
update the datasource by
            'calling the update method and passing the DataSet and
any parameters.
            OleDbDataAdapter1.Update(objdsMain, "Customers")
            OleDbDataAdapter2.Update(objdsMain, "Orders")
            OleDbDataAdapter3.Update(objdsMain, "Order Details")
        Catch eUpdate As System.Exception
            'Add your error handling code here.
            Throw eUpdate
        End Try
        'Add your code to check the returned DataSet for any errors
that may have been
        'pushed into the row object's error.
    End If
End Sub
```

And, yes, it does work. You can compile the project and try it.

Loading the Data

The load procedure is fraught with similar strangeness. Here is the unmodified procedure:

```
Public Sub LoadDataSet()
    'Create a new DataSet to hold the records returned from the call
to FillDataSet.
    'A temporary DataSet is used because filling the existing
DataSet would
    'require the DataBindings to be rebound.
    Dim objDataSetTemp As ADOBook08_01.dsMain
    objDataSetTemp = New ADOBook08_01.dsMain()
    Try
        'Attempt to fill the temporary DataSet.
        Me.FillDataSet(objDataSetTemp)
    Catch eFillDataSet As System.Exception
        'Add your error handling code here.
        Throw eFillDataSet
    End Try
    Try
        'Empty the old records from the DataSet.
        objdsMain.Clear()
        'Merge the records into the main DataSet.
        objdsMain.Merge(objDataSetTemp)
    Catch eLoadMerge As System.Exception
        'Add your error handling code here.
        Throw eLoadMerge
    End Try

End Sub
```

Right at the top of the procedure the developer makes the comment that the intermediate DataSet is needed, because if you fill the main DataSet directly you will have to rebind all of the controls. I have no idea where this is coming from except that in VB 6 this was sometimes necessary with the data-bound combo box and the OLEDB DataGrid control. It was due to a bug. This reinforces my hypothesis that this is really a lame conversion of a VB 6 program. The following procedure works just as well:

```
Public Sub LoadDataSet()
    Try
        objdsMain.Clear()
        Me.FillDataSet(objdsMain)
    Catch eFillDataSet As System.Exception
        'Add your error handling code here.
```

```
            Throw eFillDataSet
        End Try
    End Sub
```

The Add and Delete Methods

The Add and Delete methods are pretty simple. They only have to deal with the master Customers table because the cascade and update rules in the relation object in the DataSet will handle cascading deletes and updates to the detail levels.

```
    Private Sub btnDelete_Click(ByVal sender As System.Object, ByVal e
As System.EventArgs) Handles btnDelete.Click
        If (Me.BindingContext(objdsMain, "Customers").Count > 0) Then
            Me.BindingContext(objdsMain,
"Customers").RemoveAt(Me.BindingContext(objdsMain,
"Customers").Position)
        End If

    End Sub

    Private Sub btnAdd_Click(ByVal sender As System.Object, ByVal e As
System.EventArgs) Handles btnAdd.Click
        Try
            'Clear out the current edits
            Me.BindingContext(objdsMain, "Customers").EndCurrentEdit()
            Me.BindingContext(objdsMain, "Customers").AddNew()
        Catch eEndEdit As System.Exception
            System.Windows.Forms.MessageBox.Show(eEndEdit.Message)
        End Try

    End Sub
```

Delete simply removes the current row from the Customers table. Add first ends and, pending edits, then is uses AddNew to append a new blank row to the Customers table. There is one potentially quirky thing about this code, and possibly ADO .NET as well. The Order Number column in the orders database is an autoincrement field. This means that it automatically adds 1 to the last order number when appending new rows. Suppose there are multiple users adding rows to the table? How does it handle the incrementing of the numbers by multiple users if the DataSet is disconnected while the users are adding rows? There will be a lot of duplicate key errors. The best practice in this situation may be to not include the AutoIncrement fields in the DataSet. Then the numbers would be generated when the DataSet is updated to the database instead of at runtime. You could also use a different DataSet to display the rows from and another one to update with. Or you could update the rows manually using a command object and SQL. These are interesting questions that the Data Form wizard does not address very well. This reinforces my statement that I would not use the data for wizard to generate code for any serious application.

There is another issue with adding and deleting master-detail structures. The order in which the updates are performed is different for each operation. In a delete operation, we want to delete the lowest level of detail first, then the next lowest, and so on. The reasoning being that we will violate relational integrity rules if we try to delete the top level first. For example, if we tried to delete the row from the Customers table, we would get an integrity violation because the detail rows require a row in the master table.

In an add operation, the opposite is true; we want to add the highest level first, in this case the Customers row. This is for the same reason as previously stated: If we try to add a lower level first, we will get an integrity violation.

One would think that a way to avoid this issue is to use DRI on the database itself. This makes some sense, but then look what would happen. We are using cascading rules in our DataSet. When we delete the Customers row in the DataSet, all the orders and order details are also deleted. Then when we go to update the database, we update only the Customers table, thinking that the other tables will get cleaned up because of the DRI rules in the database. In reality, you get an integrity violation. When the Customers row in the database is deleted, it also deletes all the child rows, but then along comes the program and tries to delete them again, failing, of course. Now the rows are still marked as deleted in the DataSet but are actually deleted in the database. This is a strange situation.

One way around this might be to delete the Customers row and not touch the other rows. Let the database cascade the delete down to the detail tables. Then simply call the `AcceptChanges` method on the orders and order details tables in the DataSet. This is not a great way to do it because you can never be certain that the database and DataSet are in synch.

Another idea would be to pull only the added rows into another DataSet using the `GetChanges(DataRowState...)` method. This seems to be the easiest to implement and does not depend on whether the database has DRI rules defined. First pull all the deleted rows into a temporary DataSet and update them, then pull all the added or modified rows and update them. Here is the modified code:

```
Public Sub UpdateDataSet()
        Dim ds As ADOBook08_01.dsMain

        'Stop any current edits.
        Me.BindingContext(objdsMain, "Customers").EndCurrentEdit()
        Me.BindingContext(objdsMain, "Orders").EndCurrentEdit()
        Me.BindingContext(objdsMain, "Order Details").EndCurrentEdit()
        If objdsMain.HasChanges Then
            Try
                'There are changes that need to be made, so attempt to
update the datasource by
                'calling the update method and passing the DataSet and
any parameters.
                ds = objdsMain.GetChanges(DataRowState.Deleted)
                If Not ds Is Nothing Then
                    OleDbDataAdapter3.Update(ds, "Order Details")
                    OleDbDataAdapter2.Update(ds, "Orders")
                    OleDbDataAdapter1.Update(ds, "Customers")
                End If
                ds = objdsMain.GetChanges(DataRowState.Added Or
DataRowState.Modified)
                If Not ds Is Nothing Then
                    OleDbDataAdapter1.Update(ds, "Customers")
                    OleDbDataAdapter2.Update(ds, "Orders")
                    OleDbDataAdapter3.Update(ds, "Order Details")
                End If
                objdsMain.AcceptChanges()
            Catch eUpdate As System.Exception
                'Add your error handling code here.
                Throw eUpdate
            End Try
            'Add your code to check the returned DataSet for any errors
that may have been
            'pushed into the row object's error.
        End If
    End Sub
```

With this change we can handle either condition. Notice how with the add and modify section we can combine the parameters using an OR (addition) operation.

Using the Data Form wizard, we have seen how to bind controls to a DataSet and DataTable. Now let's look into other objects we can bind controls to.

BINDING TO OTHER OBJECTS (ARRAYS, LISTS, ETC.)

In addition to DataTable and DataViews, we can bind controls to simple arrays and list objects. A list object is any object that implements the `IList` interface. Besides the array, some other objects that implement the interface are the DataView, the ArrayList, and the CollectionBase (from which all collections are derived). So you see that we can bind controls to many more objects than we could in VB 6. You can also create your own bindable object just by implementing the interface yourself

To demonstrate this, let's create a new project, ADOBook08-02. Add controls to the default form to make it look like Figure 8.10.

Binding to a single-dimension array is really simple. We cannot use any design-time methods to bind to an array because the array is not part of the component model. We must initialize the binding at runtime. This is a simple task. The following lines of code demonstrate the process:

```
    Private mList() As String

    Private Sub Button1_Click(ByVal sender As System.Object, ByVal e As
System.EventArgs) Handles Button1.Click
        Me.BindingContext(mList).Position += 1
    End Sub

    Private Sub Button2_Click(ByVal sender As System.Object, ByVal e As
System.EventArgs) Handles Button2.Click
        Me.BindingContext(mList).Position -= 1
    End Sub
```

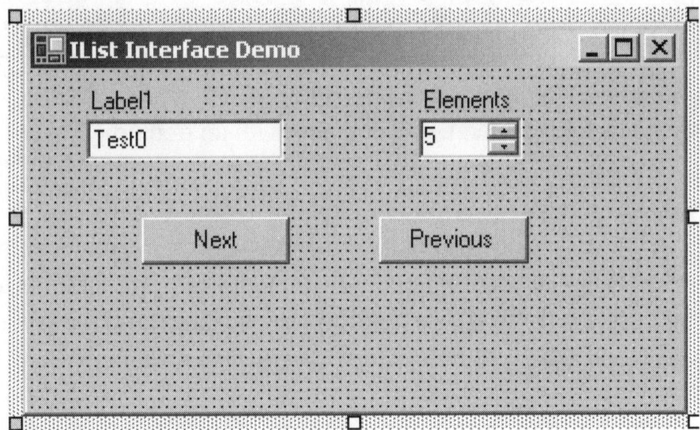

FIGURE 8.10 Bound array form.

```
    Private Sub NumericUpDown1_ValueChanged(ByVal sender As Object,
ByVal e As System.EventArgs) Handles NumericUpDown1.ValueChanged
        Dim i As Integer

        TextBox1.DataBindings.Clear()
        ReDim mList(NumericUpDown1.Value)
        For i = 0 To NumericUpDown1.Value
            mList(i) = "Text" & i
        Next
        TextBox1.DataBindings.Add("Text", mList, "")
    End Sub
```

This is actually the entire program. This binds the text box to the array. The UpDown control allows us to vary the array size at runtime. As we click the Next and Previous buttons, the text box displays the values of the different elements of the array. Notice that when we create the binding, we supply an empty string to the property name parameter of the `Add` method. If we were binding to a DataTable, we would supply the column name here, but since this is a single-dimension array there is no property name to bind to. As far as I can tell, the documentation does not explicitly tell you this anywhere. I noticed that the parameter accepts an empty string and just tried it. If you try to use any other property of the string array, it fails. Any mention of this in the documentation would have saved me half a day of digging. But that's why you bought this book, isn't it?

It is not possible at this time to bind to a multidimensional array, at least not easily. One possibility would be to copy each column (Dimension 2) into a separate array and then bind to that, but the code to keep them in synch would get pretty complex and prone to errors. If you must bind to a two-dimensional array it would be better to use a DataTable object. Then you would be able to bind to the columns with no trouble.

In the object-oriented world, arrays are passé. The gods of OOP would rather you use collections in place of arrays. Collections, the OOP theory goes, are easier to manipulate, manage memory better, and are faster than arrays. I might buy into the first two arguments, but I find it hard to believe that they are faster. If you must use arrays, then do so, but be aware that they may disappear in some future revision. Java does not now natively support arrays, and even those in VB are pseudo-arrays; that is, they are really collections disguised as arrays. The only real arrays left can be found in C or C++ unmanaged code.

THE BINDING CLASS

The `Binding` class and the `BindingCollection` facilitate data binding on the control's side. We saw some of this in the previous example of binding to an array. We can actually see the contents of the `Binding` collection if we click the Advanced tab of a control with a `DataBindings` property. This looks like Figure 8.11 for the TextBox control.

As you can see, you can bind almost any property to a bindable object. This could come in very handy if you wanted to be able to create forms at runtime using data stored in database tables or XML files.

The `Bindable` attribute we've mentioned is actually only used to make a property appear in the `DataBindings` area of the Properties window and allow it to be bound at design time. Any property can be bound at runtime.

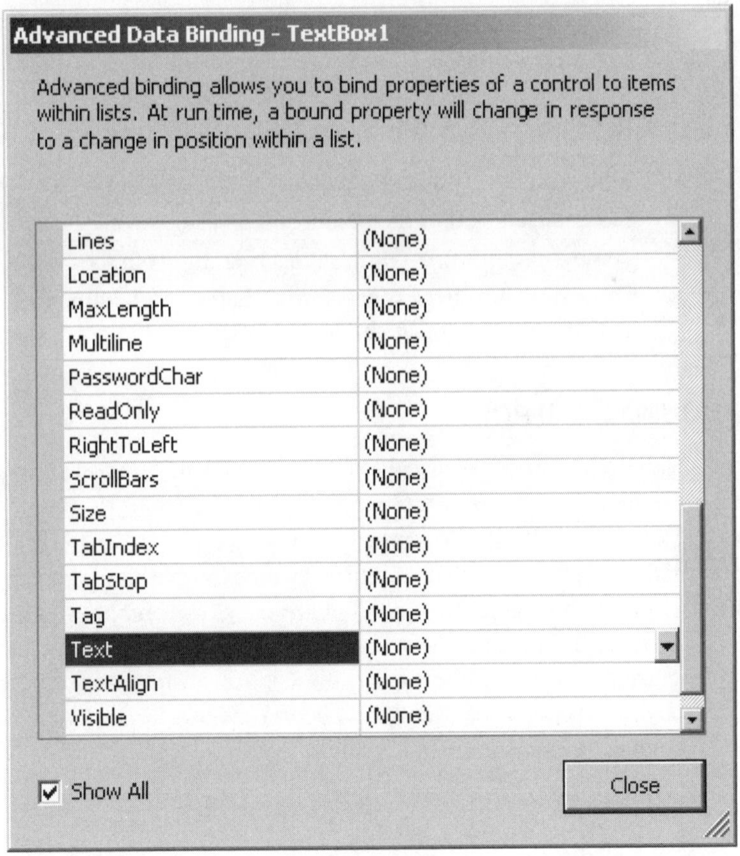

FIGURE 8.11 The Data Binding collection editor.

Well, almost any property: In order to be able to be bound, a property must be a basic data type and return only a single value. You can't bind to complex objects or an array of values, for example. The reasons for this should be obvious.

The Binding class supports the following properties and events:

- Control—Returns the control the binding is attached to.
- DataSource—Gets the DataSource object for the binding.
- IsBinding—Returns a value indicating if the binding is active. The `Suspend` and `Resume` binding methods of the BindingContext control this.
- PropertyName—The name of the property of the control the binding applies to.
- Format Event—Fires when the control needs to update its display of the data.
- Parse Event—Fires when the control is going to update the data source with a new value.

The BindingCollection supports the following methods:

- Add— Adds a new binding object to the collection.
- Clear—Clears all of the bindings for this control.
- Remove; RemoveAt—Removes a binding from the collection.
- CollectionChanged Event—Fires when the collection changes, through an `Add` or `Remove` method.

SIMPLE BOUND CONTROLS

Now let's switch gears and begin looking at the controls provided by Visual Studio .NET. There are two types of bound controls: simple and complex. Simple bound controls typically bind single properties to one `DataSource` and `DataColumn`. The TextBox is an example of a simple bound control. Complex bound controls can bind to a `DataSource` and multiple `DataColumns`. In the case of a complex bound control, the `DataSource` is typically bound to a collection in the control, instead of a single property. An obvious example of a complex bound control is the DataGrid. The simple bound controls are the following:

- TextBox
- Label
- LinkLabel
- Button

- CheckBox (CheckAlign, Tag, Text, Checked)
- RadioButton (CheckAlign, Tag, Text)
- PictureBox (Tag Property Only, Image Property can be bound through Binding collection)
- Panel (tag property only)
- ListView (tag only)
- TreeView (tag only)
- Tab Control (tag only)
- DateTimePicker (Checked, Tag, Text—Returns string representation of date; Value—Returns Date data type)
- MonthCalendar (tag only)
- ScrollBars (value property)
- Splitter (tag only)
- Domain and Numeric UpDown (text and value)
- TrackBar (value)
- ProgressBar (value)
- RichTextBox (text)
- ToolBar (tag)
- StatusBar (text, single panel only)
- Crystal Report Viewer (tag only)

With all these controls, other bindable properties are available through the Binding collection, which can be accessed at design time by clicking the advanced ellipsis button under DataBindings in the Properties window. I would not consider a control that only allows binding to the tag property data bound. Now let's look at some specific controls.

Text Boxes, RichTextBoxes, and Labels

Controls, like text boxes and labels that display text directly, are among the most popular of bound controls, because they can display the text from an individual field of a table, which means you can tailor your application's data display field by field.

You can use the data in any of these controls to update a database (note that a label may not be changed directly by the user, of course, but you can change the contents of a label under programmatic control).

To use these controls, you just work with the `DataBinding` properties. You can bind the `Text` property to the DataSource by expanding the `DataBindings` node in the Properties window and then dropping down this

`Text` property. Select the `DataSource` and column you wish to bind to. We've already seen examples of binding text boxes to data sources. You can use the first project from this chapter (ADOBook08-01) for these examples (see Figure 8.12).

The process is the same for the RichTextBox and the labels.

Check Boxes

You can bind check boxes to Boolean (True/False) fields in databases, and the check box will be checked or unchecked to match the value in that field. (Technically, check boxes actually have three states: checked [True], unchecked [False], and grayed [indeterminate]).

Instead of binding to the `Text property`, we can bind the CheckBox to the `Checked` or `CheckState` properties, as well as `CheckAlign` and `Text`. These properties work as follows:

- Checked—Returns the Boolean true if the box is checked or false if the box is cleared. If the box is indeterminate (grayed) it returns false because it is not checked. You should use this property to bind to a Boolean database field.

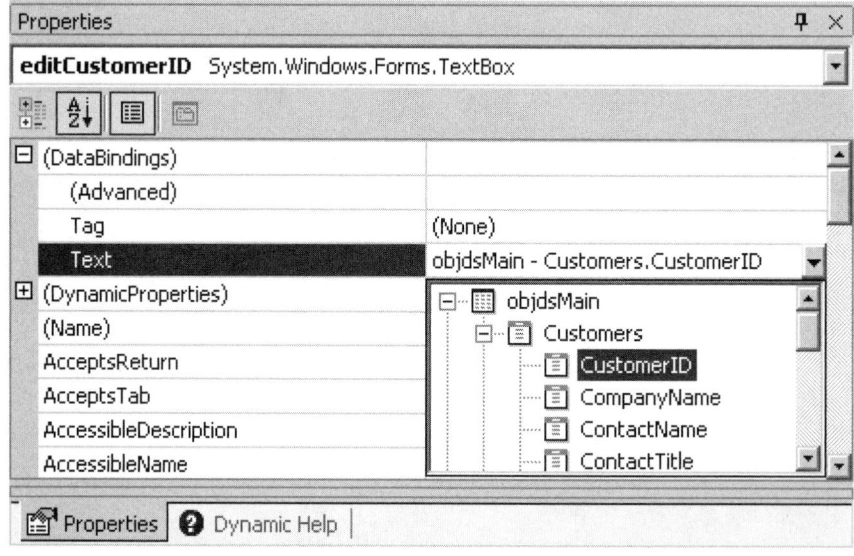

FIGURE 8.12 Selecting a data source.

- CheckedState— Returns an enumeration that corresponds to the actual state of the check box, checked, unchecked, or indeterminate.
- CheckAlign— An enumeration that determines when the check appears relative to the caption (or text). `Right` or `Left` are the values.
- Text—The text that appears as the caption of the check box.

Picture Boxes

Picture boxes can no longer bind to images stored in databases as they could with VB 6. There does not seem to be any way to manage binary data in a database with ADO .NET. The only way to do this would be to store the images in disk files and then store a path name in the database. As each row is made current, you can then use the `FromFile` method of the picture box to get the image into the control. The `FromFile` method supports URLs as well as standard Windows paths.

DateTimePickers and MonthViews

DateTimePickers let the user select dates and times, and MonthViews present the user with a small calendar. The DateTimePicker supports the following bound properties:

- Checked—Returns True if the date value is checked. The `ShowCheck-Box` property of the control must be set to true.
- Text—Returns a `Text` representation of the date formatted according to the `Format` property. Use this to bind the control to a String SQL data type (nvarchar).
- Date—Returns a date data type. Use this property to bind the control to a DateTime SQL data type.

Complex Bound Controls—ListBoxes, ComboBoxes, and the DataGrid

The complex bound controls allow the control to be bound to more than one column at a time. The DataGrid displays multiple rows of data from a DataTable. The ListBox and ComboBox can display a single column but multiple rows from that column.

ListBoxes and ComboBoxes

The ListBox and ComboBox controls automatically populate their lists from a DataSource. They can also bind their `Text` property to a column in a DataTable. A combo box is a combination of a list box and a text box. The text box can be bound to one column, while the list box can get its list from another table. Likewise, the list box gets its list from a DataTable. It can also bind its `Text` property (which is the value of the current row of the list) to another DataTable.

Binding the List

The `DataSource`, `DisplayMember`, and `ValueMember` properties affect the list portion of the combo box. These apply to both the combo box and the list box:

- `DataSource`—The DataSet and DataTable or DataView to draw data from.
- `DisplayMember`—The value to display in the text portion of the combo box and the list. The typical use for this is to display a description for an underlying code value.
- `ValueMember`— The underlying code value that will be stored in the database.

Binding the Data

The Binding collection properties that can be bound though the Properties window are for binding the selections in the combo box or list box to the database.

- `SelectedItem`—Returns the `ListItem` object of the selected item.
- `SelectedValue`—Returns the `ValueMember` value of the selected item.
- `Text`—The string displayed in the text box portion of the control. NOTE: This does not necessarily have to correspond with any item in the list, if the DropDownStyle of the control is a dropdown list. If it is drop-down list then the `Text` property will be one of the `DisplayMember` values in the current list. Applies to the ComboBox only.

For the ListBox, the `Text` property refers to the displayed text in the selected item in the list even though it is not listed in the Properties window. This is the same behavior as the VB 6 list box. It will be the same as the `SelectedItem` value for the ListBox so it is not listed as a separate bindable property.

You can search the ComboBox control by entering text into the text box of the control. That value is located in the list, and the current list item is set to that item if it is found. If the item is not found, the `SelectedValue` property is set to null. The ListBox control also has an automated search mode.

THE DATAGRID

We have left the DataGrid control as a separate topic because the control is quite complex. It is the most robust grid control ever provided out-of-the-box from Microsoft. It is probably as robust as some of the third-party grid controls of only a couple of revisions back. The DataGrid has no unbound mode. It must be bound to a DataSource. But before you get excited, think for a minute. Since we can now create DataSets on the fly and use them in place of obsolete structures like arrays, we really can use the grid unbound —to a database that is. All we have to do is create a DataTable or a DataSet, populate it with whatever way we want, and bind it to our grid. This is the same effect as an unbound grid control in previous versions of VB, but now we do not have to worry about using different techniques if the grid is bound or unbound. Also the DataSource is separate from the presentation component which is better architecturally.

Since we don't have to worry about database specifics, we can limit our discussion to the presentation capabilities of the grid. These are numerous, but admittedly they were not easy to find. Say good-bye to the design editors of previous grid controls. There is no visual design tool for the grid. The way we VB programmers are, I wouldn't be surprised if one of you came up with one. There's a suggestion for a project for any of you with free time.

To fully demonstrate the DataGrid's capabilities, we will need a demo project. We'll start with our familiar UI, as in Figure 8.13.

You can get ADOBook08-03Starter from the web site. To save time we will not go though all of the details of creating the project. We will also omit the database update code. We are going to concentrate on the presentation capabilities of the DataGrid control.

Data Grid Demo

CustomerID	CompanyNa	ContactName	ContactTitle	Address	City	Region
ALFKI	Alfreds Futter	Maria Anders	Sales Repres	Obere Str. 57	Berlin	
ANATR	Ana Trujillo E	Ana Trujillo	Owner	Avda. de la C	México D.F.	(null)
ANTON	Antonio More	Antonio More	Owner	Mataderos 2	México D.F.	(null)
AROUT	Around the H	Thomas Hard	Sales Repres	120 Hanover	London	Test
BERGS	Berglunds sn	Christina Ber	Order Admini	Berguvsväge	Luleå	(null)
BLAUS	Blauer See D	Hanna Moos	Sales Repres	Forsterstr. 57	Mannheim	(null)
BLONP	Blondesddsl	Frédérique Ci	Marketing Ma	24, place Klé	Strasbourg	(null)
BOLID	Bólido Comid	Martín Somm	Owner	C/ Araquil, 67	Madrid	(null)
BONAP	Bon app'	Laurence Leb	Owner	12, rue des B	Marseille	(null)
BOTTM	Bottom-Dollar	Elizabeth Lin	Accounting M	23 Tsawasse	Tsawassen	BC
BSBEV	B's Beverage	Victoria Ashw	Sales Repres	Fauntleroy Ci	London	(null)
CACTU	Cactus Comi	Patricio Simp	Sales Agent	Cerrito 333	Buenos Aires	(null)

Load

FIGURE 8.13 The starter project.

The TableStyle Class

There are two ways of customizing the default display of the DataGrid control.

- Use a custom DataView and bind the grid to it. That works for filtering and sorting, but you cannot customize the visual display of the DataGrid that way. The DataView is really intended for customizing the data itself, not the visual display of the DataGrid.
- Create a collection of custom TableStyle objects that we can use to alter the grid's appearance without touching the underlying data.

Previous VB grid controls had a Columns collection that had properties such as `Format`, `Visible`, `Width`, and so forth for affecting the appearance of the grid. You could use the property page editor to change the values of these properties. There were also Style objects and a Styles collection that you could use to store alternate display formats that the user could switch to. This was a bit confusing. Which should I use, a custom style or the Columns collection? In this version, all of the appearance-related properties have been moved into the TableStyle class, Hopefully this will eliminate the confusion. Incidentally, the Columns collection has gone away as well. In keeping with the architecture of the DataSet, you now get the value of data in the grid using the `Item` property. This property is indexed by row and column. There is also a `CurrentRowIndex` property that returns the row index of the row the pointer in the indicator column is on. So to access a given column in the current row the code is as follows:

```
TextBox1.Text = DataGrid1.Item(DataGird1.CurrentRowIndex, 3)
```

This returns the data in the first row, fourth column. We get the native representation of the data converted to a string for display in the text box. It uses the default Windows format unless changed.

One flaw in this system is that you can no longer access a column by its name. In previous DataGrids, the Column collection contained named column objects. The physical layout of the grid could change by a user moving columns around, and so forth, but the column could still be accessed by its name. Now, the user can no longer move columns at runtime. In my experience, no user actually used this feature, but it was still nice to have and be able to offer users the ability to customize the grid at runtime. Now we will have to purchase a third-party grid control if we want this feature.

Setting Up TableStyles

There are two ways to set up TableStyles: in design mode or programmatically at runtime. Let's look at doing it at design time first.

Let's take our starter project and add some buttons. Make the form look like Figure 8.14.

Since this book is in black and white, the color of the alternating rows is dark teal (0, 192, 192 in RGB notation). You can use the direct `AlternatingRowColor` property to set this up. In our TableStyle object, we will use a different color just because we can!

To create our TableStyle object, we will open the collection editor. Do this by clicking the ellipsis button on the `TablesStyles` property in the Properties window as in Figure 8.15.

Once we click the button the now-familiar collection editor opens. Click the Add button to add a new TableStyle object to the collection as in Figure 8.16.

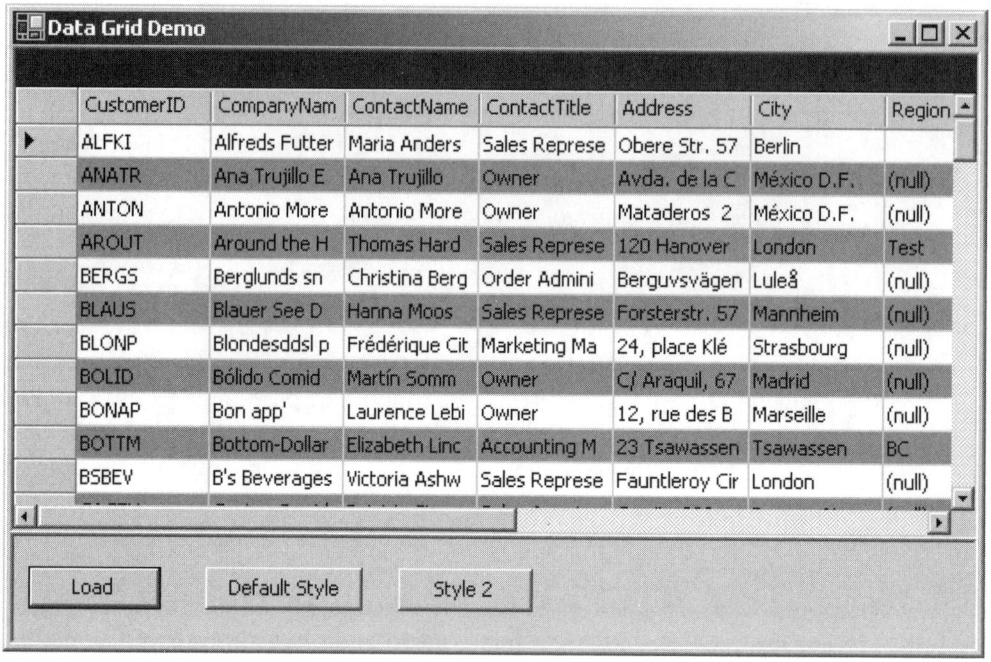

Data Grid Demo

CustomerID	CompanyNam	ContactName	ContactTitle	Address	City	Region
ALFKI	Alfreds Futter	Maria Anders	Sales Represe	Obere Str. 57	Berlin	
ANATR	Ana Trujillo E	Ana Trujillo	Owner	Avda. de la C	México D.F.	(null)
ANTON	Antonio More	Antonio More	Owner	Mataderos 2	México D.F.	(null)
AROUT	Around the H	Thomas Hard	Sales Represe	120 Hanover	London	Test
BERGS	Berglunds sn	Christina Berg	Order Admini	Berguvsvägen	Luleå	(null)
BLAUS	Blauer See D	Hanna Moos	Sales Represe	Forsterstr. 57	Mannheim	(null)
BLONP	Blondesddsl p	Frédérique Cit	Marketing Ma	24, place Klé	Strasbourg	(null)
BOLID	Bólido Comid	Martín Somm	Owner	C/ Araquil, 67	Madrid	(null)
BONAP	Bon app'	Laurence Lebi	Owner	12, rue des B	Marseille	(null)
BOTTM	Bottom-Dollar	Elizabeth Linc	Accounting M	23 Tsawassen	Tsawassen	BC
BSBEV	B's Beverages	Victoria Ashw	Sales Represe	Fauntleroy Cir	London	(null)

Load | Default Style | Style 2

FIGURE 8.14 The form ready for the TableStyles demo.

At this point, we can edit global properties of the grid like the `AlternatingBackColor`. Let's change it to light aqua (192, 255, 255 in RGB notation). Before we can use the TableStyle, it must have at least one column defined. It does not inherit the columns of the default grid when you create the object, which is annoying. This is where a designer would come in handy. You have to manually create your columns. This can be a tedious task of pointing and clicking. To define your columns, we have to open yet another collection editor. Do this by going to the `GridColumnStyles` property and clicking the ellipsis button as in Figure 8.17.

When the `GridColumnStyle` editor opens, click the Add button. One column is added to the TableStyle. Do this five more times to add five columns. The editor will now look like Figure 8.18.

The way we bind a `GridColumnStyle` to a column in a DataTable is though the `MappingName` property. If we drop down the list in the property pane, we will be able to select columns from the DataSource as in Figure 8.19.

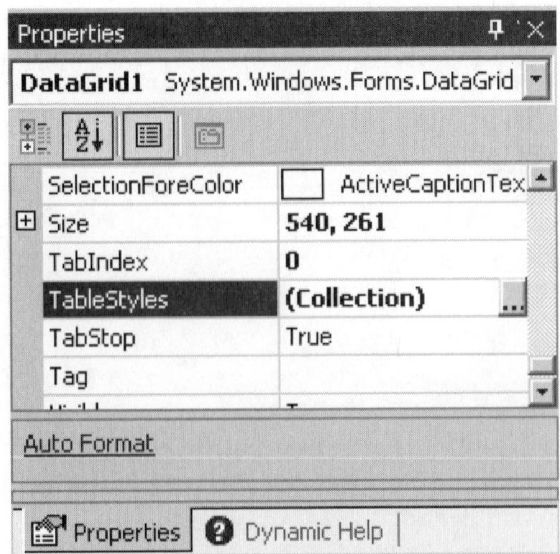

FIGURE 8.15 Accessing the TablesStyles collection.

Note that when we click the Add button, there are two choices for the kind of column we can add. The default, DataGridTextBoxColumn, adds a normal text style column to the grid. The other choice, DataGridBoolColumn, adds a column with a check box in it. This is for columns that have a `true` or `false` value. This is set up so you can add your own column editors to the system by subclassing the DataGridColumn abstract class. This is beyond the scope of this book, but if you want to look into it there are instructions in the Help files. Choose which type you wish to display by dropping down the button as in Figure 8.20.

Now go through all of the columns and enter the following column names in the `MappingName` properties: `CustomerID`, `CompanyName`, `ContactName`, `ContactTitle`, `Phone`.

Close all the editors. Next we have to make a TableStyle active. This isn't as obvious as you would think nor is it very well implemented. The way I would have implemented this would have been to have an `ActiveTableStyle` property on the main grid control and then set this to the index or name of the style you wish to use. That way only one style could be active at any given time, which is what I would assume you would want. Another good way would have been to have an `Activate` method on the TableStyle object itself. Calling it would activate the TableStyle and deactivate any currently active TableStyle.

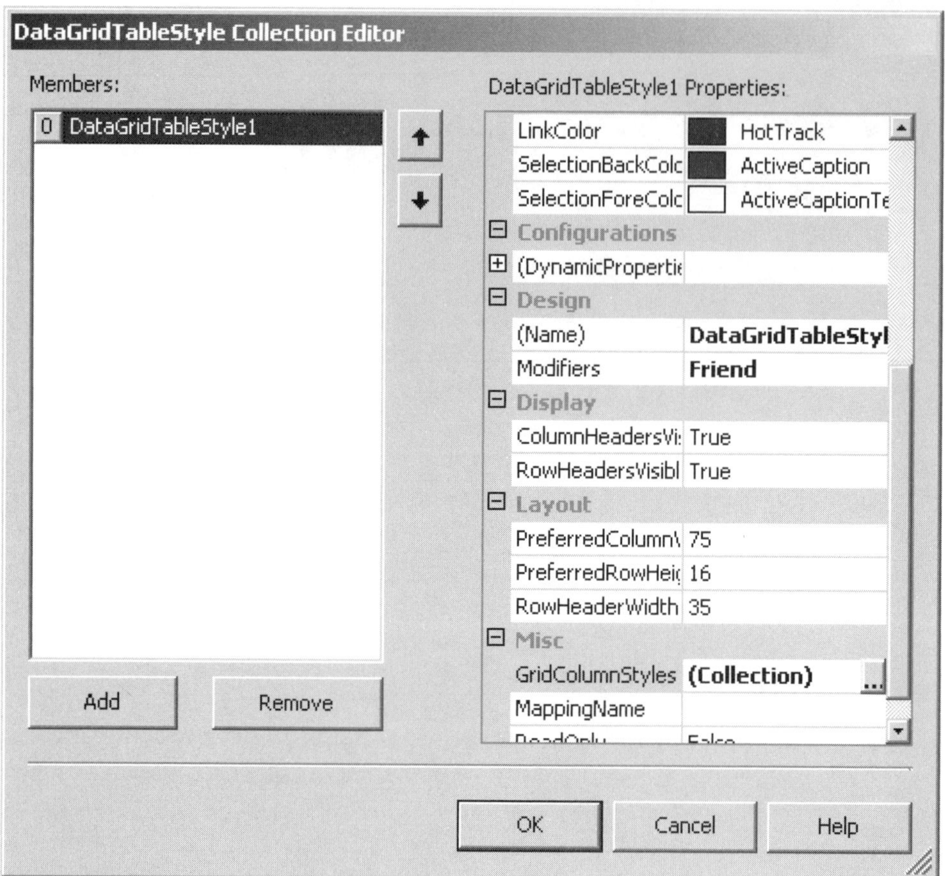

FIGURE 8.16 The TableStyles collection editor.

The way the developers chose to do this is through the `MappingName` property of the TableStyle object itself. When you set the MappingName to a table, the TableStyle is displayed in the grid. We already set the names of the columns in the ColumnStyles. Doesn't this imply the table we are going to use? What if we set the `MappingName` property to a table other than the one we used for the ColumnStyles? It seems to me this should drill down; that is, by setting the DataSource of the grid itself we imply the available DataTable for the TableStyles. Then we set the `MappingName` on the TableStyle object to one of those tables, and then the `MappingName` of the ColumnStyle to an available column from the table. But this is not how it works at all. And what if you set more that one TableStyle object to the same `MappingName`? Which one gets used? The answer is that you will throw an error if you try to

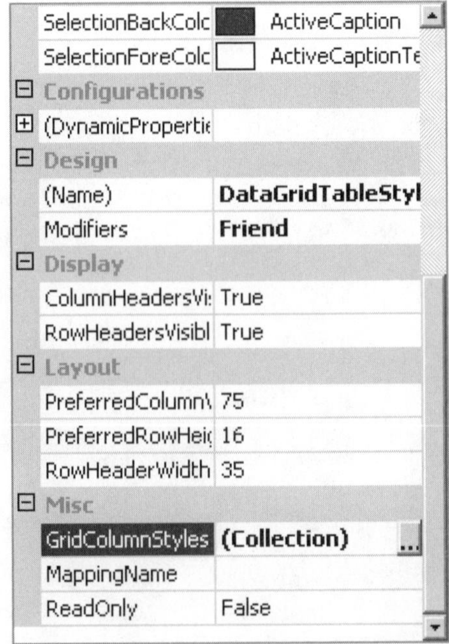

FIGURE 8.17 Accessing the GridColumns collection.

set the `MappingName` of two different TableStyles to the same name. You first have to clear out the active one, then set the new one. This is a really strange way of doing it.

I remember years ago when there was a lot of experimentation with GUIs, one came out as an alternative to the Windows 3.1 program manager called New Wave. It had some nice ideas that were eventually incorporated into the Windows 95 shell, but one of the weird things it did was require the user to drag the trash can to an object such as a file to delete it. I remember some cynical reviewer remarking that "in real life we don't 'apply the trash-can to the garbage,' we throw the garbage in the trash." It is painfully clear that this might be the reason no one remembers the "New Wave" shell. I hope the same will not be said some day about the DataGrid and it's odd Table-Style architecture.

Making It Work

Now let's add a few lines of code to the project to make it work. The code is all in the button click event procedures and is pretty simple, so I'll just show it here:

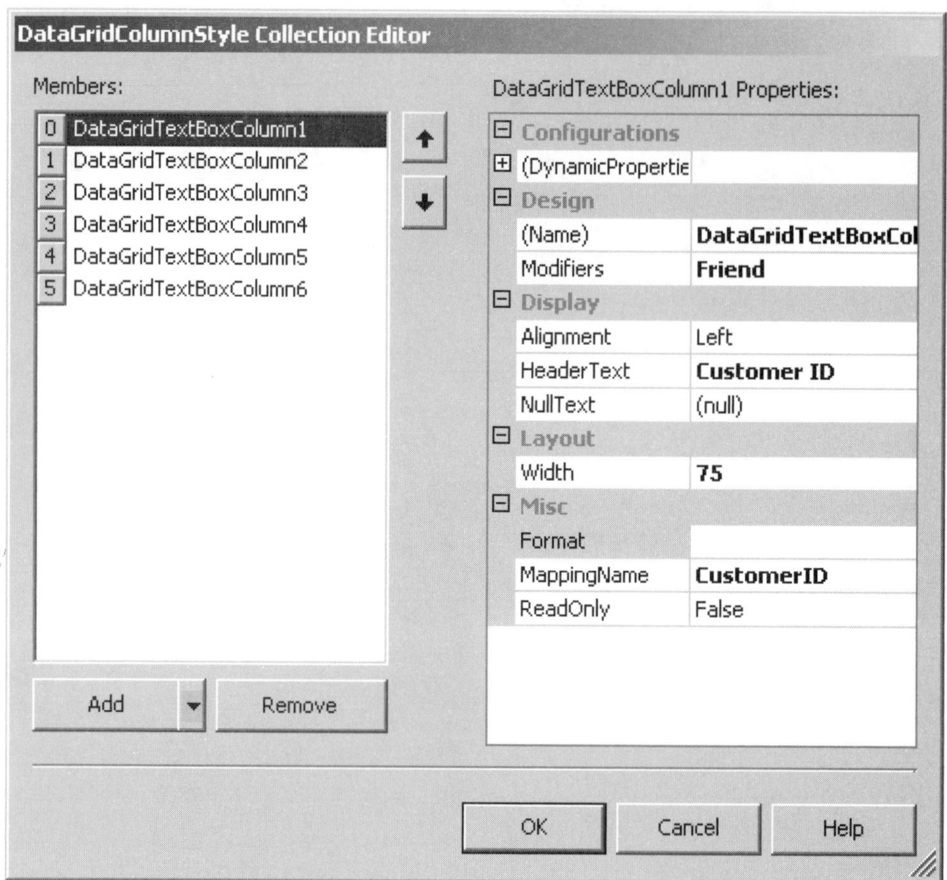

FIGURE 8.18 The GridColumnStyle editor.

```
    Private Sub Button1_Click(ByVal sender As System.Object, ByVal e As
System.EventArgs) Handles Button1.Click
        SqlDataAdapter1.Fill(DsCust1)
    End Sub

    Private Sub Button3_Click(ByVal sender As System.Object, ByVal e As
System.EventArgs) Handles Button3.Click
        DataGrid1.TableStyles(1).MappingName = ""
        DataGrid1.TableStyles(0).MappingName = "Customers"
    End Sub

    Private Sub Button2_Click(ByVal sender As System.Object, ByVal e As
System.EventArgs) Handles Button2.Click
```

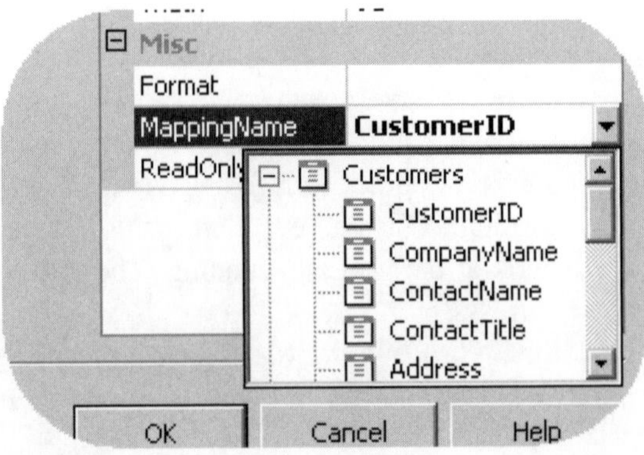

FIGURE 8.19 Setting the `MappingName` property.

```
        DataGrid1.TableStyles(0).MappingName = ""
        DataGrid1.TableStyles(1).MappingName = ""
    End Sub
    Private Sub Button4_Click(ByVal sender As System.Object, ByVal e As
System.EventArgs) Handles Button4.Click
        DataGrid1.TableStyles(0).MappingName = ""
        DataGrid1.TableStyles(1).MappingName = "Customers"
    End Sub

    Private Sub frmGridDemo_Closing(ByVal sender As Object, ByVal e As
System.ComponentModel.CancelEventArgs) Handles MyBase.Closing
        If DsCust1.HasChanges Then
            If MsgBox("Save Changes?", MsgBoxStyle.YesNo) =
MsgBoxResult.Yes Then
                SqlDataAdapter1.Update(DsCust1)
            End If
        End If
    End Sub
```

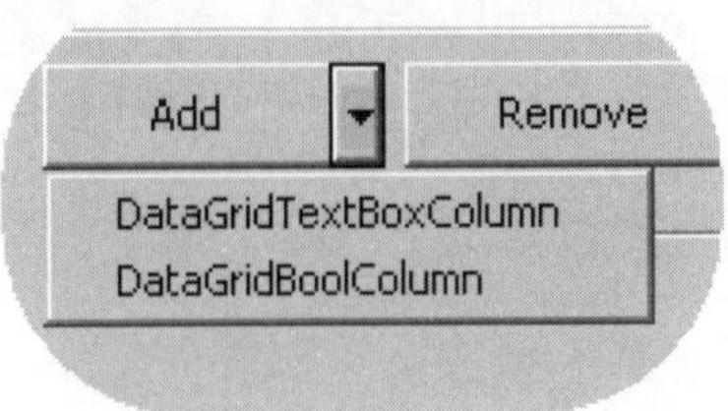

FIGURE 8.20 Selecting the column type.

Notice that to get back to the default grid display, we simply set the `TableMapping` property of all the TableStyle objects in the collection to the null string. By the way, if we set the `TableMapping` property to an invalid name, such as a table that doesn't exist, no error occurs. As a matter of fact, nothing at all happens. Another strange behavior.

The last bit of code in the Closing event allows us to save the data to the database. Now let's look at the program running. The grid with the default settings looks like Figure 8.21.

When we click the Style 1 button, we set the `TableMapping` property of the first TableStyle object to `Customers`. The grid then appears as in Figure 8.22.

Besides the different columns, the alternating row color is now light aqua. Let's look at Style 2 (see Figure 8.23).

To go back to the original display, click Default Style. This clears all the TableMapping settings and restores the original view.

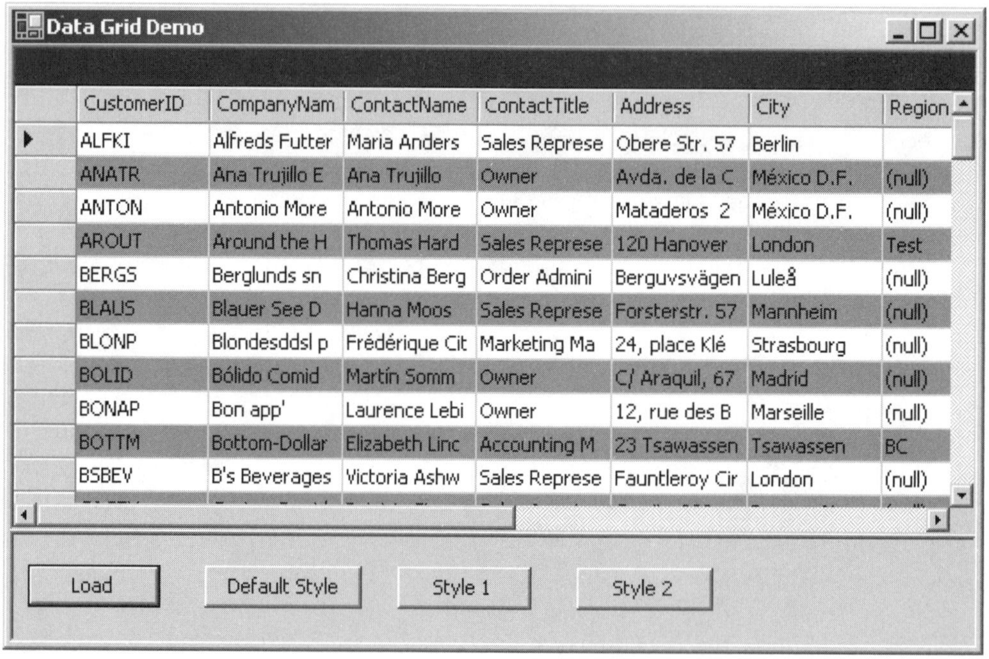

FIGURE 8.21 The grid with the default style.

Data Grid Demo

Customer ID	Company	Contact	Title	Phone	
ALFKI	Alfreds Futter	Maria Anders	Sales Represe	030-0074321	(null)
ANATR	Ana Trujillo E	Ana Trujillo	Owner	(5) 555-4729	(null)
ANTON	Antonio More	Antonio More	Owner	(5) 555-3932	(null)
AROUT	Around the H	Thomas Hard	Sales Represe	(171) 555-77	(null)
BERGS	Berglunds sn	Christina Berg	Order Admini	0921-12 34 6	(null)
BLAUS	Blauer See D	Hanna Moos	Sales Represe	0621-08460	(null)
BLONP	Blondesddsl p	Frédérique Cit	Marketing Ma	88.60.15.31	(null)
BOLID	Bólido Comid	Martín Somm	Owner	(91) 555 22 8	(null)
BONAP	Bon app'	Laurence Lebi	Owner	91.24.45.40	(null)
BOTTM	Bottom-Dollar	Elizabeth Linc	Accounting M	(604) 555-47	(null)
BSBEV	B's Beverages	Victoria Ashw	Sales Represe	(171) 555-12	(null)
CACTU	Cactus Comid	Patricio Simps	Sales Agent	(1) 135-5555	(null)

Load | Default Style | Style 1 | Style 2

FIGURE 8.22 The grid with Style 1 displayed.

Sorting Data

There are two ways to sort the data in a DataGrid: by single column or by multiple columns. The easier way is to allow the user to sort by clicking the column headings. This works the same way as Windows Explorer in Detail View, the first click sorts ascending, the second click sorts descending. The direction of the sort is indicated by a 3D arrow pointing up or down. The main drawback to this method is that the user can only sort by one column at a time. Also, you cannot control which columns the user is allowed to sort on. If we want to do this we will have to use a little code. This will demonstrate how to use the `HitTest` method to determine where the mouse was clicked over the grid.

The `HitTest` Method

In the previous version of the grid, there was a HeadClick event that fired and returned the column index of the column that was clicked. There were also other click events. Rather than have so many events, the designers decided to

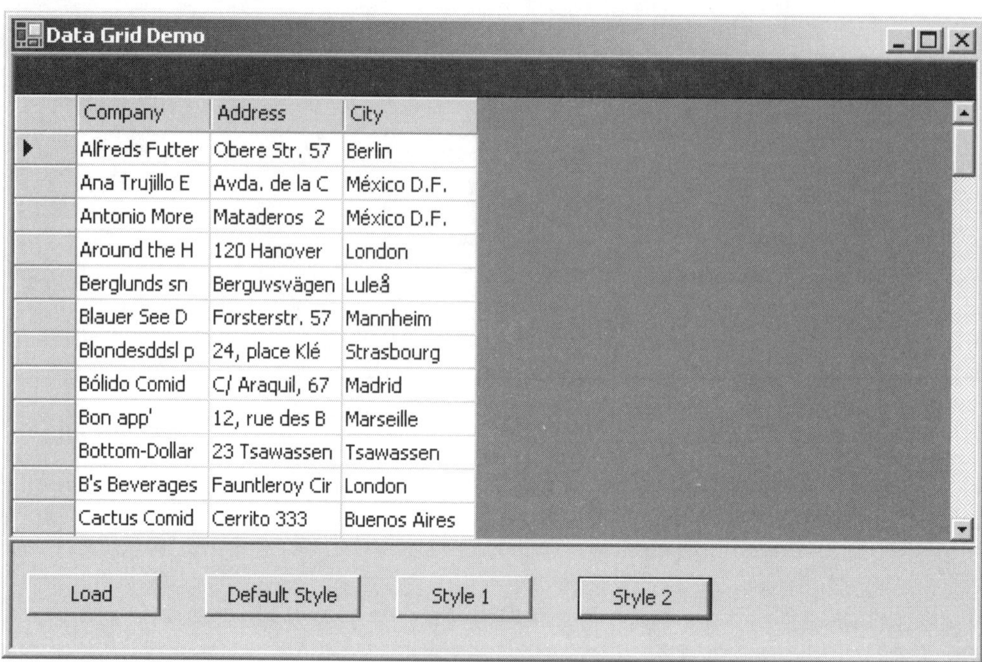

FIGURE 8.23 The grid with Style 2 displayed.

let the programmer figure out where the click occurred. There are already the mouse events that return *x* and *y* coordinates to where the mouse was when the event took place. All we need is a way to determine where in the control the mouse was clicked. The designers provided this in the form of the `HitTest` method. You pass it the *x* and *y* coordinates, and it returns a HitTestInfo object that contains the row, column, and type enumeration. The type enumeration will tell you where on the grid the click occurred. Examples are the column heading, in a cell, and so forth. You can then use this information to determine the DataTable column that you are positioned over and use that information to either sort the column or do nothing if it is a column you do not want to allow the user to sort on.

To do this, first add a DataView object to the designer. Set the `DataTable` property to the Customers table. Then change the `DataSource` property of the DataGrid to the DataView object. You may have noticed by now that binding to a DataView will be a standard practice in the future. I can't see any reason not to use one as they are so versatile. Also, we have to set the `AllowSorting` property of the grid control to false. This disables the default behavior of sorting on the clicked column automatically. We must do this so we can control where the sorting is allowed.

Next we have to add some code to the MouseUp event of the DataGrid. Here is the code:

```
Private Sub DataGrid1_MouseUp(ByVal sender As Object, ByVal e As
System.Windows.Forms.MouseEventArgs) Handles DataGrid1.MouseUp
        Dim ht As DataGrid.HitTestInfo

        Try
            ht = DataGrid1.HitTest(e.X, e.Y)
            If ht.Type = DataGrid.HitTestType.ColumnHeader Then
                If DsCust1.Customers.Columns(ht.Column).ColumnName =
"ContactName" Or _
                   DsCust1.Customers.Columns(ht.Column).ColumnName =
"CustomerID" Then
                    DataView1.Sort =
DsCust1.Customers.Columns(ht.Column).ColumnName
                End If
            End If
        Catch errobj As Exception
            MessageBox.Show(errobj.Message)
        End Try
End Sub
```

Even though it might appear complicated it is really simple. The event passes a MouseEventArgs object, which contains the *x* and *y* coordinates of the mouse position as properties. These properties are then passed to the `HitTest` method of the DataGrid. This returns the HitTestInfo object. The HitTestInfo object has a `Type` property which tells us where the user clicked on the grid. It also returns the column index. So if the user clicked in the column header, we can use the column index to get the name of the column from the underlying DataSet. We can then test the column name to see if it is one of the columns we want to allow the user to sort by. If it is we set the `Sort` property of the DataView to the column name. If not, we just do nothing.

We can make one more change to emulate the default behavior of the DataGrid, which is to alternate between ascending and descending sorts each time the heading is clicked. We need to make one more change to the procedure.

```
    Private Sub DataGrid1_MouseUp(ByVal sender As Object, ByVal e As
System.Windows.Forms.MouseEventArgs) Handles DataGrid1.MouseUp
        Dim ht As DataGrid.HitTestInfo
        Static strDirection() As String
```

```
        Try
            ReDim Preserve strDirection(DsCust1.Customers.Columns.Count
- 1)
             ht = DataGrid1.HitTest(e.X, e.Y)
             If ht.Type = DataGrid.HitTestType.ColumnHeader Then
                 If DsCust1.Customers.Columns(ht.Column).ColumnName =
"ContactName" Or _
                    DsCust1.Customers.Columns(ht.Column).ColumnName =
"CustomerID" Then
                     If strDirection(ht.Column) = "" Then
strDirection(ht.Column) = "Asc"
                     DataView1.Sort =
DsCust1.Customers.Columns(ht.Column).ColumnName & " " &
strDirection(ht.Column)
                     If strDirection(ht.Column) = "Asc" Then
strDirection(ht.Column) = "Desc" Else strDirection(ht.Column) = "Asc"
                 End If
             End If
        Catch errobj As Exception
             MessageBox.Show(errobj.Message)
        End Try
    End Sub
```

What this does is create a static string array to store that last sort direction of each column. The keyword `Static` makes the variable retain its values between calls to the method. We use the `Redim Preserve` statement to set up the array initially. Then we simply toggle the value of the element that corresponds to the column index between `Asc` and `Desc`. We then append this value to the `Sort` property value.

Sorting Multiple Columns

In order to sort multiple columns, we need a way to select the columns we want to sort. This version of the grid does not have any column selection mechanism so we will have to invent one. Let's make it so that if the user right-clicks on the column header it selects the column. We will need a way to store the selected column names in a temporary collection until we apply the sort. Once the sort is applied, we will clear the collection. We can use a ListBox to display the columns we want to sort on. For now we will limit our demonstration to ascending sorts. We will leave it up to you to modify the code to sort either way. You don't want us to have all the fun, do you?

The procedure for the user is right-click on the column he wishes to sort on in the most-significant to least-significant order. So the first column clicked will be the outermost sort, the next column within that, and so on. As the user clicks on the columns they will be added to the collection and the ListBox. If a column is clicked twice it will not be added the second time. Once the user has finished selecting, he can click the Sort button to apply the sort. After the user clicks the sort button, if he clicks another column heading the list clears and prepares for the next sort sequence. Again it sounds complicated but much of the work is already done. Here is the modified code and the button click event for the Sort button. The new code is in bold.

```
    Private Sub DataGrid1_MouseUp(ByVal sender As Object, ByVal e As
System.Windows.Forms.MouseEventArgs) Handles DataGrid1.MouseUp
        Dim ht As DataGrid.HitTestInfo
        Static strDirection() As String

        Try
            If e.Button = MouseButtons.Left Then
                ReDim Preserve
strDirection(DsCust1.Customers.Columns.Count - 1)
                ht = DataGrid1.HitTest(e.X, e.Y)
                If ht.Type = DataGrid.HitTestType.ColumnHeader Then
                   If DsCust1.Customers.Columns(ht.Column).ColumnName =
"ContactName" Or _
                      DsCust1.Customers.Columns(ht.Column).ColumnName =
"CustomerID" Then
                        If strDirection(ht.Column) = "" Then
strDirection(ht.Column) = "Asc"
                        DataView1.Sort =
DsCust1.Customers.Columns(ht.Column).ColumnName & " " &
strDirection(ht.Column)
                        If strDirection(ht.Column) = "Asc" Then
strDirection(ht.Column) = "Desc" Else strDirection(ht.Column) = "Asc"
                    End If
                End If
            ElseIf e.Button = MouseButtons.Right Then
                ht = DataGrid1.HitTest(e.X, e.Y)
                If ht.Type = DataGrid.HitTestType.ColumnHeader Then
                    If mCols Is Nothing Then
                        ReDim mCols(0)
                    Else
                       ReDim Preserve mCols(mCols.GetUpperBound(0) + 1)
                    End If
                    If mCols.IndexOf(mCols,
DsCust1.Customers.Columns(ht.Column).ColumnName) < 0 Then
                        mCols(mCols.GetUpperBound(0)) =
DsCust1.Customers.Columns(ht.Column).ColumnName
                        ListBox1.DataSource = mCols
                    End If
```

```
                    ListBox1.DataSource = mCols
                End If
            End If
        Catch errobj As Exception
            MessageBox.Show(errobj.Message & vbCrLf & errobj.StackTrace)
        End Try
    End Sub

    Private Sub Button5_Click(ByVal sender As System.Object, ByVal e As
System.EventArgs) Handles Button5.Click
        DataView1.Sort = Join(mCols, ", ")
        Erase mCols
    End Sub
```

There is one more line of code that needs to be added and that is a declaration of the string array mCols. It is a simple `Private mCols() As String`. Notice that we are using the ability to bind a control to an array to populate the ListBox automatically. It saves us having to constantly maintain the list in the ListBox.

There are a couple of items worth noting. First, I use the `IndexOf` method of the array object to test if a proposed new element exists in the array. If it does, the method returns the index. If it doesn't, the method returns `–1`. This is a handy method. It beats looping through the array and testing each item, although that's probably what it does internally. But it's code I didn't have to write.

Also, notice the use of the Join function. This is a holdover from VB 6 that was kept in the language. This function takes a string array and converts it to a delimited string. The delimiter can be any character or characters you desire, although the most common is probably the comma. It has a companion function, Split, that takes a delimited string and converts it into any array. I'm glad they left these in, because the `string class` methods that are supposed to replace them only take single-character delimiters, which is a big deficiency.

There is a lot more to the DataGrid than we have looked at, but I think I have given you enough to whet your appetite. As you can see, with a little code you can really do a lot with this grid control. Before you go out and drop some big bucks on one of the third-party controls, why not look into enhancing the one that came with Visual Studio. Now that VB is fully object oriented, you could subclass the control and add some of these techniques to the existing class to create your own customized version. Have fun!

SUMMARY

In this chapter we have seen how to create data-bound Windows Forms. We have looked at data binding. We have seen that with the data binding mechanism in Windows Forms, there is no longer any reason to bypass it. Gone are the days of working around the deficiencies of the data binding of prior versions of VB. Windows Forms provides a very robust binding mechanism that if used properly will yield very robust database applications.

CHAPTER 9

Data Binding in Web Forms

Now we will move on to Web Forms. We have not done too much with Web Forms until now. Because of this I will be a little more detailed in my instructions when it comes to creating the example projects. But relax, because in the .NET world, creating a Web Form is very similar to creating a Windows Form. As a matter of fact, because of the nature of the Web, Web Forms are much simpler than Windows Forms in many ways. For one thing, we do not have to respond to every move the user makes when entering data because there are no events that fire back to the server, due to the limitations of web-based architecture. As with Windows Forms, there are many controls that can be bound, and there is a Web DataGrid control. The difference is that these controls separate the programmatic functionality from how they are rendered. All these controls render themselves by emitting standard HTML. For example, the DataGrid ends up creating a standard HTML table when it is sent to the client. This is very similar to the old design-time ActiveX controls we used in Visual InterDev.

THE LIFE CYCLE OF A WEB FORM

The biggest difference between Windows Forms controls and Web Forms controls is that while the Web Forms control is visibly displayed on the user's screen, no instance of the control exists on the server. This seems to be a difficult concept for many programmers to grasp. It is not a new concept either, because it was just as true with ASP. It makes sense when you understand that all server-side scripts or compiled programs only execute for brief moments at a time. Usually it is the amount of time between a request and a response. This is very different from Windows programs which execute for as long as the user wants, until they close the program.

Why am I going into this in a discussion of Web forms data binding? Because in order to understand data binding you have to understand the life cycle of the controls (see Figure 9.1). The controls actually only exist for very brief periods of time between requests and responses. This is why there are no events in Web controls like keystroke or mouse events. They have no where to go!

Requests and Responses

The concept that you have to grasp about web-based applications is that they consist of a series of requests and responses. It really isn't an event-driven model the way Windows is. A request comes from the user and goes to the server. The response is what the server sends back to the user. Requests can have the form of the user entering a URL is the address box, clicking a link, or posting a form by clicking the Submit button. The response is usually HTML but it can also be a command like a redirect.

It's interesting but this is really not much different from the old CICS and COBOL on IBM mainframes. Basically, the user filled out the screen and then submitted it to the queue, where a COBOL program was waiting to process the input. Once processed, the COBOL program would then send another screen back to the terminal. The more things change, the more they remain the same, right?

MAINTAINING SESSION STATE

The main thing to understand here is that Web Forms (or the code behind the Web Forms) have to execute each time a request comes from the user. They process the request and then terminate. This makes things like module-level variables unusable for storing data that must persist for the entire session. Ah! A new word, session. Web applications use something called *session state* to maintain context between requests. The session state is maintained by IIS itself, so we don't have to worry about the program terminating and losing its data.

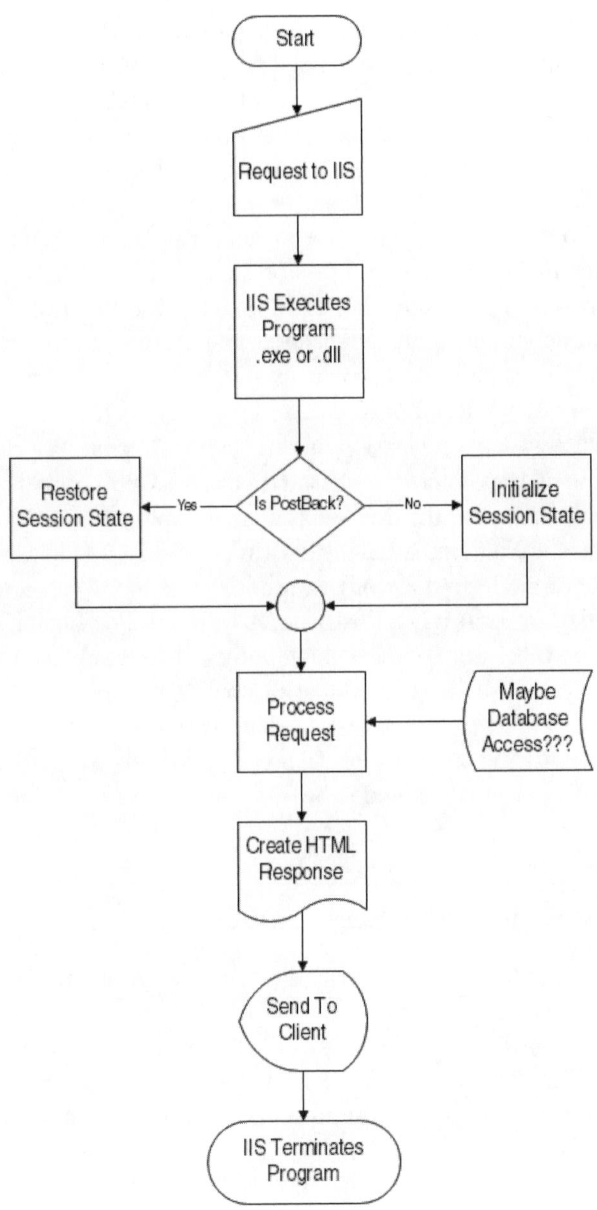

FIGURE 9.1 Web Form life cycle.

The session exists outside the memory space of the executing code, so it is not lost. There is an intrinsic object called the Session object that is accessible from any Web Form's code that can be used to store persistent session data. A session is defined as the time span between when the user first loaded a page within the web application and when the user jumps to a page outside the scope of the application. This could be to another server or to another application on the same server. Usually once the user loads a page from another web site, the session is considered terminated. Since your web server has no way of knowing that the user has left, this is usually handled by a timeout. So it is possible for a user to leave a site and then return right away (within the timeout) and retain session state. The session timeout is usually pretty long—sometimes as high as 30 minutes—so the user doesn't lose the session while still using the application. In a typical intranet or secure site it will usually be shorter, because the user is expected to be more active on the site. If you've ever left a page on the screen and then returned, and it made you reauthenticate, you probably hit the session timeout.

All this is important to understand because Web Forms have to recreate themselves every time the user sends a request to the server. The life cycle of a Web Form is diagrammed in the drawing in Figure 9.1. Fortunately, there is a property of the form that you can use to determine if the form is executing for the first time or if it is a PostBack. A form is a PostBack if it has already executed and the user did something without leaving the site that made the form rerender itself. It is important to note that even with a PostBack, the form still must reexecute and restore all of its state data. That is one very useful function of the `IsPostBack` property. If it is a PostBack, you must retrieve all the data you stored in Session variables or in cookies on the user's machine.

Setting Up Internet Information Server 5.0

Before we start building sample applications, we must have IIS installed and running If you have not set up the IIS on your machine, you should do so now. To set up IIS on a Windows NT 4.0 machine, you must download (or obtain on CD-ROM from MSDN or another source) the Options Pack. This contains IIS 4.0, but when you install the components upgrade from Visual Studio it will include IIS 5.0 with Windows 2000 and XP Pro; IIS is installed by default. If for some reason it is not (such as an OEM installation that did not install it), you can install it by going into control panel, add/remove programs, and then clicking the Windows Components button in the installer applet.

Once you have installed IIS, rerun the component update so that IIS can respond to ASP .NET requests properly. This mainly involves adding the appropriate software and creating the application Mappings. This is a list of file extensions and associated programs and .dlls that IIS loads when that type of page is requested. It is similar to file associations in the Windows file system. In order to tell if IIS is properly configured, you can check the Mappings page. To do this, right-click on My Computer and then click Manage in the context menu. This opens the computer management console as in Figure 9.2. Expand the tree and find the node shown.

Right-click on the node and open the Properties pages. Select the Directory tab and then click the Configuration button as in Figure 9.3.

Once you have clicked the Configuration button, the Application dialog opens as in Figure 9.4.

Make sure the correct associations are present as in Figure 9.5. If they are not you should reinstall the component update.

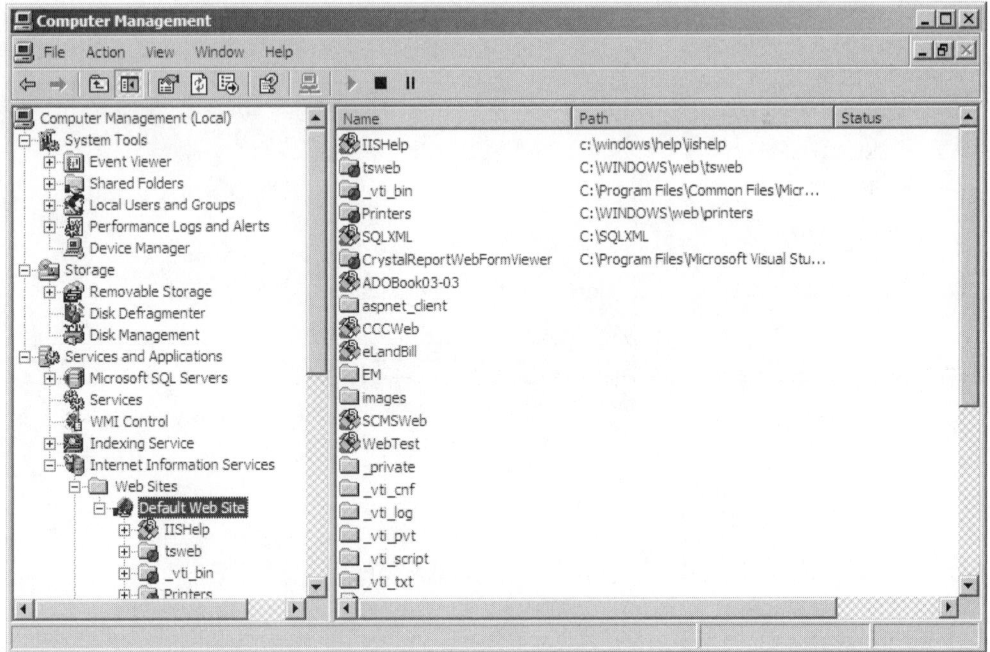

FIGURE 9.2 Managing IIS from the management console.

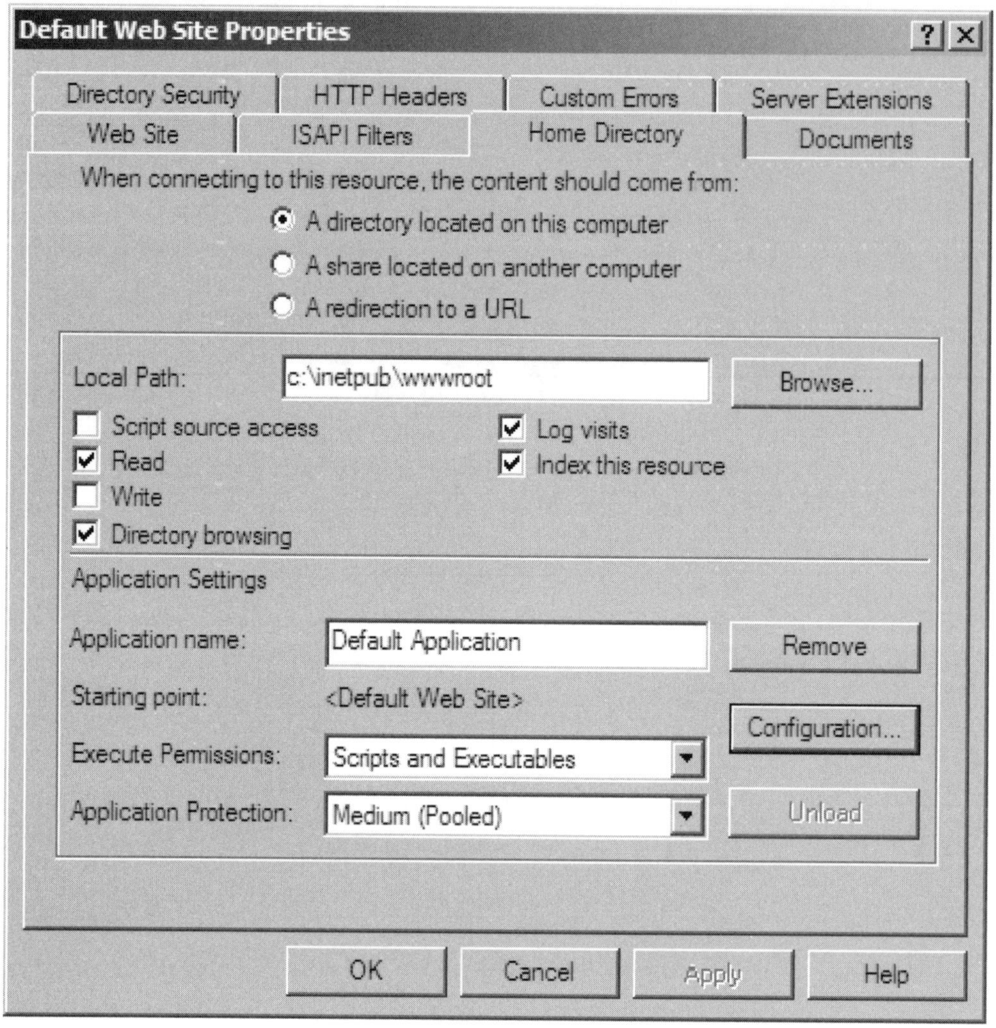

FIGURE 9.3 IIS web site Properties page.

ASP .NET and HTML–Universal Browser Support

It may seem on the surface that ASP .NET doesn't offer much more than ASP. After all, they both end up at the same place and there is nothing you couldn't do in ASP that you can do in ASP .NET. The main advantage of ASP .NET over ASP is the programming model. Instead of writing ASP scripts or VB web classes you can write your code in Visual Basic or C# and

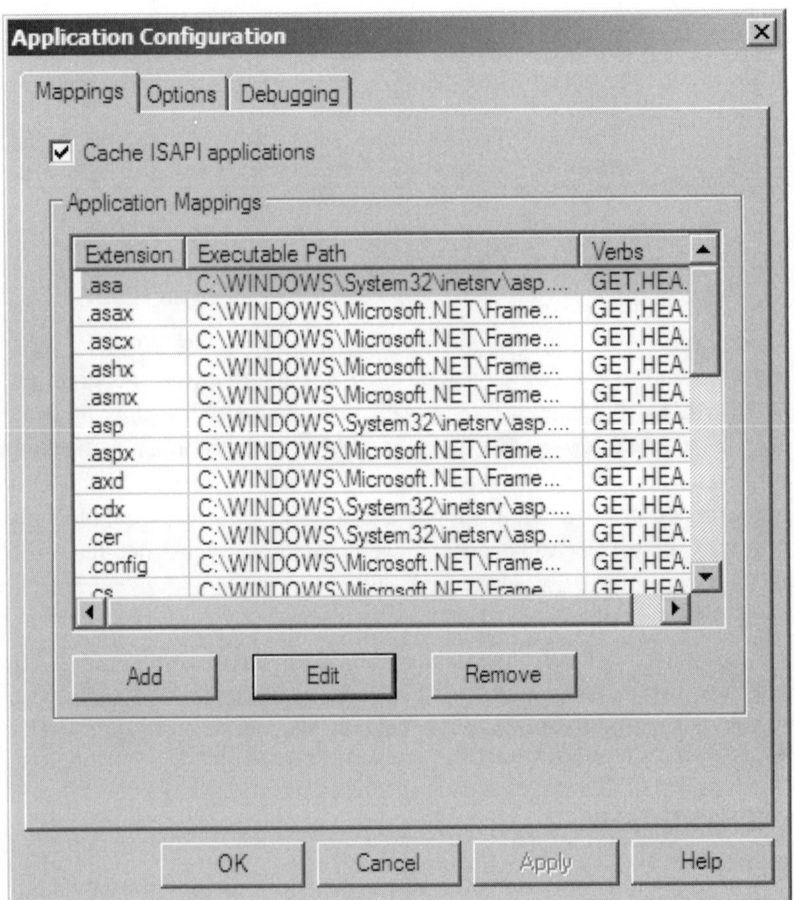

FIGURE 9.4 The Application Configuration dialog.

it renders the HTML for you. You are relieved of having to use the `Response.Write` method to create HTML yourself; ASP .NET does it for you behind the scenes. Well, actually it does a little more than that.

ASP .NET attempts something that has been very elusive ever since there was more than one web browser, universal browser support. Many previous incarnations of ASP and other vendors' tools have made this claim, only to fail miserably. No matter what, you had to write browser-specific code in order to make sure all of your users had a positive experience. What you ended up with was these Viewed Best With… disclaimers on web pages or a lowest common denominator experience that would work with the most common browsers, Internet Explorer or Netscape. If you had some other browser, good luck.

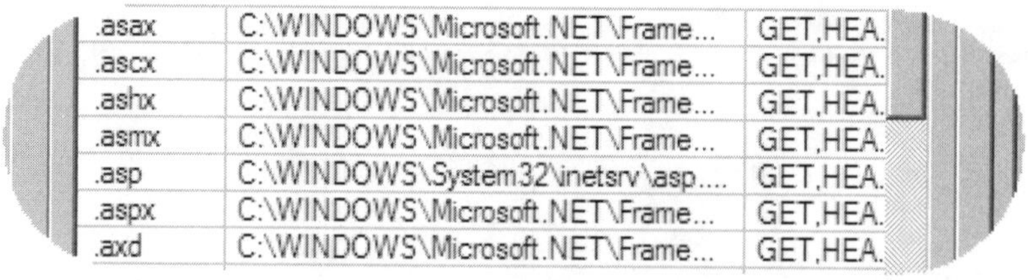

.asax	C:\WINDOWS\Microsoft.NET\Frame...	GET,HEA.
.ascx	C:\WINDOWS\Microsoft.NET\Frame...	GET,HEA.
.ashx	C:\WINDOWS\Microsoft.NET\Frame...	GET,HEA.
.asmx	C:\WINDOWS\Microsoft.NET\Frame...	GET,HEA.
.asp	C:\WINDOWS\System32\inetsrv\asp....	GET,HEA.
.aspx	C:\WINDOWS\Microsoft.NET\Frame...	GET,HEA.
.axd	C:\WINDOWS\Microsoft.NET\Frame...	GET,HEA.

FIGURE 9.5 The ASPX associations.

Universal browser support is supposed to address this problem. ASP .NET is supposed to detect the browser type and automatically generate the correct HTML for the browser. How well does it work? It seems to work okay for IE and Netscape 4 and above. I tried it with Konquerer, the Web browser that comes with Linux and KDE, and it worked—sort of. Most forms rendered except it didn't seem to support the absolute positioning. It blew my visual design all to pieces because it went to flow layout, but the form worked, and some of my framesets came out really wacky, with paragraphs in the wrong places.

So, does ASP .NET solve the universal browser support problem? Not in my book. Microsoft needs to work on it some more. ASP .NET pages are still best viewed in Internet Explorer.

THE DATA-BOUND WEB FORM

Now that we've laid the groundwork, we can begin discussing how data binding works in a Web Form. Remember that the form as displayed on the user's screen is standard HTML. This means that all of the binding must be done before the HTML is emitted and transferred to the client. This is accomplished by the controls emitting their tags with the value attribute set to the value of the current row and column in the DataSet to which the control is. So you can see that the data binding can only be one-way. When the user posts the form back to the server, the data comes back in the Request.Forms ("ControlName") format, so there is no way to support two-way binding.

Creating the Project

Let's create our demo project called ADOBook09-01. Since this is a web project, you will have had to set up your machine to run web applications. Create the new project. When prompted, select Web Forms as in Figure 9.6.

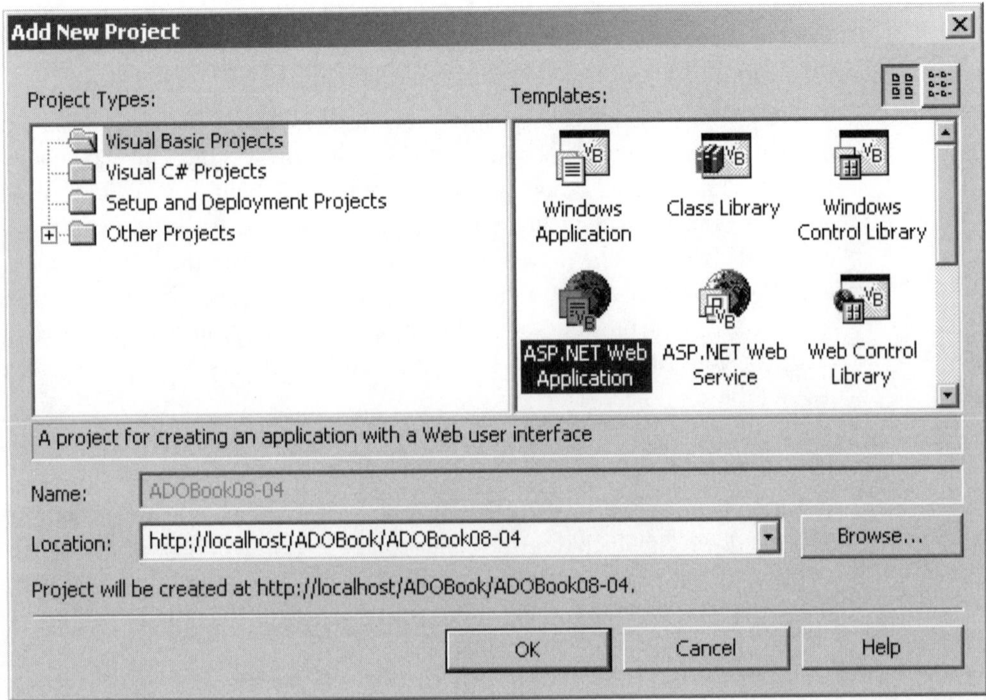

FIGURE 9.6 Creating an ASP .NET application.

Notice that it creates the project on the Web. You could just as easily have used the web address of another server, an application development web server, for example. The project is created in the folder pointed to by the web address. In many cases this is c:\inetpub\wwwroot\<path to application>. Once the project is created, it creates a default Web Form called webform1. The Web Form consists of two parts, the HTML page and the VB code module associated with it. Notice that the project is a class library, which will compile to a DLL.

The first part of creating our data-bound form is to add the requisite data components. We will need a DataAdapter, Connection, and at least one DataSet. To add the DataAdapter, drag an SqlDataAdapter from the toolbox and drop it on the form. Go through all the wizard pages and use the Customers table from the Northwind database. Next, we will create another DataAdapter using the Customers table. This time, we will only create an SQL `Select` statement. When you mark the columns to use in the `Select` statement, only select the CustomerID and CompanyName columns. We will use this DataAdapter to populate the list portion of a combo box.

Next we will create the visual design of our form. This is similar to creating a Windows Form. You can drag objects from the toolbox and drop them on the form. We will make our form look like Figure 9.7.

If you designed Web Forms in previous versions of Visual Studio, you know that absolute placement of controls on a form was difficult. Somebody finally listened, because now the placement is the default. If you still want to autoflow your form elements, you can, just change the `PageLayout` property of the form to `FlowLayout.` Flow layout is when the browser determines the final placement to the elements on the page, and the elements flow just like text, wrapping to the next line if necessary. With absolute positioning or grid layout, the controls will never move. Scroll bars will appear in the user's browser if necessary.

The Specification

The way the form will work is that the user will select a company name from the drop down, at which time the controls on the form will fill with the details of the selected company. The user can then edit the record and save it by clicking the Submit button. The user can also delete the record by clicking the

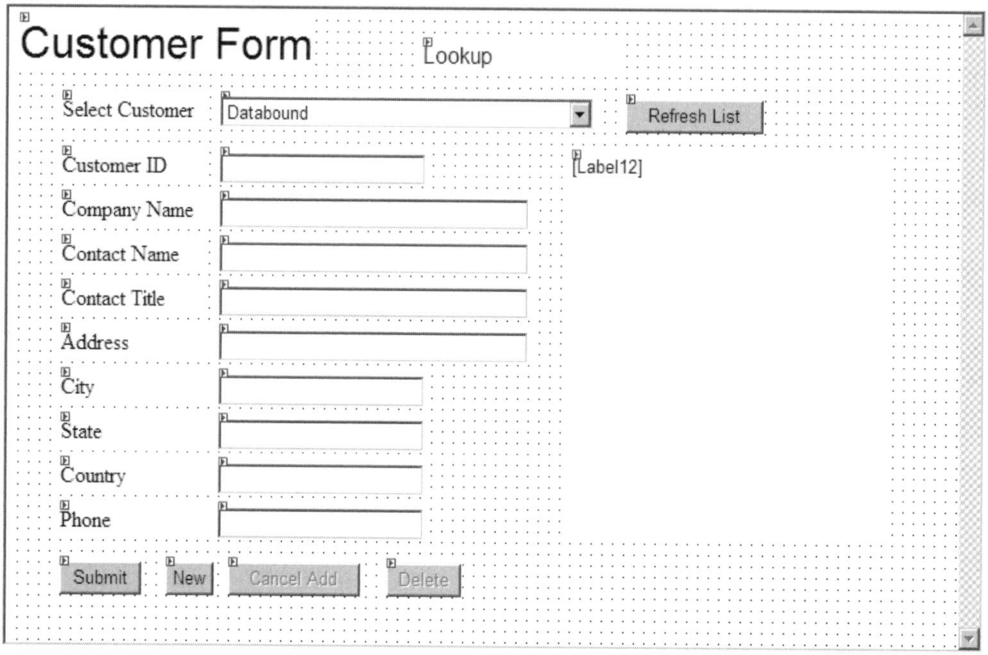

FIGURE 9.7 The visual design of the Web Form.

Delete button. If the user wants to add a new record, he or she can click the New button. This clears the fields and allows the user to enter a new record.

To save the new record the user would click Submit. The form has two "modes." The default is LookUp mode. In this mode the user can select records from the drop down. In LookUp mode, the CustomerID field is read-only. The other mode is Add. In this mode the drop down is disabled and the user can enter a new CustomerID as well as the other information. The mode is indicated at the top of the screen by a label control. If the user wants to abort adding a new record, he or she can click the Cancel Add button. The Refresh List button repopulates the list of the drop down with fresh data. The various buttons will enable and disable themselves based on the current context of the form.

Binding Controls

Binding controls in Web Forms is a little different than in Windows Forms. We will start with a simple text box. A quick look at the property windows for a web text box and it is easy to see that this is not your Windows Forms text box. Many of the properties have to do with HTML and how the control is rendered. Let's use the CustomerID columns to begin with. Select the first text box on the page, TextBox1. To bind the text box to a column in the DataSet, click on the ellipsis button in the `DataBindings` property. This opens the binding editor as in Figure 9.8.

Leave Simple Binding selected and find the CustomerID column in the tree. You have the option of including a custom format string as well. This is useful for date and numeric fields. If you notice the grayed-out text box, you will see a peculiar looking statement. This is actually the HTML that gets placed in the tag on the web page that is also created. You can override the generated HTML and type in your own custom binding expression here. Here is the full tag for TextBox1 in HTML:

```
<asp:textbox id=TextBox1 style="Z-INDEX: 100; LEFT: 160px; POSITION:
absolute; TOP: 104px" runat="server" Text='<%# DataBinder.Eval(DsCust1,
"Tables[Customers].DefaultView.[0].CustomerID") %>'></asp:textbox>
```

Notice the text after the text= attribute. This is the same thing that we saw in the custom DataBinding area of the DataBinding dialog in Figure 9.8. Now go ahead and create the bindings for the other controls on the form.

We need to bind the dropdown control's list to a list of customers. The idea here is that the user will choose a customer from the list, then the details will display for editing. To bind the list portion of the drop down, we use the

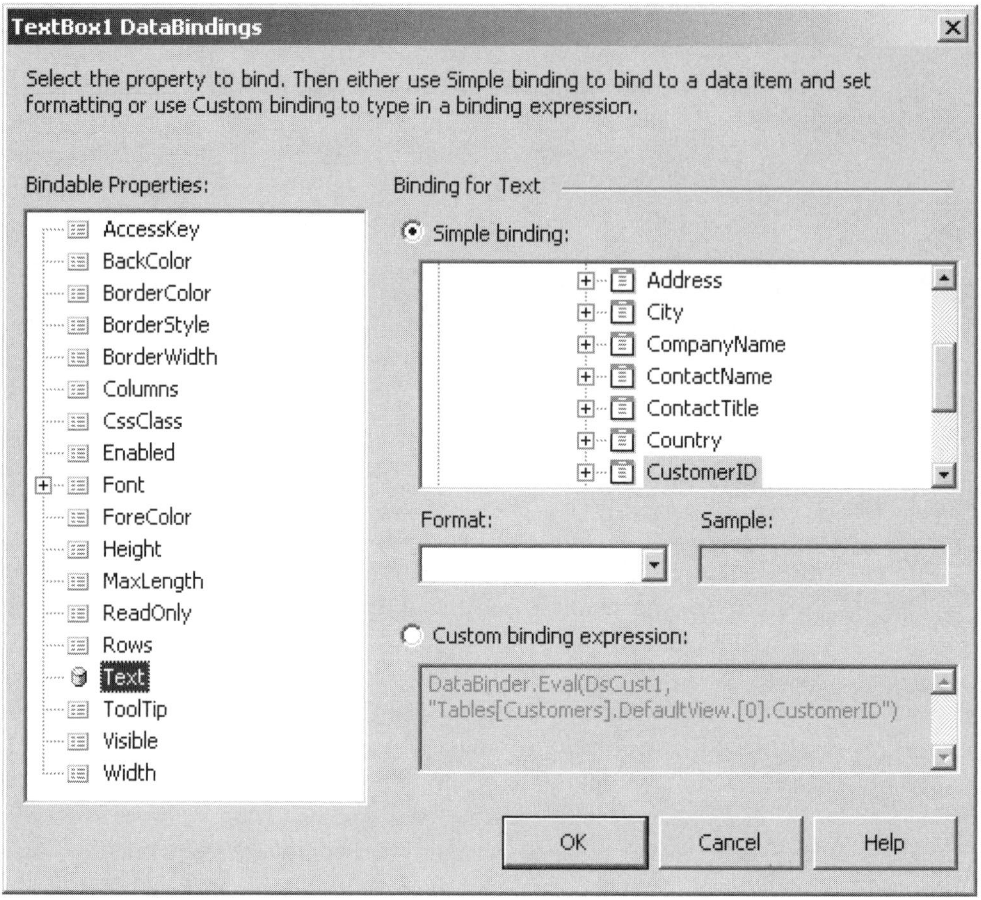

FIGURE 9.8 The DataBindings editor.

`DataSource` and `DataTextField` and `DataValueField` properties. The DataSource is where we put the DataSet name. The DataMember is where we put the DataTable name. Use dsCustList1 as the DataSource and Customers as the DataMember.

The DataTextField is the column we want to display in the list. This should be a descriptive column. We will use the CompanyName column in our list. For the `DataValueField` property we will use the CustomerID, since this is the primary key of the Customers table in the database. Do not bind the drop down to the main table in dsCust1. We are using this control as a selector only. The editable control will be the text box.

Now comes the fun part of getting it all working. There are two things we have to do on form start-up. The first thing is to determine if we are starting the form for the first time or if this is a PostBack. We do this with the

IsPostBack property of the form itself. Then we have to initialize the form or restore its state. The page load event for the form ends up looking like the following code snippet.

```
    Private Sub Page_Load(ByVal sender As System.Object, ByVal e As
System.EventArgs) Handles MyBase.Load
        If Not IsPostBack Then
            SqlDataAdapter2.Fill(DsCustList1)
            Session("CustList") = DsCustList1
            Drop downList1.DataBind()
            Session("IsAdding") = False
        End If
    End Sub
```

This initializes the DataSet that contains the rows that will populate the list portion of the dropdown box. It also initializes some Session variables. A Session variable is a value that is stored by the IIS, rather than in the program's data space. This is so we can preserve values across requests, as we said before. It is stored in an object called Session. The Session object does not have to be created because it is automatically passed to the form from the IIS. Notice that we can save an entire DataSet in a Session variable. We don't have to worry about cleanup because IIS will automatically dereference the variable when the session timeout expires, then the CLR's garbage collector will destroy the object. This is a big advantage over using ActiveX .dlls, which, despite Microsoft's claims to the contrary, never worked as well as ASP applications. It was common for orphaned applications to remain active indefinitely; the only solution was to reboot the server. Notice that there is no code path if it is a PostBack because this is taken care of elsewhere in the code.

Now that we have the list populated, we can display the page. This happens automatically with ASP .NET pages. Unlike older ASP applications, there is no need to use the Response object to write the HTML stream. Now the form is displayed inside the web browser. Remember, the program has now terminated. When the page is first displayed it looks like Figure 9.9.

The next problem to solve is how to get the data into the fields on the page. It's very simple, thanks to a property of the DropdownList control (and many other web controls) called AutoPostBack. Normally, web controls don't fire events back to the server every time the user does something with them. Remember what we've been saying all along about the program terminating once the page has been sent to the client. If web controls fired similar events to Windows Forms controls, we would be executing, processing, and terminating the server-side program for each keystroke. This would be terri-

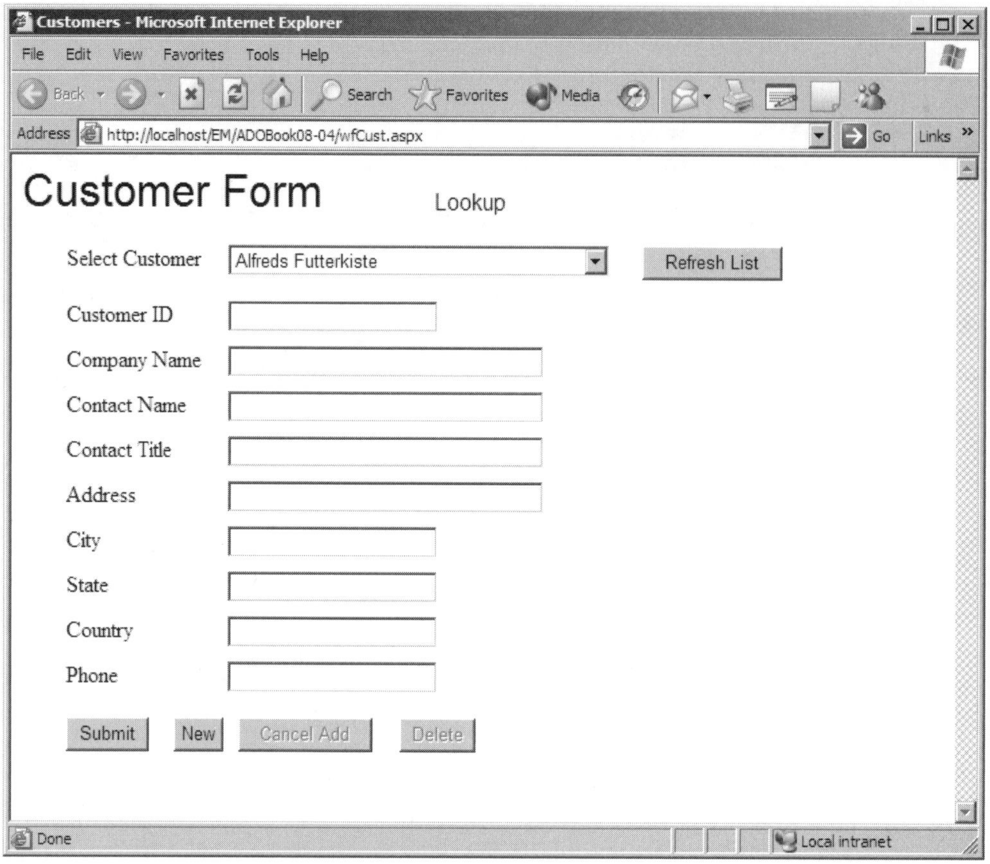

FIGURE 9.9 The Web Form at runtime.

bly inefficient. But there is a way to make web controls cause a PostBack to occur. A PostBack is different from an event, because the PostBack acts as if the user clicked the Submit button. It includes parameters in the request that indicate which control caused the posting and which procedure to execute when the program executes. It's a kind of pseudoevent.

So to make the application respond to the user selecting an item from the list of the DropdownList we set the control's `AutoPostBack` property to true. Now the question becomes, which event procedure runs? If you look at the list of available events, only one really fits the bill. It's the SelectedIndex-Changed event as in Figure 9.10.

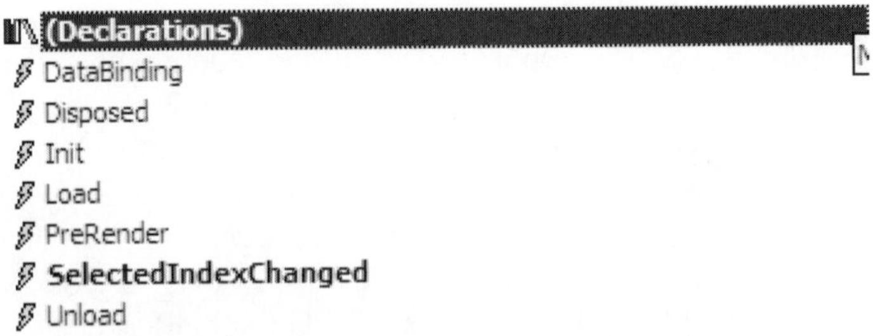

(Declarations)
DataBinding
Disposed
Init
Load
PreRender
SelectedIndexChanged
Unload

FIGURE 9.10 DropdownList events.

The code for this event is as follows:

```
    Private Sub Drop downList1_SelectedIndexChanged(ByVal sender As
System.Object, _
        ByVal e As System.EventArgs) Handles Drop
downList1.SelectedIndexChanged
        If Me.IsPostBack Then
           SqlDataAdapter1.SelectCommand.Parameters("@CustID").Value =
Drop downList1.SelectedItem.Value
            Session("selIndex") = Drop downList1.SelectedIndex
            SqlDataAdapter1.Fill(DsCust1)
            Me.DataBind()
            Button5.Enabled = True
            Session("dsCust1") = DsCust1.Copy
        End If
    End Sub
```

It's important to understand the order of events when this occurs. Why does the Page_Load event fire? Remember, the program is executing all over again. The Page_Load event fires when the code starts, not when the page is displayed on the user's browser. If I seem repetitive on this it is because it is difficult for many programmers who are used to Windows Forms to get used to how Web Forms work. Many programmers automatically associate Page_Load with Form_Load and while similar, they are not the same. Form_Load only fires once when the form is first loaded. Page_Load can fire many times during the time a Web Form is in use by the user. So when Page_Load fires, we don't want to reload the DataSet that contains the data for the list. What we do is bypass this code if it is a PostBack.

Next the DropdownList event fires. Here is where we do most of the processing for getting the selected record. The code to fetch the record is standard and we have seen it many times before. Unlike Windows Forms, you have to call DataBind, a special method of the Web Form to cause the binding to take effect. Then we enable the Delete button and save a copy of the DataSet in a Session variable. Once this procedure exits, we are almost ready to display the form.

There is one more thing to do.

Remember, we reexecuted the code. Nowhere did we repopulate the DropdownList control. If we want the control to keep displaying the list, we have to rebind it every time the code runs. Just before ASP .NET is ready to send the HTML to the user, it fires the Form_PreRender event. This fires so that you have a chance to do any final processing before the form HTML is created. At this point all we have to do is restore the dsCustList DataSet from the Session variable we stored it in and then rebind it to the DropdownList.

In our last step we restore the selected index so the list still appears to the user to be unchanged. Here is the code.

```
    Private Sub Page_PreRender(ByVal sender As Object, ByVal e As
System.EventArgs) Handles MyBase.PreRender
        If IsPostBack Then
            DsCustList1 = Session("CustList")
            Drop downList1.DataBind()
            Drop downList1.Items(Session("selIndex")).Selected = True
        End If
    End Sub
```

Let's try it. Run the program. When you select a customer from the list, the data should fill the form. It should appear seamless. It happens so fast that the form does not appear to redisplay, but it does. Figure 9.11 shows how the form looks filled in.

So far so good. We've been able to display data. Now we must add the code to be able to update the database. Here is where the one-way read-only data binding glares back at you.

```
  Private Sub Button1_Click(ByVal sender As System.Object, ByVal e As
System.EventArgs) Handles Button1.Click
    Try
      DsCust1 = CType(Session("dsCust1"), dsCust).Copy
      DsCust1.Customers.Rows(0)("CompanyName") = TextBox2.Text
      DsCust1.Customers.Rows(0)("ContactName") = TextBox3.Text
      DsCust1.Customers.Rows(0)("ContactTitle") = TextBox4.Text
      DsCust1.Customers.Rows(0)("Address") = TextBox5.Text
      DsCust1.Customers.Rows(0)("City") = TextBox6.Text
      DsCust1.Customers.Rows(0)("Region") = TextBox7.Text
      DsCust1.Customers.Rows(0)("PostalCode") = TextBox8.Text
      DsCust1.Customers.Rows(0)("Country") = Textbox9.Text
      DsCust1.Customers.Rows(0)("Phone") = TextBox10.Text
      SqlDataAdapter1.Update(DsCust1)
```

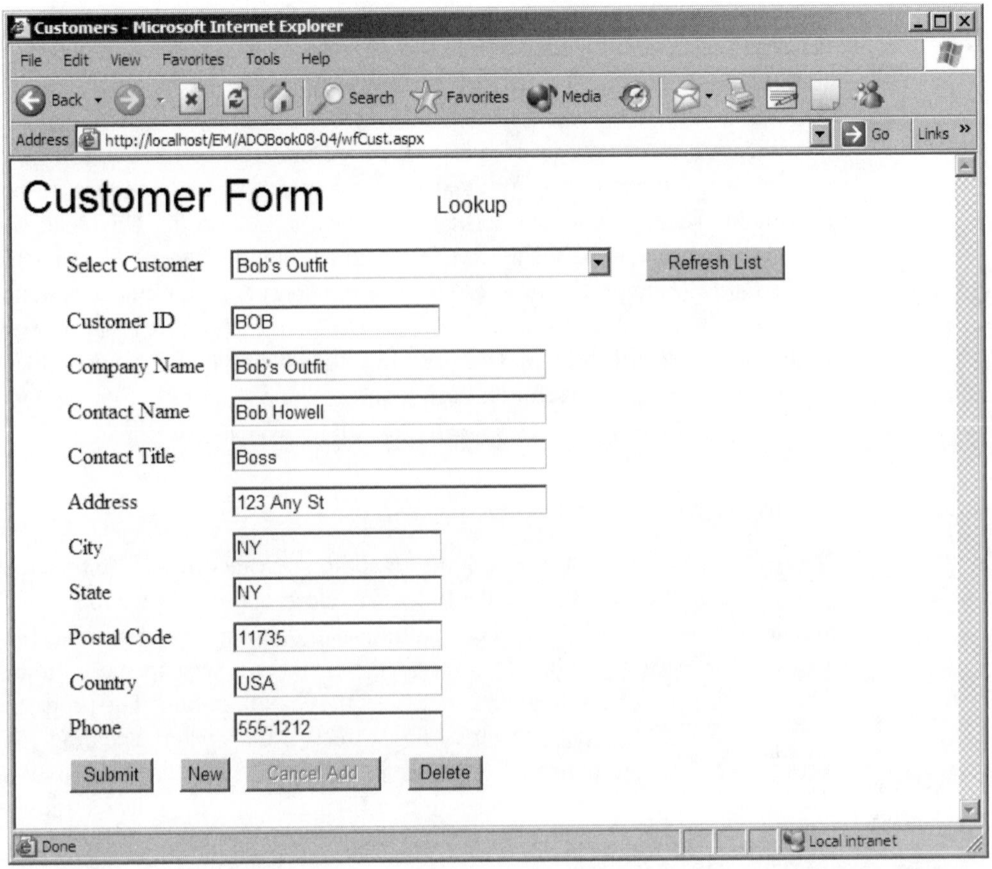

FIGURE 9.11 The form filled in.

```
        Session("dsCust1") = DsCust1.Copy
        TextBox1.ReadOnly = True
        Drop downList1.Enabled = True
        Button3.Enabled = True
        Button2.Enabled = False
        Button4.Enabled = True
        lblError.Text = ""
    Catch errobj As Exception
        lblError.Text = errobj.Message & vbCrLf & errobj.StackTrace
    End Try
End Sub
```

It is smart enough to restore the TextBox values to the `Text` property of each control. It is not smart enough to restore the bound values to the DataSet. To me this is strange. I understand the architectural reasons why data binding in Web Forms is one way. What I don't understand is why, if they can reestablish the association between the `Text` property of the web control and its HTML counterpart on the client's browser, they can't take it one step further and reestablish the data bindings as well.

What we have to do, besides restoring the DataSet from the Session variable, is assign the values of the text boxes to their associated values in the DataTable. Then we call the normal `Update` method on the DataAdapter. And, yes, we have to save the DataSet again and repopulate the DropdownList control. We have to do it every time. Fortunately for us, it happens quite quickly. However, this is one of the reasons I am still not a big fan of web applications. Imagine a large database of customers and having to download the list to the user's browser after each request. You couldn't use this method. For really robust UIs, Windows Forms are still the way to go.

Adding New Records

Our next task is to incorporate support for adding new records. To do this, the user will click the New button, the fields will clear, and the user will be able to enter the new record. The add operation is a two-part process. First, the user clicks the New button. This clears the fields and sets up the buttons. After the user has entered the data, he clicks the Submit button. The program must take a different path when adding a record than when updating the record, so we must remember that we are in Add mode between requests. We will use a Session variable for this purpose. Figure 9.12 shows how the screen looks in Add mode.

The code for the New button is as follows:

```
Private Sub Button3_Click(ByVal sender As System.Object, ByVal e As
System.EventArgs) Handles Button3.Click
     Try
        ClearScreen()
        Session("IsAdding") = True
        lblNew.Text = "Add New"
        TextBox1.ReadOnly = False
        Drop downList1.Enabled = False
                Button3.Enabled = False
        Button2.Enabled = True
        Button4.Enabled = False
        Button5.Enabled = False
     Catch errobj As Exception
        lblError.Text = errobj.Message & vbCrLf & errobj.StackTrace
     End Try
End Sub
```

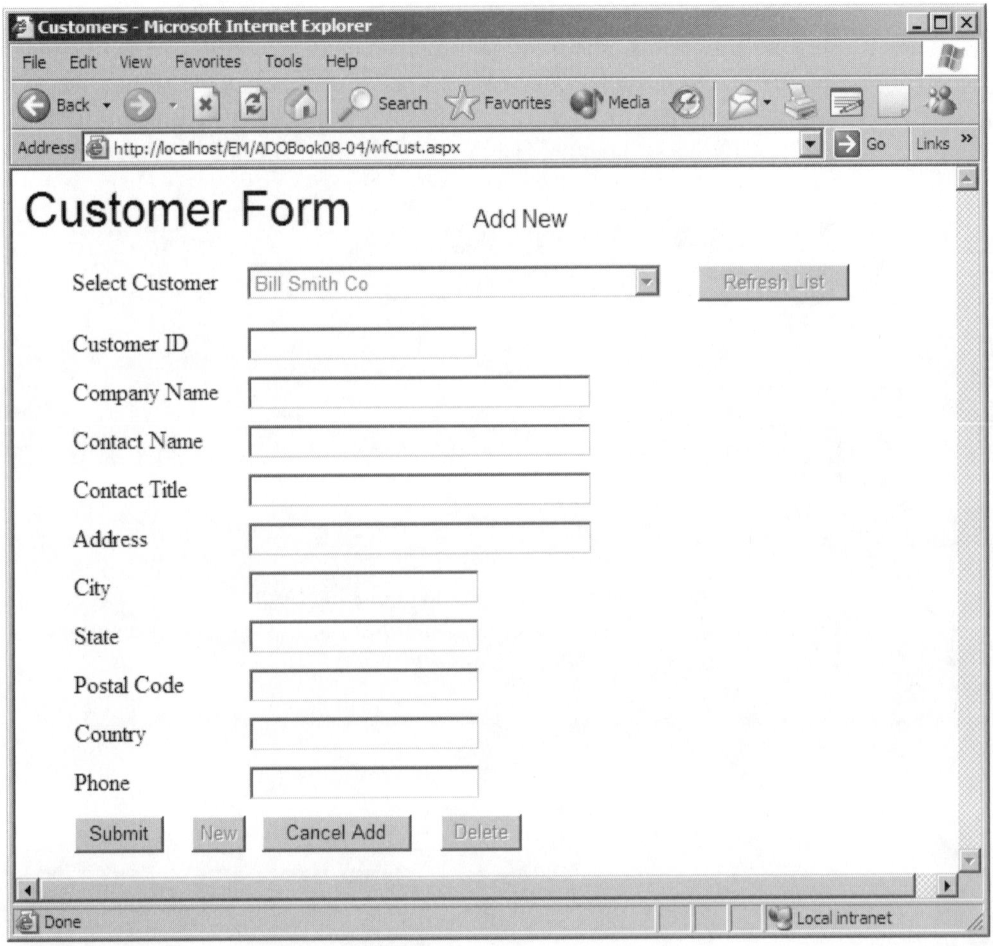

FIGURE 9.12 The customer form in Add mode.

```
Private Sub ClearScreen()
    TextBox1.Text = ""
    TextBox2.Text = ""
    TextBox3.Text = ""
    TextBox4.Text = ""
    TextBox5.Text = ""
    TextBox6.Text = ""
    TextBox7.Text = ""
    Textbox8.Text = ""
    Textbox9.Text = ""
    TextBox10.Text = ""
    lblError.Text = ""
End Sub
```

This code enables or disables buttons and controls, clear the fields, and sets the Session variable IsAdding to True. It does not do anything at all to the database or DataSet. That comes when the user clicks Submit. If the user decides not to add the record and clicks Cancel Add, the procedure does the opposite of the Add button. Here is the code for canceling:

```
Private Sub Button2_Click(ByVal sender As System.Object, ByVal e As
System.EventArgs) Handles Button2.Click
     ClearScreen()
     lblNew.Text = "Lookup"
     TextBox1.ReadOnly = True
     Drop downList1.Enabled = True
     Session("IsAdding") = False
     Button3.Enabled = True
     Button2.Enabled = False
     Button4.Enabled = True
     Button5.Enabled = True
End Sub
```

Once the user enters the fields and clicks the Submit button, the code is a little more involved. Here is the updated Submit button procedure after adding the code to support adding a record:

```
Private Sub Button1_Click(ByVal sender As System.Object, ByVal e As
System.EventArgs) Handles Button1.Click
     Try
          If Not Session("IsAdding") Then
               DsCust1 = CType(Session("dsCust1"), dsCust).Copy
               DsCust1.Customers.Rows(0)("CompanyName") = TextBox2.Text
               DsCust1.Customers.Rows(0)("ContactName") = TextBox3.Text
               DsCust1.Customers.Rows(0)("ContactTitle") = TextBox4.Text
               DsCust1.Customers.Rows(0)("Address") = TextBox5.Text
               DsCust1.Customers.Rows(0)("City") = TextBox6.Text
               DsCust1.Customers.Rows(0)("Region") = TextBox7.Text
               DsCust1.Customers.Rows(0)("PostalCode") = Textbox8.Text
               DsCust1.Customers.Rows(0)("Country") = Textbox9.Text
               DsCust1.Customers.Rows(0)("Phone") = TextBox10.Text
          Else
               Session("dsCust1") = Nothing
               DsCust1 = New dsCust()
               DsCust1.Customers.AddCustomersRow( _
                TextBox1.Text, _
                TextBox2.Text, _
                TextBox3.Text, _
                TextBox4.Text, _
                TextBox5.Text, _
                TextBox6.Text, _
                TextBox7.Text, _
```

```
                Textbox8.Text, _
                Textbox9.Text, _
                TextBox10.Text)
        End If
        SqlDataAdapter1.Update(DsCust1)
        Session("IsAdding") = False
        Session("dsCust1") = DsCust1.Copy
        Button2_Click(Button2, New System.EventArgs())
    Catch errobj As Exception
        lblError.Text = errobj.Message & vbCrLf & errobj.StackTrace
    End Try
End Sub
```

The first thing it does is check the Session variable IsAdding. If this is false, we do the normal update code that we had before. If it is true, we do not restore the old DataSet; instead we create a new empty one. We then use the `AddCustomersRow` method of the typed DataSet to add a new row to the Customers table, which started out empty since we created a DataSet. We then fall out of the `If` statement and the same code we had previously executes. First it calls the `Update` method of the DataAdapter, then it executes the Cancel Add button click event, which puts the form back into Look-up mode.

In order to include our new record in the DropdownList control, we need to refresh its list. We can do this by clicking the Refresh List button. The code for this is as follows:

```
  Private Sub Button4_Click(ByVal sender As System.Object, ByVal e As
System.EventArgs) Handles Button4.Click
    DsCustList1.Clear()
    SqlDataAdapter2.Fill(DsCustList1)
    Session("CustList") = DsCustList1
    Drop downList1.DataBind()
  End Sub
```

Deleting Records

To delete a record, the user simply clicks the Delete button with a record displayed on the screen. The code for this button follows:

```
  Private Sub Button5_Click(ByVal sender As System.Object, ByVal e As
System.EventArgs) Handles Button5.Click
    DsCust1 = CType(Session("dsCust1"), dsCust).Copy
    DsCust1.Customers.Rows(0).Delete()
    SqlDataAdapter1.Update(DsCust1)
    ClearScreen()
    Session("dsCust1") = Nothing
    Button4_Click(Me, New System.EventArgs())
  End Sub
```

First we restore the DataSet from the Session variable. Then we delete the row. Since we know we are always dealing with a one-row DataTable we can assume we are on row zero. Note that it is important to use the `Delete` method and not one of the `Remove` methods because the `Remove` methods remove the row from the collection whereas the `Delete` method marks the row as deleted but does not actually remove it. This is important because the `Update` method of the DataAdapter looks for rows marked deleted. It cannot delete removed rows because they no longer exist in the collection.

Web Forms are a definite improvement over previous web programming technologies, but there still could be improvements. Getting rid of the stateless model would be good. What if we could have the code executing continually on the server side, so the browser could communicate with it in real time? These are all things that can be addressed via Web Services, which we will look at in the next chapter. Next we will take a more detailed look at the data binding in simple controls and complex controls, such as the Web DataGrid.

The Simple Web Controls

The simple web controls support binding a single column to a single property. Just about every property of these controls can be bound to different columns. We already looked at the data bindings editor earlier. Let's look again (Figure 9.13).

Notice that you can bind to data columns, but you can also bind to page elements. If you scroll down the simple binding tree view you will see what I mean (see Figure 9.14).

I have a confession to make: I am not really a web guru. My expertise is in native Windows applications. It's not that I don't see the value in web applications. Quite the contrary. I'd be a fool not to acknowledge that web applications have become a mainstay of e-commerce as well as corporate intranets and the like. But I also still believe that the web is not God's gift to the computer challenged. The impression you get from listening to the hype about the Web is that it solves all of the problems with software distribution, user training, user's having to learn complex applications, and myriad other issues. It does address some of these. Web applications do alleviate distribution woes. They are sometimes easier to use. But with these benefits there is the ever present trade-off.

Web application UIs still don't come remotely close to the kind of UI I can build in a native Windows application. Simple things that we take for granted like on-the-fly input editing, complex queries, look-up screens, real-time database updates, and multiuser concurrency handling are all orders of

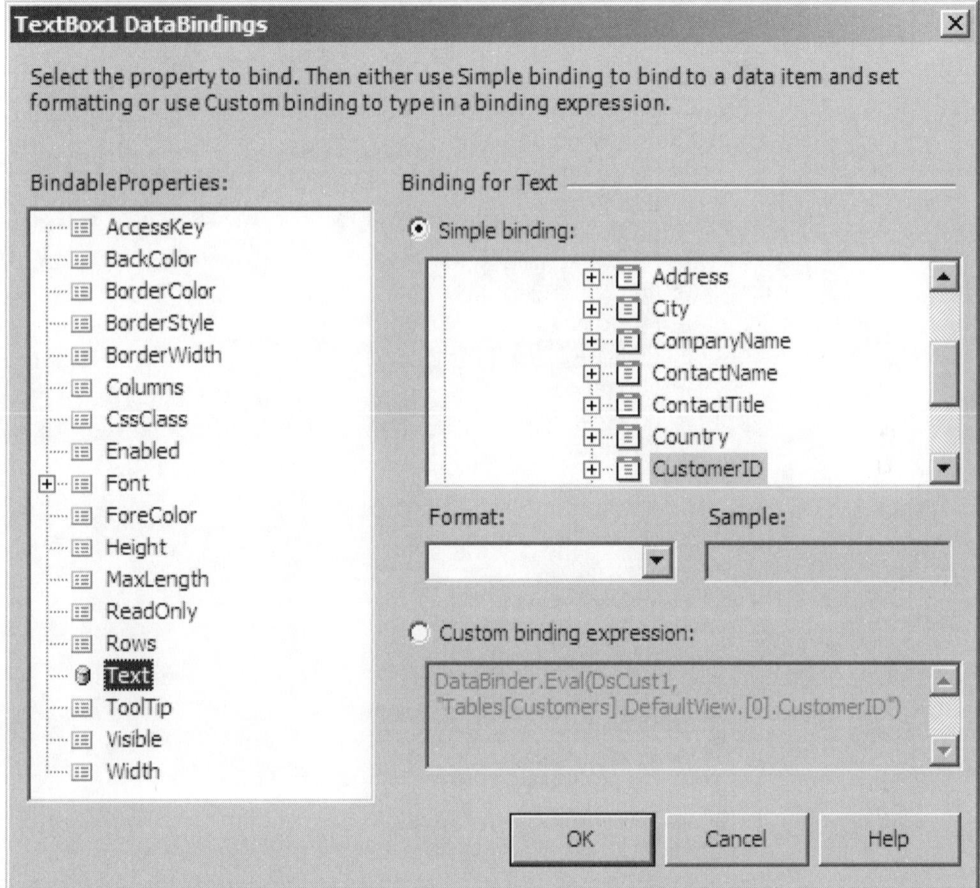

FIGURE 9.13 The data bindings editor for the TextBox.

magnitude more difficult, if not impossible, with web applications. I'm not saying they *can't* be done. I just don't see how with the stateless nature of the Web.

I've said all this because I can't see why in heck you would *ever* want to data-bind a text box to the `AcceptChangesDuringFill` property (or any other property) of a DataAdapter.

The simple web controls and the most likely binding properties are:

- `TextBox`—`Text` property.
- `Label`—`Text` property.
- `Button`—`Text` property.
- `LinkButton`—`Text` property.

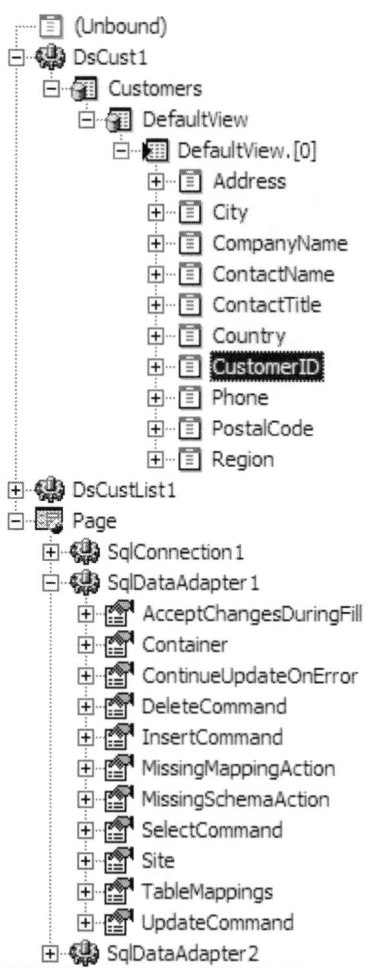

FIGURE 9.14 The binding tree showing the page items.

- `ImageButton`—This one's interesting. You can data-bind the `ImageURL` property to a text column in the database. So you can store the URL of the image in a database column, then just by changing the database you can change the image displayed in the button. This is true of all the controls that show images.
- `Hyperlink`—You can not only bind the `Text` property, but the URL of the link as well. This is useful for dynamically changing the linked URL at runtime.
- `CheckBox - RadioButton` —The `Checked` property is most likely to be bound to a Boolean database field. You can also bind the `Text` property which is the label displayed next to the check box.

- `Image`—`ImageURL` property, as with the ImageButton.
- `Panel`—Can be bound; I can't see why you would.
- `Calendar`—`SelectedDate` property. There are many other useful properties that can be bound to date ranges, and so forth. I'll leave it to you to investigate on your own.
- `AdRotator`—This control displays a series of banner ads on the page. The ads are contained in a file and you can bind the `AdvertismentFile` property of the control to a database field.
- `Validator controls`—These controls are used to display custom field validation messages to the user. You can bind the `ErrorMessage` property to a database field.

THE COMPLEX WEB CONTROLS

The complex web controls support binding to multiple columns or rows of a DataSource. The most obvious example is the Web DataGrid. Other examples are the DropdownList, the list box, the DataList, the CheckBoxList, and the RadioButtonList. We've already seen the DropdownList in action. The list box is virtually identical except that the list is always showing. The CheckBoxList and RadioButtonList are the same as the list box except items are selected using check boxes or radio buttons.

I am glossing over these controls because we covered the Drop downList and the rest are similar and rather easy to grasp. I want to spend the rest of the section talking about two very interesting controls, the Web DataGrid and the DataList control.

The Web DataGrid is the web counterpart of the Windows Forms grid. Since it is HTML-based it has distinct differences, but the basic concept is the same. It displays data in a table format and allows editing of the data as well as some other nice features. The DataList is similar to the DataGrid, except that you can embed other web controls in the DataList to create a customized grid. You can use any of the simple bound web controls to create the rows in the grid. This makes it a very versatile control. It has its drawbacks though and we will see how to decide when to use the DataGrid or the DataList control.

The DataRepeater is similar to the DataList control, except that it is entirely HTML-based. To configure the control, you must switch to HTML view and enter HTML directly. Because this book is not about HTML, I decided not to include this control. It also seems somewhat redundant; how many data listing controls do you need? You HTML gurus may find it better than the other grid-style controls for your use. If so, enjoy. This book is about database access and Visual Basic, so that's where I'm concentrating.

THE WEB DATAGRID

The Web DataGrid provides a way of displaying and editing data in a tabular format. It emulates the behavior of the Windows Forms DataGrid control by implementing a paging technique whereby the grid automatically recreates the underlying DataSource each time the user wants to scroll to the next page of records. While not terribly efficient, the effect is decent. As long as there are only a few records in the DataSource the performance of the grid is not too bad. We cannot simply scroll through the rows as with the Windows Forms DataGrid because of that darn stateless problem again. There is a way to take control of the paging mechanism and implement your own paging logic to improve performance.

The control also supports a type of in-place editing and updating. All of these features require a considerable amount of configuration on the programmer's part, and they all require some behind-the-scenes code support. Unlike the Windows Forms DataGrid, almost nothing is automatic. It's as if Microsoft provided the hooks but left the actual implementation up to the programmer. This makes the control versatile, but not so easy to use. Hopefully, this section will clear up some of the basic techniques and get you started being productive with the control.

To demonstrate the control, let's create a web application project and name it ADOBook09-02. Once the project is created, delete the default form that it provides. We will copy the previous project's form into this project to use as a starting point. Use Windows Explorer to copy the files highlighted in Figure 9.15 to the new project folder. Remember you must look in your web server's root folder to find the path to your project. Your project may not be under the EM folder like mine. I put all my projects in a folder that has meaning to me, just in case some other vendor uses the same project name as I did. In this case EM is the abbreviation of my company name. Sometimes I will use a client's stock ticker symbol.

Once the files have been copied, you must include them in your project. The easiest way to do this is to click the Show All Files button in the Solution Explorer and then right-click each file and select Include In Project.

One more thing. You may have noticed that I have my wwwroot folder shared. This is normally a really bad thing to do. The reason I have it shared is because I am on a private internal class C network using the 192.168.1.0 subnet. This is a private subnet and cannot be accessed by the outside world unless I open a hole in my firewall, which I haven't. Because I develop on two different machines, I have chosen to take some liberties so I can easily share files between them. Do not do this yourself unless you really know what you are doing with TCP/IP networking. You could open your network to attack.

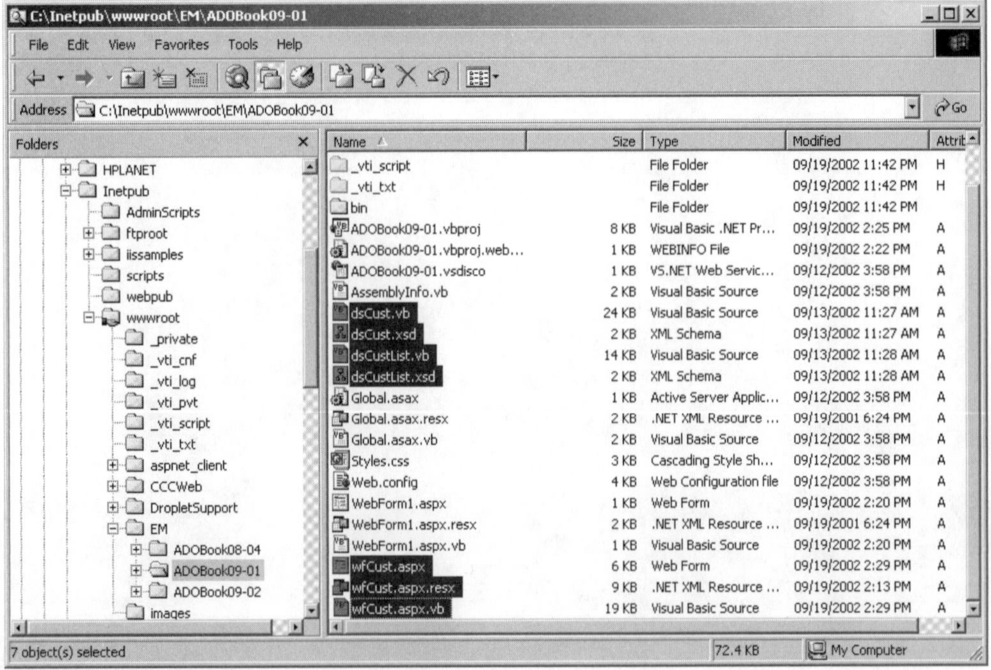

FIGURE 9.15 Files to move for new project.

Once we have the project configured properly, let's open the wfCust form. We will be chopping and hacking it down. Delete most of the fields and buttons until your form looks like Figure 9.16.

Next we will add a DataGrid to our form. You can just drag it from the toolbox onto the form. The grid will be used to display all the orders for each selected customer. So we will also need another SqlDataAdapter and another DataSet. We could also just use an existing DataSet, but let's create a new one for the exercise. Let the wizard create the DataAdapter normally. Only include the following columns from the Orders table in the select query: OrderID, OrderDate, RequiredDate, ShippedDate, ShipVia, and Freight. If you want to get fancy you could create a join to the Order Details table and summarize the details total into the query using a subquery and a Group By. But let's keep it simple for now. Use this SQL statement when creating your DataAdapter:

```
SELECT     OrderID, CustomerID, OrderDate, RequiredDate, ShippedDate,
ShipVia, Freight, ShipName
FROM        Orders
WHERE     (CustomerID = @CustomerID)
```

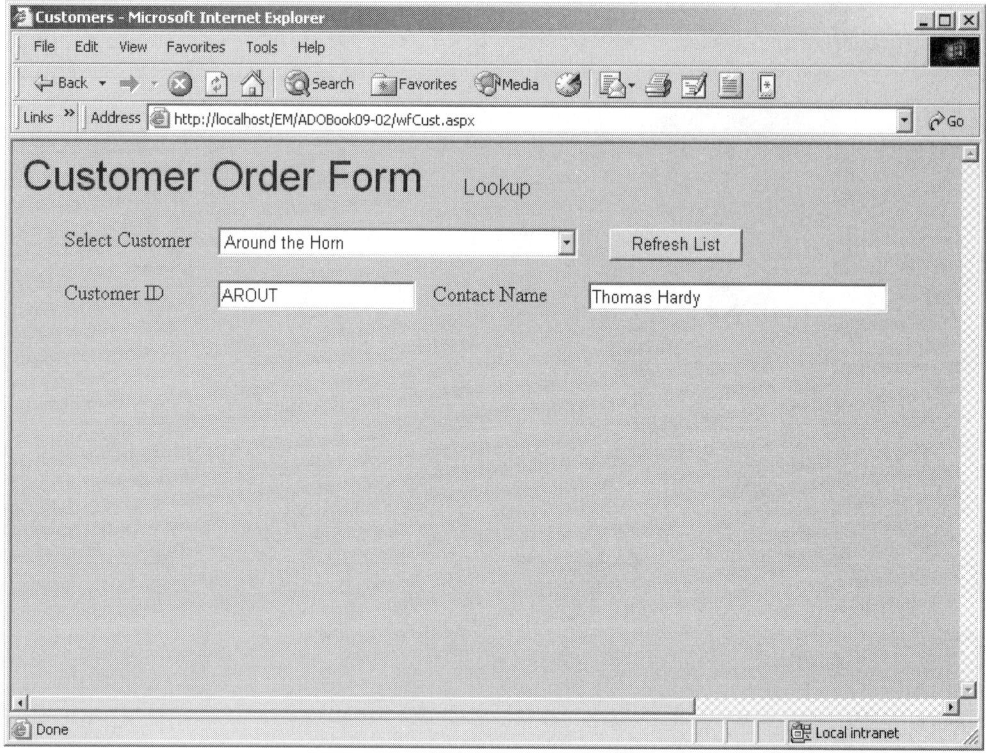

FIGURE 9.16 The new stripped-down form.

The parameter is so we can select the rows for the customer chosen using the DropdownList.

When you first drop the grid on the form, all you get is an ugly HTML table as in Figure 9.17.

We will make our grid look really pretty in no time. When we are done, it will look like Figure 9.18.

Setting the Visual Appearance

It's too bad this book's illustrations are in black and white. The grid is in complementary shades of blue on a gray background. It looks real sharp. So how do we make it look so nice? It was easy. You could set numerous properties to the different colors manually, but you can also choose from a set of predefined styles. To do this, select the grid, then click the Auto Format... link at the bottom of the Properties window. See Figure 9.18.

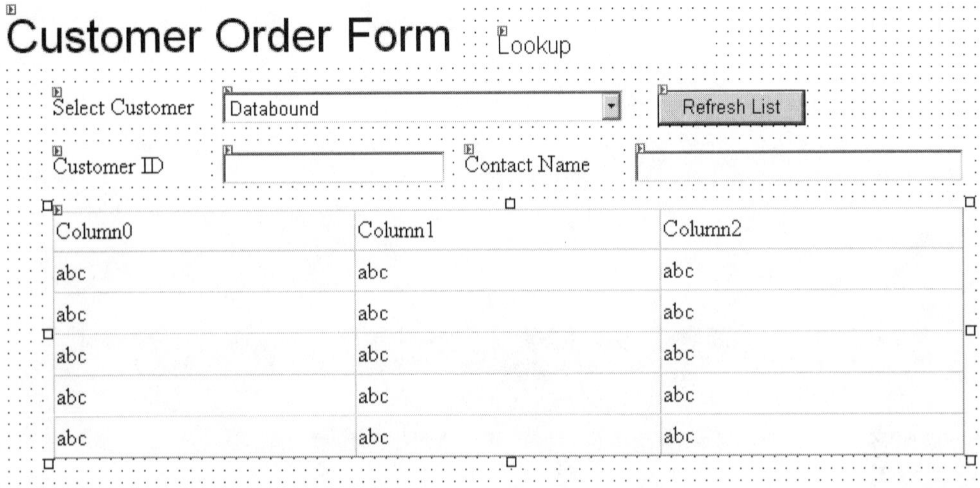

Customer Order Form Lookup

Select Customer	Databound	Refresh List
Customer ID		Contact Name

Column0	Column1	Column2
abc	abc	abc
abc	abc	abc
abc	abc	abc
abc	abc	abc
abc	abc	abc

FIGURE 9.17 The raw grid control.

While you are at it set up the DataSource properties as shown in Figure 9.19. When you click the autoformat link, a window opens which allows you to select from several styles.

Once you have set all this up, your grid should look something like Figure 9.21 in Design mode.

It's an improvement, but we still need to tweak it a little. There are two things glaringly wrong with the grid: the date display is ugly and the grid is bottomless.

In the date display we don't need the time component and the fields are all wrapping. This makes the rows too tall. We describe the grid as bottomless, meaning that if there were 50 rows, we would get a page that was really long, because the grid will display all 50. This also means that we cannot count on any two pages being the same length. There is a way of dealing with this called paging. It allows the grid to show only so many (configurable) rows at a time. It also then displays paging controls at the bottom of the grid to allow the user to navigate between pages.

First we will deal with the display issues. Notice that there is a Columns collection with this grid. You can use this to open a property builder that will assist us in configuring our display. Open the property builder by clicking the link at the bottom of the Properties window right next to the autoformat link. The property builder opens as in Figure 9.22.

Notice that Create Columns Automatically at runtime is checked. This is the default behavior. With this selected, the grid will simply take all of the columns in the DataSource and display them using default settings. We don't

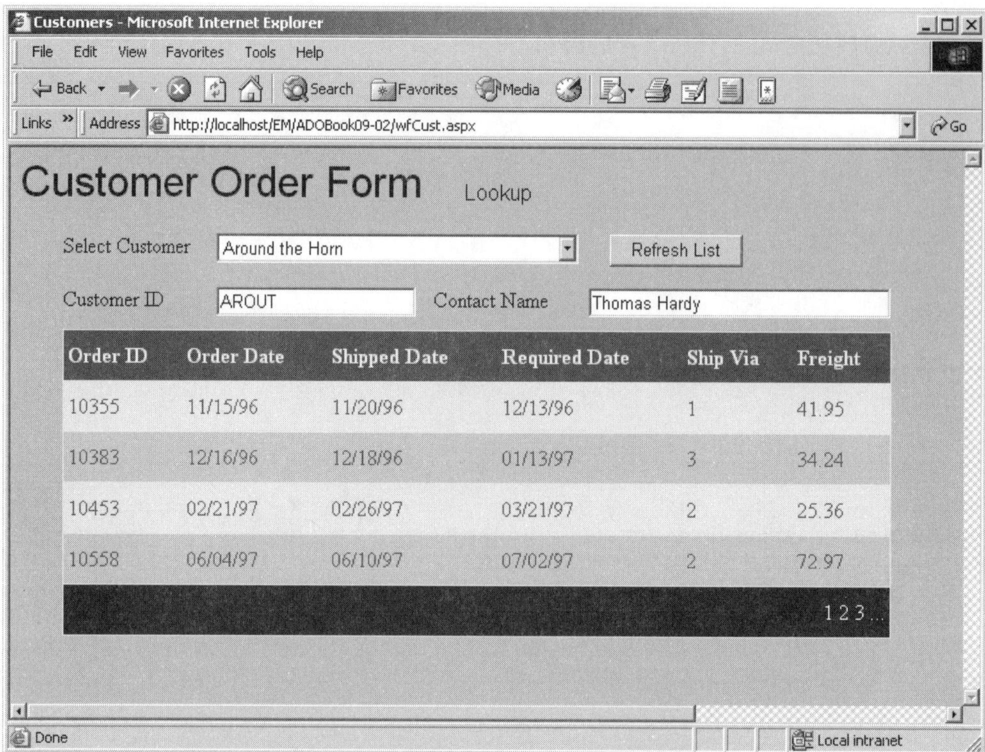

FIGURE 9.18 The form with the formatted grid control.

want this behavior, so let's uncheck the box. Now we have to select the columns we want to display. We do this by selecting the fields in the Available Columns list and moving them to the Selected Columns list using the arrow button as in Figure 9.23.

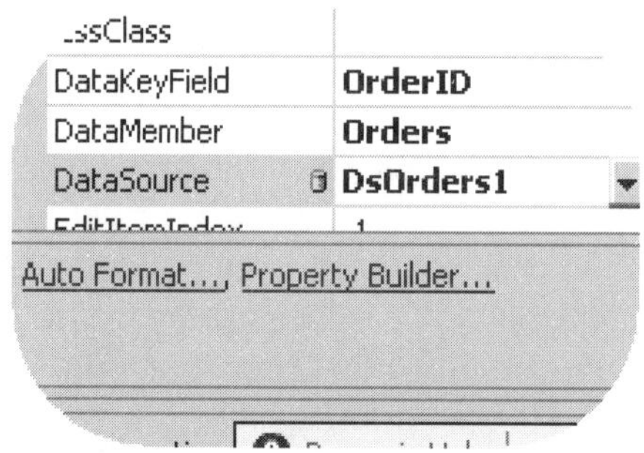

FIGURE 9.19 The Auto Format... link.

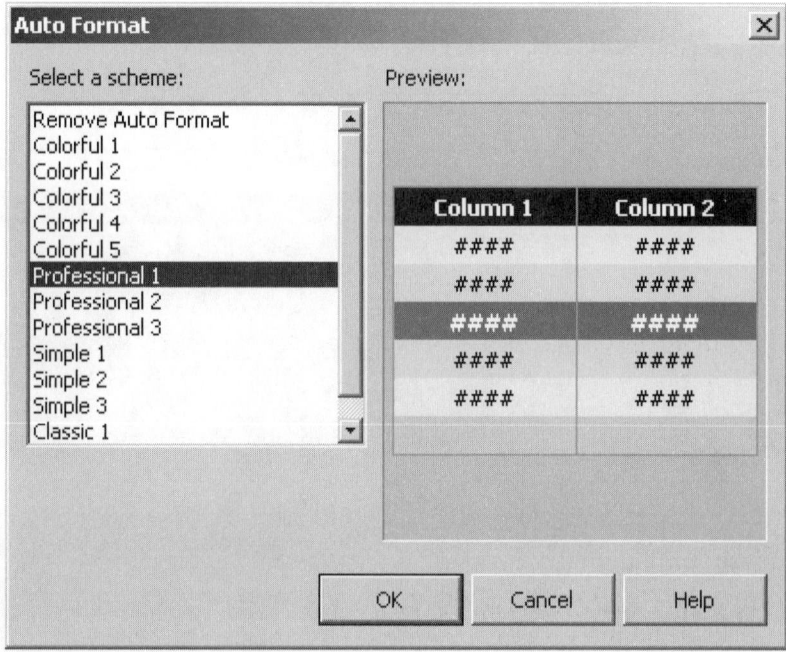

FIGURE 9.20 The Auto Format dialog.

Next we want to change the date display format. This took me quite a while to figure out, and I'll show you why. If you are not a web guru, this will pay for the book right now. My instinct when setting up the date format was to use a standard Visual Basic format string. This is how all the other grids do it. Let's see what happens when I tried it as in Figure 9.24.

When I run the program, look what happens in Figure 9.25.

What happened? Why did it display the literal format string instead of formatting the date? It turns out that there are whole other sets of formatting expressions you must use with Web Forms. These are documented, but they are really hard to find. In the documentation for the Web DataGrid it tells you to use them, but does not provide a link to them. The correct date format is {0:d}. These are regular expression format strings. If any of you ever used the print function in C these may be familiar to you. They can be used in the `WriteLine` method of the console object to format output in a similar way you would use placeholders in the print C function. If we use the correct format string the display comes out right. Enter the expression as in Figure 9.26.

Next we want to make sure the lines don't wrap within each cell if the data is too long. We do this using the Format page of the builder as in Figure 9.27.

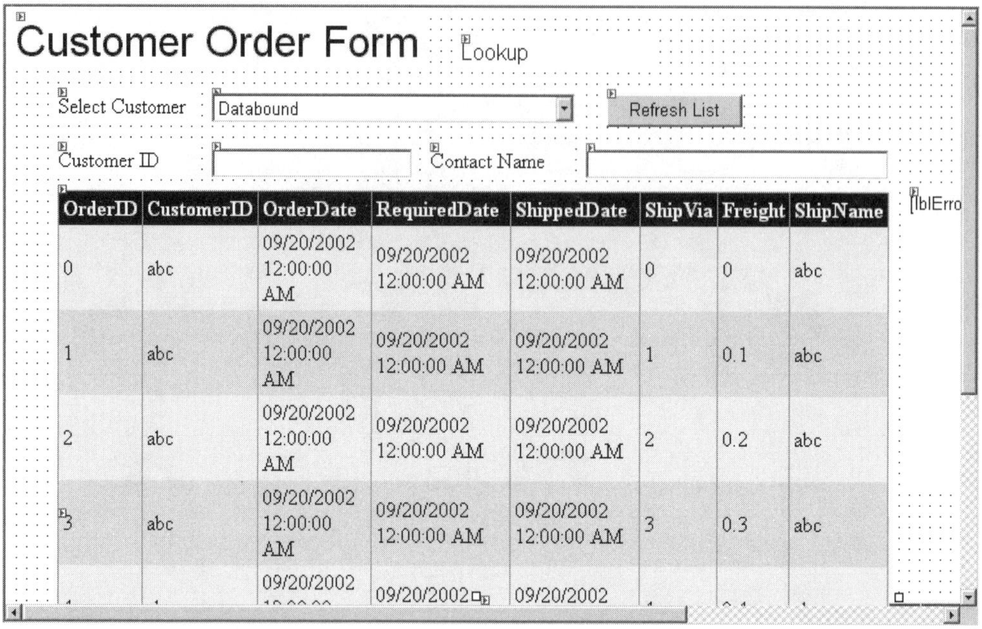

FIGURE 9.21 The roughed-out DataGrid.

There are many items we can format. The one we're interested in is the "Wrap text within cell" check box. You have to uncheck this item for each column in the tree view control. You must do this in two places for each column, the header and the item.

Now we have to implement the paging mechanism we mentioned earlier. This will ensure that no more than four lines appear in the grid at any one time. To do this, we must first enable paging. With the property builder still open, select the Paging page of the builder. This page appears as in Figure 9.28.

Check the Allow Paging button and change Page Size to four. That's all we have to do in the designer to implement paging. We still have to add code to implement it behind the scenes, but not very much. After adding the paging feature your grid should look like Figure 9.29 in Design mode.

Let's close the builder and open the code window. If you have not already done so, delete all the event procedures for any buttons we have removed and remove any references to controls we have deleted. The first thing we need to do is add the code to populate the DataSet that is the grid's DataSource. The likely place for this is the DropdownList's SelectedIndexChanged event, which we are already using to get the customer's record.

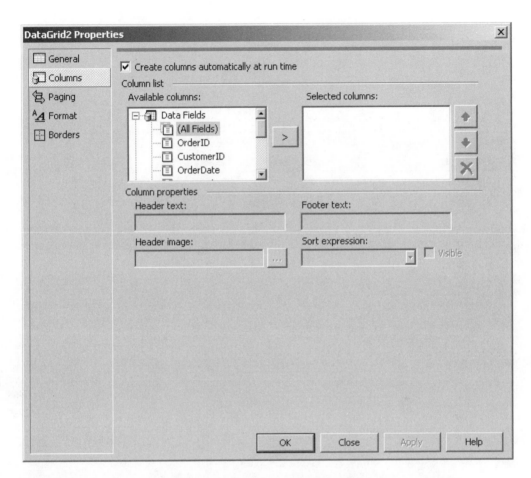

FIGURE 9.22 The DataGrid property builder with default settings.

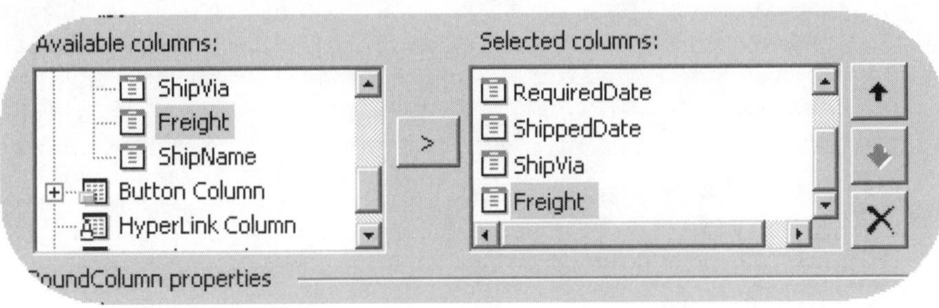

FIGURE 9.23 Selecting columns for display.

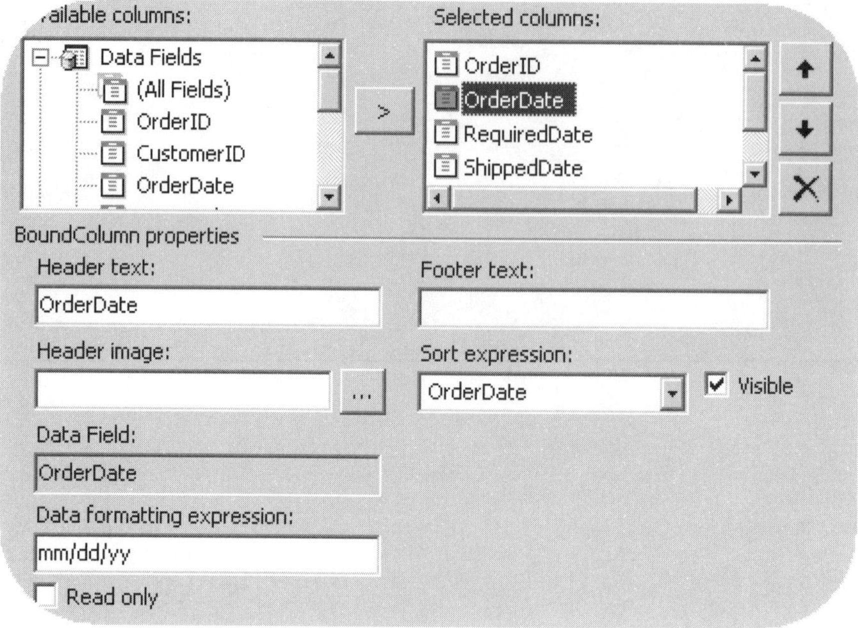

FIGURE 9.24 The wrong way to format a date.

Add the following code to the procedure:

```
Private Sub Drop downList1_SelectedIndexChanged(ByVal sender As
System.Object, ByVal e As System.EventArgs) Handles Drop
downList1.SelectedIndexChanged
     If Me.IsPostBack Then
          SqlDataAdapter1.SelectCommand.Parameters("@CustID").Value =
Drop downList1.SelectedItem.Value
          Session("selIndex") = Drop downList1.SelectedIndex
          SqlDataAdapter1.Fill(DsCust1)
          SqlDataAdapter3.SelectCommand.Parameters("@CustomerID").Value
= Drop downList1.SelectedItem.Value
          SqlDataAdapter3.Fill(DsOrders1)
          Me.DataBind()
     End If
End Sub
```

Let's also do a little refactoring. Change the Page_PreRender event to look like this:

```
  Private Sub Page_PreRender(ByVal sender As Object, ByVal e As
System.EventArgs) Handles MyBase.PreRender
          If IsPostBack Then
```

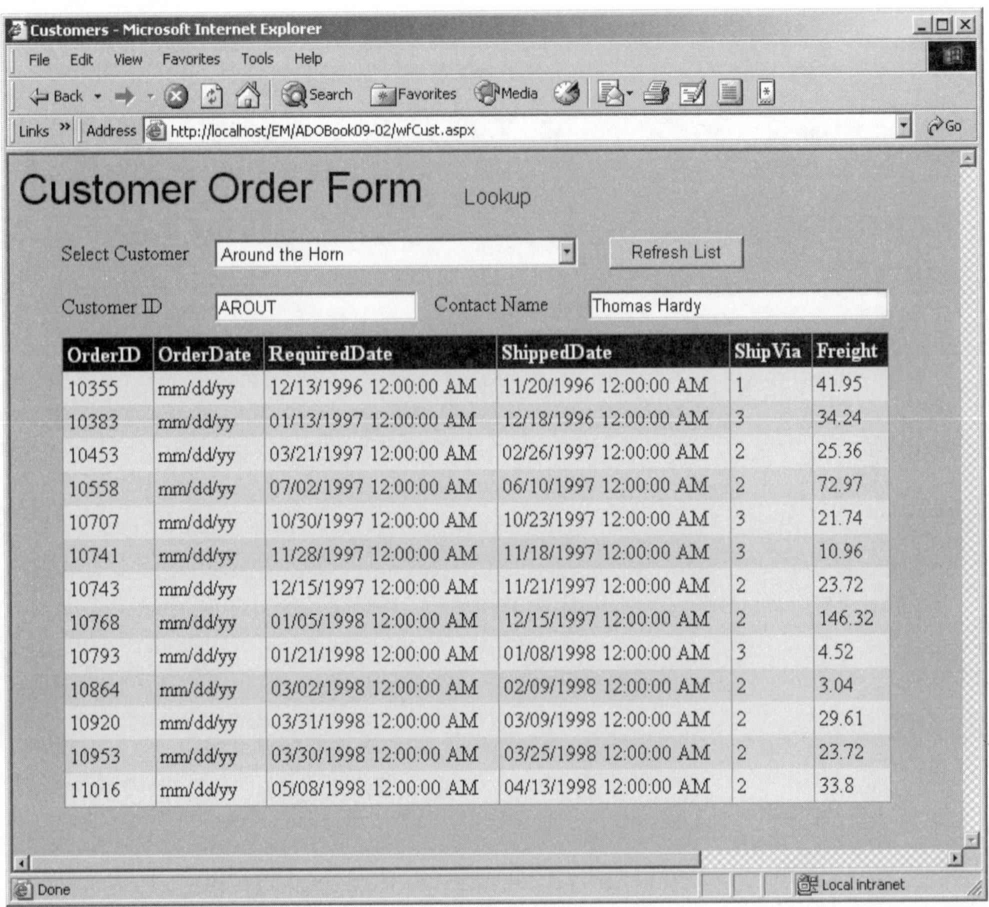

OrderID	OrderDate	RequiredDate	ShippedDate	ShipVia	Freight
10355	mm/dd/yy	12/13/1996 12:00:00 AM	11/20/1996 12:00:00 AM	1	41.95
10383	mm/dd/yy	01/13/1997 12:00:00 AM	12/18/1996 12:00:00 AM	3	34.24
10453	mm/dd/yy	03/21/1997 12:00:00 AM	02/26/1997 12:00:00 AM	2	25.36
10558	mm/dd/yy	07/02/1997 12:00:00 AM	06/10/1997 12:00:00 AM	2	72.97
10707	mm/dd/yy	10/30/1997 12:00:00 AM	10/23/1997 12:00:00 AM	3	21.74
10741	mm/dd/yy	11/28/1997 12:00:00 AM	11/18/1997 12:00:00 AM	3	10.96
10743	mm/dd/yy	12/15/1997 12:00:00 AM	11/21/1997 12:00:00 AM	2	23.72
10768	mm/dd/yy	01/05/1998 12:00:00 AM	12/15/1997 12:00:00 AM	2	146.32
10793	mm/dd/yy	01/21/1998 12:00:00 AM	01/08/1998 12:00:00 AM	3	4.52
10864	mm/dd/yy	03/02/1998 12:00:00 AM	02/09/1998 12:00:00 AM	2	3.04
10920	mm/dd/yy	03/31/1998 12:00:00 AM	03/09/1998 12:00:00 AM	2	29.61
10953	mm/dd/yy	03/30/1998 12:00:00 AM	03/25/1998 12:00:00 AM	2	23.72
11016	mm/dd/yy	05/08/1998 12:00:00 AM	04/13/1998 12:00:00 AM	2	33.8

FIGURE 9.25 The bad date format.

```
            DsCustList1 = Session("CustList")
            Drop downList1.DataBind()
            Drop downList1.Items(Session("selIndex")).Selected = True
        Else
            SqlDataAdapter2.Fill(DsCustList1)
            Session("CustList") = DsCustList1
            Drop downList1.DataBind()
        End If
        Session("dsCust1") = DsCust1.Copy
        Session("dsOrders1") = DsOrders1.Copy
    End Sub
```

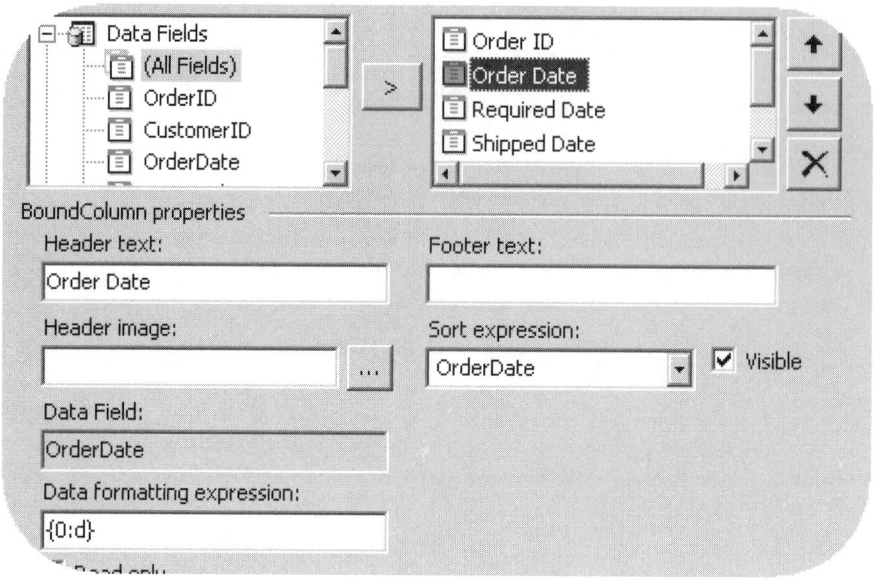

FIGURE 9.26 The correct expression.

We can then delete the Page_Load code. It is no longer needed. One thing the documentation never tells you is that you *must* save all of your DataSets in Session variables between requests. This is best done in the PreRender event as that is the last event that the code executes before creating the HTML.

Now let's add the code to support the paging. This is code is quite simple, as the grid does most of the work for you.

```
Private Sub DataGrid1_PageIndexChanged(ByVal source As Object, ByVal
e As System.Web.UI.WebControls.DataGridPageChangedEventArgs) Handles
DataGrid1.PageIndexChanged
      DsOrders1 = CType(Session("dsOrders1"), dsOrders).Copy
      DataGrid1.CurrentPageIndex = e.NewPageIndex
      DataGrid1.DataBind()
End Sub
```

The DataGrid has a PageIndexChanged event which fires when the user clicks one of the paging buttons. You must first restore the DataSet. Remember, this is a PostBack, so the program reexecutes all over again. Next, assign the new page index to the current page index of the DataGrid. The new page index is passed to the event through the `DataGridPageChangeEventArgs` parameter. Then call the `DataBind` method. This causes the grid to

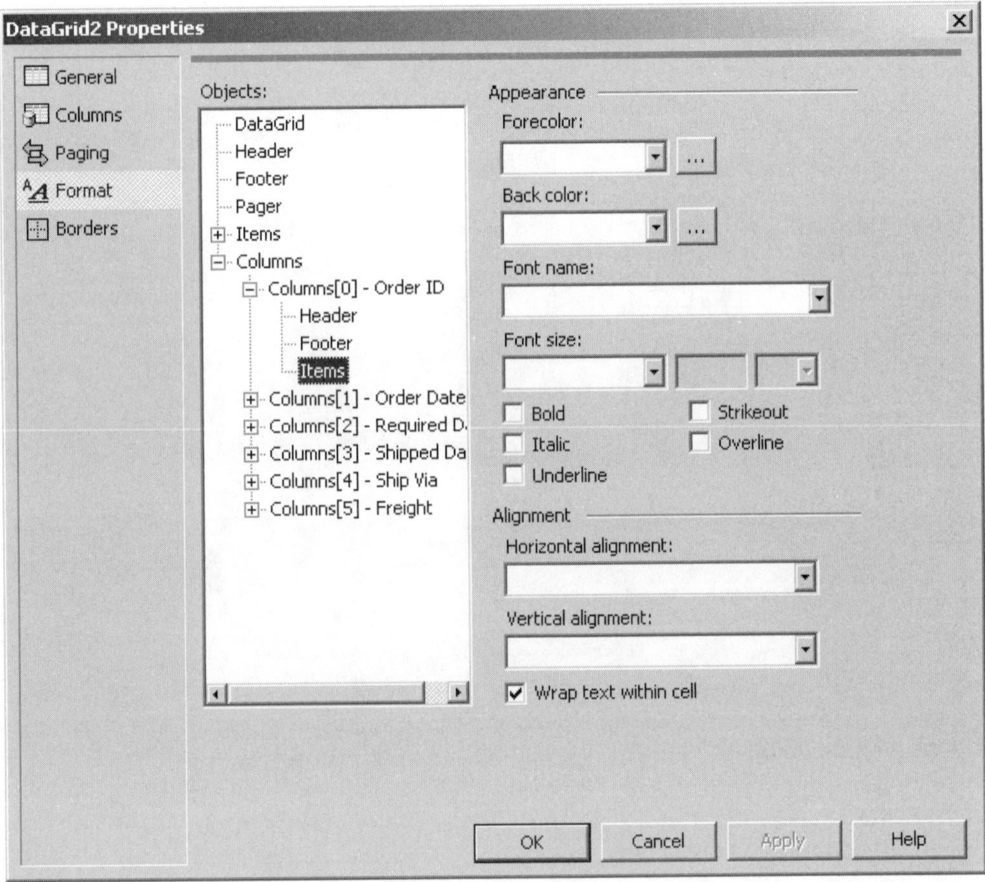

FIGURE 9.27 The Format page.

recreate the DataSet and position itself on the first row of the new page. It then reads the next four rows (because that is what we told the grid to display on each page) and then data binds them to the grid. Then it sends the page back to the client. The finished product looks like Figure 9.30.

Adding In-Place Editing Capabilities

The DataGrid is capable of in-place editing as well. In-place editing emulates the ability of the Windows Forms grid to allow the user to directly edit the cells of the grid. We say emulate because it is not quite the same as the Windows Forms grid. The way this works is that the user must put the desired row into an Edit mode first. This is done by clicking a button on the desired

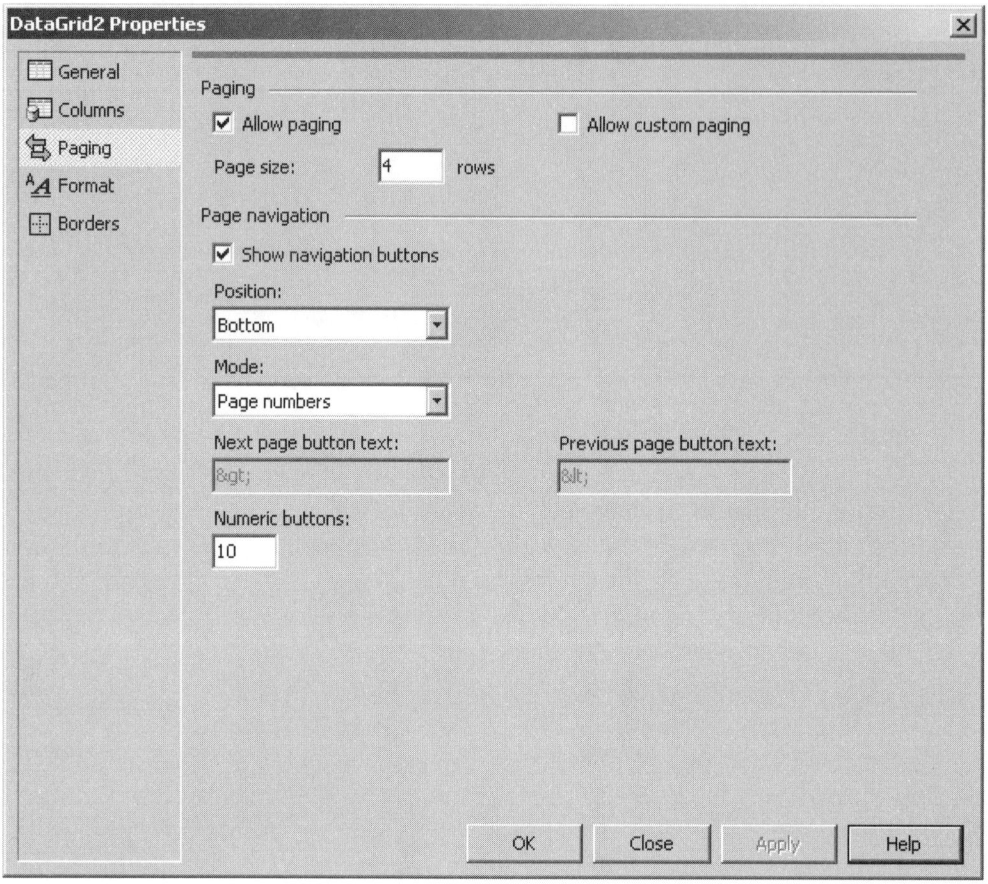

FIGURE 9.28 The Paging builder page.

row. The row then changes from static text to text boxes in each cell. The user then edits the data and clicks an Update button to save the data and put the row back into static text mode. To add this ability, we first have to add some controls to the grid. When we are finished, the grid, at runtime, will look like Figure 9.31.

The first step in implementing in-place editing is to add the buttons to the grid. To do this we will use the familiar property editor. Open it by clicking on the ellipsis in the `Columns collection` property. Expand the tree on the available columns list until you find the Button Column node. Add the Edit, Update, and Cancel buttons to the selected columns list as in Figure 9.32.

You can also go ahead and add a Delete button to the selected columns. Use the arrow buttons (Figure 9.33) to move the button columns to the top of the list. This will ensure that they appear to the left of the data columns.

Order ID	Order Date	Shipped Date	Required Date	Ship Via	Freight
0	09/20/02	09/20/02	09/20/02	0	0
1	09/20/02	09/20/02	09/20/02	1	0.1
2	09/20/02	09/20/02	09/20/02	2	0.2
3	09/20/02	09/20/02	09/20/02	3	0.3
1 2					

FIGURE 9.29 The finished grid control.

You end up with a grid that, when in Design mode, looks like Figure 9.34.

Once we've added the buttons, we must add the code to implement them. The way this works is a little interesting. When the user clicks one of the buttons, the DataGrid does a PostBack to the server and raises an event. It is then

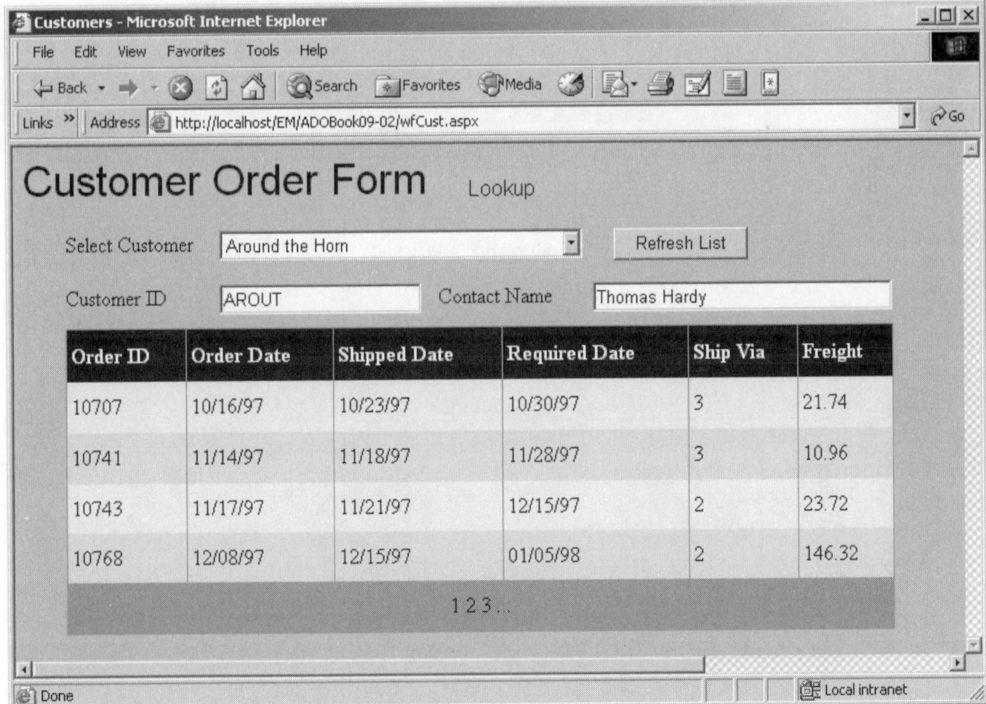

FIGURE 9.30 The finished read-only grid.

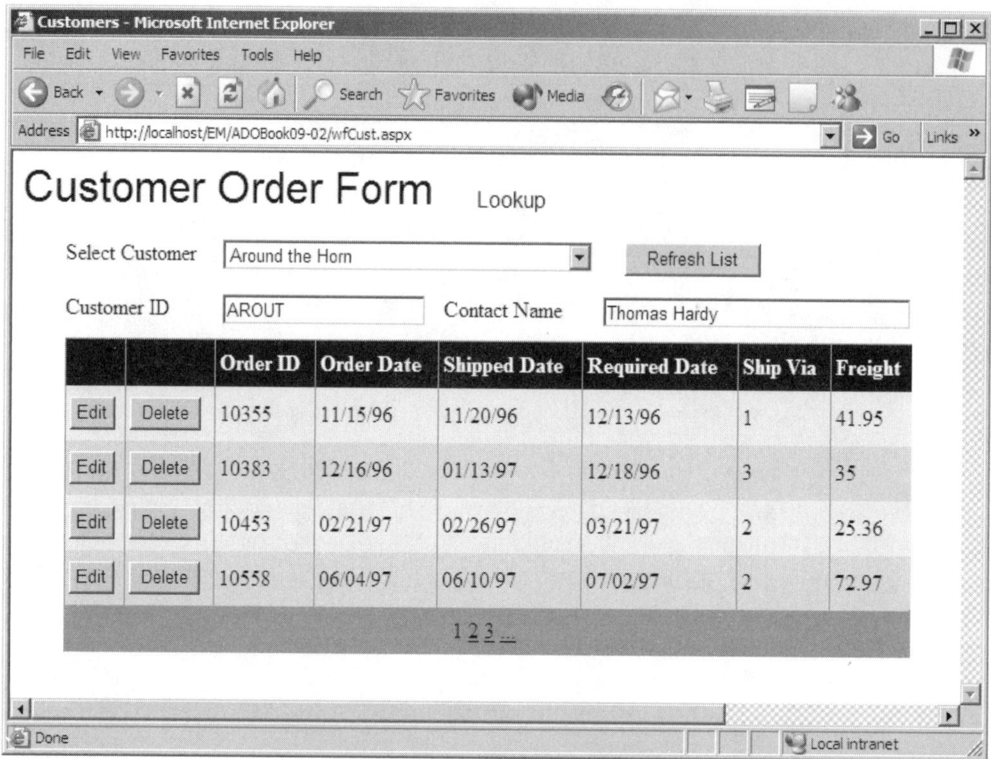

FIGURE 9.31 Grid with edit controls added.

up to the programmer to respond to the event. This is similar to the paging feature we looked at in the last section. The EditCommand event is raised. The programmer then must set the grid's `EditItemIndex` property to the row that is being edited. Here is the procedure:

```
  Private Sub DataGrid1_EditCommand(ByVal source As Object, _
    ByVal e As System.Web.UI.WebControls.DataGridCommandEventArgs)
Handles DataGrid1.EditCommand
    DataGrid1.EditItemIndex = e.Item.ItemIndex
    DataGrid1.DataBind()
  End Sub
```

It is necessary to rebind the grid after each of these events, just like with the paging event. The DataGridCommandEventArgs class passes the index of the row clicked as shown in the code. When this completes, the row changes into a row of text boxes for editing. The Edit button changes to Update, and a Cancel button appears as in Figure 9.35. This happens automatically by setting the EditItemIndex.

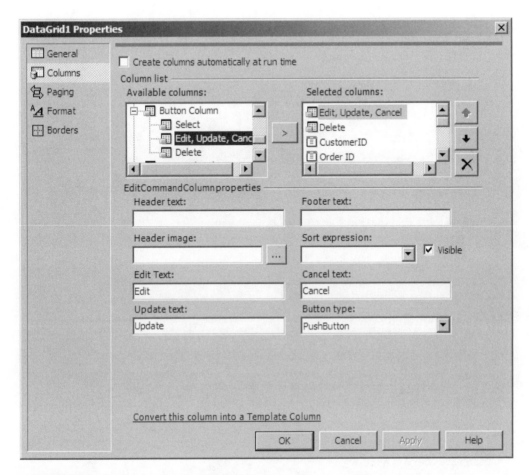

FIGURE 9.32 Adding buttons to the grid.

If the user clicks the Edit button on another row, it has the effect of canceling the edit on the original row and starting an edit on the new row. Now we must respond to the Update button being clicked. To do this we must use the UpdateCommand event. Here is the code:

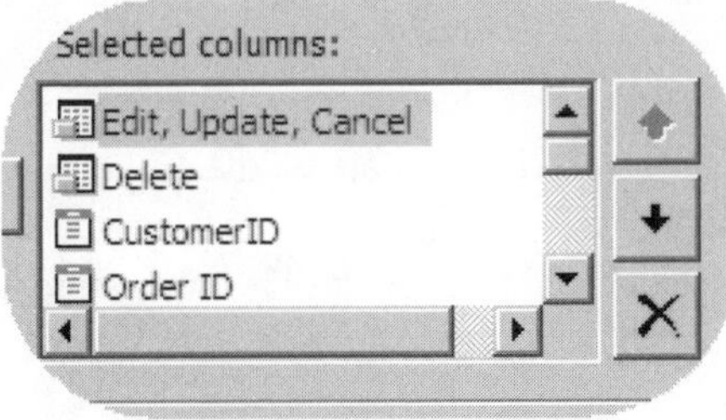

FIGURE 9.33 The arrow buttons.

		Order ID	Order Date	Shipped Date	Required Date	Ship Via	Freight
Edit	Delete	0	09/23/02	09/23/02	09/23/02	0	0
Edit	Delete	1	09/23/02	09/23/02	09/23/02	1	0.1
Edit	Delete	2	09/23/02	09/23/02	09/23/02	2	0.2
Edit	Delete	3	09/23/02	09/23/02	09/23/02	3	0.3
				1 2			

FIGURE 9.34 The grid with the buttons added.

```
Private Sub DataGrid1_UpdateCommand(ByVal source As Object, ByVal e As
System.Web.UI.WebControls.DataGridCommandEventArgs) Handles
DataGrid1.UpdateCommand
  Dim i As Integer

  Try
    For i = 3 To e.Item.Cells.Count - 1
      If Not DsCust1.Orders.Columns(i - 3).ReadOnly Then
        DsCust1.Orders.Rows(e.Item.ItemIndex)(i - 3) =
CType(e.Item.Cells(i).Controls(0), TextBox).Text
      End If
    Next
    SqlDataAdapter3.Update(DsCust1)
  Catch errobj As Exception
    lblError.Text = errobj.Message & vbCrLf & errobj.StackTrace
    Exit Sub
  End Try
  DataGrid1.EditItemIndex = -1
  DataGrid1.DataBind()
End Sub
```

Since we do not know which column the user might have changed, we can loop through all of them. You must test each column to see whether or not it is read-only. Attempting to assign to a read-only column will throw an exception. We must also coerce each column to a text box. An interesting thing is the Controls collection that is part of the Cells collection's `Item` property. In this case we are referencing the first and only member of the collection. However, this implies that there can be more than one control per cell. Is this true? I'll leave it up to you to find out. Hint: Look at custom column templates.

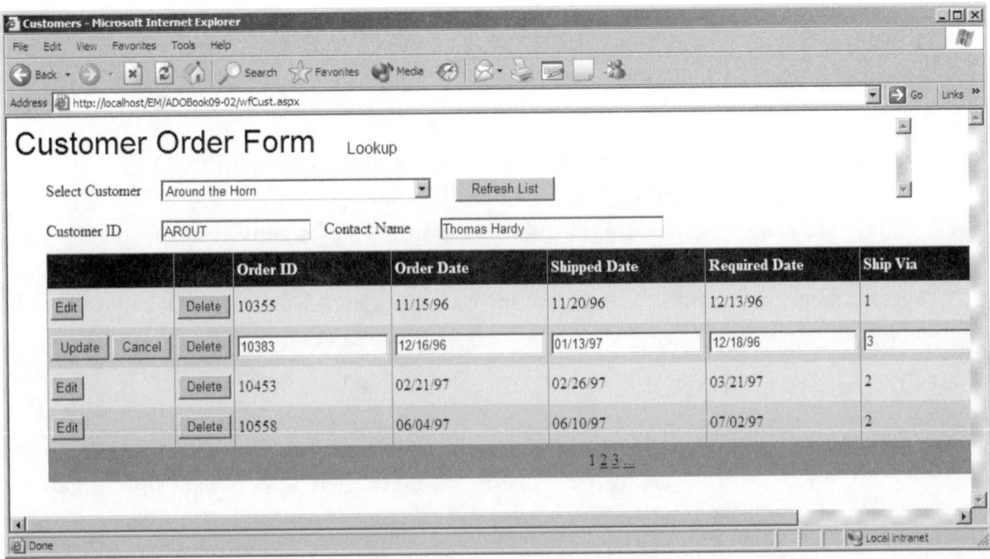

FIGURE 9.35 The grid in Edit mode.

Once we have assigned our values to the DataTable rows item, we can then make the database update using the usual `Update` method of the DataAdapter. If all this succeeds, we take the row out of Edit mode.

To cancel the edit on a row, we just need to respond to the CancelCommand event and set the EditItemIndex to –1. This takes all rows out of Edit mode. For completeness, here is the code.

```
Private Sub DataGrid1_CancelCommand(ByVal source As Object, ByVal e As
System.Web.UI.WebControls.DataGridCommandEventArgs) Handles
DataGrid1.CancelCommand
  DataGrid1.EditItemIndex = -1
  DataGrid1.DataBind()
End Sub
```

You can also delete rows from the grid. To do this, we respond to the DeleteCommand event. Here is the code to delete a row.

```
Private Sub DataGrid1_DeleteCommand(ByVal source As Object, ByVal e As
System.Web.UI.WebControls.DataGridCommandEventArgs) Handles
DataGrid1.DeleteCommand
  Try
    DsCust1.Orders.Rows(e.Item.ItemIndex).Delete()
    SqlDataAdapter3.Update(DsCust1)
  Catch errobj As Exception
    lblError.Text = errobj.Message & vbCrLf & errobj.StackTrace
```

```
        Exit Sub
    End Try
    DataGrid1.DataBind()
End Sub
```

Remember, we use the `Delete` method, not one of the `Remove` methods. As you can see, the DataGrid is a very powerful control. We have only scratched the surface, but we have given you enough to whet your appetite and to encourage you to explore on your own. Next we will look at another approach at presenting repeating data, the DataList control.

THE DATALIST CONTROL

The DataList control is similar to the DataGrid, but allows for more control at a lower level. There is no paging ability either. If you want this capability, you will have to build it yourself. The control works in a similar manner to the DataGrid, and has a similar event model. Where it differs is in the way you design the rows. You have much more control than with the DataGrid. Each row of the control is a separate page document, and you can use any controls you want. There are no columns, each control stands by itself. You can mix text boxes, DropdownLists, labels, and so forth on any row. Not only that, but each row has different mode templates, so for Edit mode you show one template and regular View mode another. Think of the DataList as repeating rows of separate groups of controls.

Let's create a project for working with the DataList control called ADOBook09-03. Create the project in the normal way, then copy the DataSets and the form into the new project folder from ADOBook09-02. Include them in the new project the way we did before. In case you forgot, click the Show All Files button in the Solution Explorer toolbar and then right-click the files and Include In Project. You may then delete the default form created with the project. When you have the previous project's form in the project, delete the grid control. Now go into the code and delete all the grid control's event procedures.

Configuring the DataList

Configuring the DataList control turns out to be an adventure in eye-hand coordination. To configure the control visually, you have to switch back and forth between the control's normal design-time view and an Edit Templates view. The Edit Templates view is accessible only through the right mouse button. The only other way to configure the control is via HTML view, and unless you happen to be an HTML guru, this is no simple task. Here is the HTML required to configure the DataList control as shown in Figure 9.36.

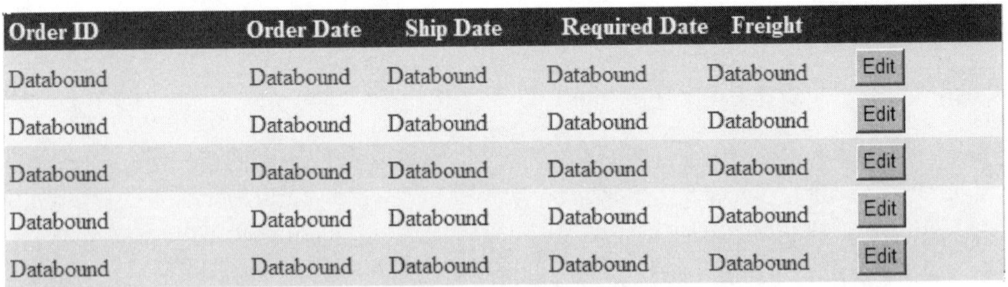

Order ID	Order Date	Ship Date	Required Date	Freight	
Databound	Databound	Databound	Databound	Databound	Edit
Databound	Databound	Databound	Databound	Databound	Edit
Databound	Databound	Databound	Databound	Databound	Edit
Databound	Databound	Databound	Databound	Databound	Edit
Databound	Databound	Databound	Databound	Databound	Edit

FIGURE 9.36 The DataList control.

```
<asp:datalist id=DataList1 style="Z-INDEX: 111; LEFT: 40px; POSITION:
absolute; TOP: 136px" runat="server" Width="734px" DataSource="<%#
DsCust1 %>" DataMember="Orders" GridLines="Both" DataKeyField="OrderID"
CellPadding="3" BackColor="White" BorderWidth="1px" BorderStyle="None"
BorderColor="#E7E7FF" >
<SelectedItemStyle Font-Bold="True" ForeColor="#F7F7F7"
BackColor="#738A9C"></SelectedItemStyle>
  <HeaderTemplate>
    <asp:Label id="Label5" runat="server" Width="158px">Order ID</
asp:Label>
      <asp:Label id="Label6" runat="server" Width="102px">Order Date</
asp:Label>
      <asp:Label id="Label7" runat="server" Width="102px">Ship Date</
asp:Label>
      <asp:Label id="Label8" runat="server" Width="110px">Required
Date</asp:Label
      <asp:Label id="Label3" runat="server" Width="110px">Freight</
asp:Label>
  </HeaderTemplate>
  <AlternatingItemStyle BackColor="#F7F7F7"></AlternatingItemStyle>
  <ItemStyle ForeColor="#4A3C8C" BackColor="#E7E7FF"></ItemStyle>
  <ItemTemplate>
      <asp:Label id=Label9 runat="server" Text='<%#
DataBinder.Eval(Container, "DataItem.OrderID", "{0}") %>'
Width="160px">
          </asp:Label>
      <asp:Label id=Label11 runat="server" Text='<%#
DataBinder.Eval(Container, "DataItem.OrderDate", "{0:d}") %>'
Width="88px">
          </asp:Label>
      <asp:Label id=Label12 runat="server" Text='<%#
DataBinder.Eval(Container, "DataItem.RequiredDate", "{0:d}") %>'
Width="104px">
```

```
            </asp:Label>
        <asp:Label id=Label13 runat="server" Text='<%#
DataBinder.Eval(Container, "DataItem.ShippedDate", "{0:d}") %>'
Width="104px">
            </asp:Label>
        <asp:Label id=Label14 runat="server" Text='<%#
DataBinder.Eval(Container, "DataItem.Freight", "{0:C}") %>'
Width="96px">
            </asp:Label>
        <asp:Button id="Button1" runat="server" Text="Edit"
CommandName="edit"></asp:Button>
          </ItemTemplate>
          <FooterStyle ForeColor="#4A3C8C" BackColor="#B5C7DE"></
FooterStyle>
          <HeaderStyle Font-Bold="True" ForeColor="#F7F7F7"
BackColor="#4A3C8C"></HeaderStyle>

          <EditItemTemplate>
     <asp:TextBox id=Textbox2 runat="server" ReadOnly="True" Text='<%#
DataBinder.Eval(Container, "DataItem.OrderID", "{0}") %>'>
            </asp:TextBox>
     <asp:TextBox id=Textbox9 runat="server" Text='<%#
DataBinder.Eval(Container, "DataItem.OrderDate", "{0:d}") %>'
Width="96px">
            </asp:TextBox>
     <asp:TextBox id=Textbox10 runat="server" Text='<%#
DataBinder.Eval(Container, "DataItem.RequiredDate", "{0:d}") %>'
Width="104px">
            </asp:TextBox>
     <asp:TextBox id=Textbox11 runat="server" Text='<%#
DataBinder.Eval(Container, "DataItem.ShippedDate", "{0:d}") %>'
Width="96px">
            </asp:TextBox>
     <asp:TextBox id=Textbox12 runat="server" Text='<%#
DataBinder.Eval(Container, "DataItem.Freight", "{0:C}") %>'
Width="102px">
            </asp:TextBox>
     <asp:Button id="Button2" runat="server" Text="Update"
CommandName="update"></asp:Button>
     <asp:Button id="Button3" runat="server" Text="Cancel"
CommandName="cancel"></asp:Button>
  </EditItemTemplate>
</asp:datalist>
```

Not for the faint of heart, even for HTML freaks. Figure 9.36 shows the DataList in design mode.

At runtime, the control looks like Figure 9.37.

As we said before, the tricky thing about configuring the control is setting up the templates. To begin, drop a DataList control on your form. The raw control doesn't look like much (see Figure 9.38).

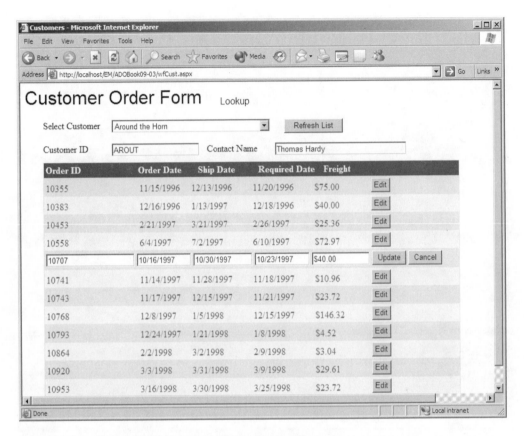

FIGURE 9.37 The DataList at runtime with a row in Edit mode.

In order to get the DataList to look usable, we have to add at least one item template. We do this by right-clicking the control and then selecting Edit Templates|Item Templates from the context menu. See Figure 9.39. I told you this would be an adventure with the mouse! This converts the control to Template Editing mode. What you see (Figure 9.40) is a set of four empty templates. You must add controls to these templates and then bind them to a DataSource.

NOTE—In the examples the control is DataList2. That is because I have already configured the control and mine is called DataList1. So the code will say DataList1, but the graphics might show DataList2.

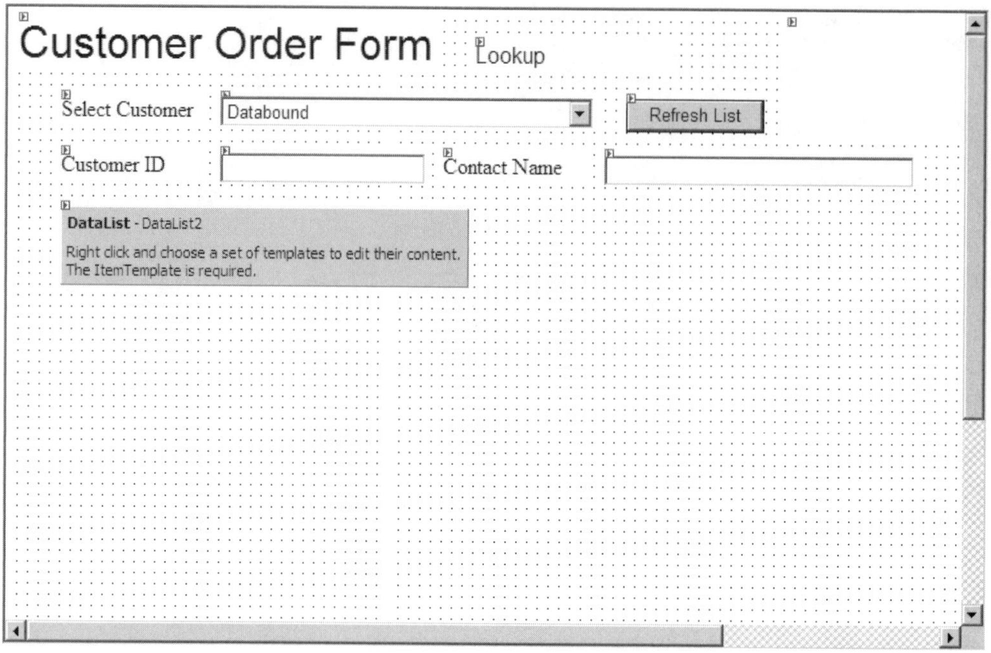

FIGURE 9.38 The raw DataList control.

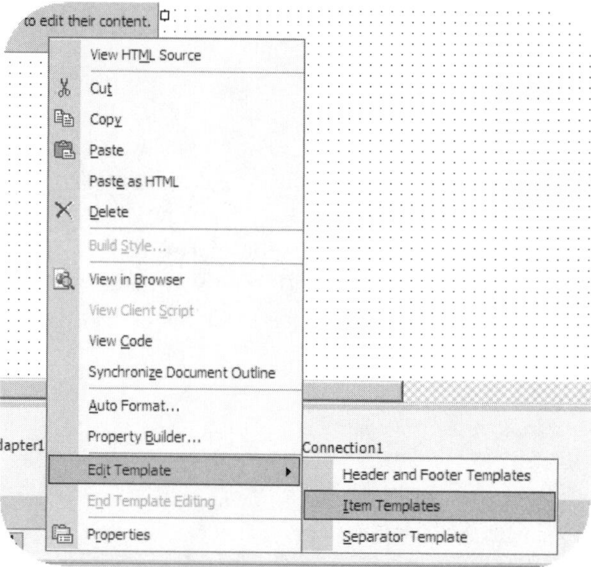

FIGURE 9.39 Finding the Edit Template command.

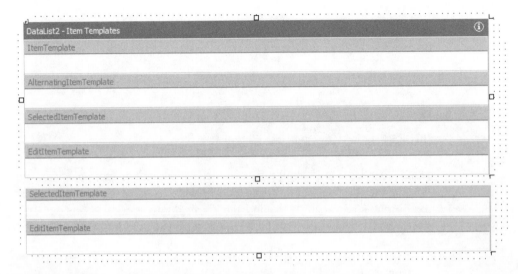

FIGURE 9.40 The DataList in Edit Template mode.

Figure 9.40 shows the control in the Edit Template mode.

What you see are four available item templates. The only one you must create is ItemTemplate. If your control is read-only that would be enough. If you want your control to support in-place editing, you also must create the EditItemTemplate. Typically, you would use static controls like labels for the ItemTemplate, and text boxes (or other editable control) for the EditItemTemplate. We add controls to the templates the normal way, by dragging them from the toolbox. The tricky part is binding to the data source. You must first set the DataSource of the control, just as we did with the DataGrid. This must be done with the control in normal design mode (not in Template Editing mode). Exit Template Editing mode by selecting End Template Editing from the context menu. Now you can set up the DataSource as in Figure 9.41.

Once the DataSource is set up, go back into Template Editing mode. Now we will add control to the ItemTemplate. As we said, we want to use static controls here. You could use editable controls as well, then you would

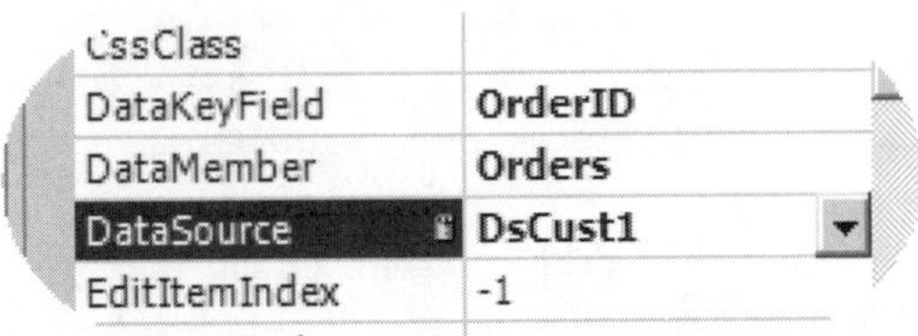

FIGURE 9.41 Setting the DataSource.

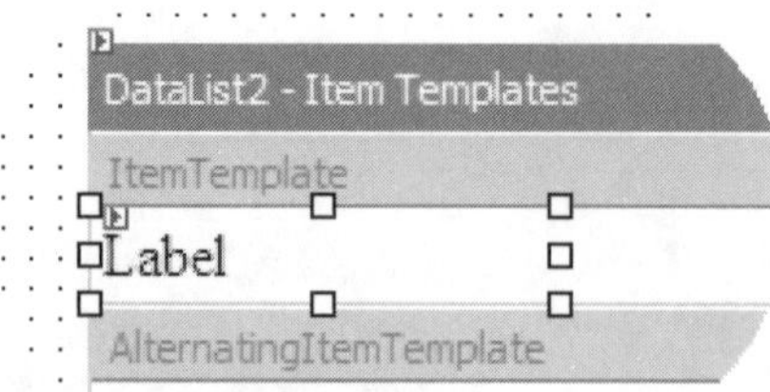

FIGURE 9.42 A label in the Item Template.

be able to edit all rows at all times. But let's stick with the normal static data until the user clicks an Edit button, like with the DataGrid. This would enable you to put some security behind the form, allowing only those with the proper privileges to update data. Figure 9.42 shows a label added to the ItemTemplate.

Now we have to bind the label to the DataSource. This is where it is a little different than we're used to. To bind the control, open the normal DataBinding dialog using the Property window. The dialog appears as in Figure 9.43.

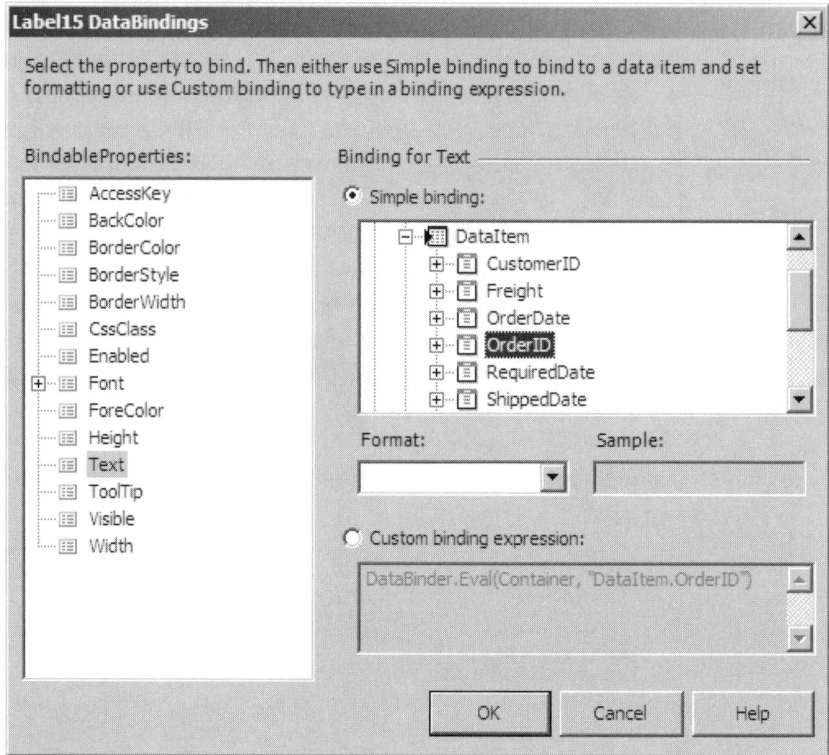

FIGURE 9.43 The DataBindings dialog.

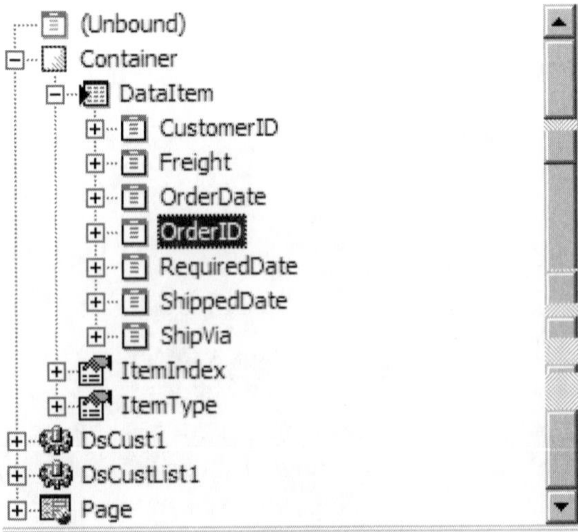

FIGURE 9.44 The full tree control.

We do not bind the control directly to the DataSet. Instead we expand the container node and then the DataItem mode. This shows the columns bound to the control itself. We then choose from one of these columns, in this case the OrderID. The full list of options is shown in Figure 9.44.

When you complete the ItemTemplate, it will look like Figure 9.45.

The next question you may ask is "How do we set up the buttons to fire the events?" We have to use the `CommandName` property of the button. The DataList is set up to respond to certain predefined commands and fire the events based on the property value. The commands are as they would seem: `Edit`, `Update`, and `Cancel`. There are also `Select` and `Delete` com-

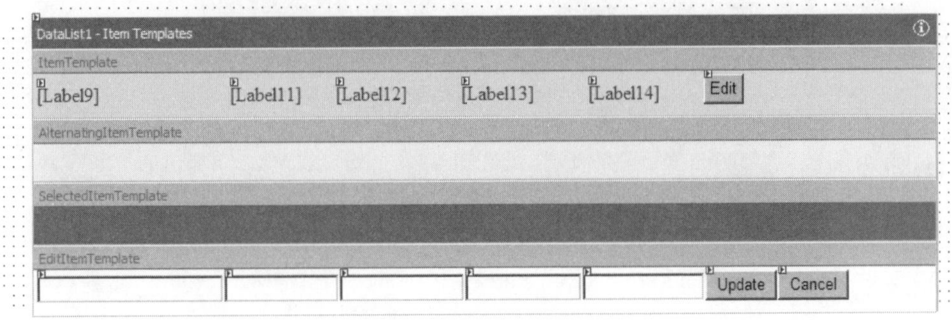

FIGURE 9.45 The control with the templates complete.

BorderWidth	
CausesValidation	True
CommandArgume	
CommandName	**edit**
CssClass	

FIGURE 9.46 The CommandName property.

mands but we will not be using those in this example. Set the property for the Edit button as in Figure 9.46.

One of the problems I had with this control was setting up the headings. It is very difficult to get the headings to align properly with the controls because you cannot edit the headings and the controls at the same time. You have to jump back and forth using trial and error. The heading is created using another template editor, Headers and Footers (see Figure 9.47).

Once this is done, we can add the code to the events. I will show all of the events here, because the code is almost the same as for the DataGrid.

```
   Private Sub DataList1_UpdateCommand(ByVal source As Object, ByVal e
As System.Web.UI.WebControls.DataListCommandEventArgs) Handles
DataList1.UpdateCommand
     Dim i As Integer

     Try
       DsCust1.Orders.Rows(e.Item.ItemIndex)("OrderDate") =
CType(e.Item.FindControl("TextBox9"), TextBox).Text
       DsCust1.Orders.Rows(e.Item.ItemIndex)("RequiredDate") =
CType(e.Item.FindControl("TextBox10"), TextBox).Text
       DsCust1.Orders.Rows(e.Item.ItemIndex)("ShippedDate") =
CType(e.Item.FindControl("TextBox11"), TextBox).Text
```

FIGURE 9.47 The Header and Footer template editor.

```
      DsCust1.Orders.Rows(e.Item.ItemIndex)("Freight") =
CType(e.Item.FindControl("TextBox12"), TextBox).Text
      SqlDataAdapter3.Update(DsCust1)
    Catch errobj As Exception
      lblError.Text = errobj.Message & vbCrLf & errobj.StackTrace
      Exit Sub
    End Try
    DataList1.EditItemIndex = -1
    DataList1.DataBind()
  End Sub

  Private Sub DataList1_EditCommand(ByVal source As Object, ByVal e As
System.Web.UI.WebControls.DataListCommandEventArgs) Handles
DataList1.EditCommand
    DataList1.EditItemIndex = e.Item.ItemIndex
    DataList1.DataBind()
  End Sub

  Private Sub DataList1_CancelCommand(ByVal source As Object, ByVal e
As System.Web.UI.WebControls.DataListCommandEventArgs) Handles
DataList1.CancelCommand
    DataList1.EditItemIndex = -1
    DataList1.DataBind()
  End Sub
```

The only difference is in the UpdateCommand event. Instead of looping through the cells (there are no cells), we use the `FindControl` method of the UpdateCommandEventArgs' `Item` property. This allows us the get a reference to the text box using its name and then directly assigns the value to the DataTable's row item object. Then we do the standard `Update` method of the DataAdapter.

SUMMARY

It is certainly easier than ever for us regular VB programmers to build very robust web applications without knowing much HTML at all. The DataGrid and DataList controls provide a very versatile way of presenting repeating rows of data to the user. They even have in-place editing. Next we will look at Web Services and how they can be used to provide a programmatic interface to business systems (or any other system) via the web.

CHAPTER 10

Building XML Web Services

XML Web Services are the latest big thing if you believe all the hype. What they are really is another way to implement remote components. In the past we had remote automation, Distributed COM, and COM+. These are proprietary Microsoft technologies. XML Web Services is a standards-based technology based on SOAP and XML. The other feature of Web Services is the discovery component, UDDI and Web Services Description Language (WSDL). UDDI is itself a Web Service that allows subscribers to search for and use other Web Services. The WSDL (pronounced wisdel) document describes the Web Service and is used by UDDI and the client application to discover what interfaces (properties and methods) the Web Service exposes for client use. If it helps, you can think of the WSDL document as the analog of the type library in COM+ terminology. Of course, the WSDL document is itself an XML file.

MULTITIER APPLICATION SERVICES

The concept of the multitier application services was born with the advent of remote OLE automation. Using this technology, it became possible to use remote procedure calls to access instances of components executing on another computer. The technique appeared seamless on the client application. It was as if the remote component were running locally. This ability allowed traditional two-tier client/server applications to include a middle tier that could contain business rules, act as a proxy to the database server, and provide other services. The three tiers were traditionally labeled the database, business rules, and presentation layers. While this solved some problems, it created new ones. How do we manage all these components? How about version synchronization? The best envisioned implementation of this architecture used an extremely thin client, which had no logic of its own beyond that needed to manage the display. The fattest part of the application is located in the myriad middle-tier components.

Unfortunately, this did not work very well with native Visual Basic because VB forms were private objects and couldn't be called remotely. This made creating a thin client difficult in Visual Basic. Anytime the business rules layer changed, it inevitably would force a revision of the UI as well, forcing another rollout to thousands of clients. It was possible to create a true thin client in VB, but because of VB's forms architecture these were invariably slow and complicated. This nullified many of the benefits of three-tier architecture.

Enter the Web. Now we have a ready-made universal thin client in the web browser. However, the web browser as a thin client has its drawbacks as well. Web browsers are designed to present formatted pages of text and images to the user. They were not intended to be used as a forms engine. You are limited to the basic HTML form elements for your UI. The stateless nature of the Web forces us into a clunky programming model, where the presentation layer is disconnected from the middle tier components (ASP or ASPX Web Forms and the VB code behind them). This forces both a lowest-common-denominator approach to the UI and limits the degree of interaction possible between the server and the client. This has not changed, although it has improved some with ASP .NET.

Visual Studio .NET finally offers the ability to build a robust, native Windows-based thin client that is not limited to what is supported by the web browser. XML Web Services allows us to build server-side components that are managed by the IIS and accessible to a variety of client platforms, not limited to Microsoft products. In addition, the Web Services themselves can be hosted on a variety of platforms, not just Microsoft servers. The best part is that in order to host Web Services, your server only needs the standard HTTP Port 80 open to provide these services.

Creating an ASP .NET Web Services Project

A Web Service in Visual Studio .NET is constructed in a similar manner to an ASP .NET Web Form. There is a small HTML file and a VB code module behind it. The HTML file is not used to display anything in a browser, it is used to invoke the Web Service. Let's create an ASP .NET Web Service project so we can see what we are talking about.

Set up your web server the same way you did for the Web Forms projects. To create a Web Services project, click New Project. Name the project ADOBook10-01. When the dialog opens, select ASP .NET Web Service from the list of templates as shown in Figure 10.1.

When you click OK, the IDE creates the project. As with an ASP .NET web application, the project is created in the wwwroot subtree of your inetpub directory. When the project is created, the IDE looks like Figure 10.2.

What Do We Want It to Do?

Before we can go any further, we must decide what we want our Web Service to do. Let's stick with our Customers—Orders—Order Details paradigm. We want our service to provide an interface through which client applications can obtain information about their order status. Notice we said *provide an interface*. We are also providing data, but more importantly we are providing the interface through which the data can be obtained. This is important because if

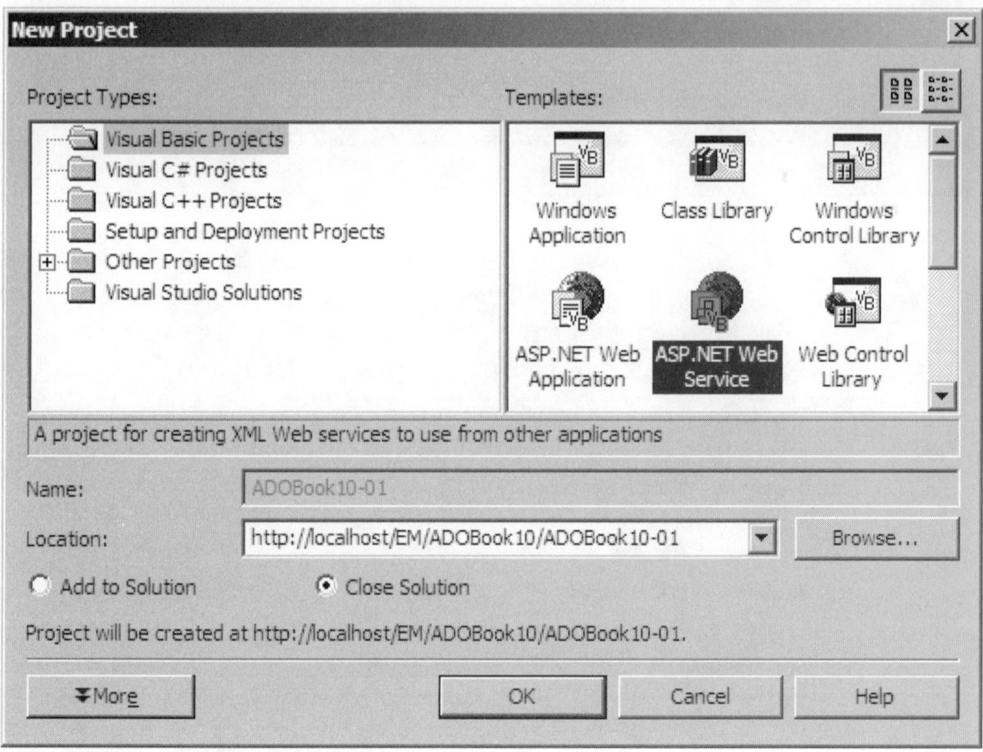

FIGURE 10.1 Creating a Web Services project.

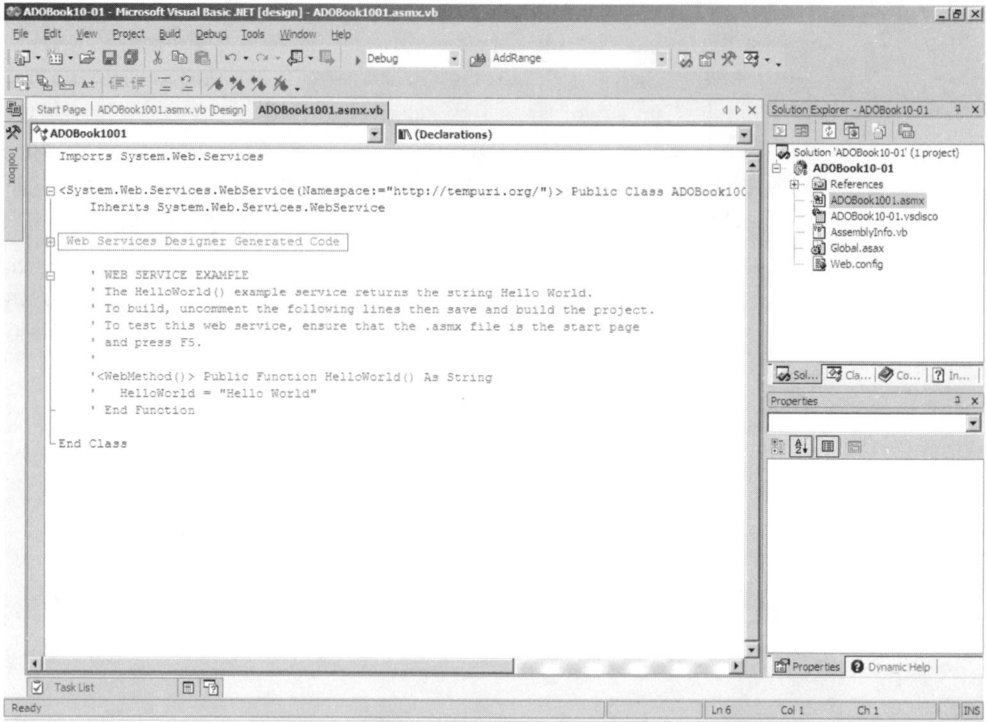

FIGURE 10.2 The IDE with a new ASP .NET Web Service.

all we wanted to do was provide the data, we could have used a web page. Instead, we are providing an interface for client applications to use to obtain the data. They can then present the data in any way they desire: via a web page, a Windows Form, a report, or even a Java UI. It doesn't matter to the Web Service.

What Can Be Passed to and from a Web Service

In order to understand what we can send back and forth to a Web Service, we must understand how the Web Service expects to communicate with the client. Remember, with Web Services everything must be able to resolve to an HTML request or XML stream. A Web Service interface is a form of remote procedure call (RPC). A request is sent to the server, and data is returned. From the client's point of view, the request takes the form of a method call. The method can only be a standard method (procedure or function). Property procedures are not supported.

The call is formatted into a request string that consists of the function name and a list of parameters. This is then sent to the server as an HTTP request. The web server looks at the request and knows to route it to the Web Service for processing. The Web Service then processes the request and returns a result. The result is formatted as an XML stream and returned to the client, which parses the stream and returns the data as the value of the function.

The data must be able to be represented as a text data stream. Fortunately, all of the .NET data types and many of the classes have this ability. The DataSet is the only data component that can be moved across HTTP connections.

Web Services cannot source events or callbacks of any kind. In the previous chapter we discussed at length why Web Forms could not communicate in real time with the web server. Web Services have the same restrictions and for the same reasons. The actual service only exists for short periods of time while processing requests, then they terminate. So you have the same concept of request/start service/process request/send results/terminate service. The life cycle of a Web Service is almost identical to that of a Web Form, with the difference being that the Web Service returns an XML stream instead of HTML. Each Web Service method must be a little program unto itself. You cannot use any module level variables to store data between requests, but you can use session variables or cookies.

THE CUSTOMERSORDERS WEB SERVICE

Since we have been working with the customers/orders/order details structure, let's continue with that and build a Web Service that returns and updates data about customer orders.

Let's rename our Web Service from the default to CustomersOrders. Do this by opening the page in design view. Web Services in Visual Studio are built using the Component Model, so we get a visual designer to work with. The only property available is the `Name` property. Change it from Service1 to CustomersOrders. Now change the file name to CustomersOrders as well. We can rename the file ins the usual manner using the Solution Explorer.

Since the Web Service class is derived from the ComponentModel class, we can add components using a visual designer. Before we can build our Web Service methods, we must first create all of the data components. We will need one SqlConnection object, four SqlDataAdapter objects, and three DataSet objects. All three DataSets will be strongly typed.

We will not go through the step-by-step details of creating the data components. By now you should be able to do that on your own. Here is how the components should be set up. Feel free to use the wizards and builders provided to speed the process.

- SqlConnection1—Connect to a convenient Northwind database.

```
    SqlDataAdapter1—Standard setup using the following Select
statement:
SELECT     CustomerID, CompanyName, ContactName, ContactTitle, Address,
City, Region, PostalCode, Country, Phone, Fax, BirthDate
FROM         Customers
WHERE      (CustomerID = @CustomerID)
```

- SqlDataAdapter2—Read-only setup. (Click Advanced tab and disable generation of `Update`, `Insert`, and `Delete` statements.) Use the following SQL statement:

```
SELECT     CustomerID, CompanyName
FROM         Customers
```

- SqlDataAdapter3—Standard setup. Use the following SQL statement:

```
SELECT     OrderID, CustomerID, EmployeeID, OrderDate, RequiredDate,
ShippedDate, ShipVia, Freight, ShipName, ShipAddress, ShipCity,
ShipRegion,
                      ShipPostalCode, ShipCountry
FROM         Orders
WHERE      (CustomerID = @CustomerID)
```

- SqlDataAdapter4—Standard setup. Use the following SQL statement:

```
SELECT     OrderID, ProductID, UnitPrice, Quantity, Discount

           FROM         [Order Details]
           WHERE      (OrderID IN
                                (SELECT     OrderID
                                  FROM          Orders
                      WHERE      CustomerID = @CustomerID))
```

- DsCust1 DataSet—Create from SqlDataAdapter1.
- DsCustList1 DataSet— Create from SqlDataAdapter2.
- DsOrders1 DataSet—Create from SqlDataAdapters 3 and 4. Create the relation between the Orders and Order Detail table the way we did in the previous chapter.

- In each of the three DataSets, add one more table called Errors. (Hint: Use the schema editor to do this.) The table has two columns, ErrorText and StackTrace, both strings. These tables will be used for error reporting; we'll see why we need to do this later.

Now it's time to begin adding our web methods. Remember the pretext; each web method must be self-contained and not rely on any outside data or services. By adding the data components to the visual designer they become module-level objects, but we are not using them to persist data between requests. They must either be passed in from the client (for the DataSet only) or recreated each time a web method is called.

The first web method we will create will be used to return our list of customers for populating the list portion of the combo box. The code looks like this:

```
  <WebMethod(Description:="Gets List of Customers for Combo Box.")> _
  Public Function GetCustomerList() As dsCustList
    DsCustList1 = New dsCustList()
    Try
      SqlDataAdapter2.Fill(DsCustList1)
    Catch errobj As Exception
      DsCustList1.Errors.Rows.Add(New String() {errobj.Message,
errobj.StackTrace})
    End Try
    Return DsCustList1
  End Function
```

This is the simplest of our methods. Notice the attribute setting before the function declaration. In order to be seen by the client, the web method must use this attribute. The `Description` argument sets the description that will display for this method when doing a UDDI query. Other than that, it is a pretty normal-looking function. Notice that we recreate the DataSet at the beginning of the function.

Let's compile and run the Web Service. Yes, we can run a Web Service in much the same way as we can run a Web Form. But the service has no UI. That's okay. Visual Studio will generate one for us (see Figure 10.3).

Incidentally, the description of the Web Service itself is set in the attribute on the declaration of the class. Here is the code for setting the description:

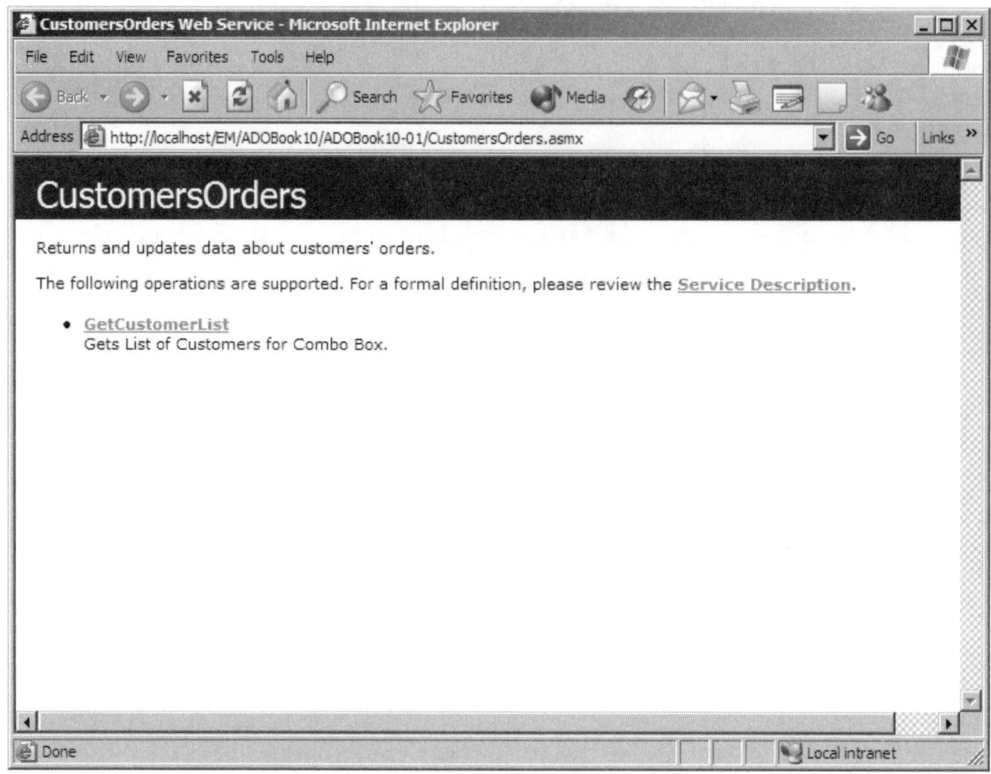

FIGURE 10.3 The Web Service introductory page.

```
Imports System.Web.Services

<System.Web.Services.WebService(Namespace:="http://
www.emanageservice.com/", Description:="Returns and updates data about
customers' orders.")> _
Public Class CustomersOrders
   Inherits System.Web.Services.WebService
```

The great thing about this page is that we can use it to test the web method. If we click on the method, we get the screen shown in Figure 10.4.

The screen virtually gives you the HTML code to invoke the method via different protocols. It also enables you to test the method by invoking it directly and then viewing the results. Not all methods can be invoked this way; they must be able to be called using the HTTP `Get` method. Still, it makes a great debugging aid. You can set breakpoints in your code and use this to invoke your method before using it in your production version. When you run the method, it returns raw XML as in Figure 10.5.

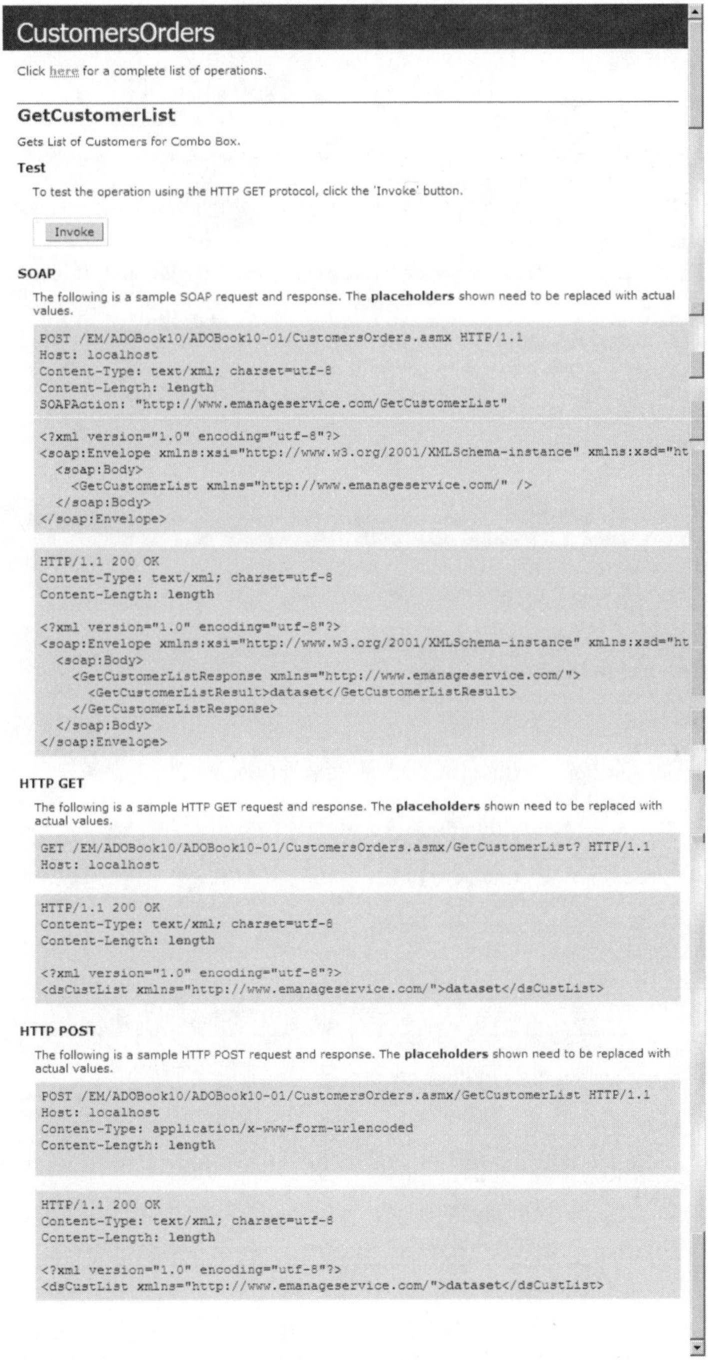

CustomersOrders

Click here for a complete list of operations.

GetCustomerList

Gets List of Customers for Combo Box.

Test

To test the operation using the HTTP GET protocol, click the 'Invoke' button.

Invoke

SOAP

The following is a sample SOAP request and response. The **placeholders** shown need to be replaced with actual values.

```
POST /EM/ADOBook10/ADOBook10-01/CustomersOrders.asmx HTTP/1.1
Host: localhost
Content-Type: text/xml; charset=utf-8
Content-Length: length
SOAPAction: "http://www.emanageservice.com/GetCustomerList"

<?xml version="1.0" encoding="utf-8"?>
<soap:Envelope xmlns:xsi="http://www.w3.org/2001/XMLSchema-instance" xmlns:xsd="ht
  <soap:Body>
    <GetCustomerList xmlns="http://www.emanageservice.com/" />
  </soap:Body>
</soap:Envelope>
```

```
HTTP/1.1 200 OK
Content-Type: text/xml; charset=utf-8
Content-Length: length

<?xml version="1.0" encoding="utf-8"?>
<soap:Envelope xmlns:xsi="http://www.w3.org/2001/XMLSchema-instance" xmlns:xsd="ht
  <soap:Body>
    <GetCustomerListResponse xmlns="http://www.emanageservice.com/">
      <GetCustomerListResult>dataset</GetCustomerListResult>
    </GetCustomerListResponse>
  </soap:Body>
</soap:Envelope>
```

HTTP GET

The following is a sample HTTP GET request and response. The **placeholders** shown need to be replaced with actual values.

```
GET /EM/ADOBook10/ADOBook10-01/CustomersOrders.asmx/GetCustomerList? HTTP/1.1
Host: localhost
```

```
HTTP/1.1 200 OK
Content-Type: text/xml; charset=utf-8
Content-Length: length

<?xml version="1.0" encoding="utf-8"?>
<dsCustList xmlns="http://www.emanageservice.com/">dataset</dsCustList>
```

HTTP POST

The following is a sample HTTP POST request and response. The **placeholders** shown need to be replaced with actual values.

```
POST /EM/ADOBook10/ADOBook10-01/CustomersOrders.asmx/GetCustomerList HTTP/1.1
Host: localhost
Content-Type: application/x-www-form-urlencoded
Content-Length: length
```

```
HTTP/1.1 200 OK
Content-Type: text/xml; charset=utf-8
Content-Length: length

<?xml version="1.0" encoding="utf-8"?>
<dsCustList xmlns="http://www.emanageservice.com/">dataset</dsCustList>
```

FIGURE 10.4 The method invocation screen.

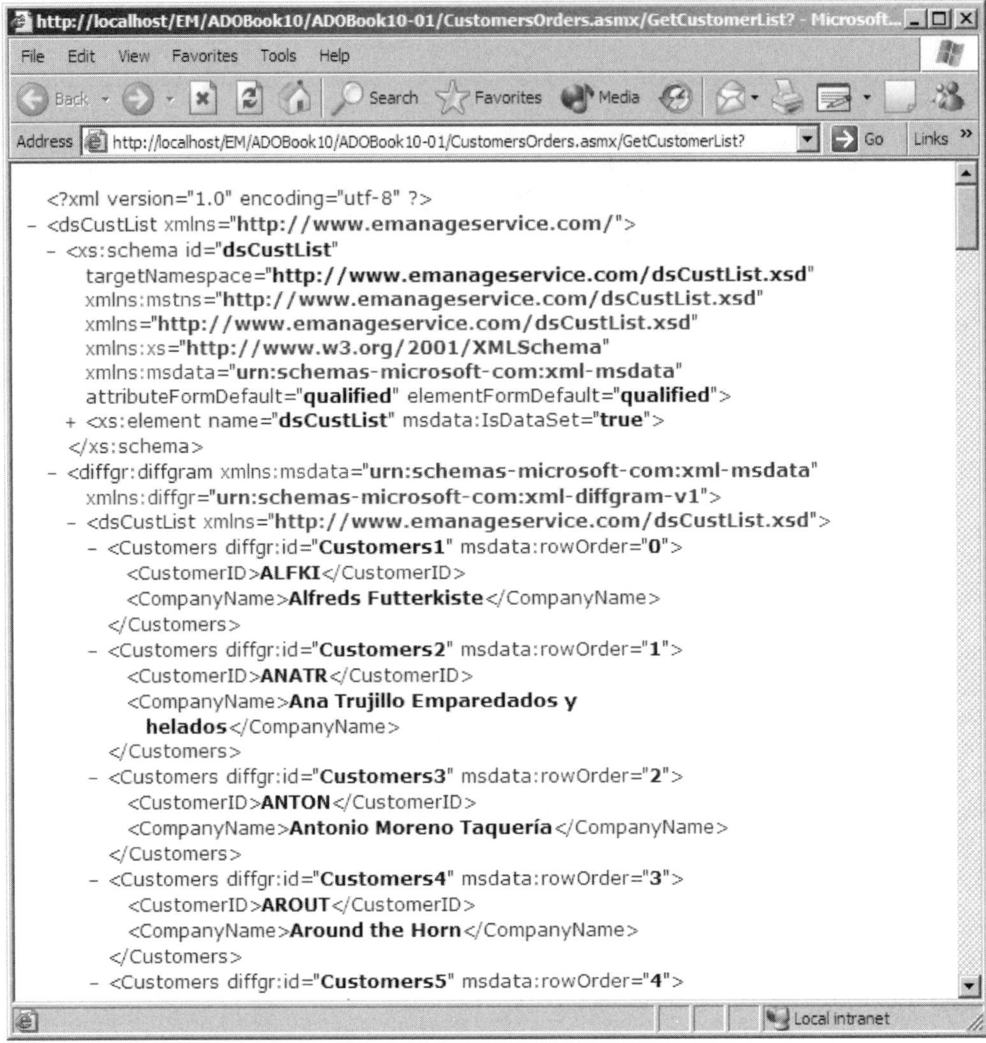

FIGURE 10.5 XML results from method invoke.

Let's add the rest of our methods. We need two more methods for now. They are:

- GetCustomer—Pass it a CustomerID and it returns a DataSet with customer details.
- GetOrders—Pass it a CustomerID and it returns all the orders and order details for the customer.

Here is the code for `GetCustomer`:

```
<WebMethod(Description:="Gets Details about a Customer.")> _
Public Function GetCustomer(ByVal strCustID As String) As dsCust
  DsCust1 = New dsCust()
  If strCustID = "" Then
    DsCust1.Errors.Rows.Add(New String() {"Customer ID is Required",
""})
    Return DsCust1
  End If
  Try
    SqlDataAdapter1.SelectCommand.Parameters("@CustomerID").Value =
strCustID
    SqlDataAdapter1.Fill(DsCust1)
  Catch errobj As Exception
    DsCust1.Errors.Rows.Add(New String() {errobj.Message,
errobj.StackTrace})
  End Try
  Return DsCust1
End Function
```

Handling Errors in Web Services

Since the CustomerID is required, the first thing we do is check to see if the caller passed a string that is not empty. If the caller did, we return an error. Now this is interesting. Error handling in a Web Service is a bit tricky because of the stateless nature of the Web. In a regular component (not a Web Service) we would throw the error back to the client or raise an event or store the error message in a module-level variable for the client to obtain later. But in a Web Service we have no such luxury. If we try to throw the error back to the client, all we get is an error page, or if it is a client application, it is ignored. We can't raise events in Web Services and we can't store the value for later retrieval. That is a bit of a kludge anyway, a holdover from the pre-ActiveX DLL days.

The best way to handle errors in a Web Service is via the DataSet itself. I include an Errors table in all my DataSets that will be used in Web Services. When I encounter an error, I simply fill the Errors table with the error message and optionally the stack trace. Then I return the DataSet to the client. It is then up to the client to interrogate the table to see if any errors occurred.

If you just throw the error back to the client, all you get is the default page shown in Figure 10.6.

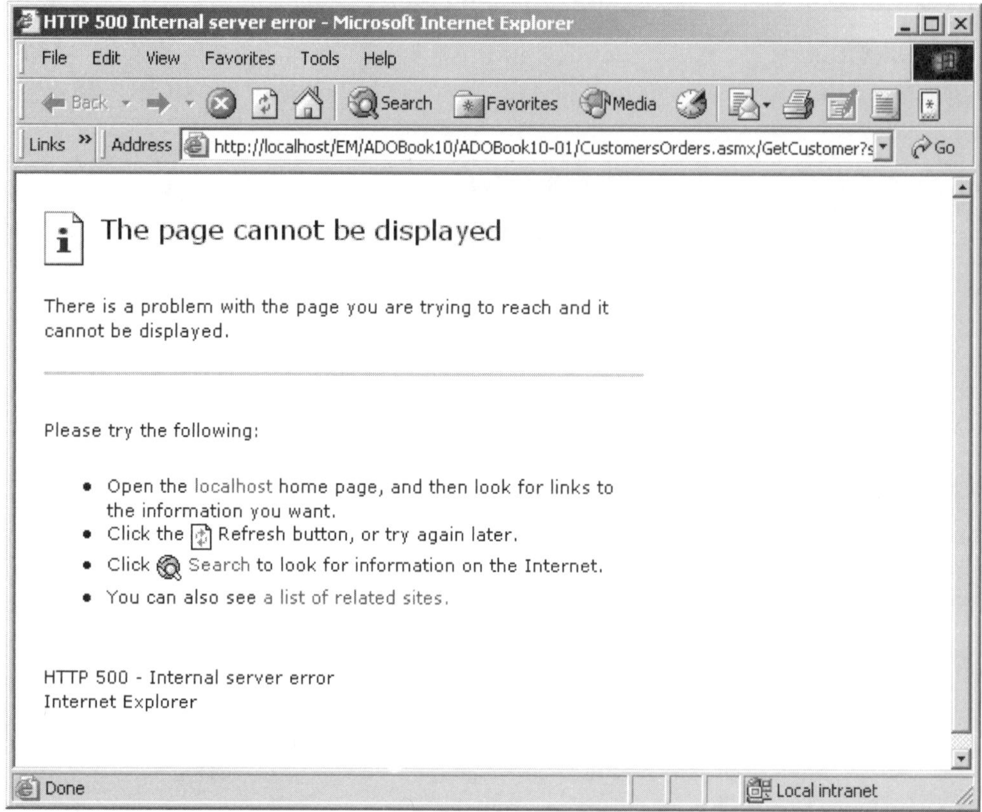

FIGURE 10.6 The error page when you throw an exception.

When you use a table to report the error, you can see what went wrong and even get the list number of the line that caused the problem. In a production environment, you might want to return less information to the client, but log the detailed information on the server for debugging purposes. Figure 10.7 shows what you get when you use the Errors table.

As you can see, you can trace the error right down to the line number. Isn't that more helpful than HTTP 500—Internal Server Error? By the way, just for this demonstration I renamed the CustomerID column CustomerIDX so it would throw the error. If you want to try this example, make sure you rename it properly when you are done.

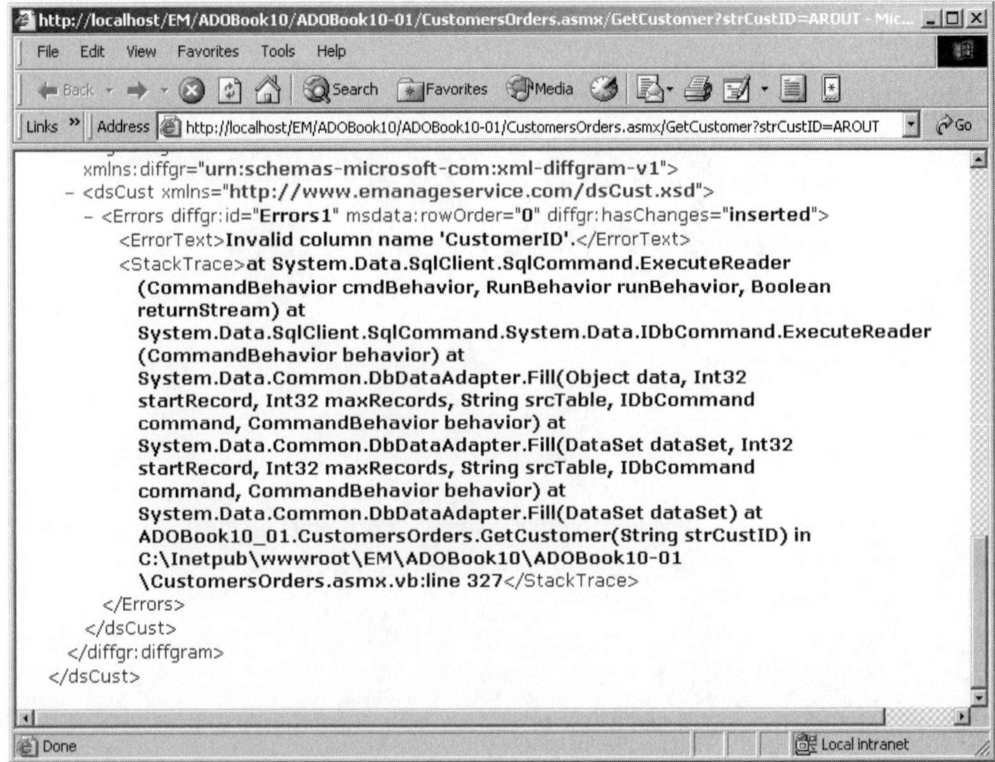

FIGURE 10.7 The XML error table returned after an error.

Getting Multitable DataSets

The Orders/Order Details relational structure is a little more complicated. Let's look at the code to retrieve the orders for a customer. Remember in our DataSet we defined the Orders table as the master table and the Order Details table as the detail table.

```
<WebMethod(Description:="Gets Orders and Details for a Customer")> _
Public Function GetOrders(ByVal strCustID As String) As dsOrders
  DsOrders1 = New dsOrders()
  If strCustID = "" Then
    DsCust1.Errors.Rows.Add(New String() {"Customer ID is Required",
""})
    Return DsOrders1
  End If
```

```
    Try
      SqlDataAdapter3.SelectCommand.Parameters("@CustomerID").Value =
strCustID
      SqlDataAdapter3.Fill(DsOrders1.Orders)
      SqlDataAdapter4.SelectCommand.Parameters("@CustomerID").Value =
strCustID
      SqlDataAdapter4.Fill(DsOrders1.Order_Details)
    Catch errobj As Exception
      DsOrders1.Errors.Rows.Add(New String() {errobj.Message,
errobj.StackTrace})
    End Try
    Return DsOrders1
  End Function
```

As with our example in the previous chapter, we retrieve all of the orders and the details for all of the orders. We then let the relational constraint we built enforce which details go with which orders. This is different than in the past when you would query the database each time the user changed rows in the master table. As a refresher, here are the SQL statements for the Select-Commands of the two DataAdapters.

SqlDataAdapter3:

```
SELECT     OrderID, CustomerID, EmployeeID, OrderDate, RequiredDate,
ShippedDate, ShipVia, Freight, ShipName, ShipAddress, ShipCity,
ShipRegion,
                     ShipPostalCode, ShipCountry
FROM         Orders
WHERE      (CustomerID = @CustomerID)
```

SqlDataAdapter4:

```
SELECT     OrderID, ProductID, UnitPrice, Quantity, Discount
FROM         [Order Details]
WHERE      (OrderID IN
                        (SELECT     OrderID
                          FROM          Orders
                          WHERE       CustomerID = @CustomerID))
```

When we execute the web method through the test interface, we get all of the order details first, then all of the order headers. Since the list is quite long I will only show excerpts. Figure 10.8 shows the order detail metadata information:

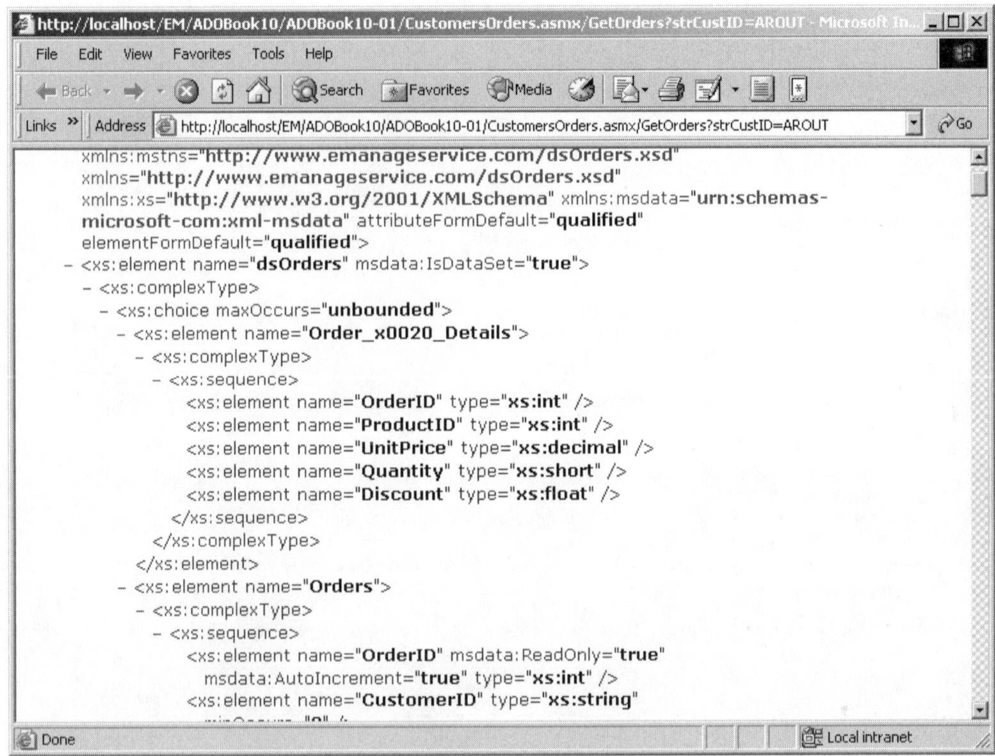

FIGURE 10.8 Order detail metadata.

In Figure 10.9 we can see some of the order details data.

Figure 10.10 shows the order header metadata.

Figure 10.11 shows the order header data. Notice the scroll bar which is toward the end of the file.

Updating Data with a Web Service

There are two main approaches to updating the database with a Web Service.

The first approach involves passing the DataSet back to the server. Of course, you would only want to pass rows that have changed, been inserted, or been deleted. You can do this with the `GetChanges` method. This would be the preferred method when using a Windows Forms client and you know your Web Service will be used only by Microsoft .NET Windows Forms clients.

The second approach, which is to pass the changed values back to the server, then let the server handle updating the database and is best if your

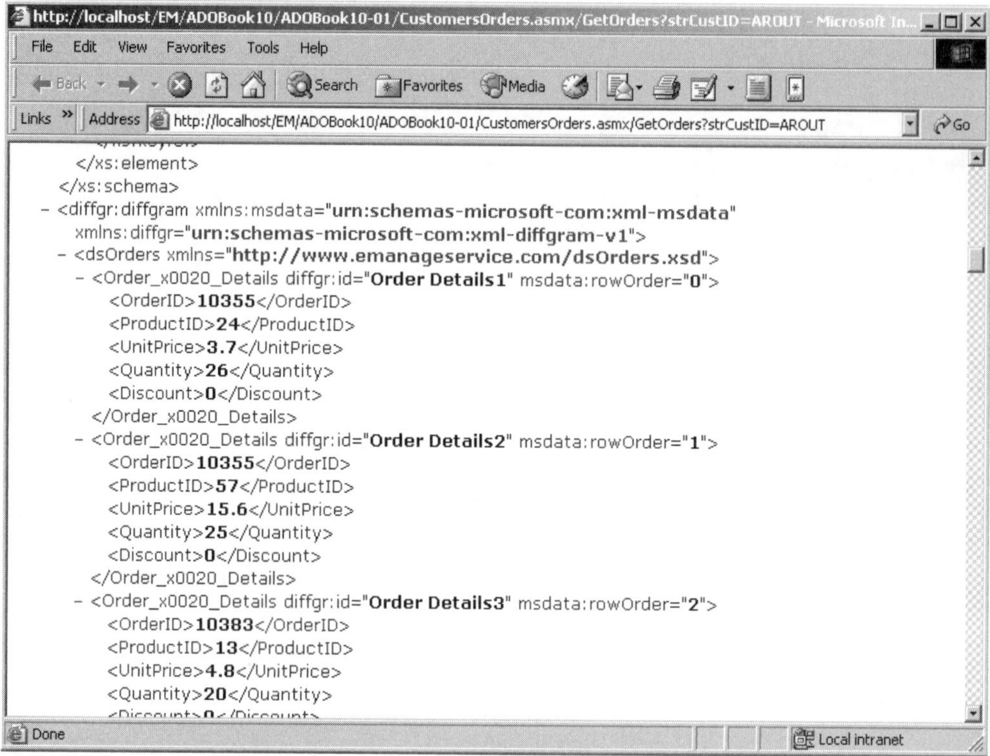
http://localhost/EM/ADOBook10/ADOBook10-01/CustomersOrders.asmx/GetOrders?strCustID=AROUT - Microsoft In...
File Edit View Favorites Tools Help
Back Search Favorites Media
Links Address http://localhost/EM/ADOBook10/ADOBook10-01/CustomersOrders.asmx/GetOrders?strCustID=AROUT Go
</xs:element>
</xs:schema>
- <diffgr:diffgram xmlns:msdata="urn:schemas-microsoft-com:xml-msdata"
xmlns:diffgr="urn:schemas-microsoft-com:xml-diffgram-v1">
- <dsOrders xmlns="http://www.emanageservice.com/dsOrders.xsd">
- <Order_x0020_Details diffgr:id="Order Details1" msdata:rowOrder="0">
<OrderID>10355</OrderID>
<ProductID>24</ProductID>
<UnitPrice>3.7</UnitPrice>
<Quantity>26</Quantity>
<Discount>0</Discount>
</Order_x0020_Details>
- <Order_x0020_Details diffgr:id="Order Details2" msdata:rowOrder="1">
<OrderID>10355</OrderID>
<ProductID>57</ProductID>
<UnitPrice>15.6</UnitPrice>
<Quantity>25</Quantity>
<Discount>0</Discount>
</Order_x0020_Details>
- <Order_x0020_Details diffgr:id="Order Details3" msdata:rowOrder="2">
<OrderID>10383</OrderID>
<ProductID>13</ProductID>
<UnitPrice>4.8</UnitPrice>
<Quantity>20</Quantity>
Done
Local intranet

FIGURE 10.9 Order details data.

Web Service is intended for general consumption by both Microsoft .NET and other platforms, which may not support DataSets, or if you will use a non–ASP .NET browser-based client.

You can't go wrong with the second method, because it will be able to handle any client platform. It does make the update a little more complex though. We will demonstrate both methods.

Passing a DataSet Back to the Web Service

Since the DataSet can be serialized as XML, it can be passed back to the Web Service. We cannot, however, use HTTP post or get. We must use a SOAP request. Because of this, we cannot use the test page to test the method. Here is the code for accepting a DataSet as a `method` parameter:

```
    <WebMethod(Description:="Updates Details about a Customer. Form 1.
Pass It The DataSet.")> _
    Public Function UpdateCustomer1(ByVal dsCust1 As dsCust) As dsCust
```

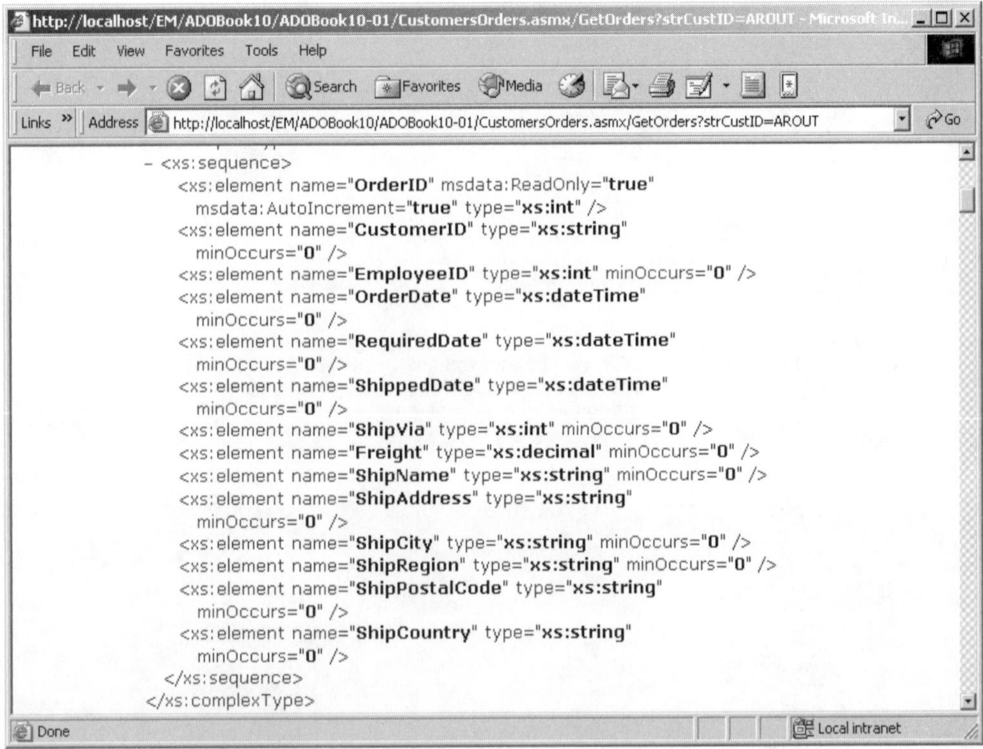
http://localhost/EM/ADOBook10/ADOBook10-01/CustomersOrders.asmx/GetOrders?strCustID=AROUT - Microsoft In...
File Edit View Favorites Tools Help
Back Search Favorites Media
Links Address http://localhost/EM/ADOBook10/ADOBook10-01/CustomersOrders.asmx/GetOrders?strCustID=AROUT Go
- <xs:sequence>
<xs:element name="OrderID" msdata:ReadOnly="true" msdata:AutoIncrement="true" type="xs:int" />
<xs:element name="CustomerID" type="xs:string" minOccurs="0" />
<xs:element name="EmployeeID" type="xs:int" minOccurs="0" />
<xs:element name="OrderDate" type="xs:dateTime" minOccurs="0" />
<xs:element name="RequiredDate" type="xs:dateTime" minOccurs="0" />
<xs:element name="ShippedDate" type="xs:dateTime" minOccurs="0" />
<xs:element name="ShipVia" type="xs:int" minOccurs="0" />
<xs:element name="Freight" type="xs:decimal" minOccurs="0" />
<xs:element name="ShipName" type="xs:string" minOccurs="0" />
<xs:element name="ShipAddress" type="xs:string" minOccurs="0" />
<xs:element name="ShipCity" type="xs:string" minOccurs="0" />
<xs:element name="ShipRegion" type="xs:string" minOccurs="0" />
<xs:element name="ShipPostalCode" type="xs:string" minOccurs="0" />
<xs:element name="ShipCountry" type="xs:string" minOccurs="0" />
</xs:sequence>
</xs:complexType>
Done
Local intranet

FIGURE 10.10 The order header metadata.

```
        Try
            dsCust1.Errors.Rows.Clear()
            If dsCust1.HasChanges Then
                SqlDataAdapter1.Update(dsCust1)
            End If
        Catch errobj As Exception
            dsCust1.Errors.Rows.Add(New String() {errobj.Message,
errobj.StackTrace})
        End Try
        Return dsCust1
    End Function
```

The advantage of this way of updating the database is that the code is fairly simple. Essentially you are getting a DataSet, then calling the `Update` method of the DataAdapter. We must first clear the Errors table in case we passed an error to the client. Also, before we invoke the method on the client side, we should call the `GetChanges` method of the DataSet so we don't

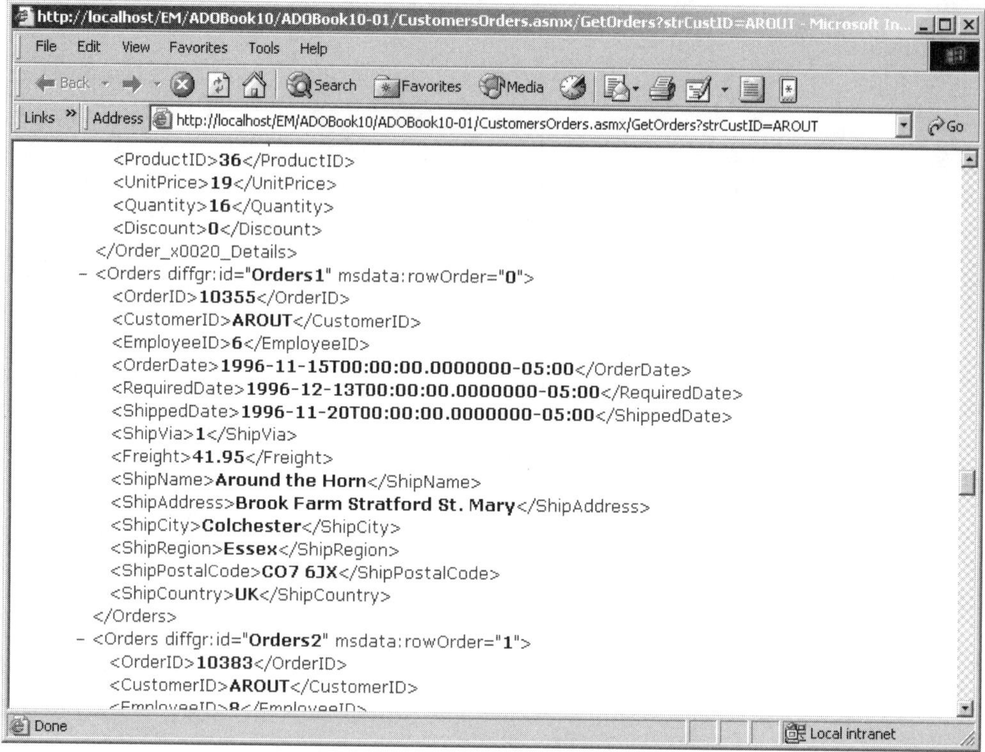
http://localhost/EM/ADOBook10/ADOBook10-01/CustomersOrders.asmx/GetOrders?strCustID=AROUT - Microsoft In...
File Edit View Favorites Tools Help
Back Search Favorites Media
Links Address http://localhost/EM/ADOBook10/ADOBook10-01/CustomersOrders.asmx/GetOrders?strCustID=AROUT Go
<ProductID>36</ProductID>
<UnitPrice>19</UnitPrice>
<Quantity>16</Quantity>
<Discount>0</Discount>
</Order_x0020_Details>
- <Orders diffgr:id="Orders1" msdata:rowOrder="0">
<OrderID>10355</OrderID>
<CustomerID>AROUT</CustomerID>
<EmployeeID>6</EmployeeID>
<OrderDate>1996-11-15T00:00:00.0000000-05:00</OrderDate>
<RequiredDate>1996-12-13T00:00:00.0000000-05:00</RequiredDate>
<ShippedDate>1996-11-20T00:00:00.0000000-05:00</ShippedDate>
<ShipVia>1</ShipVia>
<Freight>41.95</Freight>
<ShipName>Around the Horn</ShipName>
<ShipAddress>Brook Farm Stratford St. Mary</ShipAddress>
<ShipCity>Colchester</ShipCity>
<ShipRegion>Essex</ShipRegion>
<ShipPostalCode>CO7 6JX</ShipPostalCode>
<ShipCountry>UK</ShipCountry>
</Orders>
- <Orders diffgr:id="Orders2" msdata:rowOrder="1">
<OrderID>10383</OrderID>
<CustomerID>AROUT</CustomerID>
Done
Local intranet

FIGURE 10.11 Order header data.

pass too much data back to the server. Despite advances in technology, there are still many 56 KB dial-up connections in use. These typically download at 56 KB but only send at 28.8 or worse, 14.4. By limiting the amount of data you have to send back to the server you will do these users a big favor. We will see how to do this later when we build our client.

Passing Values to the Server

To make sure your Web Service can be consumed by any user on the Web (if that is your requirement) you must pass only basic data types back and forth. We didn't cover this in the earlier section on getting data, but this is true there as well. If our Web Service is to be consumed by non–.NET clients, we can't pass a DataSet down to the client either. It will not know what to do with it. We would have to pass comma-delimited strings or some other format that is universally readable.

Here is the code to pass values back to the service:

```
    <WebMethod(Description:="Updates Details about a Customer. Form 2.
Pass It The Values.")> _
    Public Function UpdateCustomer2( _
     ByVal strCustID As String, _
     ByVal strCompanyName As String, _
     ByVal strContactName As String, _
     ByVal strContactTitle As String, _
     ByVal strAddress As String, _
     ByVal strCity As String, _
     ByVal strState As String, _
     ByVal strPostal As String, _
     ByVal strPhone As String) As dsCust

        DsCust1 = New dsCust()
        If strCustID = "" Then
            DsCust1.Errors.Rows.Add(New String() {"Customer ID is
Required", ""})
            Return DsCust1
        End If
        Try
            DsCust1.Errors.Rows.Clear()

SqlDataAdapter1.SelectCommand.Parameters("@CustomerID").Value =
strCustID
            SqlDataAdapter1.Fill(DsCust1)
            DsCust1.Customers.Rows(0)("CustomerID") = strCustID
            DsCust1.Customers.Rows(0)("CompanyName") = strCompanyName
            DsCust1.Customers.Rows(0)("ContactName") = strContactName
            DsCust1.Customers.Rows(0)("ContactTitle") = strContactTitle
            DsCust1.Customers.Rows(0)("Address") = strAddress
            DsCust1.Customers.Rows(0)("City") = strCity
            DsCust1.Customers.Rows(0)("Region") = strState
            DsCust1.Customers.Rows(0)("PostalCode") = strPostal
            DsCust1.Customers.Rows(0)("Phone") = strPhone
            If DsCust1.HasChanges Then
                SqlDataAdapter1.Update(DsCust1)
            End If
        Catch errobj As Exception
            DsCust1.Errors.Rows.Add(New String() {errobj.Message,
errobj.StackTrace})
        End Try
        Return DsCust1
    End Function
```

As you can see, the code is more complex. Also, you can only update one row at a time with UpdateCustomer2, whereas the UpdateCustomer1 will push multiple updates, as well as `inserts` and `deletes`, to the database. The advantage to the UPdateCustomer2 is that it is entirely self-contained and does not rely on any external data structures. Notice that we actually create the DataSet using the passed-in CustomerID, then update it. One thing we don't check is to see if the CustomerID still exists. If someone deleted this customer, we would not have anything to update. This will throw an error; however, we would probably want to handle this condition with a little more grace.

You could also create a custom collection of classes that can be passed back and forth using XML. This would create a custom schema that any system capable of understanding XML would be able to use.

We would use similar techniques to update the orders and order details. For the sake of space, we will not go into detail about how to do this, but the same considerations apply. For the orders and details, it is definitely better to be able to pass the DataSet with only the changes back to the client. If you must do it using values, and you must pass row by row, then you will have to make multiple calls to the web method, which has its own negative issues. It is always better to use .NET clients with a .NET Web Service. You could also provide both methods and instruct your clients to use the .NET-specific methods if they are using a .NET client or to use the other methods if not.

Using Web Services with Windows Forms Clients

You can consume Web Services with Windows Forms clients. This is the most robust way of using Web Services. You have the advantage of using HTTP protocol for simplicity, yet you have all the advantages of using Windows Forms to build a robust UI.

The way we do this is almost as simple as referencing a local component. We create a reference to a Web Service. But first let's create an empty Windows Forms project and add it to the solution. Call the new project ADOBook10-02. Once the project is created we can create our web reference. This is a little different than creating a reference to a local component. To create the web reference, we point to the .asmx document on the server via a URL. Do this by right-clicking on the References node of the ADOBook10-02 project in the Project Explorer. Then select Create Web Reference as in Figure 10.12.

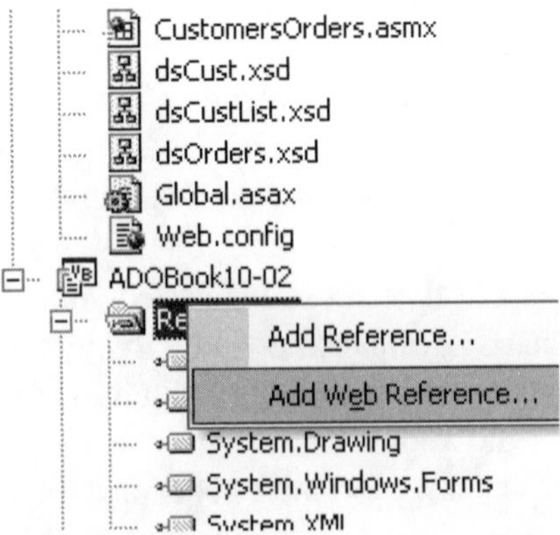

FIGURE 10.12 Adding a web reference.

When you select this item, the Web Reference dialog opens. This combines the UDDI service with the intro page we saw previously (see Figure 10.13).

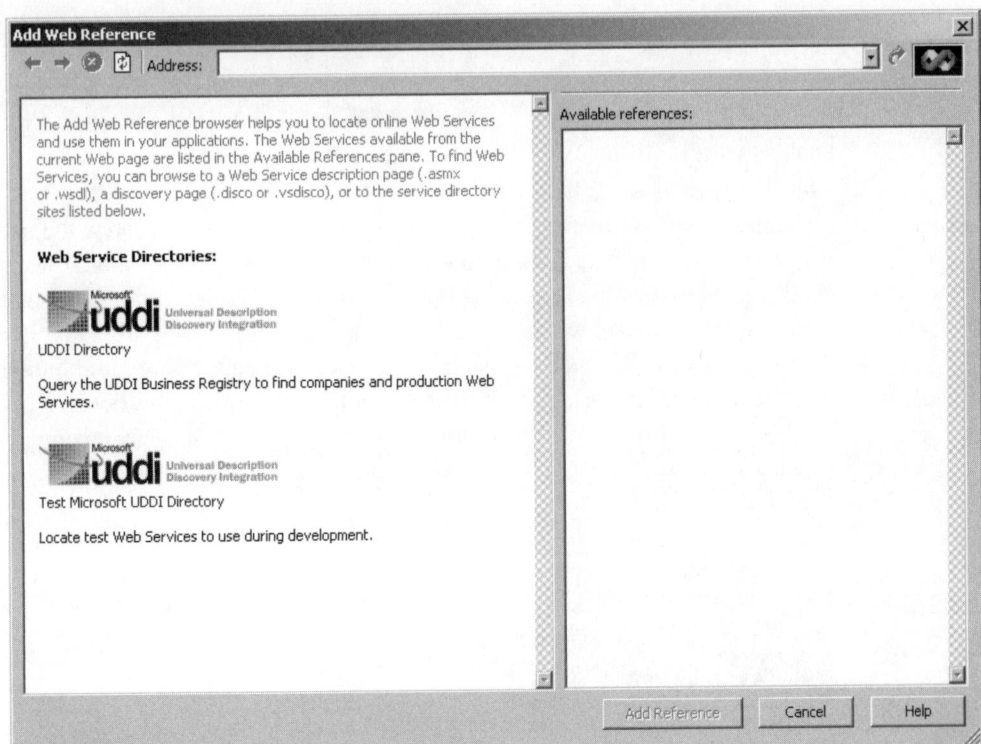

FIGURE 10.13 The Add Web Service dialog.

To add our service to the project, we must know where to point the dialog. Since we have not added it to UDDI service, we cannot simply browse for it. Enter the full URL to the service in the address box, as shown in Figure 10.14.

If you have entered it correctly, you should bring up the intro page as in Figure 10.15.

Once you have determined that this is the correct Web Service, simple click Add Reference to make it available in your project. Once you have added the reference, it appears in the Solution Explorer as in Figure 10.16.

That little mouse click did a lot of work. To create the reference, it created all of the files you see under the localhost node, plus some you don't see. The CustomersOrders.wsdl document describes the entire interface to the Web Service. Remember we said that the WSDL document is the analog of the COM type library? If we open it we will see that it is an XML document that describes the interface in three ways, HTTP get, HTTP post, and SOAP.

Second, it also downloaded the three DataSet schemas. This is so we have access to the data types locally.

Third, it creates the Reference.map document. This document is the discovery reference, which contains references to the other documents. Open it and look at it to see what we mean. It is straightforward.

Fourth, it creates a Visual Basic interface proxy class. It does this from the .map file and the WSDL document. This is a Visual Basic source file that enables us to call the Web Service methods as if they were local function calls. It wraps the calls to the Web Service for us.

Take a look at this file, but don't make any changes to it. Notice the use of the `Invoke` method. This is how we call late-bound classes in .NET. This is analogous to the `CallByName` function we had in VB 6. This class is not technically necessary; we don't have to wrap the method calls like this. But then we would have made our Web Service method calls using late-binding the way the proxy class does, and it is a lot more work. Why bother? Let Visual Studio do it for you. If, for whatever reason, you were creating a generic thin client, you could use the late-bound calls after parsing the WSDL document yourself.

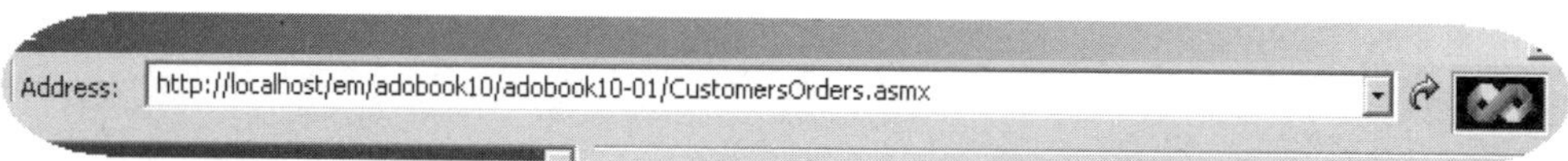

FIGURE 10.14 The URL of the Web Service.

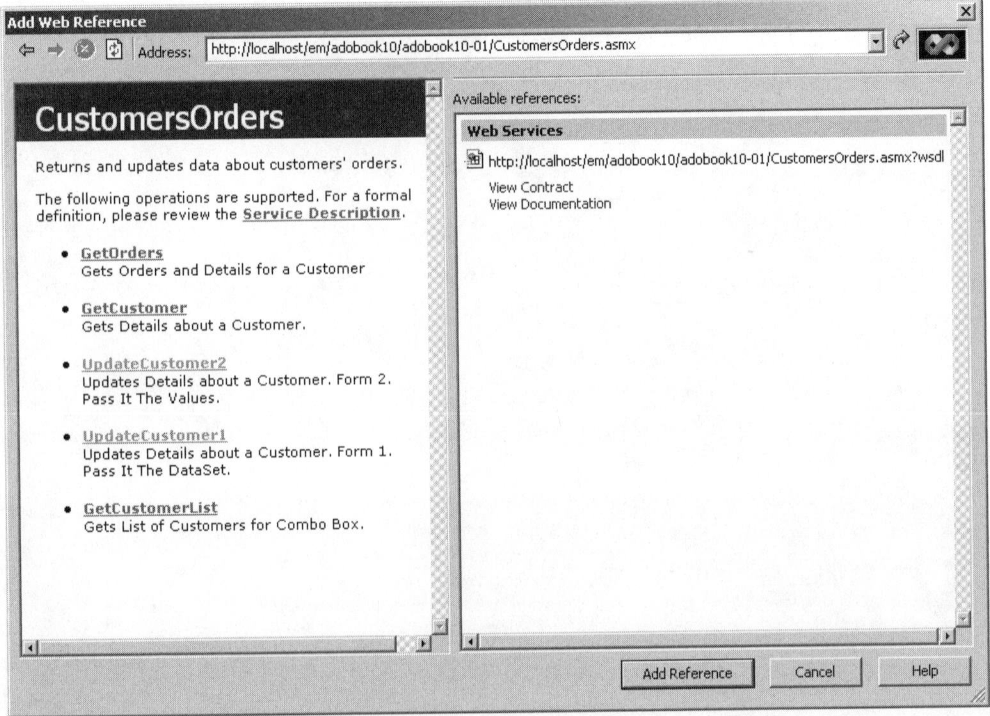

FIGURE 10.15 The Add Web Reference dialog with the Web Service found.

Let's put our Web Service to work. First step is to create our UI. We'll use a Windows Forms version of the Web Forms project we did in the previous chapter. You will have a combo box that is populated with the list of companies, and a details area that has the information about the selected company. We will have an Update button to allow changes to the details.

Now, let's add our DataSets to the form. Since we are using a Web Service, we do not need a Connection object or DataAdapters. Already we can see a benefit to using a Web Service. The client does not know about or care what kind of database we are using or where the database is located. This is a great security benefit, as well as a benefit to your application programmers. End users or application programmers do not have to have any database training or even know where the database is.

When we add a DataSet, we will use typed DataSets, but we will get our types from the Web Service. This is really neat. Remember how it downloaded the XSD schema files for the DataSets? We can use these to create our own typed DataSets locally so when we pass DataSets back and forth to the

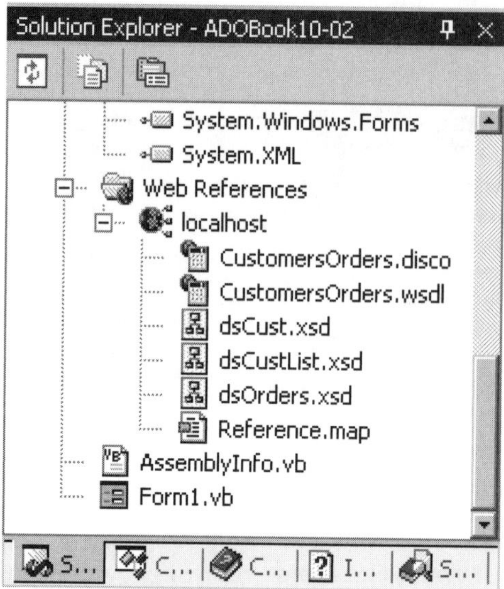

FIGURE 10.16 The Web Service reference.

Web Service, they are strongly typed. Start by dragging a DataSet from the toolbox and dropping it in the form. The DataSet dialog opens. In the drop down under Typed DataSet, you will see the DataSets from the Web Service listed. Select the one shown in Figure 10.17.

This creates DsCustList1. We will use this to bind to the list portion of the ComboBox. Next create another DataSet, this time use dsCust as the type. Don't create one for DsOrders yet.

Once we have created the DataSets, we will add a DataView object to bind our controls to. Drag one onto the form and set its DataTable property to `DsCust1.Customers`. Remember, when we bind to a DataTable, we are really binding to the default view, so instead we will use our own view. This is a best practice for general use. For the sake of space I will show you only the interface; by now we should be pretty adept at creating a Windows Form. Create the form to look like Figure 10.18. Bind the text boxes to their appropriate fields in the DataView1 object.

This is essentially the same thing we had with the Web Form, except as a Windows Form. The code to create the Web Service and call the methods for getting data follows:

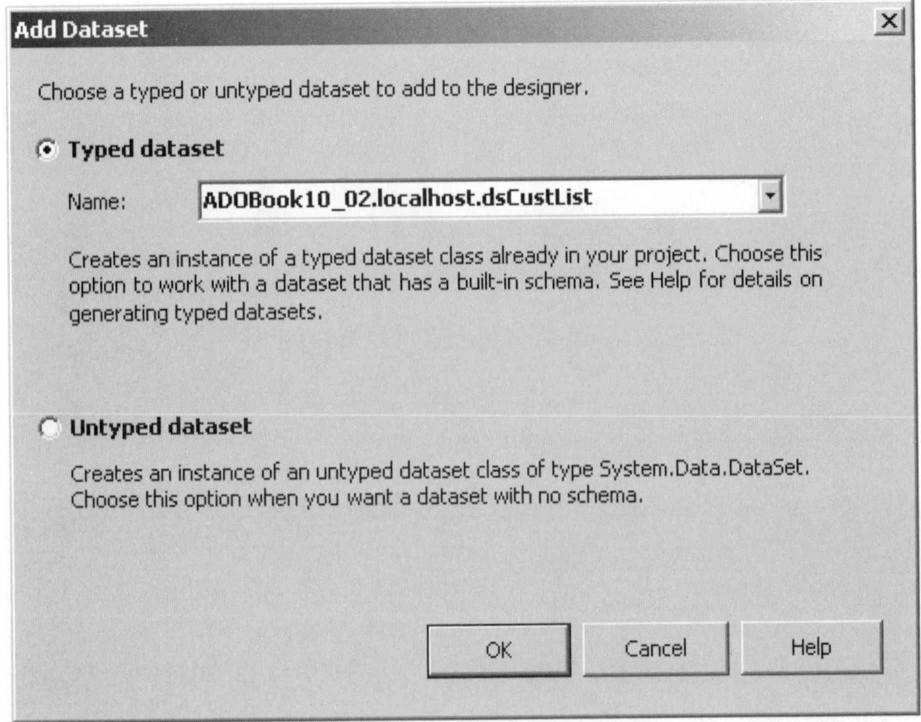

FIGURE 10.17 Creating a typed DataSet from a Web Service.

```
    Private mWebSvc As localhost.CustomersOrders = New
localhost.CustomersOrders()

    Private Sub frmCust_Load(ByVal sender As System.Object, ByVal e As
System.EventArgs) Handles MyBase.Load
        DsCustList1.Merge(mWebSvc.GetCustomerList())
    End Sub

    Private Sub ComboBox1_SelectedIndexChanged(ByVal sender As
System.Object, ByVal e As System.EventArgs) Handles
ComboBox1.SelectedIndexChanged
        DsCust1.Clear()
        DsCust1.Merge(mWebSvc.GetCustomer(ComboBox1.SelectedValue))
    End Sub
```

Notice that instead of assigning the output of the web method to the DataSet, I use the `Merge` method on the DataSet. I do this so I don't have to rebind the DataSet to all the text boxes. Think about it. We have created our

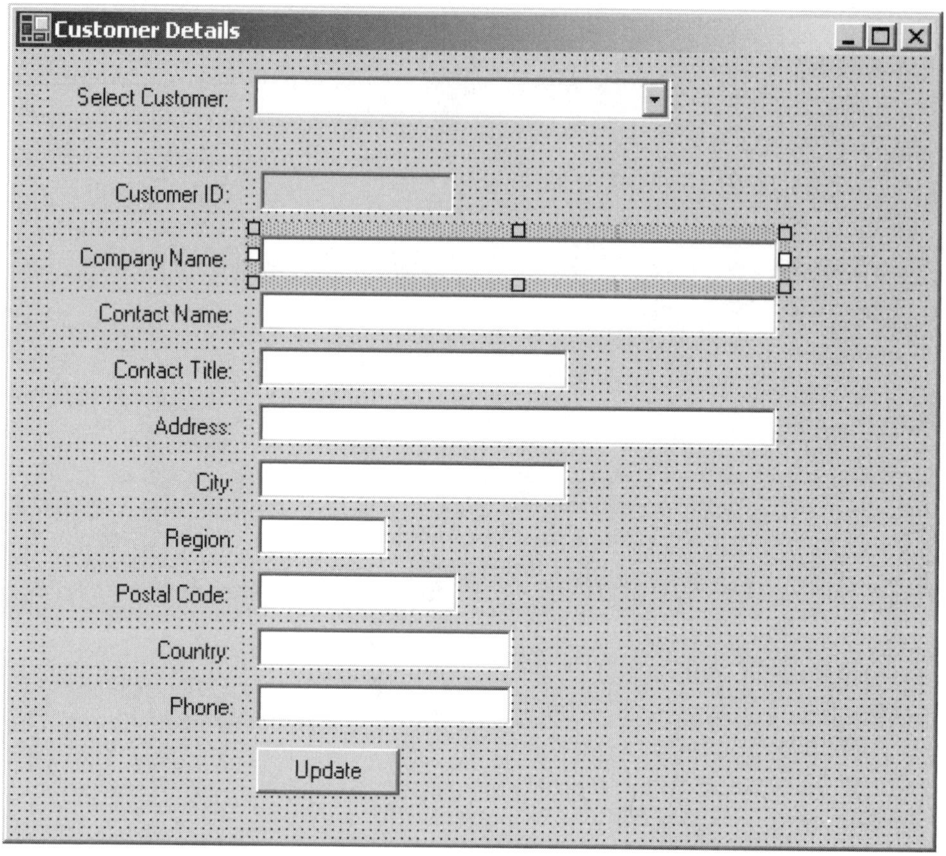

FIGURE 10.18 The UI for the Web Service Form.

DataSets using the visual designer. That means that instances of them are created automatically when the form starts. When we bind the controls to the DataSets, it is to this instance that we are binding. If we were to simply assign the DataSets to the output of the web methods, we would be effectively destroying the bound instance and creating an instance that is not bound to anything. By using the `Merge` method, we do not have to destroy the bound instance of the DataSets, and the bindings remain intact. This is true even though we are binding through a DataView. This has nothing to do with Web Services, by the way. It is just as true if we were using local data components.

We can declare our Web Service as a module-level variable. With each method invocation, the proxy class handles creating the web request and returning the data as the correct type. So even though it seems as though the Web Service is existing for the whole lifetime of the client program, it really is being created and destroyed with every method call. What does exist is the proxy class. But this is all transparent to the client application. When we compile and run the client program, we have the same functionality that we had with the Web Form. You can begin to see how by using a Web Service we can build equivalent Windows and web front ends to the same business rules fairly easily, compared to previous technologies. Figure 10.19 shows the form in action.

Now let's implement the Update button. For now, we'll just pass the DataSet back to the server. Since we made the web method return the DataSet as well, we can take advantage of the SqlDataAdapter2's refresh of the DataSet to keep the display current.

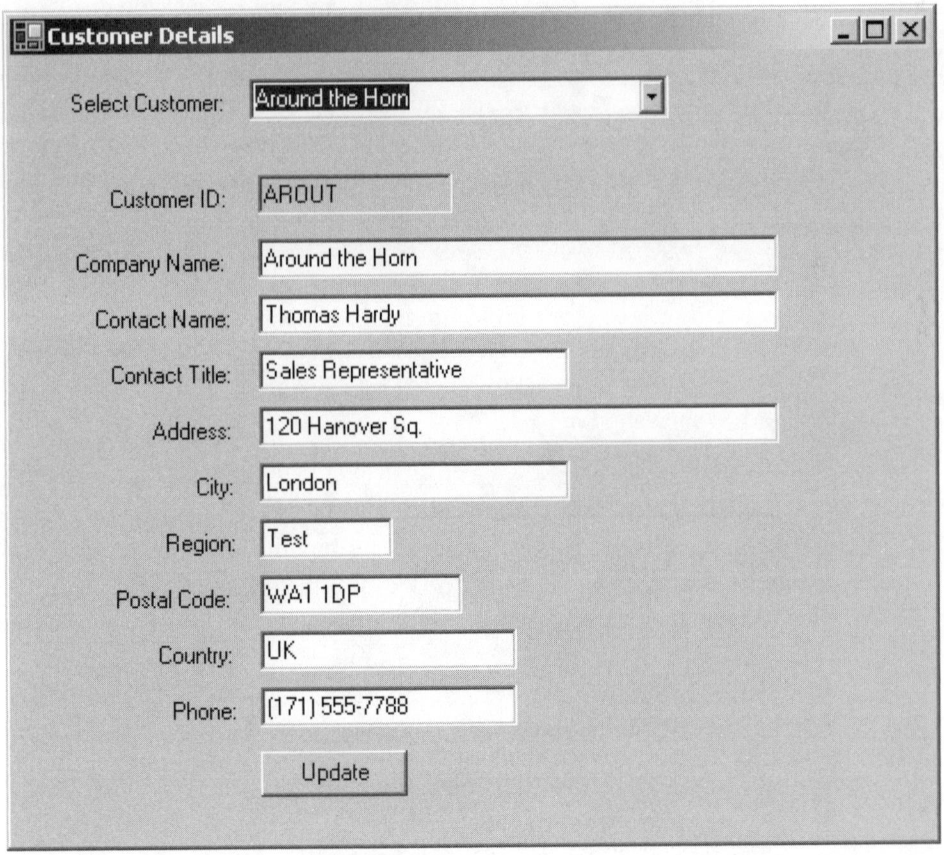

FIGURE 10.19 The Web Service Windows client.

Here is the code to do a simple update:

```
Private Sub Button1_Click(ByVal sender As System.Object, ByVal e As
System.EventArgs) Handles Button1.Click
    Dim dsTemp As localhost.dsCust

    Me.BindingContext(DataView1).EndCurrentEdit()
    If DsCust1.HasChanges(DataRowState.Modified) Then
      dsTemp = DsCust1.GetChanges(DataRowState.Modified)
      DsCust1.Merge(mWebSvc.UpdateCustomer1(dsTemp))
    End If
  End Sub
```

First, as usual, we end the pending edit. Next we see if there were any changes. If there were, we copy them to a temporary DataSet and send the temporary DataSet off to the web method. We get back another DataSet which we then merge (remember our discussion earlier) into the permanent DataSet.

Now let's add some complexity. We want to create a way of adding records to the table. Do we need a new web method? The answer after this: The first and most obvious thing we need to do is add two more buttons to the form. Label one New and the other Cancel Add. Set the `Enabled` property of the Cancel button to `False`. We want the Cancel button enabled only in Add mode. Okay, do we need a new method? No, we do not. What we already have will suffice.

As with our Web Form project in the last chapter, when the user clicks the New button, the form will clear and allow the user to enter a new record. The user can cancel the add at any time by clicking the Cancel button. The new form is shown in Figure 10.20.

Let's do the code for the New button first since it's the simplest. Here we must clear the DataSet, put the DataView into Add mode, and enable the CustomerID text box (TextBox1). We also want to disable the combo box. The user should not select another customer until he is finished adding the new one. We then want to enable the Cancel button. Here is the code for the New button and the Cancel button:

```
  Private Sub Button2_Click(ByVal sender As System.Object, ByVal e As
System.EventArgs) Handles Button2.Click
    DsCust1.Clear()
    DataView1.AddNew()
    ComboBox1.Enabled = False
    TextBox1.ReadOnly = False
    Button3.Enabled = True
    Button2.Enabled = False
  End Sub
```

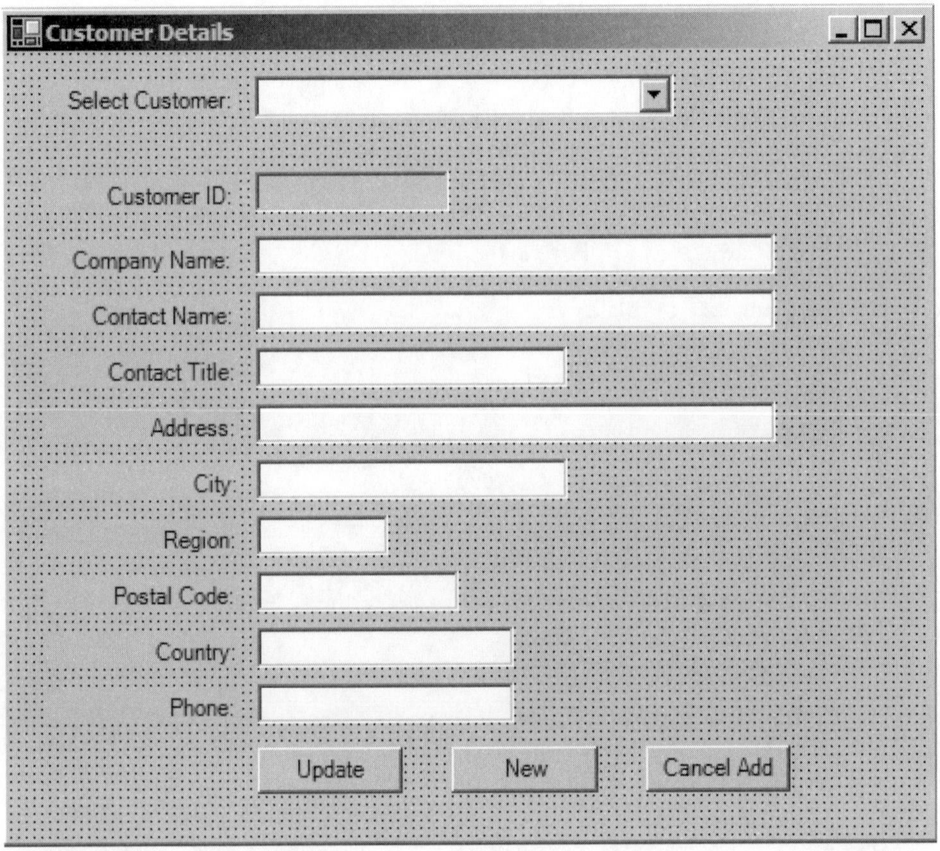

FIGURE 10.20 The finished form.

```
  Private Sub Button3_Click(ByVal sender As System.Object, ByVal e As
System.EventArgs) Handles Button3.Click
    Me.BindingContext(DataView1).CancelCurrentEdit()
    ComboBox1.Enabled = True
    TextBox1.ReadOnly = True
    Button3.Enabled = False
    Button2.Enabled = True
    DsCust1.Clear()
    ' Restore previous record
    DsCust1.Merge(mWebSvc.GetCustomer(ComboBox1.SelectedValue))
  End Sub
```

If the user cancels Add mode, we restore the last record that was displayed. Now code the most complicated part of the program. We must modify the Update button's click event to do a couple of things. First, if a record was added, we want it to refresh the dropdown list so we can see the new record. Next, if the user changes the company name field, we also want to update the list to reflect the new name. This sounds simple, and it is, but it adds some conditions to the code that prove quite interesting and some we haven't even seen yet. Here is the code:

```
  Private Sub Button1_Click(ByVal sender As System.Object, ByVal e As
System.EventArgs) Handles Button1.Click
    Dim dsTemp As localhost.dsCust
    Dim strCust As String
    Dim RePopulate As Boolean

    strCust = TextBox1.Text
    Me.BindingContext(DataView1).EndCurrentEdit()
    ' In our case it will be either/or, since we are only dealing with
a one row datatable.
    If DsCust1.HasChanges(DataRowState.Modified Or DataRowState.Added)
Then
      dsTemp = DsCust1.GetChanges(DataRowState.Modified Or
DataRowState.Added)
      ' Must test if adding a row or changed company name before we do
the update.
      If dsTemp.Customers.Rows(0).RowState = DataRowState.Added Then
RePopulate = True
      ' Since we are testing equality of two objects' VALUES we use the
"Is" operator.
      ' The "Equals" method tests to see if two variables point to the
SAME object.
      ' If they were value types we could use "=" but these methods
return objects.
      If Not (dsTemp.Customers.Rows(0)("CompanyName",
DataRowVersion.Current) Is _
          dsTemp.Customers.Rows(0)("CompanyName",
DataRowVersion.Original)) Then
        RePopulate = True
      End If
      DsCust1.Merge(mWebSvc.UpdateCustomer1(dsTemp))
      ' Only want to repopulate if added new row or changed Company
Name.
      If RePopulate Then
        PopulateList()
        ComboBox1.SelectedValue = strCust
      End If
```

```
    End If
    ComboBox1.Enabled = True
    TextBox1.ReadOnly = True
    Button3.Enabled = False
    Button2.Enabled = True
End Sub
```

I commented this code liberally, unlike my usual bad habit of not commenting at all. The trick is to know when I am adding a record, or changing the Company Name field. If either of these conditions is met, update the dropdown list, or update the database normally. The problem is that as soon as I update the database I lose visibility into what changed and what was added. So I use a Boolean variable to hold the condition, then I update the database, then I test the Boolean, and, if it is true, I refresh the list.

The way we test the conditions is interesting. To test to see if the row was newly added, I use the `RowState` property of the DataRow. This returns a `DataRowState` enumeration value that determines if the row was added, modified, and so forth. Next, to find out if the user modified the Company Name field, we use another form of the `Item` method of the DataRow. We can get any of four possible values for any given column: `Current`, `Original`, `Proposed`, and `Default` values. Normally there is only a `Current` value. If the user has edited the field, or if it was changed by assignment, and `EndCurrentEdit` has *not* been called, then there are `Original` and `Proposed` values. Once `EndCurrentEdit` had been called, but the row had not yet been updated to the database, there are `Current` and `Original` values. Whether or not there is a default value depends on how the field was defined. Since we have already called the `EndCurrentEdit` method, we will only have `Current` and `Original` values. We can then compare these values for any field to determine if it has changed. If we run the program, we can now change and add rows to the database. Just make sure you use a unique company ID value.

Master-Detail Data

We looked at master-detail data in the chapter on Windows Forms. We can add more code to support a DataGrid control without too much trouble. This time we do need to add a new web method to our Web Service. We need a method to update the Orders and Order Details tables. This will also demonstrate what we must do if we make a change to a Web Service. Add the following web method to the Web Service:

```
<WebMethod(Description:="Updates Customer Order Info.")> _
Public Function UpdateOrders(ByVal dsOrders1 As dsOrders) As dsOrders
  Try
    dsOrders1.Errors.Rows.Clear()
    If dsOrders1.HasChanges Then
      SqlDataAdapter3.Update(dsOrders1.Orders)
      SqlDataAdapter4.Update(dsOrders1.Order_Details)
    End If
  Catch errobj As Exception
    dsOrders1.Errors.Rows.Add(New String() {errobj.Message,
errobj.StackTrace})
  End Try
  Return dsOrders1
End Function
```

After we compile the Web Service, we must refresh the web reference in the client form. This is because we changed the contract, and the client needs to know. It must regenerate its proxy class to include the new web method.

This brings up an interesting point about Web Services. We need to understand more than ever the concept of the WSDL document and interface contract. We had a similar issue with COM objects and interfaces. Once we have published a Web Service, it is very important not to change any existing web method. This is because your service may be in use by any number of users, and if you change the parameters of a web method, you will break hundreds of applications that rely on your service. This can result in angry customer service calls if they are paying for using the Web Service. If you need to modify a service, you can create one that has the new functionality and instruct your users to use the new service if they need the new functionality. This way you don't break existing applications.

Next we add our grid control to the form. In order to do this, we have to rearrange the controls so we get a good fit. Figure 10.21 shows the form with the DataGrid on it.

I used the AutoConfigure option of the grid control and chose Professional3. I then set the `BorderStyle` property to `Fixed3D`. I also enclosed the three buttons in a panel and then docked the panel to the bottom of the form. You also need to add another DataSet. Select Localhost.dsOrders when the DataSet configuration dialog opens. Set the `DataSource` property of the grid to `DsOrders1` and the `DataMember` property to Orders. Since there is a relation from Orders to Order Details, the grid will automatically be configured as a master-detail grid.

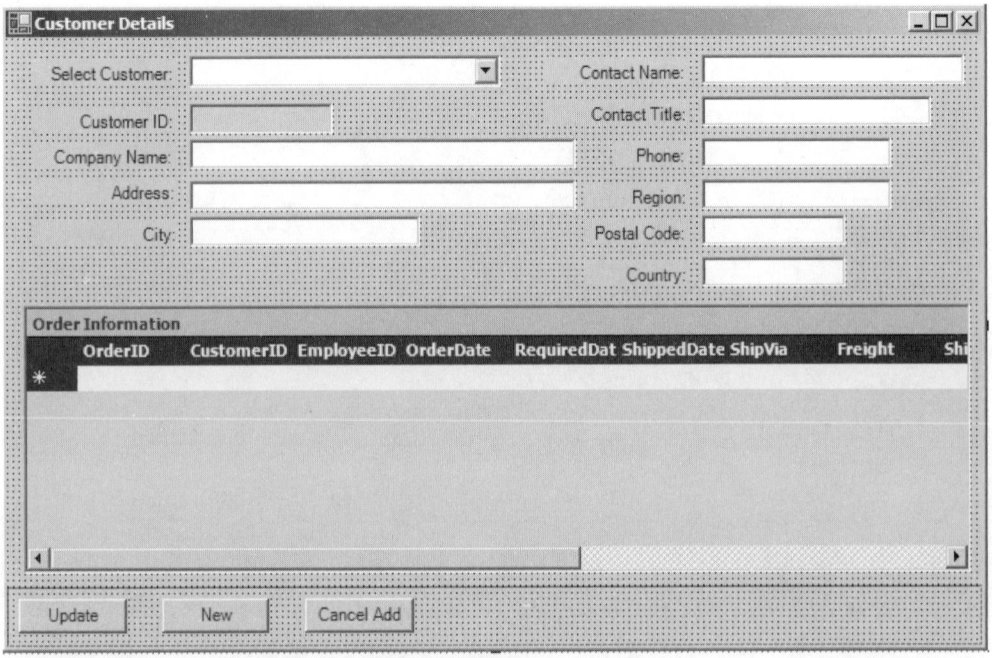

FIGURE 10.21 The form with order information.

Now we need the code to populate the grid. As it turns out, this is quite simple. We need to add two lines of code to the ComboBox's SelectedItemChanged event:

```
  Private Sub ComboBox1_SelectedIndexChanged(ByVal sender As
System.Object, ByVal e As System.EventArgs) Handles
ComboBox1.SelectedIndexChanged
    DsCust1.Clear()
    DsCust1.Merge(mWebSvc.GetCustomer(ComboBox1.SelectedValue))
    DsOrders1.Clear()
    DsOrders1.Merge(mWebSvc.GetOrders(ComboBox1.SelectedValue))
  End Sub
```

You can test the application now if you like. Notice that it takes a lot longer for the form to start. This is because we now have to get all of the order and order detail rows each time we change items in the drop down. This first time is a little slow, but once the program is running, it is very quick. Here is where you need to plan carefully if you know you will be using a slow network connection. You may not want to download the entire set of orders and details to the client at once.

Next we need to modify the Update button's click event to handle updating the order information. We only want to do this if needed, and we only want to pass changes back to the Web Service to conserve bandwidth in case of the slow connection. The new click event for the Update button is:

```
  Private Sub Button1_Click(ByVal sender As System.Object, ByVal e As
System.EventArgs) Handles Button1.Click
     Dim dsTemp As localhost.dsCust
     Dim dsTemp1 As localhost.dsOrders
     Dim strCust As String
     Dim RePopulate As Boolean

     strCust = TextBox1.Text
     Me.BindingContext(DataView1).EndCurrentEdit()
     ' In our case it will be either/or, since we are only dealing with
a one row datatable.
     If DsCust1.HasChanges(DataRowState.Modified Or DataRowState.Added)
Then
        dsTemp = DsCust1.GetChanges(DataRowState.Modified Or
DataRowState.Added)
        ' Must test if adding a row or changed company name before we do
the update.
        If dsTemp.Customers.Rows(0).RowState = DataRowState.Added Then
RePopulate = True
        ' Since we are testing equality of two objects' VALUES we use the
"Is" operator.
        ' The "Equals" method tests to see if two variables point to the
SAME object.
        ' If they were value types we could use "=" but these methods
return objects.
        If Not (dsTemp.Customers.Rows(0)("CompanyName",
DataRowVersion.Current) Is _
           dsTemp.Customers.Rows(0)("CompanyName",
DataRowVersion.Original)) Then
           RePopulate = True
        End If
        DsCust1.Merge(mWebSvc.UpdateCustomer1(dsTemp))
        ' Only want to repopulate if added new row or changed Company
Name.
        If RePopulate Then
           PopulateList()
           ComboBox1.SelectedValue = strCust
        End If
     End If
     Me.BindingContext(DsOrders1).EndCurrentEdit()
     If DsOrders1.HasChanges(DataRowState.Modified Or DataRowState.Added
Or DataRowState.Deleted) Then
```

```
        dsTemp1 = DsOrders1.GetChanges(DataRowState.Modified Or
DataRowState.Added Or DataRowState.Deleted)
        DsOrders1.Merge(mWebSvc.UpdateOrders(dsTemp1))
    End If
    ComboBox1.Enabled = True
    TextBox1.ReadOnly = True
    Button3.Enabled = False
    Button2.Enabled = True
End Sub
```

The new code is bolded and in italics. If you test the code, you can make changes to the Orders grid, and when you click Update, the changes are sent back to the Web Service, which updates the database.

Next, we take a quick look at Web Forms, and then, that's it! You're a Web Services expert!

USING WEB SERVICES WITH WEB FORMS CLIENTS

Web Forms clients to Web Services sounds redundant. Why not just access the data directly in the Web Form? It is transparent to the user anyway, right? Yes, but you are missing the point of Web Services. What if a Web Service existed that was published by one of your company's vendors? The Web Service enabled you as a programmer to access data about your company's order status with this vendor. You can present this data in any way you wish. Suppose you had a requirement to build a robust Windows interface for use in-house, but needed a web interface as well for your road warriors to use. By using the Web Service you can build both interfaces and they will conform to the business rules defined by the vendor.

To keep it simple, we will use the same Web Form we used in the previous chapter. We will merely change the code to use the Web Service we just built for our Windows Form. To refresh our memories, Figure 10.22 shows the form we will use from ADOBook09-02.

For this project, create a new project in the same solution we have been using, with the Web Service and the Windows Form in it. Next, go to Windows Explorer and copy the Web Form from ADOBook09-02 into ADOBook10-03. Now in the Solution Explorer, include the form in the project using the Show All Files button. (We've done this before, right?) Now add the web reference as we did in the Windows Forms project. It's the same process.

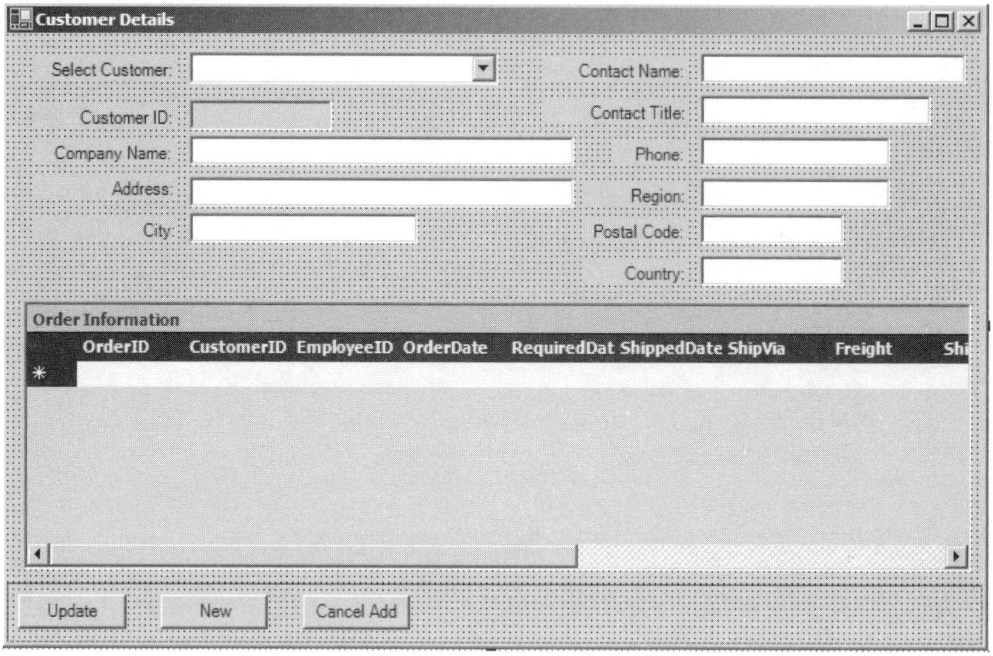

FIGURE 10.22 The Web Form for the Web Service.

Next, make this the startup project and the Web Form the startup form. You can delete the default Web Form that was created when we created the project. Now let's do something drastic. Open the Web Form in Design mode. Delete the DataAdapters and the Connection object. Add a new DataSet as a dsOrders type the same way we did in the Windows Form. Now go through the code and change the references to dsCust1 and dsCustList1 to reference the classes from the Web Service, just like in the Windows Form. There is one change: The Orders table is no longer in dsCust1. It is now in dsOrders1. You should change the code to reflect this.

Now search for each reference to the DataAdapters. We must change these to get the data from and update it to the Web Service. The whole program follows. We have already done all of this so I don't think it needs much explanation.

```
  Private mWebSvc As localhost.CustomersOrders = New
localhost.CustomersOrders()

  Private Sub Page_Load(ByVal sender As System.Object, ByVal e As
System.EventArgs) Handles MyBase.Load
```

```
    If Not IsPostBack Then
      Session("IsAdding") = False
      DsCust1 = New localhost.dsCust()
      Session("dscust1") = DsCust1.Copy
      DsOrders1 = New localhost.dsOrders()
      Session("dsorders1") = DsOrders1.Copy
      DsCustList1 = New localhost.dsCustList()
      Session("dscustlist1") = DsCustList1.Copy
    Else
      DsCust1 = CType(Session("dscust1"), localhost.dsCust).Copy
      DsOrders1 = CType(Session("dsorders1"), localhost.dsOrders).Copy
    End If
  End Sub

  Private Sub DropDownList1_SelectedIndexChanged(ByVal sender As
System.Object, ByVal e As System.EventArgs) Handles
DropDownList1.SelectedIndexChanged
    If Me.IsPostBack Then
      Session("selIndex") = DropDownList1.SelectedIndex

DsCust1.Merge(mWebSvc.GetCustomer(DropDownList1.SelectedItem.Value))

DsOrders1.Merge(mWebSvc.GetOrders(DropDownList1.SelectedItem.Value))
      Me.DataBind()
    End If
  End Sub

  Private Sub Page_PreRender(ByVal sender As Object, ByVal e As
System.EventArgs) Handles MyBase.PreRender
    If IsPostBack Then
      DsCustList1 = Session("CustList")
      DropDownList1.DataBind()
      DropDownList1.Items(Session("selIndex")).Selected = True
    Else
      DsCustList1.Merge(mWebSvc.GetCustomerList())
      Session("CustList") = DsCustList1
      DropDownList1.DataBind()
    End If
    Session("dsCust1") = DsCust1.Copy
  End Sub

  Private Sub ClearScreen()
    TextBox1.Text = ""
    TextBox3.Text = ""
    lblError.Text = ""
  End Sub
```

```
  Private Sub Button4_Click(ByVal sender As System.Object, ByVal e As
System.EventArgs) Handles Button4.Click
    DsCustList1.Clear()
    DsCustList1.Merge(mWebSvc.GetCustomerList())
    Session("CustList") = DsCustList1
    DropDownList1.DataBind()
  End Sub

  Private Sub DataGrid1_PageIndexChanged(ByVal source As Object, ByVal
e As System.Web.UI.WebControls.DataGridPageChangedEventArgs) Handles
DataGrid1.PageIndexChanged
    DsCust1 = CType(Session("dscust1"), localhost.dsCust).Copy
    DataGrid1.CurrentPageIndex = e.NewPageIndex
    DataGrid1.DataBind()
  End Sub

  Private Sub DataGrid1_EditCommand(ByVal source As Object, ByVal e As
System.Web.UI.WebControls.DataGridCommandEventArgs) Handles
DataGrid1.EditCommand
    DataGrid1.EditItemIndex = e.Item.ItemIndex
    DataGrid1.DataBind()
  End Sub

  Private Sub DataGrid1_UpdateCommand(ByVal source As Object, ByVal e
As System.Web.UI.WebControls.DataGridCommandEventArgs) Handles
DataGrid1.UpdateCommand
    Dim i As Integer
    Dim dsTemp As localhost.dsOrders

    Try
      ' This only works if the order of the grid columns is the same as
the
      ' order of the columns in the DataTable.
      For i = 3 To e.Item.Cells.Count - 1
        If Not DsOrders1.Orders.Columns(i - 3).ReadOnly Then
          DsOrders1.Orders.Rows(e.Item.ItemIndex)(i - 3) =
CType(e.Item.Cells(i).Controls(0), TextBox).Text
        End If
      Next
      dsTemp = DsOrders1.GetChanges(DataRowState.Modified)
      DsOrders1.Merge(mWebSvc.UpdateOrders(dsTemp))
    Catch errobj As Exception
      lblError.Text = errobj.Message & vbCrLf & errobj.StackTrace
      Exit Sub
    End Try
    DataGrid1.EditItemIndex = -1
    DataGrid1.DataBind()
  End Sub
```

```
  Private Sub DataGrid1_CancelCommand(ByVal source As Object, ByVal e
As System.Web.UI.WebControls.DataGridCommandEventArgs) Handles
DataGrid1.CancelCommand
    DataGrid1.EditItemIndex = -1
    DataGrid1.DataBind()
  End Sub

  Private Sub DataGrid1_DeleteCommand(ByVal source As Object, ByVal e
As System.Web.UI.WebControls.DataGridCommandEventArgs) Handles
DataGrid1.DeleteCommand
    Dim dsTemp As localhost.dsOrders

    Try
      DsOrders1.Orders.Rows(e.Item.ItemIndex).Delete()
      dsTemp = DsOrders1.GetChanges(DataRowState.Deleted)
      DsOrders1.Merge(mWebSvc.UpdateOrders(dsTemp))
    Catch errobj As Exception
      lblError.Text = errobj.Message & vbCrLf & errobj.StackTrace
      Exit Sub
    End Try
    DataGrid1.DataBind()
  End Sub
```

As you can see, we are using the same web methods we used in the Windows Forms project, combined with the techniques we use for Web Forms, such as saving session state, and so on. The great thing is that your web programmers do not have to know any SQL at all! Just document your Web Service well and give them what they need.

SUMMARY

That ends the discussion of Web Services, although we have only scratched the surface here. Again my hope is that your appetite is whetted for you to dig further, but with what you already have you can become a competent Web Services programmer or consumer. In the next and final chapter we will build a data control, similar to that in previous versions of Visual Basic. This will demonstrate how to use ADO .NET in Visual Basic .NET user controls.

CHAPTER 11

Creating Your Own Data Control

In this chapter, we will create our own .NET version of the VB 6 ADO Data Control, an exercise designed to demonstrate the robust features of ADO .NET. Up until now, we have investigated the ADO .NET components and we have built simple forms using these components. We have discovered that ADO .NET is a much more robust tool than ADO. We have also discovered that it is inherently more complicated. Creating a simple data form with bound controls now requires a minimum of three ADO .NET Data Components, where ADO only required one.

For those of us used to the RAD tools of VB 6, VB .NET seems a bit daunting. I was never a big proponent of using data-bound controls in previous versions of VB because, while you could create a working application faster using data-bound controls, you also relinquished a lot of control over what was happening in the background. I admit that as a programmer, I am a control freak. I *like* to control what goes on behind the scenes. I have, however, used the old data control in a few circumstances. One good use was as a navigation control. It made a good visual control for navigating a table or RecordSet. This was especially true when used in conjunction with the ADO DataGrid control. Another good use was when I needed to create a simple stand-alone form for quick data entry, and I didn't have time to fool with too much code.

I never used it in enterprise class applications for widespread distribution though, except as a navigation control. And that leads me to ask this question: Why did Microsoft choose to omit a navigation control from the Windows

Forms classes? Was it to keep the "script kiddies" away? Who knows? Anyway, Microsoft's omission is our opportunity. By creating our own control, we will put to use many of the components and techniques of ADO .NET.

My only reservation is that you will create this control, and then use it in your production applications. While I have no problem with this from the standpoint of ethics, I do want to make this disclaimer: This control is for instructional purposes only. Any use beyond this is at your peril. I have debugged the code sufficiently for instructional use, but I have not performed a full battery of tests on it. If you use the control, you will be responsible for making sure that it is tested and ready to use in a production environment.

About UserControls

We will create our data control by subclassing a UserControl. This is a base class from which all visual controls derive. The UserControl class provides a visual drawing space upon which other controls may be placed. It also provides many of the properties and methods you would expect any control to have. In some ways, it is similar to a form. The difference is that the control must be *hosted.* That is, it must reside on a *container.* This container may be a form, or another UserControl.

To cover all of the bases, we will be creating what we call a compound control, or a control made up of a group of existing controls. There is another type of control called a painted control. In this type, the control author is responsible for fully creating the visual interface graphically. These controls typically derive from the Control class and are beyond the scope of this book.

VB 6—If you have created controls in VB 6 you have a head start with .NET UserControls. In many ways, VB 6 UserControls were more complex to develop than VB .NET controls. Since VB .NET supports full inheritance and since all IDE designers generate real VB code that you can see, silly things like PropertyBags, the extender object, and the ambient object go away. Property values that are set in the IDE Property window are simply assigned during form initialization. It's right there in the code. We no longer have to worry about persistence; it's automatic. All controls are now compiled into plain .dll files. There is no longer an .ocx file extension for custom controls. If you've programmed in VB long enough, you know that there was no difference between an ActiveX .dll and .ocx. The extension is just a convention used to distinguish visual components from nonvisual ones. I've even used some controls that were compiled as .dlls, probably just to draw the ire of Microsoft.

CREATING THE PROJECT

Shall we begin? Start by closing any open projects or solutions. Create a project. When prompted, select Windows Control Library. Name the project DataControl. This will create a Windows Control Library project with a default UserControl class called UserControl1.vb. Select UserControl1.vb in the Project window and open the code view. Notice that the control is just a class that inherits from windows.forms.UserControl. Change the programmatic name of the class to ucDataNav for data navigator. Do this by simply overtyping UserControl1 with ucDataNav right in the source code. To be consistent let's also change the source code file name to match. Do this right in the Project window. Note two things: Changing the name in the window renames the disk file and there is no code except that which was generated by the designer. This is collapsed in the region labeled Windows Form Designer Generated Code. Yet there are already lots of properties listed in the Properties window. Where did they come from? As with forms, they are defined in the base class. Ah, the beauty of inheritance.

CREATING THE VISUAL INTERFACE

We will want our control to resemble the old ADO Data Control. This includes four navigation buttons and a caption area. When we open the designer we see a blank drawing area. We are going to put four command buttons on the control, but first look at the Properties window. There is no `BorderStyle` property. We want our control to be able to have some kind of border. The solution is to use a panel control, a container control used to group other controls. Conveniently it has a `BorderStyle` property. Drop a panel control onto the UserControl. Next, find the `Dock` property of the panel control. The `Dock` property allows a control to be parked against one or all of the inner borders of the container. For you VB 6 programmers, it is similar to the `Align` properties some controls had except that it also has a `Fill` property that allows the control to automatically fill and resize with the container.

Click the dropdown button and a strange-looking object appears. The object represents six buttons that correspond to the Dock type enumeration. The choices are Fill, Top, Bottom, Right, Left and None. Click the button in the middle. This is the Fill option which eliminates having to write custom code in the resize event of the control. Set the `BorderStyle` property to Fixed3D (this creates a sunken effect) and change the name of the panel to pnlMain.

Next we will add four buttons and name them cmdFirst, cmdPrevious, cmdLast, and cmdNext. Name them in this order so that I can demonstrate something later on. Blank out the `Text` properties of the buttons. On the web site, there are four icons which I created for you in the project folder: first.ico, previous.ico, next.ico, and last.ico. Copy these to your working folder.

Select each button and find the `Image` property. Click the ellipsis (…) button and a File Open dialog appears. Assign each icon to its respective button or, if you don't feel like doing this, use the `Text` property and less-than and greater-than signs. It looks cheesy but then you're the only one looking at it. Use << for first, < for previous, > for next, and >> for last. Select the `FlatStyle` property of each button and set it to Popup.

Select cmdFirst. Now we will Dock the button to the left edge of the panel. This is something you couldn't do in VB 6 where controls could only be aligned on forms and UserControls. Now controls can be Docked on most containers. (The frame is the only exception, I think.) Next Dock cmdPrevious left as well. Dock cmdLast and cmdNext to the right. Now the control is starting to resemble the old data control.

Wait a minute! The cmdNext button is all the way to the right and cmdLast is toward the center. What happened? Try to drag cmdNext toward the center. It won't move. Unlike the VB 6 `Align` property, you can't change the position of the aligned controls by dragging. What then determines the order in which they Dock? Actually, it's the order the controls were created, something I found out the hard way. I was trying like crazy to rearrange some Docked controls. It wouldn't work so I deleted and recreated them. That's when I noticed the pattern. You do not have to know in what order you want the controls to stack when they're Docked before dragging them onto the form. You can use the Bring To Front and Send To Back menu items in the Format menu.

There also is a back-door way to change the Docking order. This is useful if you need to rearrange numerous controls and are tired of clicking the mouse. Open the Code window for the control. Expand the region Windows Form Designer Generated Code. Scroll down past—and ignore—the comment Do Not Change the Code in This Section… Ignore it because you are rearranging the code, not changing it. Scroll to where you find a comment pnlMain. Find the line of code that looks like this:

```
Me.pnlMain.Controls.AddRange(New System.Windows.Forms.Control() _
  {Me.lblText, Me.cmdPrevious, Me.cmdFirst, Me.cmdNext, Me.cmdLast})
```

Make sure the order of the controls appears as in this line. The real reason they appear in the z-order they do is because of the order they appear in this line of code. Incidentally, this line of code adds the controls to the Controls collection of the *panel,* not the UserControl! That's correct, all container controls now have their own Controls collection. Another interesting thing about this line of code is that the function call passes an array of controls made up on the fly. There is no longer an array function to create a variant array (there are no variants any longer). Instead the syntax resembles the C++ style. The curly braces contain the elements of the array.

By the way, I didn't lie when I said it was the order that the controls were added that determines the stacking order. The designer composes this statement and the controls are added to the array list in the order they are added to the form. Simply changing the order in the list does not seem to affect the designer in any way. If you want to make sure, then change the order the controls are declared and initialized as well. When you tab back to the designer, you will see that they now appear correctly.

The last thing we want to do to complete the look of the ADO Data Control is add a label. This label will display whatever caption we choose, often a record position indicator. Drop the label in the center of the panel. Name it lblText. Set the `Dock` property to fill. Set the `Text` property to Record: Our visual design is now finished. Notice that the controls all resize automatically. We didn't have to write any resizing code at all! Your control should appear as in Figure 11.1. You can compile the project now.

CREATING A TEST HARNESS

Next we will create a test harness project to try out our control on. If you've never been part of an electrical engineering team, the term *test harness* might seem strange. In a prior life (so it seems) I once worked as a test technician in an electronics plant. We used test harnesses, which were specially designed pieces of equipment, to provide controlled input to a component. The output can be compared to a known set of expected parameters. This way we had a controlled way of determining whether a component was performing as expected. We will do the same thing with our test harness.

FIGURE 11.1 The visual design of the Data Control.

In our case, the harness will simply be a Windows Form. We will put controls on the form that test all of the functions of the Data Control. Let's add a new project to our solution. When prompted, choose Windows Application. The IDE creates a project and adds it to the solution. Change the name of the project to TestBed and the name of the form to frmCtlTest. Right-click on the References node in the Project Explorer. Select Add Reference. The References dialog opens. Choose the Project tab and select the DataControl project. This assumes that you have compiled the DataControl project. If not, compile it now. Now if you open the form designer for frmCtlTest, and then open the toolbox, you will see the ucDataNav listed under Windows Forms. Select this control and drop it on your form.

If you've done everything correctly up to this point, the control should paint itself on the form and resemble the old ADO Data Control as in Figure 11.2. Try resizing the control. See the buttons stretch and shrink. Of course it does absolutely nothing right now. Next we will add the functionality to the control. This is where we will really learn something.

ADDING THE FUNCTIONALITY

Before we begin coding, it would be a good idea to review the functionality of a data navigator control. Since we are incorporating the functionality of the ADO Data Control, we will review that as well. Even if you never used any of the data controls from previous versions of VB, you should still review this information because it will act as our functional specification.

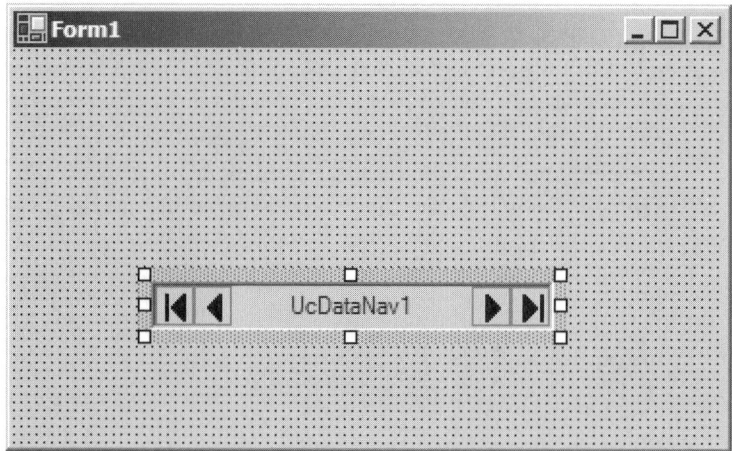

FIGURE 11.2 The test harness with the cata control on it.

A Data Navigator

Strictly speaking, a data navigator is a relatively simple idea. It should provide the user with the ability of moving through a collection of rows in a table. The First button moves to the beginning of the data rows. The Previous button moves one record backward. The Next button moves one record forward. The Last button moves to the last row in the collection. Although it would normally be used for database records, it could be used for arrays or any other collection of data. The control would need to be able to be bound to a data table or collection of some type and would also need to be able to be bound to a set of controls on the form. Our data navigator will provide all of this functionality and much more.

The VB 6 ADO Data Control

The ADO Data Control is more than a simple navigation control. It can act as a stand-alone visual control that would handle all of the details of connecting to, accessing, and updating database tables. Although you could (and I usually did) create your RecordSets outside the control and then assign the control's `RecordSet` property a reference to the externally created RecordSet, you didn't have to. The control would do it all for you with no code whatsoever. This is also the goal of our navigation control. It will contain all of the ADO .NET objects required to connect, access, and update the database with almost no code in the host form at all. It will also provide the mechanism through which the controls on the host form can be bound to the control. In addition to providing insight into the ADO .NET components, it will give a great deal of insight into the object-oriented capabilities of VB .NET.

VB 6–Differences

Although our new control will mimic many of the functions of the VB 6 control, there will be some differences. The VB 6 control would automatically update the database with a connected RecordSet as soon as the user moved off the current row to another row. Since ADO .NET DataSets are disconnected, this will not happen. The DataRow in the DataTable will be updated, but the database will not. A separate method needs to be implemented to take care of updating the database with changes. We will create an `UpdateChanges` method for this purpose. The VB 6 control could manage at most one table. The ADO .NET DataSet can manage multiple tables. Since our control is best suited to managing one table at a time, we will create the `BoundTable` property. This will get or set an index value that determines which DataSet table we will be binding to. It will default to zero. In addition we need to provide for a DataAdapter. We will give our control the ability to create its own DataAdapter or be provided one already created by the programmer. As the VB 6 control exposed its RecordSet, we will also expose the DataSet. This way the user will have maximum flexibility to create a DataSet externally, and then supply it to the control. If this sounds ambitious, it is, but it will demonstrate the flexibility of ADO .NET.

CREATING THE COMPONENTS

The first thing to do is add the data components to form. Add an SqlConnection, an SqlDataAdapter, and a DataSet. Cancel out of the wizard for the SqlDataAdapter. When the DataSet configuration wizard appears, select untyped DataSet and click OK. Name the SqlConnection mConnection, the SqlDataAdapter mAdapter, and the DataSet mDataset. Close the Designer window and open the Code window.

Data Navigation

Now it's time to start writing code. The first bit of functionality to add is the ability to connect to a database. We will use our Connection object for this. First create a property to expose the Connection object to the world. This will have an interesting effect we will look at later on:

```
Public Property Connection() As SqlClient.SqlConnection
  Get
      Connection = mConnection
  End Get
  Set(ByVal Value As SqlClient.SqlConnection)
      mConnection = Value
  End Set
End Property
```

Next create a separate property to get and set a ConnectionString. This is really a convenience feature. You'll see why in a minute. Add the following property:

```
Public Property ConnectionString() As String
    Get
        If Not mConnection Is Nothing Then
            ConnectionString = mConnection.ConnectionString
        End If
    End Get
    Set(ByVal Value As String)
        mstrConn = Value
```

```
            If mstrConn = mConnection.ConnectionString Then Exit
Property
            If mConnection.State = ConnectionState.Open Then _
                                                  mConnection.Close()
            mConnection.ConnectionString = mstrConn
        End Set
    End Property
```

The way this works is simple. If you change the ConnectionString, the control closes any open connection and assigns the value to the `ConnectionString` property of the Connection object. Now compile the project. Open frmCtlTest. Select the data navigator control. Look at the Properties window. Scroll down until you see the `Connection` property. Click the plus sign. Look at what it did! It created a `Connection` property that expands to reveal all of the properties of the Connection object. Try doing that with your VB 6. With this functionality the users of your control can assign their own Connection object to the control, or just use the built-in one. See Figure 11.3.

Now let's assign a ConnectionString to the control. But, who can remember all the arcane syntax of a ConnectionString? I have been programming in VB since VB 1 and I still have to look some of them up. Not to worry: You can have the Connection object generate the string for you. First create a user connection. Hover the mouse pointer over the Server Explorer. It should roll out. If you have a slower machine it might take a few seconds if this is the first time you've accessed it, because it has to refresh all of its connections. If you don't have it rolled up, then open it from the toolbar. Next click the Connect to Database button. The familiar ADO Database Connection dialog appears. Connect to the Northwind database. Figure 11.4 shows how mine looked.

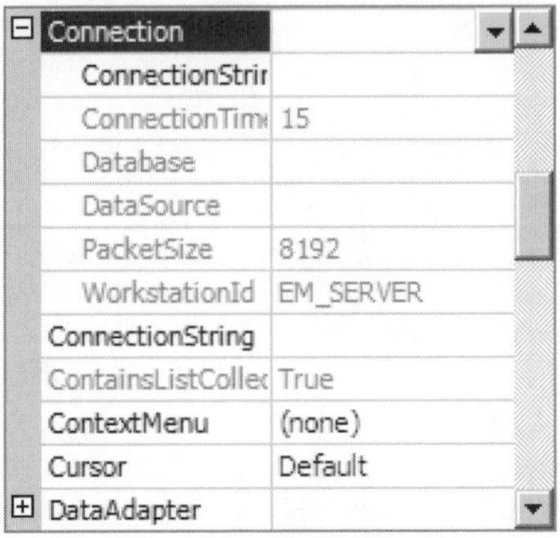

⊟ Connection	
ConnectionStrir	
ConnectionTim	15
Database	
DataSource	
PacketSize	8192
WorkstationId	EM_SERVER
ConnectionString	
ContainsListCollec	True
ContextMenu	(none)
Cursor	Default
⊞ DataAdapter	

FIGURE 11.3 The Connection property.

Now go to the Properties page and click on the `ConnectionString` property of the Connection object. Do *not* click on the one we added. In the drop-down the list, you will see the connections we added. Select the Northwind one. Both `ConnectionString` properties are now populated with correctly formed ConnectionStrings. Note that we did all of this just by exposing the Connection object through a simple property. Now add properties for the DataAdapter and the DataSet. Your code should look like this:

```
Public Property DataAdapter() As SqlClient.SqlDataAdapter
    Get
        DataAdapter = mAdapter
    End Get
    Set(ByVal Value As SqlClient.SqlDataAdapter)
        mAdapter = Value
    End Set
End Property

Public Property DataSet() As DataSet
    Get
        DataSet = mDataSet
    End Get
    Set(ByVal Value As DataSet)
        mDataSet = Value
    End Set
End Property
```

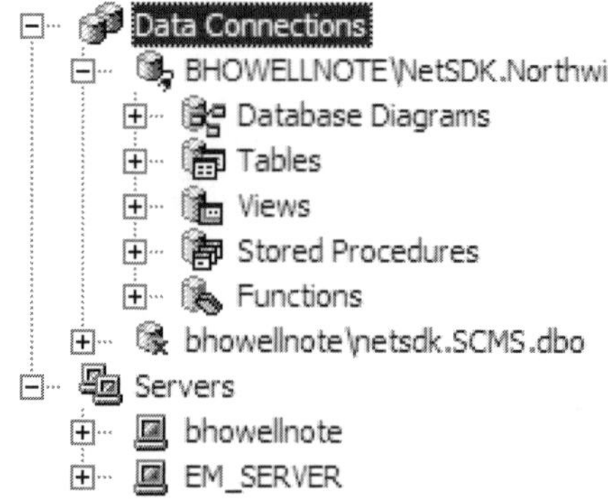

FIGURE 11.4 Selecting the Data Connections.

Pretty straightforward, eh? Now we can see all of the properties of the adapter and the DataSet in the Properties window—once we've compiled the control. This is the easy part. The more difficult tasks will follow.

Let's take a break from the database programming to take care of one small detail. We want to add a `Text` property to our control so we can update the caption between the navigation buttons. You'll notice that the UserControl has a `Text` property that we can override. Click Overrides in the component list at the top of the Code window, then drop down the procedures list to see it. Select the `Text` property. The Code window creates the procedure stub for you. Make the procedure look like this:

```
Public Overrides Property Text() As String
    Get
        Text = lblText.Text
    End Get
    Set(ByVal Value As String)
        lblText.Text = Value
    End Set
End Property
```

This will assign the string to the `Text` property of the label control. Now compile the project. Open the form designer for frmCtlHost again. Select the data navigator control. Look at the Properties window. There is no `Text` property! What gives?

The `Text` property of the UserControl base class has an *attribute* that prevents the property from displaying in the Properties window. Since we overrode this property, our class inherited the attribute. What is an attribute? An attribute is a class object that you can attach to a class, procedure, property, or member that affects how that object behaves. You can, obviously, do many things with attributes. In this case the attribute controls the design-time behavior of the property. If you open the object browser and select the `Text` property of the UserControl, you will see its attributes listed. One of them is System.ComponentModel.BrowsableAttribute. It is set to False. We have to override this behavior, so add the following line (in bold) just before the property procedure:

```
<System.ComponentModel.BrowsableAttribute(True)> _
    Public Overrides Property Text() As String
        Get
            Text = lblText.Text
        End Get
        Set(ByVal Value As String)
            lblText.Text = Value
        End Set
    End Property
```

Now compile the project. Switch back to frmCtlTest and select the navigator. You will now see the `Text` property in the Properties window.

How did I know this? By digging until I found it. I can't find a list of predefined attributes listed anywhere in the VB or .NET documentation. They are all documented, but not very usefully. For example, a list of attributes that can be applied to properties would be nice.

VB 6—VB 6 had a menu item called Procedure Attributes in the Tools menu. This is where you found the capability to control things like appearing in the Properties window and whether or not a property was bindable. Interestingly, VB 6 also supported attributes but in a different way. Since VB 6 Forms package objects were private and pre-declared, the attributes were expressed differently. If you ever opened a VB 6 form or UserControl using Notepad (or another text editor), you could see the attributes before each procedure if any were used. They had an arcane syntax and were not documented. Since these could all be set using the Procedure Attributes menu item, there was never any need to manually edit them. It would have been nice if Microsoft included such a feature in the .NET IDE, but it didn't. Maybe in the first service pack.

Event Handlers

The next task is to put some code behind the navigation buttons. We could just double-click on each button and then add the code to the click event, but why be normal? I would rather we have all our navigation code in one procedure so we can find it easily. In VB 6 we would have done this with a control array, but VB .NET doesn't support control arrays. What are we to do?

VB .NET does support something called a *delegate*. If you're familiar with C or C++, you know that you can create a function pointer and then call the function through the pointer. A function pointer is a variable that contains the *address* of the entry point of the function. A VB .NET delegate is similar to a function pointer in C++. It is a *reference type* that points to a procedure. The biggest difference is that the delegate is a lot smarter than a simple pointer. In C++ the compiler does nothing to validate the pointer. In other words, you can very easily create a pointer to nowhere. This was often the cause of the General Protection Fault error that plagued the early days of Windows.

In VB .NET, the compiler validates the delegate to make sure it points to a valid procedure. It also validates that the parameter signature of the delegate and the target procedure match. The best part is that you can assign several controls' events to the same delegate. What this means in simple terms is that several controls' click events can all call the same procedure. We no longer need control arrays. The programmer jargon for this is wiring up events. When we attach an event to a procedure we say we've *wired* the event to procedure *x*.

We will use the `AddHandler` statement to create a delegate and assign the control's click event to it. First we have to create the subprocedure that will receive the events. The only requirement of the delegate is that the parameter signatures match the event's and that the procedures not return a value. Since the click event is a standard event it passes two parameters, the sender As Object and the EventArgs object as EventArgs. So let's create our procedure:

```
Private Sub NavButtons(ByVal sender As Object, ByVal e As EventArgs)

End Sub
```

Don't worry about the contents of the procedure yet. The next question is where to put the `AddHandler` statements. They have to appear after the buttons are created but before anyone can click a button. The best place is in the constructor of the class. Expand the region labeled Windows Forms Designer Generated Code. Right at the top you will find Public Sub New().This is the default (and only) constructor. Add the `AddHandler` statements right after the comment that says Add Any Initialization After the InitializeComponent() Call.

```
Public Sub New()
   MyBase.New()

   'This call is required by the Windows Form Designer.
   InitializeComponent()

'Add any initialization after the InitializeComponent() call

' Assign Navigation Buttons to same click event handler
    AddHandler cmdFirst.Click, AddressOf NavButtons
    AddHandler cmdPrevious.Click, AddressOf NavButtons
    AddHandler cmdNext.Click, AddressOf NavButtons
    AddHandler cmdLast.Click, AddressOf NavButtons

End Sub
```

Notice the use of AddressOf in the statement. This does the same thing as in VB 6 right? Wrong! In VB 6 it returned the address of a procedure, and it could only be a procedure in a standard module. In VB .NET it returns an actual delegate, and it can refer to any procedure that does not return a value, no matter what kind of module it is in. This is not the only way to create a delegate, but the other ways are beyond the scope of this book. Now when we click any of the navigation buttons we will call the NavButtons procedure. How do we know which button was clicked? There is no index parameter to test. The answer is the sender object. It is passed as an object type (which is the root base class of the whole .NET class library) so it can accept any type of object. Since we know we are passing a button, we can typecast the sender to a button and then test the name property to see which button was clicked.

COMPLETING THE TEST HARNESS

Let's complete the test harness. We already have our data navigator control on the form. Now we need a control to display and manipulate our data. The best choice is the DataGrid control. Go ahead and drop a DataGrid control on the form. Set the `Dock` property to Top. Select the navigator control and set its `Dock` property to `Top` as well. Oops, the navigator went to the top of the form above the grid! This is the same problem we had before with the buttons. Simply use the Bring to Front or Move to Back commands.

Add two more buttons to the form. Name one cmdUpdate and change its `Text` property to `Update`. Name the other cmdCancel and change its Text property to Cancel Changes. If you want, although it is not necessary, you can put the buttons in a nested panel structure so that they stay to the right when the control is resized. Look at my code to see how this is done. Your form should look something like Figure 11.5:

INITIALIZATION CODE

Before we continue, let's finish the initialization code. Go back to the constructor. After the code we added to wire the events, let's add this code:

```
mSQLBuilder = New SqlClient.SqlCommandBuilder(mAdapter)
mAdapter.SelectCommand = New SqlClient.SqlCommand("", mConnection)
mAdapter.InsertCommand = New SqlClient.SqlCommand("", mConnection)
mAdapter.DeleteCommand = New SqlClient.SqlCommand("", mConnection)
mAdapter.UpdateCommand = New SqlClient.SqlCommand("", mConnection)

mDataSet.Tables.Add()
```

These initializers just precreate the objects mentioned so they show up in the Property window correctly. Before the region add the following declarations. The region statement is shown for a point of reference:

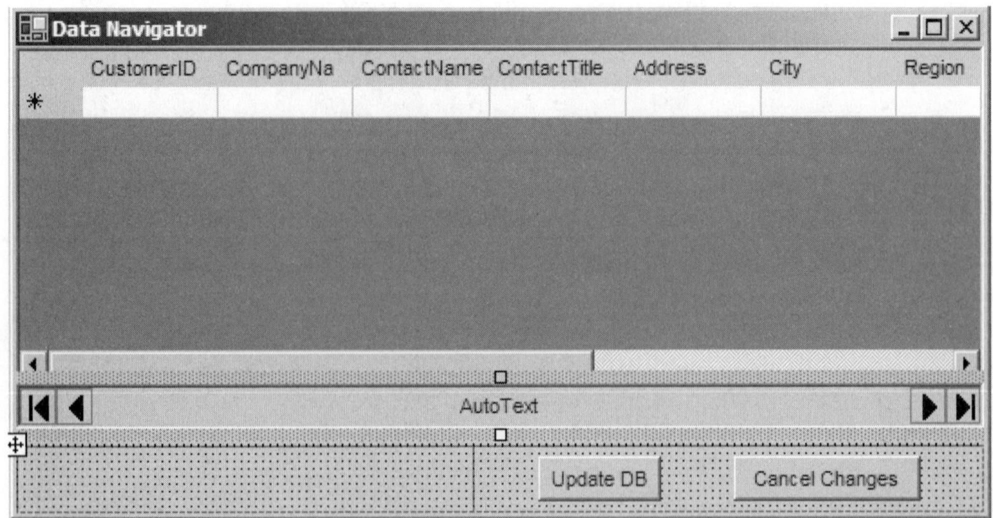

FIGURE 11.5 The completed test harness.

```
    Private mSQLBuilder As SqlClient.SqlCommandBuilder
    Private mstrConn As String
    Private mintBoundTable As Integer = 0
    Private mblnAutoText As Boolean

    Public Event BoundTableChanged(ByVal intBoundTable As Integer)
    Public Event DataSetFilled(ByVal dsDataSet As DataSet)
    Public Event PositionChanged(ByVal intNewRow As Integer)

#Region " Windows Form Designer generated code "
```

Don't worry about what these are for yet, especially the SqlCommandBuilder object. We will discover what they do shortly.

Reading the Data and Schema

Before the control does anything, it has to be able to read the schema from the database based on the `Select` statement. Let's create a public subprocedure and call it ReadData. We want the procedure to behave a little differently when the control is displayed in a form designer than when it is running in an application. When the control is in a designer, we don't want to read data from the database. What we really want to do is to read the schema. The DataAdapter has a method just for this purpose called FillSchema. The question is, how do we detect if the control is in a designer or in design mode?

If you never developed controls in VB 6, you might be wondering what the heck I'm talking about. This can get a little confusing so please be patient. Controls execute in two modes, User and Design. When a control is in Design mode, it is sitting on a form that is being designed or open in the form designer. The *control* is actually executing. The *form* is being designed. The control is executing in Design mode.

When a control is in User mode it is running in the actual application. The control is executing in User (or application) mode. Both modes refer to a compiled control executing. One is executing in a designer, the other is executing in an application. Got It? Good, you're half way there!

In VB 6, you could access a property of the ambient object called UserMode. This returned a value that indicated how the control was running. VB .NET controls no longer need the ambient object, so they have a `Direct` property called `DesignMode` which returns True if the control is running in a designer. So here is our ReadData procedure. We also will add a few more support procedures:

```
Public Sub ReadData()
    Try
        If mAdapter.SelectCommand.CommandText = "" Then Exit Sub

        If mDataSet.Tables.Count > 0 Then
            mDataSet.Tables.RemoveAt(mintBoundTable)
        End If
        If Me.DesignMode Then
            mAdapter.FillSchema(mDataSet, SchemaType.Source, _
                                mintBoundTable)
        Else
            mAdapter.Fill(mDataSet, mintBoundTable)
            RaiseEvent DataSetFilled(mDataSet)
            UpdatePosition()
        End If
    Catch errobj As Exception
        Throw errobj
    End Try
End Sub

Private Sub UpdatePosition()
    If Not Me.ParentForm Is Nothing Then
        If mblnAutoText Then
            lblText.Text = "Record: " & _
                 Me.ParentForm.BindingContext(Me).Position + 1 & _
                   " of " & _
                   mDataSet.Tables(mintBoundTable).Rows.Count
```

```
        End If
    End If
End Sub

Public Property AutoText() As Boolean
    Get
        AutoText = mblnAutoText
    End Get
    Set(ByVal Value As Boolean)
        mblnAutoText = Value
        Me.Text = "AutoText"
    End Set
End Property

Public Property SelectCommandText() As String
    Get
        SelectCommandText = mAdapter.SelectCommand.CommandText
    End Get
    Set(ByVal Value As String)
        mAdapter.SelectCommand.CommandText = Value
        ReadData()
    End Set
End Property
```

It's pretty straightforward. If there is no `Select` statement assigned, the procedure exits. If the DataSet already has any table objects, then they are removed. We could also have used mDataset.Clear. This would clear all of the DataTables from the DataSet. If the DataSet were created outside the control and then passed in via the `DataSet` property, this is not what we would want to happen. We really want to remove only the bound table, or the table we will use to bind controls to. We want to leave any other tables alone.

Next we check to see if we are in Design mode. If we are, we want to get the schema from the database, but not the actual data. If we are not, we grab the whole kit and caboodle. We then fire an event that notifies the host that we have replaced the data in the `DataSet`. We then call a procedure that updates the `Text` property with Record: *n* of *x* if we have the `autoText` property turned on. The `autoText` property is a Boolean value that indicates if we want the `Text` property automatically updated when the DataTable's current row changes. If any errors occur they are thrown back to the calling procedure.

THE NAVIGATION PROCEDURE

Next let's fill in the code for the NavButtons event procedure. The code appears as follows:

```
Private Sub NavButtons(ByVal sender As Object, ByVal e As EventArgs)
      Dim intNewRow As Integer
      Try
Me.ParentForm.BindingContext(mDataSet, _
                                    mintBoundTable).EndCurrentEdit()
intNewRow = Me.ParentForm.BindingContext(Me).Position
Select Case CType(sender, Button).Name
    Case "cmdFirst"
        intNewRow = 0
    Case "cmdPrevious"
        If intNewRow > 1 Then
         itNewRow -= 1
        Else
               intNewRow = 0
        End If
    Case "cmdNext"
          If intNewRow < _
             mDataSet.Tables(mintBoundTable).Rows.Count - 1 Then
              intNewRow += 1
          Else
              intNewRow = _
                 mDataSet.Tables(mintBoundTable).Rows.Count - 1
          End If
      Case "cmdLast"
          intNewRow = mDataSet.Tables(mintBoundTable).Rows.Count - 1
 End Select
 If Me.ParentForm Is Nothing Then Exit Sub
 Me.ParentForm.BindingContext(Me).Position = intNewRow
 RaiseEvent PositionChanged(intNewRow)
 UpdatePosition()
      Catch errobj As Exception
 Throw errobj
      End Try
End Sub
```

The first line after the `Try` statement ends any pending edits on the parent form. We have to use the binding context of the parent form because that is where the data is displayed. If we used the binding context of the UserControl it would not do anything because no edits were made in the UserControl itself. Next we get the current position of the data row. Again we use the parent form's binding context. Next we determine which button fired the event.

We typecast the sender object to a button type and then get the name property. The `Select Case` statement then takes over control. Instead of directly setting the row position, we use an intermediate variable to hold the results of a calculation that determines the new row. The new row is determined via an offset from the current row. If the new row would be beyond the last row, then we use the row index of the last row. If it would be negative or before the first row (row zero), then we use zero as the new row index.

Finally, we set the position using the parent form's binding context. We then call UpdatePosition to set the `Text` property and fire the Position-Changed event.

EXPOSING THE DATA TABLE TO THE WORLD

Let's compile the control. Open the form designer for frmCtlTest. If no connection or `Select` statement is set, then set them to Northwind and Select * From Customers, respectively. Now click on the DataGrid. Find the `DataSource` property. Drop down the list. What gives? The data control is not listed as a valid data source. What gives?

We have to implement an interface. What do we mean by implementing an interface? If you've designed ActiveX components in VB 6 you will have some idea. An interface is simply a predefined set of method signatures. This differs from a base class because the interface defines the methods. It cannot have any functionality and it cannot be inherited from. When we implement an interface, we are saying, "My class will contain these methods, and they have to be defined."

Okay, so which interface do we implement? IlistSource of the component model. This interface has two methods, `GetList` and `ContainsListCollection`. ContainsListCollection returns True if the component supplies a list. GetList returns the actual list object. Add the following code to the top of the class. The class declaration should look like this when you're finished:

```
Public Class ucDataNav
    Inherits System.Windows.Forms.UserControl
    Implements System.ComponentModel.IListSource
```

Notice there is a syntax error under System.Component-Model.Ilist-Source. Hover the mouse pointer over the code and see that one of the methods is not defined. Remember what we said about interfaces. When you implement an interface you are saying that your class will support all of the methods of the interface. So open the list of the components drop down at the top of the code window. You will see the interface listed. Select it. Now open the list of the procedure drop down. Click ContainsListCollection. A read-only property is created. Have the property return True.

```
    <System.ComponentModel.BrowsableAttribute(False)> _
    Public ReadOnly Property ContainsListCollection() As Boolean _
        Implements
System.ComponentModel.IListSource.ContainsListCollection
        Get
            ContainsListCollection = True
        End Get
    End Property
```

Also add the attribute to prevent the property from showing in the Property window. Now do the same thing for the `GetList` method. But what do we want to return from this function? The DataTable object's DefaultView object is derived from the System.Collections.Ilist class, which is what GetList wants to return. Is my head sore!

```
Public Function GetList() As System.Collections.IList Implements _
            System.ComponentModel.IListSource.GetList
        GetList = mDataSet.Tables(mintBoundTable).DefaultView
End Function
```

Now compile the control and go back to the frmCtlTest designer. Look at the DataGrid's `DataSource` property. If you open the list, you will see the data navigator listed. Can we enable it to list the control and the tables in a tree view? Yes, we can. If you have a valid Connection and SQL `Select` statement assigned, when you select the DataSource the grid should populate its columns.

LET'S TRY IT!

If you haven't already done so, set the TestBed project to be the startup project. Now run the program. The DataGrid should populate with the contents of the Northwind Customer table. Try clicking the navigation buttons. The pointer should move accordingly and the caption should update with Record: *n* of *x* (assuming the `autoText` property is set to True). Notice there is no user-supplied code in the test form. All of this functionality comes from the navigator control (see Figure 11.6).

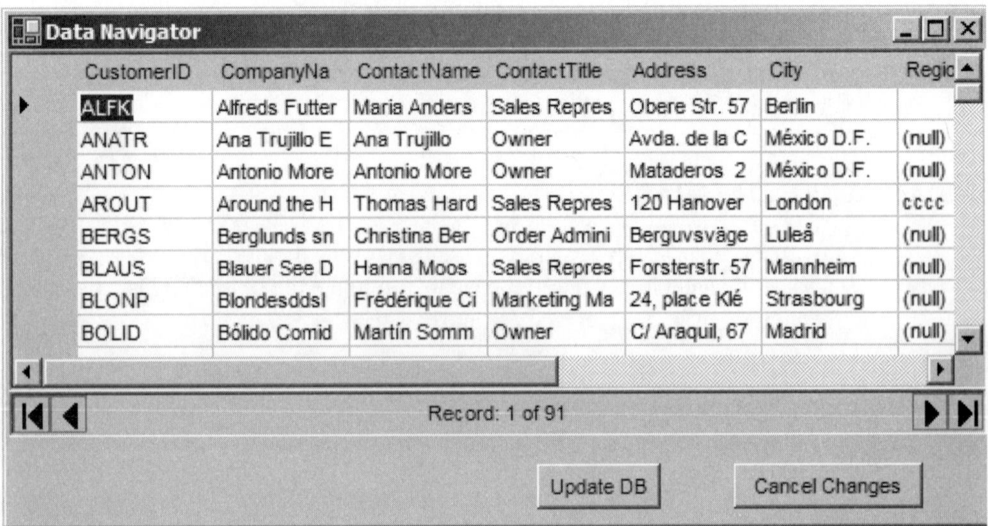

CustomerID	CompanyNa	ContactName	ContactTitle	Address	City	Regic
ALFK	Alfreds Futter	Maria Anders	Sales Repres	Obere Str. 57	Berlin	
ANATR	Ana Trujillo E	Ana Trujillo	Owner	Avda. de la C	México D.F.	(null)
ANTON	Antonio More	Antonio More	Owner	Mataderos 2	México D.F.	(null)
AROUT	Around the H	Thomas Hard	Sales Repres	120 Hanover	London	cccc
BERGS	Berglunds sn	Christina Ber	Order Admini	Berguvsväge	Luleå	(null)
BLAUS	Blauer See D	Hanna Moos	Sales Repres	Forsterstr. 57	Mannheim	(null)
BLONP	Blondesddsl	Frédérique Ci	Marketing Ma	24, place Klé	Strasbourg	(null)
BOLID	Bólido Comid	Martín Somm	Owner	C/ Araquil, 67	Madrid	(null)

FIGURE 11.6 The running test harness.

Click on the Selector column of the grid and move the pointer that way. Oops! The record counter does not get updated. The VB 6 Data Control had the same problem. The control has no way of knowing that you changed the position in the grid. The grid does notify its parent form through the CurrentCellChanged event. We can use this event to notify the navigator control that the user clicked a new row in the grid. As it turns out, the binding context position does change, but the binding context does not notify the form of this. I think there still needs to be some work done to ADO .NET in the next release. So if you add the following code to the DataGrid's CurrentCellChanged event, the caption will update properly:

```
Private Sub DataGrid1_CurrentCellChanged(ByVal sender As Object, _
        ByVal e As System.EventArgs) Handles
DataGrid1.CurrentCellChanged
UcDataNav1.Text = "Record: " & _
    Me.BindingContext(UcDataNav1).Position + 1 & _
    " of " & UcDataNav1.DataTable.Rows.Count
End Sub
```

Now if you run the project you will see the caption change when you click on the grid directly. This is great but let's try something else. Try changing something in the grid. Now close the form and run the project again. The value reverted to its old value! Do you remember that we said ADO .NET

DataSets are disconnected? When we updated the grid, we changed the data in the underlying DataTable, but we did nothing to change the data in the database itself. Unlike the old ADO Data Control, we will have to add more functionality to make this happen.

Updating the Database

To make this easier, we are going to create a method that we will call to update the database. We could probably emulate the old ADO Data Control's behavior, but instead let's create an `UpdateChanges` method:

```
Public Sub UpdateChanges()
    Dim dsTemp As DataSet

    Try
        If mAdapter.InsertCommand.CommandText = "" And _
            mAdapter.UpdateCommand.CommandText = "" And _
            mAdapter.DeleteCommand.CommandText = "" Then
             Exit Sub
        End If
        Me.ParentForm.BindingContext(Me).EndCurrentEdit()
        If mDataSet.HasChanges Then

mAdapter.Update(mDataSet.Tables(mintBoundTable).GetChanges)
            mDataSet.AcceptChanges()
            mDataSet.Clear()
            mAdapter.Fill(mDataSet, mintBoundTable)
        End If
    Catch errobj As Exception
         Throw errobj
    End Try
End Sub
```

First the procedure tests if the update commands have been created. If not it exits, assuming the control is read-only. If any of the commands are created, it attempts the update. It ends the current edit using the binding context. This is equivalent to the user moving off the row in the DataGrid. Then it checks to see if there were any changes. If there were, the `HasChanges` property of the DataSet returns True. Then we call the `Update` method of the DataAdapter. We use the `GetChanges` method of the DataSet to only send the changes back to the server. This reduces network traffic. Then we call the `AcceptChanges` method of the DataSet. This makes the pending changes permanent. We clear the DataSet and refill it from the database. We don't have to do this, but it refreshes the data and verifies that the data was updated.

Every example I've seen does this, but it seems redundant and would have an adverse affect on network traffic. I've tried it both ways and both work fine. The only valid reason for doing this is so we can see any changes other users may have made to the database. I prefer a `Refresh` method for this but it depends on how volatile (how often the database is updated) the data is. If this table is being changed by hundreds of users simultaneously, then it is better to leave it in.

Compile the control. Now open frmCtlTest's code window. Double-click the Update button we created earlier. Add the following code to the event procedure:

```
Private Sub cmdUpdate_Click(ByVal sender As System.Object, _
    ByVal e As System.EventArgs) Handles cmdUpdate.Click
    Try
        UcDataNav1.UpdateChanges()
    Catch errobj As SqlClient.SqlException
        MsgBox(errobj.Message & vbCrLf & errobj.Procedure & _
                vbCrLf & errobj.StackTrace)
    End Try
End Sub
```

Now run the project. Repeat the test we did earlier. Change something in the grid. Click the Update button. Close the program and run it again. What? The data still did not change! It did not update because there is no SQL command in the DataAdapter's UpdateCommand object. Now we have a choice, we can either create one manually (sigh!) or we can have the system create one for us. As it turns out, the library provides a class that does this very thing. Remember the SqlCommandBuilder object we created way back when? That is what it does. When you use the DataAdapter's configuration wizard to create the command objects, it uses this class. Add this procedure to the control:

```
Private Sub GenerateSchema()
    Try
        If mAdapter.SelectCommand.CommandType = _
          CommandType.StoredProcedure Then
            mAdapter.SelectCommand.Parameters.Clear()
            mSQLBuilder.DeriveParameters(mAdapter.SelectCommand)
        Else
            mSQLBuilder.RefreshSchema()
            mAdapter.UpdateCommand = mSQLBuilder.GetUpdateCommand
            If Not mAdapter.UpdateCommand Is Nothing Then
                If mAdapter.UpdateCommand.CommandType = _
          CommandType.StoredProcedure Then

mSQLBuilder.DeriveParameters(mAdapter.UpdateCommand)
```

```
                    End If
                End If
                mAdapter.InsertCommand = mSQLBuilder.GetInsertCommand
                If Not mAdapter.InsertCommand Is Nothing Then
                    If mAdapter.InsertCommand.CommandType = _
            CommandType.StoredProcedure Then

mSQLBuilder.DeriveParameters(mAdapter.InsertCommand)
                    End If
                End If
                mAdapter.DeleteCommand = mSQLBuilder.GetDeleteCommand
                If Not mAdapter.DeleteCommand Is Nothing Then
                    If mAdapter.SelectCommand.CommandType = _
            CommandType.StoredProcedure Then

mSQLBuilder.DeriveParameters(mAdapter.DeleteCommand)
                    End If
                End If
            End If
        Catch errobj As Exception
            MsgBox(errobj.Message & vbCrLf & errobj.StackTrace)
        End Try
    End Sub
```

We will use three functions of the command builder. The `RefreshSchema` method generates the `Insert`, `Update`, and `Delete` SQL statements based on the Select statement. Since the SQL Builder object exists independently of the DataAdapter, the commands don't automatically propagate into the DataAdapter's command objects. That is what the `GetxxxCommand` methods do. They return precreated command objects. These are then assigned to the Insert, Update, and Delete commands respectively.

The other method, `DeriveParameters`, is only used if the select command is a stored procedure. It gets the parameter list from the stored procedure. It has to access the database to do this so there is network overhead involved. I haven't tested the control with this functionality so I don't know if it will work.

Next we have to determine when to call GenerateSchema. Since it requires a `Select` statement to base its other commands on, a good place would be the `SelectCommandText` property procedure. Make the procedure look like this:

```
    Public Property SelectCommandText() As String
        Get
            SelectCommandText = mAdapter.SelectCommand.CommandText
        End Get
```

```
    Set(ByVal Value As String)
        mAdapter.SelectCommand.CommandText = Value
        GenerateSchema()
        ReadData()
    End Set
End Property
```

Now compile the control. Open the frmCtlTest designer. Drill down to the DataAdapter's command objects. If we did everything right, the `Insert`, `Update`, and `Delete` SQL statements should be populated. Open up one of the SQL statements in the query designer. See, it created all the parameters for you! Open the Parameters property page. There they all are! The command builder class is a powerful class that can be used in many other applications. If you learned nothing else from this exercise, this alone would be worth it.

Final Testing

Now let's run the project. Change one of the values in the grid. Click the Update button. Close the form and run it again. Notice the data does change now. You can try deleting a row and inserting a new row as well. They all work. One last thing. Suppose we want to roll back the edits we've made. We can add one more method to the control:

```
Public Sub CancelChanges()
    Try
        Me.ParentForm.BindingContext(Me).CancelCurrentEdit()
        mDataSet.RejectChanges()
    Catch errobj As Exception
        Throw errobj
    End Try
End Sub
```

Call this method from the Cancel Changes button's click event. The `CancelCurrentEdit` method of the binding context ends the edit of the current row without saving the changes. It is equivalent to the user clicking the Escape key while the DataGrid has the focus. The `RejectChanges` method of the DataSet does just that. It cancels all changes made to the DataSet since the last `Fill` command was executed. Let's compile it and try it out. Run the project. Make some changes to the grid data. Click the Cancel Changes button. The data reverts to its previous state. Deleted rows reappear and inserted rows disappear.

Summary

In this chapter, we created a data navigation control that emulates the behavior of the VB 6 ADO Data Control. In doing so we were able to demonstrate many of the things we learned earlier in the book, and some new things. We also created a very useful control that we can use in our own projects. As stated previously, do your own testing on the control before you use it in any production applications.

Now you're a competent Visual Basic .NET database programmer. I hope you found this book helpful and enjoyable. Unlike other books, I attempted to give you the truly useful information, while skipping the marketing hype and obscure or arcane features that most of us will never use. I did not attempt to cover every nook and cranny of ADO .NET. I wanted to get you started. Now it is up to you to take it from here.

Index

A

B

C

D

E

F

N

O

P

Q

R

S

T

U

V

W